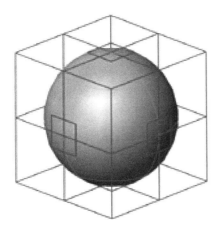

AutoCAD® in 3 Dimensions Using AutoCAD® 2005

Stephen J. Ethier
Christine A. Ethier

CADInnovations (www.viziwiz.com)

PEARSON
Prentice
Hall

Upper Saddle River, New Jersey
Columbus, Ohio

Library of Congress Cataloging-in-Publication Data

Ethier, Stephen J.
   AutoCAD in 3 dimensions using AutoCAD 2005 / Stephen J. Ethier, Christine A. Ethier.
      p. cm.
   ISBN 0-13-152562-X
   1. Computer graphics. 2. AutoCAD. 3. Three-dimensional display systems. I. Ethier,
Christine A. II. Title.

T385.E3859 2005
620'.0042'0285536—dc22

2004050310

Executive Editor: Debbie Yarnell
Managing Editor: Judith Casillo
Production Editor: Louise N. Sette
Production Supervision: Lisa Garboski, *bookworks*
Design Coordinator: Diane Ernsberger
Cover Designer: Jim Hunter
Cover Art: Stephen J. Ethier
Production Manager: Deidra Schwartz
Marketing Manager: Jimmy Stephens

This book was set in Dutch 801 and Swiss 721 by *The GTS Companies*/York, PA Campus. It was printed and bound by Courier Kendallville, Inc. The cover was printed by Phoenix Color Corp.

Disclaimer:

The publication is designed to provide tutorial information about AutoCAD® and/or other Autodesk computer programs. Every effort has been made to make this publication complete and as accurate as possible. The reader is expressly cautioned to use any and all precautions necessary, and to take appropriate steps to avoid hazards, when engaging in the activities described herein.

Neither the author nor the publisher makes any representations or warranties of any kind, with respect to the materials set forth in this publication, express or implied, including without limitation any warranties of fitness for a particular purpose or merchantability. Nor shall the author or the publisher be liable for any special, consequential or exemplary damages resulting, in whole or in part, directly or indirectly, from the reader's use of, or reliance upon, this material or subsequent revisions of this material.

Pearson Prentice Hall™ is a trademark of Pearson Education, Inc.
Pearson® is a registered trademark of Pearson plc
Prentice Hall® is a registered trademark of Pearson Education, Inc.

Pearson Education Ltd.
Pearson Education Singapore Pte. Ltd.
Pearson Education Canada, Ltd.
Pearson Education—Japan

Pearson Education Australia Pty. Limited
Pearson Education North Asia Ltd.
Pearson Educación de Mexico, S. A. de C.V.
Pearson Education Malaysia Pte. Ltd.

10 9 8 7 6 5 4 3 2 1
ISBN:0-13-152562-X

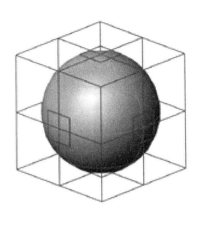

This text is dedicated
first,
to each other,
a tenacious bond between the best of friends
and
a wonderful 3-dimensional marriage.

Next,
to our strongest supports,
Dorothy and Vic Evans,
for
unfailing help,
intelligent guidance,
and unconditional love.

And, finally,
in memory of my father,
George Ethier,
who was always there for me.

Stephen and Christine Ethier

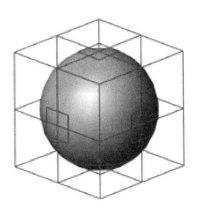

Preface

Our own interest in CAD began many years ago, when "technological revolution" was not yet a household phrase. It was our feeling then that computerized drawing would drastically change the field of drafting and design, but we couldn't have guessed the far-reaching implications of the changes. Today, drafting students—although still being introduced to work on the boards—are universally exposed to the computer early in the game and are being hired into the job market based on their familiarity with and skill in this area. And, as always, in this skill-intensive age, the more information we have, the better we are able to compete.

AutoCAD® in 3 Dimensions Using AutoCAD® 2005 was written to provide the information students need to compete in a competitive job market. The text covers AutoCAD 2005 and is a hands-on, lab- and exercise-intensive look at all the important concepts needed to draw in true 3D. It is our hope that even the beginner, who has had only an introduction to CAD, will be able to pick up this text, follow the activities and the labs, and turn to the book for answers to possible questions—leaving the instructor relatively question-free!

Features

To aid student understanding of AutoCAD, the text includes the following pedagogical features:

- More than 600 illustrations of 3D drawings help students visualize the concepts.
- Part 4, Solid Modeling, gives the most thorough look at AutoCAD's Advanced Modeling Extension currently available.
- Part 7, Application Projects, includes six chapters (18–23) that act as independent labs with step-by-step guidelines. These labs cover architectural (residential and commercial), mechanical, structural, and civil projects.
- Most chapters have a series of labs that move the student from simple to complex projects (all chapters except those in Section 7, where the chapters themselves are labs). The accompanying CD-ROM contains lab openers to save student startup time.
- Chapters end with questions that test students' understanding of chapter concepts.

- Chapters also end with assignments that allow students to explore the chapter concepts interactively.
- The text is accompanied by an online *Instructor's Manual* that includes answers to chapter questions; suggestions for additional assignments and discussion topics; and chapter tests with a mix of multiple choice, true/false, matching, and short-answer questions. This online resource can be accessed at *www. viziwiz.com*. Instructors should contact their local Prentice Hall representative for the required passcode.

Organization

The text is organized into eight parts covering all aspects of three-dimensional AutoCAD:

Understanding 3D
Preparing for Construction of 3D Models
Construction of 3D Surface Models
Solid Modeling
Enhancing the Use of 3D
Presentation
Application Projects
Application Programs

There is no question that three-dimensional modeling is here to stay. In what direction it will eventually take the reader and the authors is anyone's guess, but there is no question that it will be an exciting trip.

Acknowledgments

We would like to thank the following people for their assistance with the text: Stephen Helba, whose constant guidance and considerable expertise have been invaluable; Michelle Churma, Media Development Editor, for lending us her technical know-how and her encouraging words; Debbie Yarnell, Executive Editor, for her energy and positive outlook; Pat Wilson, for her thoroughness in every manuscript check she performs; John Wadman and Bert Rioux for their special support and contributions; Patrick Daigle, a former student, for his professional work in visual media; David Fenety, a former student, for his graphic contributions to the text; Vic Evans, for his classy contribution to the introductory section of the text; David Devereaux-Weber, Craig Burgess, and Charles Michal, for their individual work in three dimensions; and those at Autodesk, who keep us posted on all that's new with AutoCAD.

We would also like to thank the following reviewers for their comments and advice: Sherwood Davis, Salt Lake Community College; Adam Jakubowski, School of Visual Arts; and Marsha Walton, Finger Lakes Community College.

We would like to extend a special thank you to Lisa Garboski for her careful and thorough accuracy check of the manuscript.

Walk-Through

AutoCAD® in 3 Dimensions Using AutoCAD® 2005

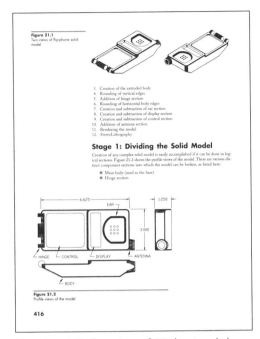

More than 600 illustrations of 3D drawings help students visualize the concepts.

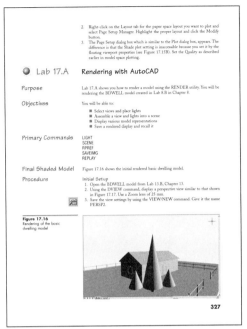

Labs at the end of each chapter create an opportunity for students to explore newly introduced concepts, step by step, from simple to more complex.

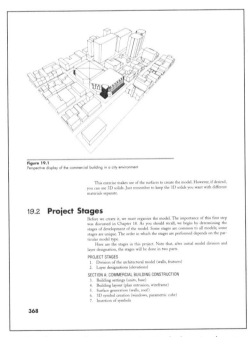

An Applications Projects section includes six chapters that act as independent labs, with step-by-step guidelines, covering architectural (residential and commercial), mechanical, structural, and civil projects.

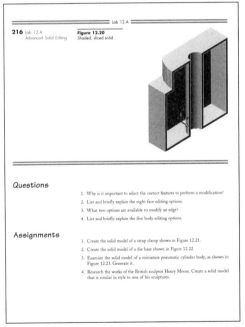

Chapters end with questions that test students' understanding of chapter concepts and with assignments that allow students to explore the chapter concepts interactively.

Coordinates

Out of your time
the ancient quest
for Holy Grail
beyond your time
to ride astride
a comet's tail
but here and now
to seek and find
new dimensions in the mind

D. V. Evans

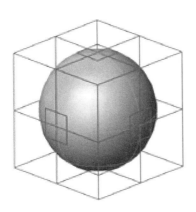

Brief Contents

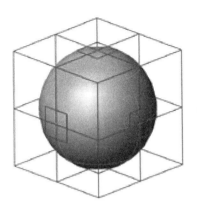

Contents

Contents   **xv**

16 Plotting   291

17 Rendering   309

Part 7 Application Projects   339

18 Architectural Project: Residential Dwelling   340

AutoCAD® in 3 Dimensions Using AutoCAD® 2005

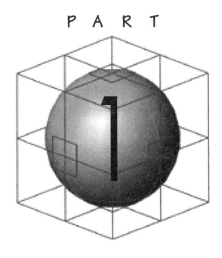

Understanding 3D

In this first part, basic 3D terminology is defined and explained to help you thoroughly understand each central concept and the many terms associated with each concept. In addition, a number of disciplines in which 3D CAD is used are discussed, and we explore how each of these disciplines would utilize the central concepts presented. It is in this discussion that the *why* of 3D CAD is disclosed: its benefits when dealing with nontechnical people, such as clients; its greater tangibility; its ability to impress; and its cost-saving benefits in design and prototype creation.

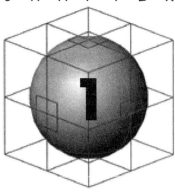

Theory Behind 3D Modeling

Overview

It is essential for 3D users to understand the concepts of extrusion, wireframe, surface models, and solid models. This chapter defines these terms and others in simple language and demonstrates them with both illustrations and diagrams.

Concepts Explored

- The purpose and benefits of 3D computer modeling
- The different model building and displaying options
- A basic vocabulary of 3D terminology

1.1 Introduction

The more tangibly a concept can be presented, the more quickly and easily it can be understood. Take the example of a pyramid: It is a difficult shape to describe, but once you have seen it in concrete form, it is easily pictured in your mind's eye. Humans learn first by knowing an object physically. Being able to touch or hold an object is the best way to understand its operation or purpose. After learning through physical interaction, humans can progress to learning through pictorial means and finally to understanding something symbolically—without contact with the actual object or even its pictorial representation.

Before three-dimensional creation on computers was possible, a model maker physically constructed a prototype of a design, either full size or to a smaller scale if, for instance, a house or bridge was being built. This allowed the designers and clients to see something tangible, something three dimensional; to interpret the ramifications of the design; and, in some cases, to actually apply operating conditions to the models and observe the results. This was a good method, and it continues to be. However, problems arise when the design needs to be altered. A new model has to be physically constructed, which is expensive and time consuming.

This is where 3D steps in. It is the ideal solution for model makers, designers, and clients alike because it allows them to construct a model whose form can be altered at will such that the results can be immediately observed. And, because computer-generated images are three-dimensional in nature, the user has the added bonus of a tool that has elements of a concrete object—its three-dimensionality—combined with the ease of creation of a pictorial image.

The art of three-dimensional construction on computers is referred to as *geometric modeling*. To save confusion, we will refer to it as *modeling* throughout this book.

A model generated on a computer consists of numeric data that describes the geometry of the object. The object geometry can include edges, surfaces, contours, or other features. Once this model database is built (created), the computer program "knows" the model has three dimensions. This allows the manipulation and display of the model in a variety of ways—some of which are not possible or not easily done with an actual physical model.

1.2 Benefits

Models provide us with a wide range of benefits. Most are described under "what-if" situations, or questions such as "What if this were changed—what would be the results?" Initially, models were created so that mechanical parts could be tested under what-if situations. This continues to be a major reason for the creation of models. Using finite element analysis (FEA), stresses can be applied to the computer model and the results graphically displayed. FEA makes use of a grid of meshes and analyzes the amount of deflection at each intersection or node point to determine allowable stresses.

With the advent of smaller, faster, and less expensive computers and powerful computer programs like AutoCAD that run on these computers, the applications of models that can be computer generated have increased by leaps and bounds. Chapter 2 details actual applications of AutoCAD 3D models. For now, consider the following examples.

Because computer models can be altered easily, a multitude of design options can be presented to a client before any construction or manufacturing takes place. In the mechanical discipline, volume and mass calculations can be done automatically when the model is altered. FEA can be applied to the model. Robotic work cells can be designed on the computer and animated to show the results of the end effector (robot's hand) paths as the robot goes through its programmed movement. In the architectural discipline, once a structure is created, the effects of sun passage can be depicted and walk-throughs can be simulated, all while the client observes. These things are not easily done with a physical miniature model. In the area of marketing, a multitude of textures or surface finishes can be applied to a model until the desired results are obtained. The benefits are virtually endless and are limited only by the imagination of the designer. And the greatest benefit is that, once the model is created, it can be used over and over again with an endless adaptability to new modifications. If the old adage is true and a picture is worth a thousand words, an animated three-dimensional model must be worth millions!

1.3 Modeling versus Drafting and AutoCAD

Exploring the possibilities of modeling is exciting. And making the transition from drafting (2D) to modeling (3D) does not have to be a difficult experience. First, to make the transition virtually painless, it is essential to understand a variety of terms, which will appear in the exercises and labs that reinforce the concepts explored in the following chapters.

The mental skills required to work in 3D are different from those needed for drawing in 2D. In drafting, the user translates the three-dimensional attributes of an object into flat two-dimensional views—top (plan), front (elevation), and side (elevation) (see Figure 1.1).

In modeling, all three dimensions are taken into consideration. This sounds complicated, but actually it allows the design to be formulated faster because the user can see the entire model at any time, instead of having to work on one view at a time.

In drafting, the creator works within two dimensions—the *X* and *Y* axes, as illustrated in Figure 1.2. In modeling, a third axis is added—the *Z* axis, as illustrated in Figure 1.3.

Both 2D and 3D creations rely on an origin point. In 2D, that origin point is described as 0,0. In 3D it's 0, 0, 0. When working with AutoCAD, the third dimension has always been available, but the program automatically assigned the *Z* coordinate

Figure 1.1
Transforming a 3D object into a 2D drawing

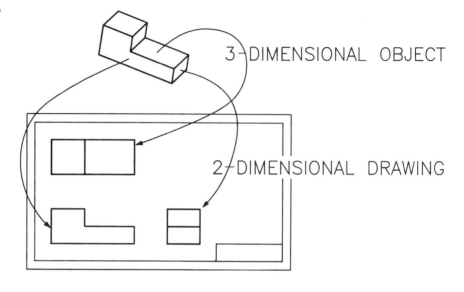

Figure 1.2
Two-dimensional axes

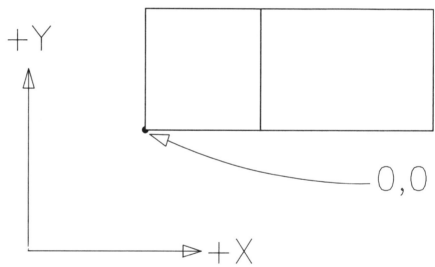

Figure 1.3
Three-dimensional axes

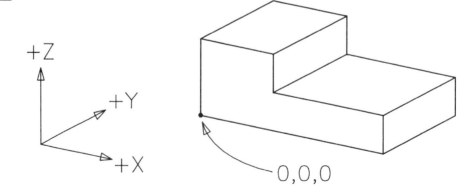

the value of 0 while working in 2D. Every entity stored the Z portion of its geometry at the 0 point. By accessing the Z value, you allow for the creation of true three-dimensional models. Coordinate entry in 3D is the same as in 2D. Coordinates can be entered with absolute values based on the origin 0,0,0 or by using relative or polar coordinates. The only difference is the addition of the third coordinate point—Z.

1.4   **Model Building Options**

In 2D drafting, the drafter used flat geometry, putting straight lines and curves into complex finished drawings. In 3D, these same simple geometric forms are used, but the third axis, Z, expands on them. The techniques learned in 2D are not forgotten; instead they are utilized in a different fashion.

Basically, the development of 3D modeling using microcomputers has followed the path from 2-1/2D line extrusions, through 3D line wireframes, to surface generations, and finally to solids. This development went hand in hand with the increasing power of the microcomputer. As the building options developed, the model database's complexity increased, putting heavier demands on the computer's processing. Although the software developers already had the techniques used to create solids on larger computers, they had to wait until the hardware (computer) caught up with the software (AutoCAD). Now, happily for users, microcomputers can make use of the most complex model creation options available—solids. There are still developments to come, but the advances to date have been revolutionary.

In our learning process, we'll follow the same path as the building options—from simple to complex. What follows is an introduction to the different building options; this will prepare us for the detailed work to come. It is up to the user to decide which of these building options would best achieve the desired effect. Luckily, they can be used in combination.

Thickness Extrusion

The first method of building a model is through the use of thickness, which is the process of taking an outline of a shape and pushing or drawing it along an axis. In CAD, this process, which is the simplest, yet one of the most useful, is the same.

As Figure 1.4 shows, an outline of a shape is drawn. Then, through a series of commands, the shape is drawn along the Z axis, forming a three-dimensional shape (see Figure 1.5). Basically, the first outline is copied along the Z axis at a set distance, and then connecting lines are automatically extended from the start and end point of each line. This connects the first outline to the corresponding points on the second, copied, outline.

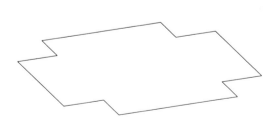

Figure 1.4
Shape-defining profile

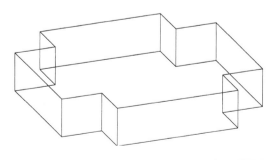

Figure 1.5
The extruded profile

The reason extrusion is the most useful process is that most graphically displayed objects are made up of an extrusion of some sort. Walls, wooden pencils, structural members, pipes, and filing cabinets are all forms of extrusions. If not the total form, then some parts of all everyday objects have extrusions. The label of 2-1/2D indicates the fact that, although not truly three-dimensional, the resulting image is amazingly close to the real thing.

Wireframe: 3D Lines

Extrusion has one basic limitation—all the extruded lines going from one outline to the next are parallel to each other. This is fine for residential walls, but what about modeling the Great Pyramid at Cheops? To draw true three-dimensional shapes, the ability to draw lines on an oblique plane must be available. A true three-dimensional line must have the possibility of a start point at one set of *X, Y, Z* coordinates and a stop point at a different set of *X, Y, Z* coordinates (see Figure 1.6).

The two *X,* two *Y,* and two *Z* coordinates must be differentiated. If a CAD program cannot do this, then it cannot create in true 3D. Drawing 3D lines to represent an object is referred to as creating a wireframe of the model. Each edge is represented by a wire. Looking at it is like looking at a skeleton of the object—you can see right through it.

Surface Generation

Now that the wireframe of the model has been created, wouldn't it be great to be able to see how it would look with some "clothes" on? This is where surface generation comes in. Wireframe is very useful during the initial complex construction of a model, but the need to see the model in a more tangible form remains. The frame must be covered with sheets of material, referred to as *surfaces,* as shown in Figure 1.7. These surfaces will display the model in an easier-to-comprehend form—the hiding of edges behind one another. This is very important in the presentation stage.

Methods of Surface Generation

There are four main methods of generating surfaces: extrusion, area definition, sweep profile, and contour mesh. Each of the methods covers a defined boundary with a surface, using semiautomatic techniques.

Surface extrusion is similar to the extrusion technique mentioned earlier, but instead of using individual connecting lines from several key vertices on one outline to the next, every possible point along the edge of one outline is used to form the

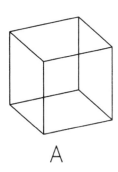

Figure 1.6
True 3D geometry

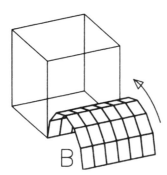

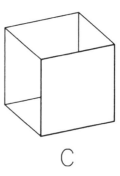

A B C

Figure 1.7
Applying a surface

Figure 1.8
Extruding a line

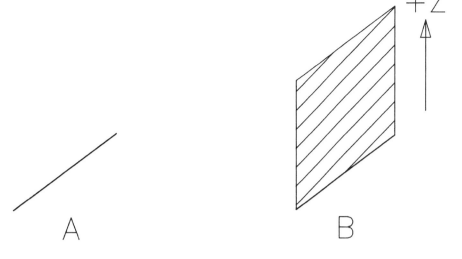

corresponding edge of the second outline, thus completing two tasks—forming the surface and forming the second profile edge (see Figure 1.8). Initially, a two-dimensional entity (line) is created, and then the entity (line) is extruded to form a surface.

In area definition, the user identifies an area to be covered with a surface by indicating the nodes (the vertices of perimeter edges) that define the area, as shown in Figure 1.9. The area can be as simple as the triangle shown in the figure or as complex as the user desires. The only limitation is that the surface be planar; that is, it must have a "two-dimensional" quality. In area definition, then, the surface generated must be flat. It is possible to form nonplanar surfaces with area definition; however, the results displayed may differ from what the user expected. Often, the surface is twisted, as if you had taken a playing card and twisted it between your left and right hands.

Sweep profile is a higher order of surface generation. It generates a multitude of surfaces based on an initially created two-dimensional profile. First, a profile is created, as in Figure 1.10A. Then, using that profile, surfaces are formed around a central axis, creating a cylindrical shape with an unlimited profile, as in Figure 1.10B. The modeled surfaces can be created through a continuous 360 degrees around the axis and any part thereof. Any semicylindrical shape can be created—wine glasses, soda bottles, light bulbs, cockpit cowls. Each surface created is planar, but because of the number of surfaces created, the contour appears to be curved. The larger the number of surfaces, the smoother the model appears. This result is similar to the drawings produced on the popular children's two-dimensional drawing toy, the Etch A Sketch. As you probably remember from your childhood sketching, the greater the number of linear bits used to draw a circle, the smoother that shape appears.

Figure 1.9
Defining a surface area

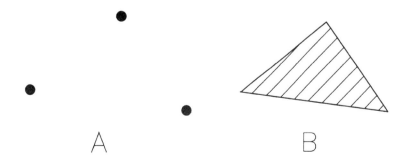

Figure 1.10
Sweeping a profile

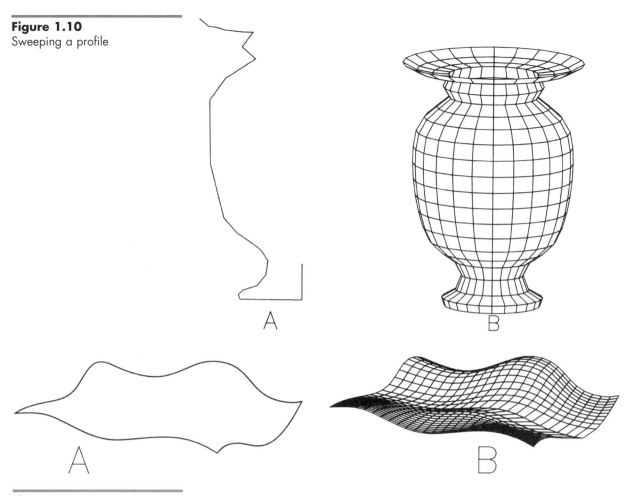

Figure 1.11
A contour mesh

Contour mesh is similar to sweep profile in that it also generates multiple surfaces. First, contour mesh generates several profiles; then, it creates surfaces to form a contoured shape, as shown in Figure 1.11. This can be quite calculation intensive because the intersection nodes that allow the blending of two or more curves to each other have to be calculated. However, the results can be quite amazing. This type of creation is used for items where irregular surfaces are the norm, such as automobiles, airplanes, and terrain modeling.

Solid Modeling

Up to this point, our discussion has focused on how wireframes are covered with flat surfaces to illustrate a model. This type of model is excellent for most applications that require only the exterior shell. Solid modeling is the culmination of the model building options. As the name implies, the user works with three-dimensional solids that have mass and density. As might be imagined, this is the most math/calculation-intensive building option, but it is the most accurate for model creation.

The process of manipulation is very simple: The user may take varied solid forms and add them together to form a complex object, as in Figure 1.12, or the user may subtract solid forms from each other to form the final object, as in Figure 1.13. In contrast to the user's simple manipulations, the CAD program is going through a lot of necessary calculations to generate the form. The resultant model, though accurate, can be time consuming and can create enormous CAD databases.

Figure 1.12
Adding two solids

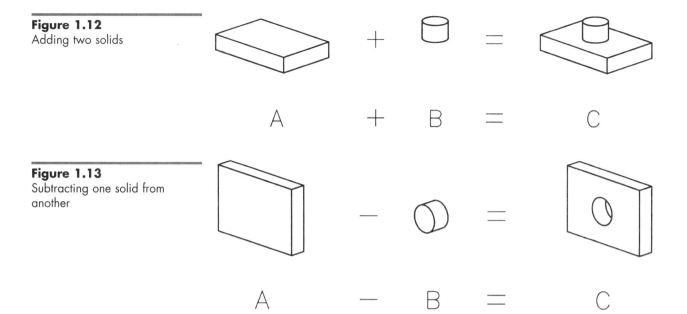

A   +   B   =   C

Figure 1.13
Subtracting one solid from another

A   —   B   =   C

1.5   Model Display Options

Just as there are a variety of building options, there are also a variety of ways in which the model can be presented on the screen to the viewer. The displaying and the building of the model are linked. Some methods of model building allow only certain methods of display. The three methods of model display representation are wireframe, edge removal, and rendering.

Wireframe is the most common way of displaying models in 3D CAD packages. Basically, it displays the model with all the edges visible to the viewer, regardless of where they are placed on the model, as shown in Figure 1.14. Think of the model as being made out of glass, so that all edges can be seen. This method is necessary for construction purposes; when constructing, it is important to be able to see where each line is going and how its path can affect other lines.

Edge removal (or, as it is commonly called, the hidden line removal option) displays the model to the viewer with foreground surfaces obstructing background surfaces. Those edges that would be obstructed by a surface between the edge and the view are not displayed. The lines or edges are not really removed, they simply are not displayed. Figure 1.15 is the same cylinder as the one shown in Figure 1.14, only in Figure 1.15 all that is visible are the unobstructed edges. The edge removal option requires surfaces or solids to function.

Figure 1.14
Wireframe display

Figure 1.15
Hidden lines removed display

Figure 1.16
A rendered display

Rendering is the technique of applying surface shades. The created surfaces are colored to accent the model, as shown in Figure 1.16. This shading can be of different types: (1) The surface can be plainly colored, based on the created surface color, or (2) the surface can be tone shaded, which is the process of giving tones to the surface color, based on different light sources, resulting in a range of light to dark tones. You can also create shadows as cast by the light sources hitting the model. Finally, rendering may assign surface textures or finishes as well. The surface can be very rough or smooth, or it may be a material such as wood, glass, or steel. The rendering option, like edge removal, requires surfaces or solids to function.

Again, it is up to the user to identify which method of display best suits the purpose of the project. But time must be considered when choosing a model display option—the more sophisticated the display, the more time required to generate it. Edge removal takes only a couple of keystrokes, whereas rendering can require the integration of a separate application program to achieve the desired results.

1.6 Model Viewing

Whereas model display defines how the model is illustrated, model viewing tells how the model is depicted according to the position of the viewer. The model will behave in a certain fashion based on the viewer position, regardless of whether it will be shown in wireframe, with edges removed, or rendered. The viewing position will determine how large or small the model appears or whether it will be shown axonometrically or perspectively.

When the model is viewed with axonometric viewing, the edges that represent the model are parallel along the *X, Y, Z* axes, as shown in Figure 1.17. In axonometric viewing, the model can be turned and viewed from any direction, and the node points that define the edges are projected orthographically (straight) toward the viewer. This is extremely useful for construction purposes.

Perspective viewing makes use of converging lines, as opposed to parallel lines, to represent the model (see Figure 1.18). This viewing represents more closely how the human eye sees the model, and it is a useful way to present the model to clients. In perspective viewing, the lines or objects that are going away from the viewer appear smaller as the distance increases, and finally they converge into a vanishing point.

In both axonometric and perspective viewing, the model can be turned to any viewing position and can be reduced or enlarged. At any point, the user can apply the type of display desired—wireframe, hidden line removed, or rendered.

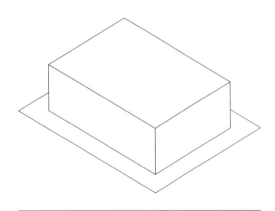

Figure 1.17
An axonometric view

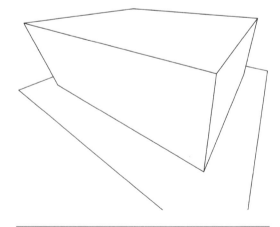

Figure 1.18
A perspective view

1.7 Working Planes

Almost all 3D creations are based on flat planes, referred to as *working planes*. Working planes form the reference point on which the building options are established. The final form is not necessarily flat, but its original creation point is built on a flat working plane (see Figures 1.19 through 1.22). In Figure 1.19, a cube has already been created. To construct a cylinder on the top of the cube, a working plane is defined, as shown in Figure 1.20; then the cylinder is added based on that working plane. Similarly, in Figure 1.21, a working plane is defined on the side of the cube

Figure 1.19
Initial cube

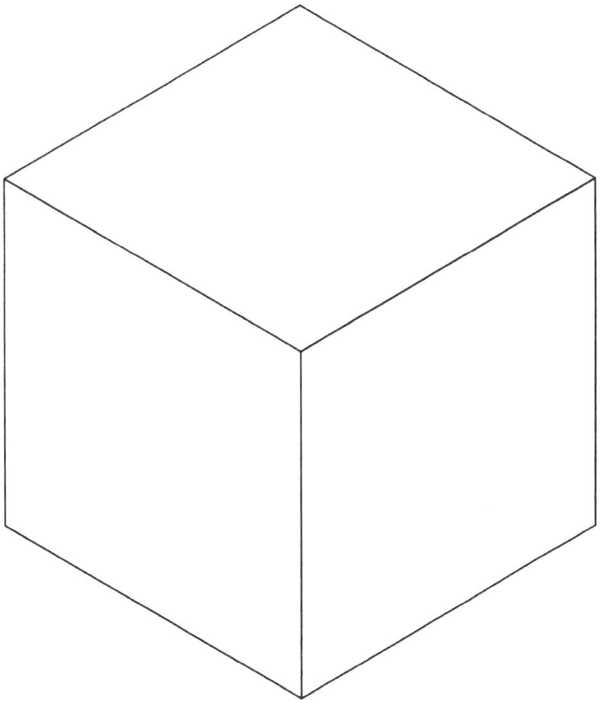

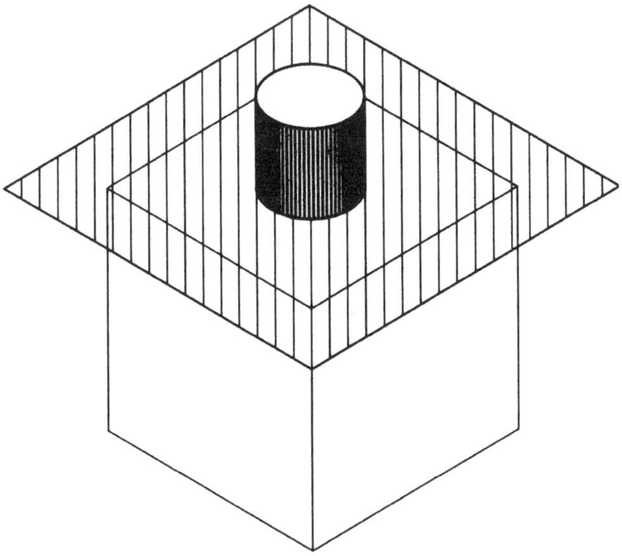

Figure 1.20
Creating a top working plane

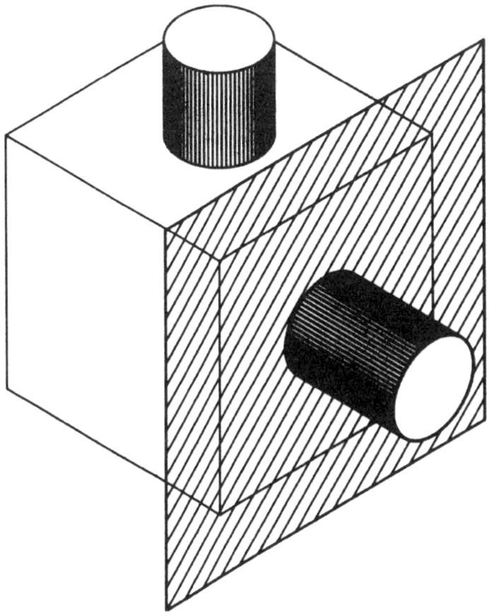

Figure 1.21
Creating a side working plane

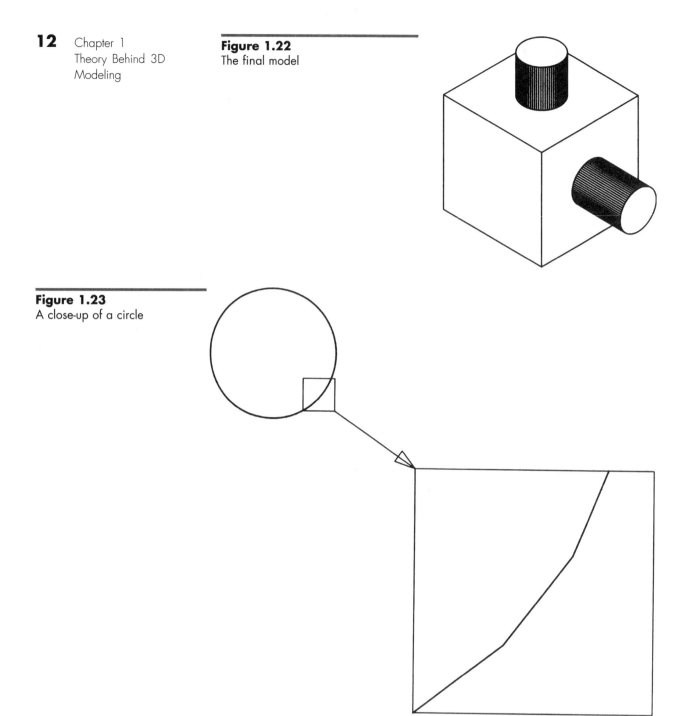

Figure 1.22
The final model

Figure 1.23
A close-up of a circle

and, from that plane, the second cylinder is added. Finally, as shown in Figure 1.22, the model is displayed.

Note that even though most curved geometry appears smooth, it is based on flat surfaces in its creation, as shown in Figure 1.23.

1.8 The Text and Lab Framework

Before we get into the thick of things, there are a few facts about the text and the labs we must note. These pointers should help you avoid unnecessary confusion when you're performing the labs. Where possible, the labs have been written in a standard format, with the major objectives and the primary commands to be used outlined for you. The labs reinforce the theories and concepts explained in the chapter through hands-on interaction.

AutoCAD Version

This text is written primarily for use with AutoCAD 2005. This does not mean that users of earlier versions are excluded. Users of previous releases will find that the majority of the text applies to them as well. If you are *not* using 2005, simply watch out for those specific areas where it has enhanced commands or rearranged menus.

3D Viewpoint Boxes

Throughout the text, you will find boxes titled "3D Viewpoint." These boxes emphasize some of the important dos and don'ts of 3D modeling. The following illustrates the concept.

3D VIEWPOINT

File Naming

When completing the labs, adopt a file naming convention that contains your initials. The length of the file name leaves space for at least two initials at the end, as in the case of the file name PLANSE, for "PLAN Stephen Ethier." It is a good idea to practice this initialing throughout the text, because it automatically distinguishes your work from others for the instructor's or your benefit.

File Referencing

As the book progresses, you will create models that build on each other. The initial labs may seem simple, but they will be used as stepping stones to more complicated model-creation techniques. When a model created in a lab or assignment is going to be used in later chapters, we explicitly mention it so that you will know of the requirement. We also mention when a previously constructed model will be required in a lab or assignment. This way, if you did not create the model the first time, you may go back, construct the model, and then use it for the required assignment.

Model Creation and the Use of Color

Virtually all the information required to construct a model is outlined in the labs. However, the mention of color for objects has been left out, mainly because this text is in black and white. Do not ignore the use of color. Models are customarily broken down into sections. You should use these sections to assign different colors; this will prove exceedingly useful when viewing the model during the construction stage. At a later time in the book, you will be creating composite models that involve, among other things, an orientation cube, wireframe techniques, 3D faces, and surface meshes. Making each of these elements a separate color is an excellent way to enhance visual distinction in the models. If you want to see one particular aspect of the model, you can turn all the other parts off, leaving only, say, the blue orientation cube or the red surface meshes. Also, when all parts are being viewed, you can distinguish each part of the model by its color on the viewing screen. Being able to distinguish the separate parts is essential during the construction phase of the more complex three-dimensional models.

Model Space and Paper Space

Within AutoCAD, there are two working environments: model space and paper space. Practically all design and creation take place in model space, and all three-dimensional work must take place in model space. Paper space is useful for preparing the model for presentation. The user creates and locates the necessary views and annotates these views in paper space. Usually, title blocks and borders are inserted in paper space. All entities created in paper space are flat, two-dimensional entities. Even the floating viewports created in paper space are flat. However, the displayed view inside the viewport can be, and often is, three-dimensional. Objects created in the two working environments are kept separate, allowing each to be modified independently.

The two environments are managed and kept separate with the TILEMODE system variable. When it is set to 1, you are working solely in model space and you will notice that the Model space tab at the bottom of the graphics screen is white, signifying it is active. If the TILEMODE system variable is set to 0, you are working in paper space and you will notice one of the Layout tabs at the bottom of the screen is white, signifying it is active.

With the Model tab active (TILEMODE = 1), any viewports you create are tiled or placed side-by-side.

With a Layout tab active, floating viewports can be created anywhere in a non-tiled fashion. Picking on the tabs switches back and forth between the model space environment and the paper space environment.

The floating viewports created in paper space contain model space views of your model. You can activate a floating viewport and manipulate the model as you would with the Model tab active. To activate a floating viewport, while in paper space, double-click inside the viewport. To return to the paper space environment, double-click in an open space outside any floating viewport.

Observe the buttons on the status line; they will change from PAPER to MODEL, letting you know which is active.

There is a new feature introduced in AutoCAD 2005. It is called Viewport Maximize and it has its own tool button on the status line when you are in a paper space layout.

When a floating viewport is active and you pick the Maximize Viewport button, the viewport is maximized to fill the screen and switched to model space for model editing. If the Paper tab is active and you double-click on the edge of the viewport it will perform the same function as clicking the Maximize Viewport button. Clicking the button again returns you to the normal paper space layout.

Tilemodes and Labs

As stated earlier, the creation of three-dimensional models must occur in model space, but it is up to you whether you choose to work in model space with TILEMODE set to 1 or 0. With TILEMODE set to 1, the working environment feels as it used to feel and, if you are just starting in 3D, this can be comforting. But with TILEMODE set to 0, you have more control over the creation of viewports and you may find this more beneficial. Basically, it is up to you to decide which method to employ. The labs do not specify which method to use unless they involve specifically practicing paper space capabilities.

Plotting

The chapter on plotting is placed later in the book so that you will have already produced some complex 3D work by that time. However, feel free to review the chapter earlier if you wish to see some of your early 3D work on paper.

Commands and Menus

Command entry in AutoCAD can be accomplished in several ways, including using the command line through the keyboard, a pull-down menu, a cursor context menu, a tool from a toolbar, a tablet menu, or a button menu.

This text concentrates on the access of commands through on-screen visual methods, acknowledging the fact that many individuals have access to a mouse rather than a digitizer for input. In addition, because of the versatility of on-screen icons (tools), more people may make use of these tools rather than the tablet method of input. Refer to the tear-out Quick Chart at the back of the book for a listing of the various toolbars used for 3D modeling. The tools are all identified for easy reference.

The commands to manipulate AutoCAD practically never change from release to release, although they are usually enhanced or added to. However, the order of pull-down menus do change from release to release, demonstrating AutoCAD's attempts to make the menus more user-friendly, although this can cause some confusion with users progressing to new releases. In any case, the method of accessing commands through the pull-down menus is given in the theoretical portion of the chapter concerned with that menu, and the use of direct commands at the command prompt, along with tools icons, are added in the labs. This should make your entry into 3D easier, regardless of which version of AutoCAD you are using.

It should also be noted that the term *pick*, which meant to press the left mouse button to pick an object or command, has now been replaced with the term *click*. So when you read an instruction such as *click a line*, it means that you are to move the cursor over the line and press the left mouse button to select the object.

Context Menu

Get in the habit of using the right-click context menu to perform functions. When you right-click, a menu appears on the screen giving you a series of options or commands. A context menu is intuitive. This means that it will present commands or options based on what you're doing.

CD-ROM and Internet Resources

The CD-ROM that's included with this book contains files that are used to assist in your practical exercises. See Appendix A about using those files. There is also a customized toolbar designed for 3D modeling. It is called A3D. Appendix A explains how to load and display the toolbar.

You'll also find many CAD resources on the www.viziwiz.com Web site. This site was created and is maintained by the authors of this book.

1.9 What's Ahead

Now that you have some grounding, you are ready to move on. Your basic understanding of the various 3D terms will enable you to master 3D construction. Before we embark on the ways in which AutoCAD can be used to accomplish the amazing feats described in the previous pages, we will explore how others have applied AutoCAD's 3D capabilities. The next chapter is devoted to actual user applications and should give you some insight in the uses of 3D. Then, Chapter 3 begins your introduction to AutoCAD's 3D commands.

Questions

1. Identify three benefits of 3D computer modeling.

2. Which discipline was the first major user of 3D? For what did it use 3D?

3. Explain what-if situations.

4. Identify the three axes that are used in 3D modeling, and explain how they are used.

5. What are the four 3D building options? How do they build on each other?

6. Surface generation can be accomplished by four different methods. Explain each.

7. What are the pros and cons of solid modeling?

8. What is the difference between displaying and viewing a 3D model?

9. Explain edge removal.

10. What is the difference between axonometric and perspective viewing?

11. What is the function of working planes?

Applications

Overview

This chapter explores the ways in which a variety of drafting and design disciplines use 3D models as well as the reasons why uses differ between disciplines. This very visual chapter includes examples from industry, business, and the arts to illustrate how these disciplines use 3D modeling techniques.

Concepts Explored

- Which 3D models are used in which disciplines
- How approaches differ when used on different model types

2.1 Introduction

As outlined in Chapter 1, the benefits of 3D modeling are numerous, and they can be applied in practically any discipline, from designing a better mousetrap to creating a digitized model to aid in the restoration of the Sphinx.

Although a variety of techniques and procedures may be used to create 3D models, each discipline relies mainly on specific techniques, depending on the design. Architects rely heavily on extrusion techniques for building walls, and they tend to use perspective views in the display of the final structure. Civil engineers use irregular 3D meshes to achieve results in terrain modeling. Mechanical manufacturers make use of solids to create accurate models of machined or welded parts and use axonometric views to detail the model. Structural designers rely on the use of 3D parametric symbols for the construction of structural members.

In the following pages, a myriad of disciplines and applications are discussed, and these examples show some of the possible hows of construction. As these discussions progress, we'll use a number of terms with which you probably are not yet acquainted. Although we cite a chapter and sometimes a section reference for each term, don't feel an obligation to follow up each reference at this point. These terms are included for two reasons: First, they give you a brief taste of things to come and a better understanding of how each of these constructions is achieved through specific AutoCAD commands. Second, after completing later chapters and learning the terms by using the commands within your own constructions, you can come back to Chapter 2 with a greater understanding of the terms.

2.2 Model Illustrations

From Two Dimensions to Three Dimensions

The drawings shown in Figures 2.1 and 2.2 show the ease with which a line drawing can be turned into a three-dimensional model.

Figure 2.1A shows a two-dimensional floor plan. By adding thickness to the wall lines, the 2D plan can easily be turned into 3D, as shown in Figure 2.1B. Using this fast method, you can get a "feel" for room volumes.

Figure 2.2A shows a two-dimensional profile of a soft-drink can. By revolving the profile around its center axis, it turns into a three-dimensional model, as shown in Figure 2.2B. Figure 2.2C shows the effect of rendering the 3D model.

Building Complex

When constructing a model of a building complex, such as the one shown in Figure 2.3, a model maker uses a variety of 3D techniques. Extruded lines (Chapter 5) are used for flat, rectangular surfaces such as the vertical building walls and retaining wall tops, whereas irregularly shaped flat surfaces created with 3D faces (Section 7.3) are used to cover the variable surfaces, such as roof tops and sloped retaining walls. In the case of surfaces that radiate from a central point, such as the main entrance-way, the polygon-mesh-generating RULESURF (Section 8.3) command automates the process. To construct items such as the rectangular-box–shaped skylights, simply specifying the shape and size desired automatically creates a 3D object (Section 8.2) to suit.

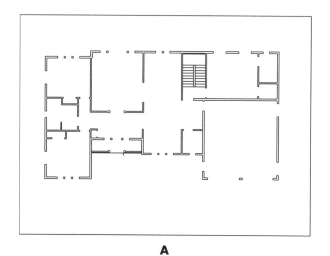

A

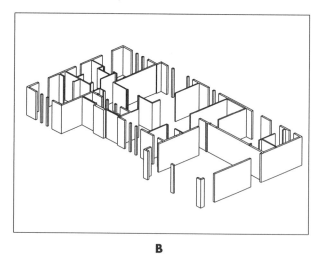

B

Figure 2.1
2D floor plan to 3D model using thickness

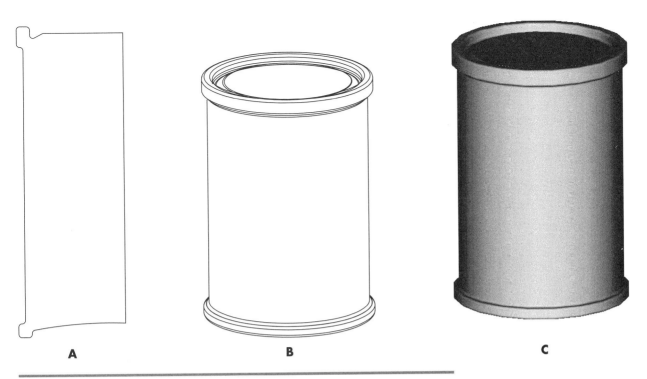

Figure 2.2
2D profile to 3D model using revolution and rendering

A   B   C

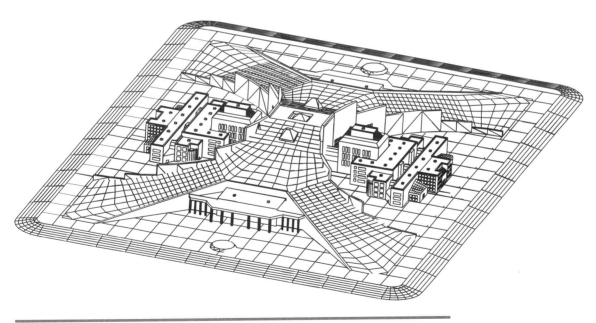

Figure 2.3
Model of a building complex (hidden lines removed)
Source: Student project

Park and Streetcar Station

The drawing shown in Figure 2.4, which was prepared by Pietz and Michal Architects in Keene, New Hampshire, and created by modeler Charles Michal, displays a complex park setting generated with a variety of extruded lines and circles (Chapter 5). Because the trunks of the trees are tapered and truncated, a truncated cone is used (Section 8.2). The leaf structure of the trees could be made from the linking of flat, irregular surfaces constructed from 3D faces (Section 7.3). When the design requires a series of parallel surfaces such as the walkways, the TABSURF (Section 8.3) command creates them automatically. After this drawing was produced, it was rendered (Chapter 17) in ink and pencil to enhance its artistic appearance for 3D animated walk-throughs on video tape.

Steel Arch Bridge

With bridges such as the one modeled in Figure 2.5, symmetry is the key. The bridge shown here is a very impressive structure, but it can be broken down into unique pieces to make the task of 3D construction easier. Because of the many related members, parametric symbols (standard designs that can be applied to differing sets of parameters; Chapter 14) can be employed to make the job of construction proceed more quickly. Parametric symbols could also be used for the light standards, and the roadway could be created by drawing its profile and then extruding it to form its length (Section 14.2).

Figure 2.4
Model of a park setting with streetcar station (hidden lines removed)
Source: Courtesy of Pietz and Michal Architects

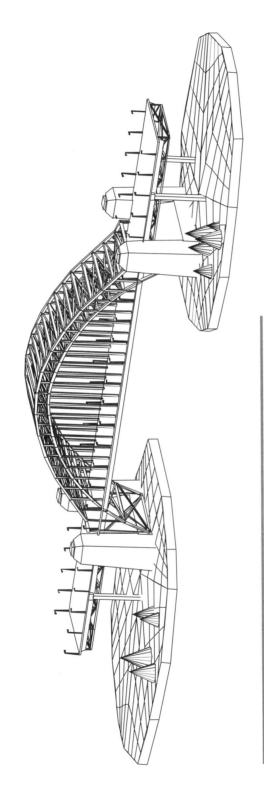

Figure 2.5
Steel arch bridge model (hidden lines removed)
Source: Student project

Office Layout

The office layout model in Figure 2.6, generated by Charles Michal of Pietz and Michal Architects, uses many extruded lines and forms in the construction of the office furniture and cabinets (Chapter 5). The rounded reception desk, which is the focal point of the drawing, uses an extruded arc in a most effective way.

Turboprop Airplane

For the creation of the airplane shown in Figure 2.7, a wireframe skeleton is constructed initially. Once this is done, the skeleton controls the automatic application of surface skins, relying heavily on Coons surface patches created by the EDGESURF command (Section 8.3), to construct such items as the wings and tail pieces. The fuselage (body) could be constructed out of either Coons surface patches or a series of ruled surfaces using the RULESURF command.

Racing Car

The racing car body shown in Figure 2.8 is composed of many flat but irregular surfaces. This is the perfect application of the 3DFACE command (Section 7.3). Because tires are naturally round but tend to have a unique tread profile, they require the use of the REVSURF command (Section 8.3), with its ability to take a profile of any shape and revolve it about an axis to create a series of surfaces that form the final shape. The nose of the body uses radial surfaces formed with the RULESURF command. The tips of the spoilers are rounded but parallel along their lengths, requiring use of the TABSURF command (Section 8.3).

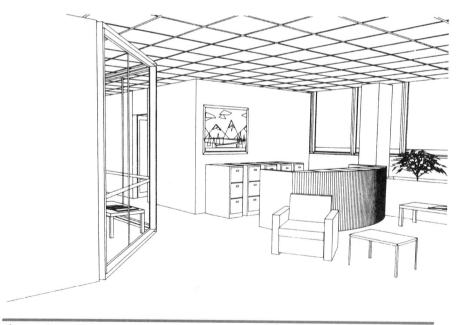

Figure 2.6
Model of an office layout (hidden lines removed)
Source: Courtesy of Pietz and Michal Architects

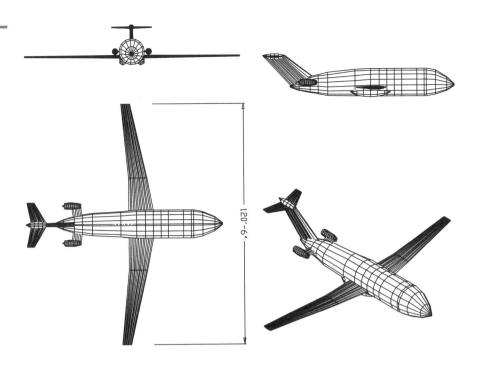

Figure 2.7
Turboprop airplane model
(hidden lines removed)
Source: Student project

120'-6'

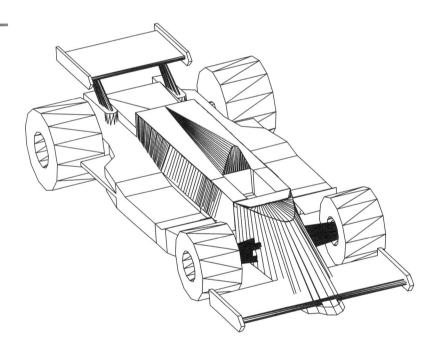

Figure 2.8
Racing car model (hidden lines
removed)
Source: Student project

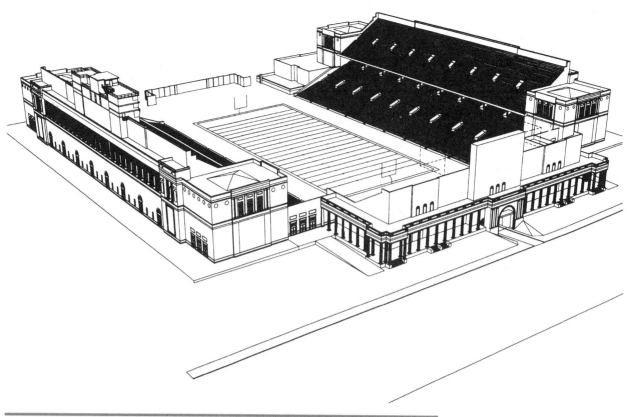

Figure 2.9
Model of Memorial Stadium at University of Illinois (hidden lines removed)
Source: Courtesy of Severns, Reid & Associates, Inc.

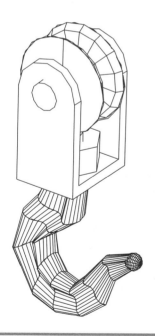

Figure 2.10
Crane hook (hidden lines removed)
Source: Student project

Memorial Stadium

The complex model of the new south stands and memorial colonnade for Memorial Stadium at the University of Illinois was created by modeler Craig Burgess from a design by architect John Severns at Severns, Reid & Associates, Inc. This model, shown in Figure 2.9, has a minimum of detail because of the building's size and complicated appearance. The stands, vomitories, and colonnades are drawn in true 3D, thereby lending themselves to the production of video walk-throughs. The stadium was a project of the University of Illinois, Urbana–Champaign. The campus architect was Roland Kehe and the project manager was George Hendricks.

Crane Hook

The model of a crane hook presented in Figure 2.10 uses a variety of surface techniques, most of which require wireframe construction to create cross–sectional profiles. Then surface techniques are applied, similar to the creation of the airplane model in Figure 2.7; the pulley wheel uses surfaces of revolution created by the REVSURF command (Section 8.3), the hook requires a combination of Coons surface patches and surface revolutions (EDGESURF and REVSURF commands), and the nut could be constructed from an extruded polygon.

Hilly Terrain

The three-dimensional construction of the model shown in Figure 2.11 relies totally on the use of topologically rectangular meshes created with the 3DMESH

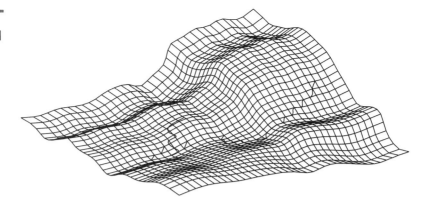

command (Section 8.3). The user or an outside program supplies all the coordinates, including elevations of all the vertices, and AutoCAD automatically links the various surfaces to generate the topographic map. Then, 3D polylines could be used to add rivers and roads.

Boardroom

A model such as the one shown in Figure 2.12 uses 3D faces (Section 7.3) for most of the construction because of the irregular flat surfaces, such as the table top and the chair backs. The pedestal supports for the table could be made of extruded polylines (Section 5.3) as could the chair columns and legs.

Antenna Tower

The model of an antenna tower depicted in Figure 2.13 is interesting in that it illustrates one of the practical purposes of 3D modeling. This 80-foot tower designed for cable television was produced by modeler David Devereaux-Weber of American Communications Consultants, Inc. The model uses a 3D approach to ensure that

Figure 2.12
Boardroom table and chairs model (hidden lines removed)
Source: Student project

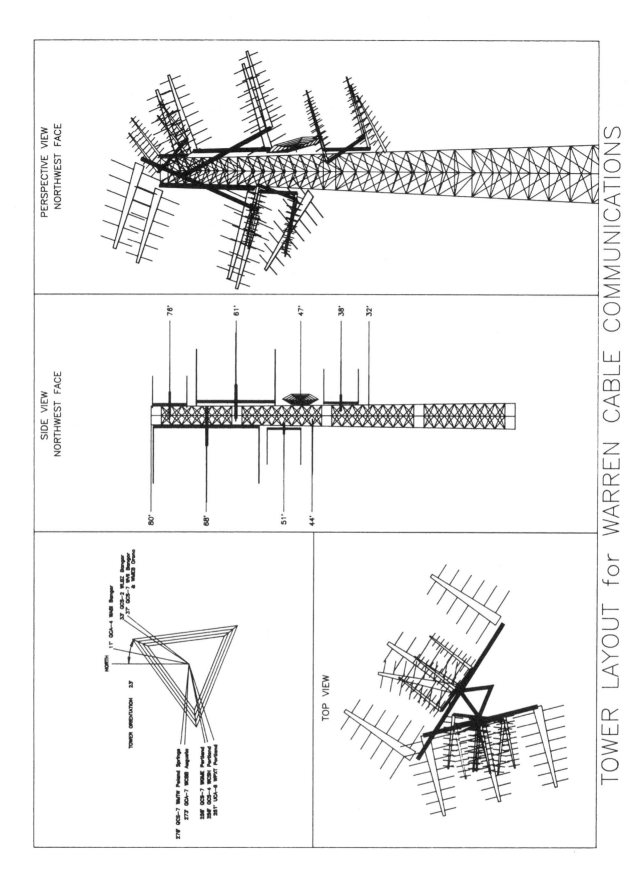

Figure 2.13

Antenna tower model (wireframe)

Source: Courtesy of American Communications Consultants, Inc.

none of the structural members of the antennas is in the same place at the same time—something that drawing in 2D could not guarantee. With the aid of this drawing created from the 3D model, the tower erector will know at what height and azimuth to install the antennas.

Diver's Helmet

The helmet shown in Figure 2.14 is composed of many curved surfaces allowing semiautomatic means to be employed in its creation. The head piece and the spherical knobs on the front of the shoulder yoke are constructed with revolved surfaces using the REVSURF command (Section 8.3). The rim of the shoulder yoke uses the RULESURF command because it requires radial surfaces. The base of the shoulder yoke is created through parallel tabulated surfaces with the use of the TABSURF command and the front of the faceplate base is made from extruded polylines that have width (Section 5.3).

Heart

The model of the heart shown in Figure 2.15 is initially created in wireframe. Wires (lines) are constructed from point to point and then 3D faces (Section 7.3) are placed over the model to allow hidden edge removal and surface shading. Terrain modeling, illustrated in Figure 2.11, could also use the 3DMESH command (Section 8.3).

Residential Dwelling

Figure 2.16 presents an attractive model of a house with attached garage. Initially constructed from extruded lines to define the preliminary model, the extrusions were replaced with 3D faces (Section 7.3) once the overall shape had been defined. 3D symbols (Chapter 13) of windows and doors were created as separate files and then inserted at all the desired locations. Finally, to accent the model, 2D hatching was applied for siding, brick, and roofing tiles.

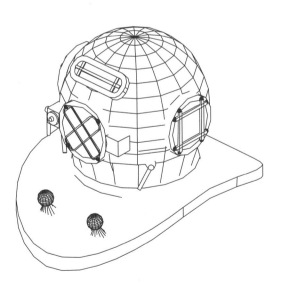

Figure 2.14
Deep sea diver's helmet model (hidden lines removed)
Source: Student project

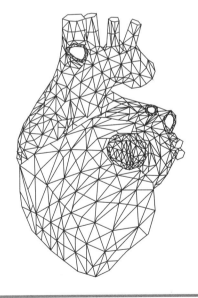

Figure 2.15
Heart model (hidden lines removed)
Source: Student project

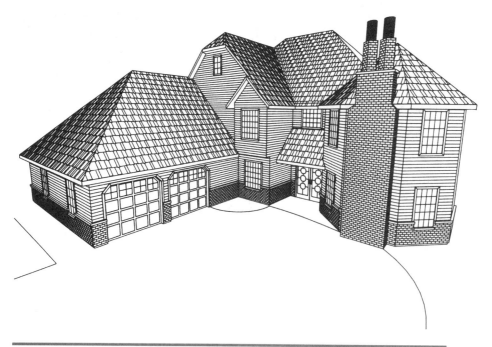

Figure 2.16
Residential dwelling model (hidden lines removed)

Miniature Pneumatic Cylinder

The miniature pneumatic cylinder body modeled in Figure 2.17 was constructed initially using solid modeling (Chapters 9 through 12). Solid three-dimensional objects such as cylinders and boxes were added to and subtracted from each other to create the final shape. Using the finished solid model, mass calculations can be performed to find its weight, its center of gravity, and much more. Because it is a solid model,

Figure 2.17
Solid model of a miniature pneumatic cylinder body (rendered)

Figure 2.18
Rendered kitchen model

its three-dimensional data could be sent to a stereolithography apparatus (SLA) and a physical, tangible part could be created. As a finishing touch to the illustration, this model was rendered (Chapter 17) inside of AutoCAD.

Kitchen

The illustration in Figure 2.18 shows a rendered kitchen model created with 3D symbols (Chapter 13). The symbols of the refrigerator, sink, cabinetry, and other similar components were created in their own files and then assembled to create the final kitchen model. These components use extruded lines capped with 3D faces. Specifically, the countertop was created with 3D faces (Section 7.3) with an opening left for the sink. The mug and coffeepot are made of revolved surfaces using the REVSURF command (Section 8.3). Once the model was finished, it was rendered using advanced rendering (Chapter 17). With advanced rendering, surface materials can make objects appear transparent or shadows can be automatically calculated and shown. Look closely at the screen of the laptop computer on the countertop; it is displaying the rendered model of the kitchen. Rendering allows the modeler to apply previously created images to 3D geometry.

Rendered House Model

Figure 2.19 shows a house model in a day scene and a night scene. This model was created with the extensive use of Regions (Chapter 7). Regions makes the creation of irregular 2D surfaces, such as the roof and walls, easy to accomplish. By using regions for the walls, window openings can be cut into the walls, allowing you to see inside the house. Note that you can create realistic renderings (Chapter 17); with the proper placement of lights, a single model can be shown in the daylight or at night. This model was the creative work of Eric Allard.

29

A   B

Figure 2.19
Day and night scene of a house

2.3 Summary

Now that you have seen what can be done with three-dimensional modeling, it's time to learn how to do it. Throughout the following chapters, you will learn and apply three-dimensional modeling techniques in a steadily advancing process until you are able to create models as complex or even more complex that those shown in this chapter. In Part 2, you will prepare yourself by learning how to move around in 3D space and how to create working planes. Then you will dig into the actual construction techniques outlined in Part 3. In Part 4 you will learn about solid modeling, building on the techniques presented in preceding chapters, but using another area of 3D modeling—the formation of models from true solids.

When you have mastered the various methods of creation, you will then learn how to produce the models more efficiently and how to present them to others in Parts 5 and 6. At this point, you'll be ready to tackle any type of 3D construction and can move on to any of the applications presented in Part 7.

Part 8 contains an introduction to three programs, Mechanical Desktop, Autodesk VIZ, and Autodesk Inventor, that can be integrated within AutoCAD or used separately to enhance your models.

Questions

1. What is the 3D modeling technique upon which architects rely so heavily? Why?

2. What technique do civil engineers most commonly use? Why?

3. What techniques described in Chapter 2 might be used when creating the model of a working farm? Explain where you would use these techniques.

4. From what you have learned of 3D modeling techniques in Chapter 2, list some 3D modeling procedures that would be helpful for the construction of a train.

5. Upon which technique do mechanical engineers rely heavily? Why?

6. Sketch a model of your own that would require at least three of the techniques already explored. Label the drawing locations where these techniques could be applied.

7. Look ahead at Figure 4.1 in Chapter 4. What 3D techniques might have been used to create these models?

Preparing for Construction of 3D Models

Before you actually create a 3D model, it is essential that you become familiar with the commands that allow movement through the 3D space created on the screen. This part includes step-by-step explanations and a number of suggested exercises to familiarize you with this three-dimensional movement. Chapters 3 and 4 introduce some simple labs that are designed to involve you quickly and prepare you for the more complex creation of geometric constructs that begin in the next part.

Display of 3D Models for Construction

Overview

The techniques you'll learn in this chapter will serve as the foundation of the skills you'll need for 3D model construction in later chapters. In simple terms, this chapter could be entitled, "how to walk around and look." The chapter instructs you in how to thoroughly explore a variety of processes for moving around the on-screen model, for viewing the model in a number of ways, and for altering the display of the model to enhance the visual imagery. In addition, this chapter gives you your first lesson in saving a 3D model.

Concepts Explored

- The difference between axonometric and perspective displays
- The importance of axonometric display in the construction phase of modeling
- The manipulation of viewpoints
- The various methods of changing the viewpoint
- Controlling the orientation of view
- The need for multiple viewports
- The creation techniques used in configuring viewports
- The application of hidden line removal to enhance the viewing of the model

3.1 Introduction

To facilitate the construction of 3D models, proper procedures for viewing need to be adopted. First, the operator needs to choose the manner in which the model will be viewed. As mentioned in Chapter 1, there are two main ways of viewing a model—axonometrically and perspectively. Although perspective views display a very realistic image of how the viewer would see the actual model (see Figure 3.1A), It is often hard to distinguish whether the geometry has been designed correctly. (For instance, are corners square or at right angles?) With axonometric views, on the other hand, it is much more apparent whether corners are square or edges are parallel to each other (see Figure 3.1B). Because of this difference, axonometric viewing is the primary method of viewing a model during the construction phase.

Let's consider some techniques of on-screen model display. Axonometric viewing makes use of orthographic techniques to view an object. With axonometric viewing, sometimes referred to as parallel projection, the object is turned on any axis and

Figure 3.1

A perspective view and an
axonometric view

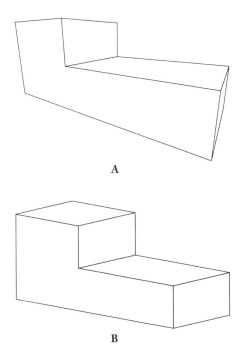

A

B

the view is projected straight toward or perpendicular to the viewer. Then it is outlined on a viewing or picture plane, thereby generating the image that shows three sides of the object. This method of on-screen display is accomplished in AutoCAD by means of the VPOINT command, which stands for viewpoint, or by using the newer interactive 3DORBIT command.

A second technique of on-screen model display utilizes multiple views of the model at one time. This technique allows the construction to move along at a faster pace because the designer can see the effects of construction on different locations on the model at the same time. You can see the three-dimensional aspect of the addition of the cylinder to the angle bracket illustrated in Figure 3.2A. At the same time, looking at Figure 3.2B, you can see that the cylinder is off-center of the horizontal plate. And, finally, observing Figure 3.2C, you can see that the cylinder is not actually touching the horizontal plate. By maintaining several different views of a model on the screen at one time, design deficiencies can be caught early in the

Figure 3.2

The need for multiple viewpoints
of the same model

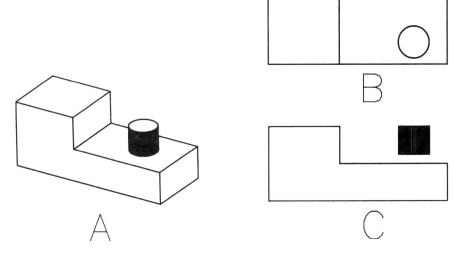

A

B

C

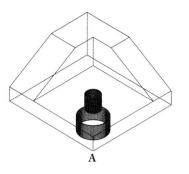
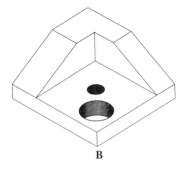
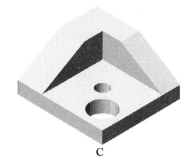

A B C

Figure 3.3
Wireframe, hidden line removed, and shaded views

design, saving time and preventing errors from accumulating. This method of on-screen display is accomplished in AutoCAD by using the VPORTS command, which stands for multiple viewports.

A third technique involves displaying the model with normally viewed obstructed edges in wireframe hidden from the viewer, thereby presenting an enhanced view. This enhanced view can clarify the construction of the model, especially when lines appear to be overlapping each other but are actually in front of or behind each other, separated by a distance. A model appears in wireframe display in Figure 3.3A; the same model is shown with edges hidden from the viewer in Figure 3.3B. It is useful to check the model construction periodically by viewing the model in this mode. This method of on-screen display is accomplished in AutoCAD by using the HIDE command, which stands for hidden line removal.

The fourth technique involves using shade modes. These modes add color and tone over the surfaces of the model, allowing you to distinguish entire surfaces (see Figure 3.3C).

3.2 View Toolbar

The easiest method of displaying and saving different views of your model is using the View toolbar shown in Figure 3.4.

Along the View toolbar there are various cube shapes with shaded surfaces. The first six cubes represent various preset orthographic views such as top and front.

The remaining four cubes represent preset common isometric views such as SW (southwest) and NE (northeast). Simply clicking one of the tools displays the desired view. All tools perform a Zoom Extents automatically.

The first tool on the View toolbar is used to save the view coordinates under a unique name. You can then recall the view at anytime. You should get used to saving views as you create them, especially when you start creating perspective views that are often time consuming to duplicate. To save a view, click the Named Views tool and the View dialog box appears as in Figure 3.5A. Clicking the New tool presents you with the New View dialog box as in Figure 3.5B. Note that the Save UCS with view box is turned off. At this stage, it's better for the beginner to turn this off. Later on when you're familiar with creating a UCS working plane, you may want to turn it back on.

Figure 3.4
View toolbar

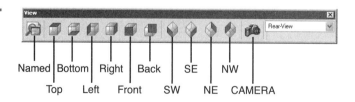

Named | Bottom | Right | Back | SE | NW
    Top   Left   Front   SW   NE   CAMERA

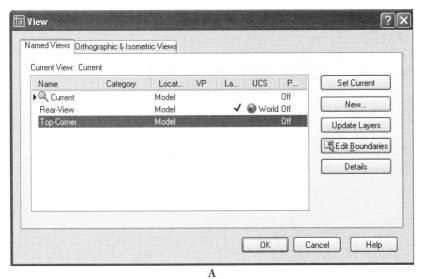

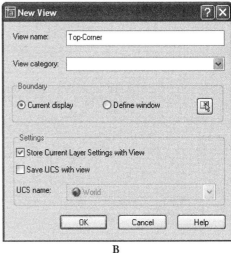

A   B

Figure 3.5
View and New View dialog boxes

To restore a view, highlight the name in the View dialog box and click the Set Current button, then the OK button.

There is also an Orthographic & Isometric Views tab, as shown in Figure 3.5A. This allows you to select preset views, although it's probably easier to use the other view tools, which we explain next.

The last tool is for generating camera views. This is explained further in later chapters.

3.3 **3D Orbit**

An interactive method for displaying a view of the model can be accomplished by using the 3DORBIT command. You can access the command by typing it on the command line, clicking it from the View pull-down menu, or using the 3D Orbit icon from the 3D Orbit toolbar.

When the command is activated, a large circle with four small circles appears on the screen (see Figure 3.6); it is referred to as the arc ball. When you move your cursor around, inside, or on the four small circles, the cursor changes to reflect the type of view rotation. Depending on where you click and drag your cursor, the view will rotate to a new position. Refer to Figure 3.6 and the following descriptions of the rotation axes.

	Circular	When you move the cursor outside the arc ball, the cursor changes to a circular arrow. When you click and drag around the outside of the arc ball, the view rotation takes place around an axis that is perpendicular to the viewing plane or screen. When you release the click button, the view rotation stops.
	Horizontal	When you move the cursor into one of the small circles on the left or right side of the arc ball, the cursor changes to a horizontal elliptical arrow. When you click and drag left or right, the view rotation takes place around a horizontal axis that is parallel to the viewing plane or screen. When you release the click button, the view rotation stops.

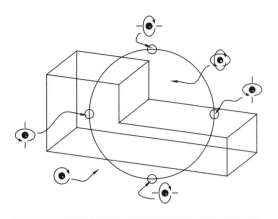

Figure 3.6
Active 3DORBIT command showing arc ball with sample cursors added

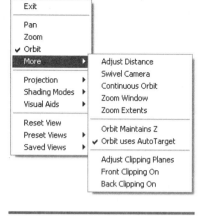

Figure 3.7
3DORBIT shortcut menu

Vertical

When you move the cursor into one of the small circles on the top or bottom of the arc ball, the cursor changes to a vertical elliptical arrow. When you click and drag up or down, the view rotation takes place around a horizontal axis that is parallel to the viewing plane or screen. When you release the click button, the view rotation stops.

Spherical

When you move the cursor inside the arc ball, the cursor changes to a combination of the horizontal elliptical arrow and vertical elliptical arrow. When you click and drag inside the arc ball, the view rotation takes place around both axes. When you release the click button, the view rotation stops.

3D VIEWPOINT

Setting the Target of the 3DORBIT

An easy way to focus on a single object when using the 3DORBIT command is to click the object just before you activate the command. Only that object will be displayed. Once you exit the command, the rest of the objects appear. Another way to set the target is to use the 3DORBITCTR command. This centers the target on a point you select.

If you right-click while the 3DORBIT command is active, a context menu similar to Figure 3.7 appears. If you click More under the 3DOrbit context menu, you are presented with more options. From this new list, you can turn on Orbit Maintains Z. This has the effect of keeping the object flat while you rotate around it using the spherical cursor rotation.

3.4 Viewpoint Manipulation

The VPOINT command is used to display accurately any viewpoint of the model. The first step in the proper viewing of a model is to identify two crucial components: (1) the center of interest (the piece of the image at which the viewer is looking) and (2) the viewer's position in relation to the model. The center of interest is set with the AutoCAD system variable TARGET. This variable is set to the default location of 0,0,0.

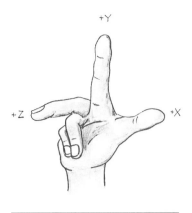

Figure 3.8
The right-hand rule

In most cases, to generate the axonometric views, all you need do is enter the position of the viewer. The VPOINT command has four methods of entering this location: (1) entering the three-dimensional *X, Y, Z* coordinates, (2) rotating the model through angles, (3) rotating the model by the use of a compass, and (4) using preset locations.

Command: **VPOINT**
Current view direction: VIEWDIR = 0. 0000,0. 0000,1. 0000
Specify a viewpoint or [Rotate]
Enter coordinates or options
<display compass and tripod>:

To help with the visualization of the model in three-dimensional space, AutoCAD uses the right-hand rule to define all coordinate systems. This rule is illustrated in Figure 3.8. To try it yourself, hold your right hand in front of the screen, with the back of the hand parallel to the screen, and make a fist. Now extend the thumb out, toward the right; this points in the positive *X* direction. Extend the index (or first) finger upward; this points in the positive *Y* direction. And, finally, extend the middle finger toward yourself; this points in the positive *Z* direction.

You can use the CAMERA command to set the center of interest and the target point using *X, Y, Z* coordinates.

3D VIEWPOINT

The VPOINT Command

The VPOINT command does not function in paper space. This is because paper space is designed for flat, two-dimensional layouts, whereas the VPOINT command is designed for 3D viewing.

VPOINT Coordinate Input

Entering coordinates to set the location of the view is an accurate way to get the required view of the model. When the VPOINT command is first selected, two things happen. First, the UCS icon dims. This is to tell the user that the entering of coordinates is based on the World Coordinate System, which is outlined in Chapter 4. In simple terms, the WCS is the main *X, Y, Z* coordinate system that keeps track of all the coordinate entries. Its 0,0,0 point is the reference point of all geometric creation.

Second, the user is prompted for the *X, Y, Z* viewpoint location. At this time, the user enters the *X, Y, Z* coordinates, which may be positive or negative and may have any numerical value (see Figure 3.9). The positive and negative values of the coordinates control whether the viewer is viewing from above or below the model, behind or in front of it, or to the right or left side of it (see Figure 3.10). *Positive* means the viewer is moving along an axis in the positive direction, away from the model. *Negative* means the viewer is moving along the axis in a negative direction, away from the model. *Zero input* means that there is no movement along that axis.

Entering a number, whether positive or negative, in only one axis generates a standard orthographic view (i.e., top, front, or side view). Entering a number in all three axes generates a pictorial axonometric view, as shown in Figure 3.11.

Because the view generated in all cases is based on parallel projection, the numerical value of the input has no effect on the size of the object. VPOINT always generates a zoom extents view. The user then makes use of the regular zoom functions to manipulate the size or placement of the view. The numerical value does have an effect on rotation of the model (see Figure 3.12). When all three axis values are set

37

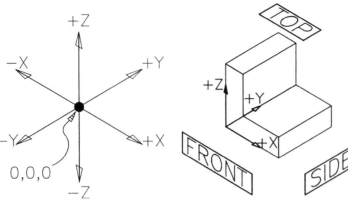

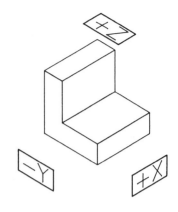

Figure 3.9
3D axes

Figure 3.10
Relation of views to axes

Figure 3.11
Viewpoints and their coordinates

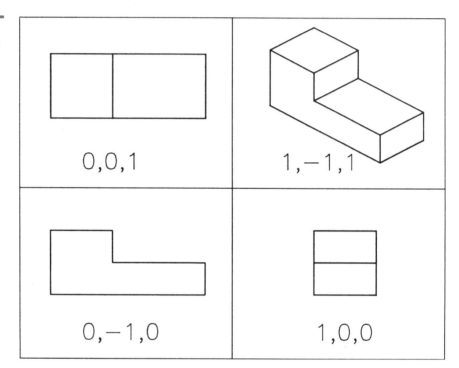

to the same quantity, whether positive or negative, an isometric view is generated. *Isometric* means all three axis angles are equal. If only two of the three axis values are the same numerical value, then a dimetric view is generated. *Dimetric* means two axis angles are different. If all three axis values are different, then a trimetric view is generated. *Trimetric* means all three axis angles are different.

VPOINT Rotation Input

Rotation input is the method of entering angular values to rotate planes away from the 0,0,0 location, as illustrated in Figure 3.13. To access this procedure, select the VPOINT command and then enter **R** for rotate at the option prompt. The user is first asked for the rotation angle (A) from the *X* axis along the *X–Y* plane. This is almost the same as a 2D rotation command. The second angle input required (B) is the rotation from the *X–Y* plane in the *Z* direction. This is similar to tilting the viewer

Figure 3.12
The three types of axonometric views

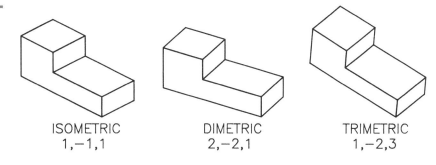

Figure 3.13
Spherical coordinates used in rotation

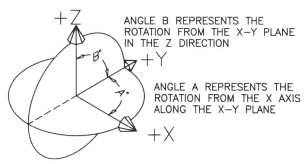

position away from the model up or down in the Z axis. After both angles are inputted, the resulting view is displayed.

VPOINT Compass Input

The compass method of input is the most visual and quickest way of displaying an axonometric view of a model using the VPOINT command. To access the compass command, enter the VPOINT command and then simply press the Enter key or select Views/3D Views/Viewpoint from the pull-down menus. At this point, the screen switches from the graphics screen to the compass input screen, which is shown in Figure 3.14A.

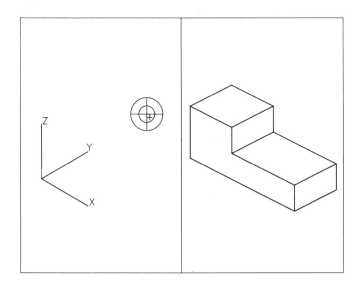

Figure 3.14A
The compass point and the resulting view above

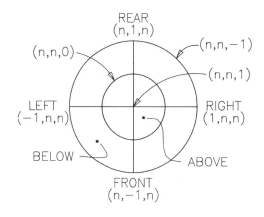

Figure 3.14B
The compass defined

39

Figure 3.15
Pull-down menu access to VPOINT

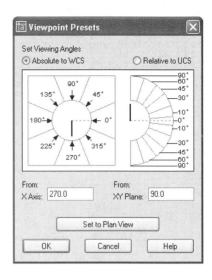

Contained in the compass input screen are two movement feedback icons. The first is the compass, which is displayed in the upper-right-hand corner of the screen. By moving the cursor, represented by a small cross, around the compass icon, a desired orientation is achieved. As the cross is moved about the compass, the second feedback icon reflects that movement. The second icon is a tripod representation of the three (*X, Y, Z*) axes. It will turn, twist, and flip based on the placement of the cursor on the compass. By moving the cursor around in a circular fashion, you can achieve a front, side, or rear view combination, either above or below the model. Figure 3.14A illustrates these views.

The compass is a two-dimensional representation of the World Coordinate System. Look at Figure 3.14B. The center of the compass represents the north pole, or the positive *Z* axis. The outer ring of the compass represents the south pole, or the negative *Z* axis. The inner ring represents the equator, or the 0 point on the *Z* axis.

VPOINT Preset Input

AutoCAD provides a pop-up dialog box containing preset viewpoints (see Figure 3.15). This box is accessible from the View pull-down menu under the 3D Views/Viewpoint Presets heading. Here, the user is presented with two feedback icons. The one on the left controls the angles from the *X* axis along the *X–Y* plane, which affects movement around the model. The one on the right controls the angles from the *X–Y* plane, which affects the viewer's elevation. The preset settings are a combination of VPOINT rotation input and VPOINT compass input, allowing for the precision of the rotation input while retaining the graphical feedback of the compass input. Exact values can be entered in the two boxes provided below the icons.

Preset Views

To make the process of displaying different views of your model easier, there are preset views that automatically set the viewpoint, such as Top, Front, and NE Isometric. These can be found under the View/3D Views pull-down menu or on the View toolbar.

3.5 The PLAN Command

To provide a quick way of displaying a plan or top view of the model, AutoCAD has included a command called PLAN. The PLAN command has two functions. The first is to display the plan view of the WCS, and the second is to display the plan

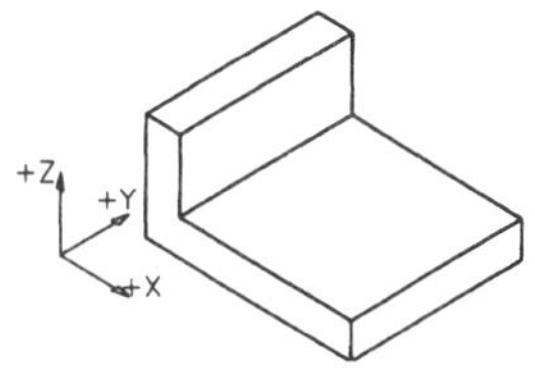

Figure 3.16
Model oriented to the *X, Y, Z*
axes

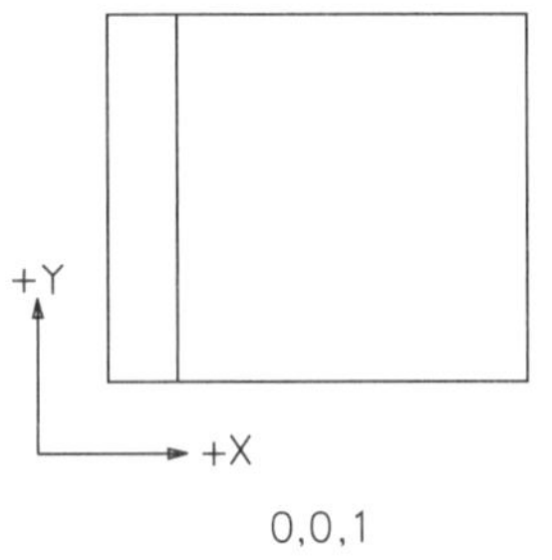

0,0,1

−0.0000001,0,1

Figure 3.17
Standard top view

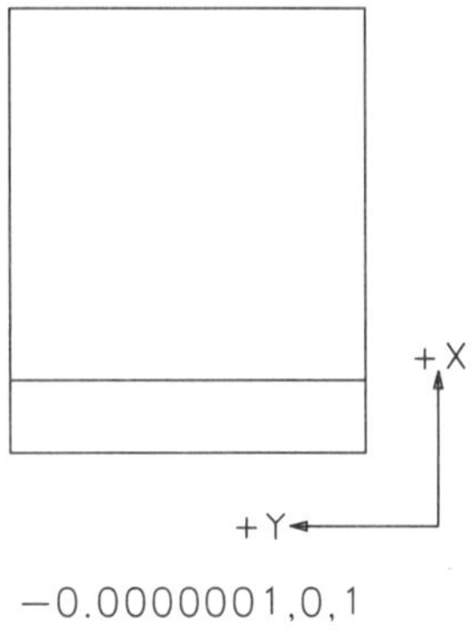

Figure 3.18
Top view turned 90°

view of the current User Coordinate System (UCS), which is explained in detail in Chapter 4. Using the WCS option of the PLAN command has the same effect as entering 0,0,1 for VPOINT coordinates.

3D VIEWPOINT

The PLAN Command

The PLAN command is a fast way of displaying the current UCS parallel with the screen. Simply type PLAN on the command line and press Enter twice.

Orientation Control

When entering coordinates to place the viewpoint for the standard orthographic views shown in Section 3.2, the final orientation of the model on the screen is always the same. However, it is not necessarily the orientation that would best suit construction or viewing. Take, for instance, the model shown in Figure 3.16. To display a top or plan view, the coordinates 0,0,1 are entered; the resulting view is shown in Figure 3.17.

It is possible to have more control over the orientation by entering almost nondiscernible values for an axis input instead of entering a zero (see Figure 3.18). The values entered to display this view were −0.0000001,0,1. A very small value for the *X* axis was given, which caused the model to be displayed with the −*X* direction pointing down. You can also use 3DORBIT to rotate the view.

Any viewpoint displayed on the screen can be saved by using the common VIEW command. Then, at any time, that viewpoint can be restored using VIEW and selecting the previously saved name.

Figure 3.19
Multiple viewports (four)

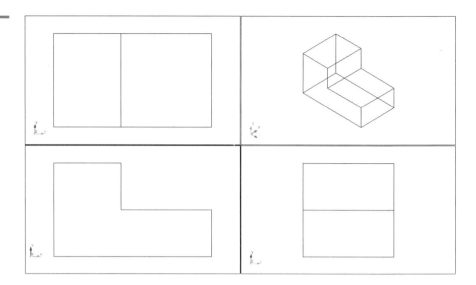

3.6 Multiple Viewports

As you probably know from your 2D drafting with AutoCAD, multiple tiled viewports are available using the VPORTS command. These viewports are useful in displaying different two-dimensional locations of a drawing. But multiple viewports are even more important to three-dimensional modeling. Not only do viewports display different locations on a drawing, but they are capable of displaying totally different viewpoints. This allows the user to observe construction of the model from different vantage points, as illustrated in Figure 3.19.

The discussion in this chapter is concerned with viewports where TILEMODE is set to 1 (model). Viewports using a tilemode set to 0 (layout — paper space) behave differently, as discussed in Chapter 16.

Viewports Dialog Box

To display multiple viewports, use the VPORTS command, click the View/Viewports/New Viewports pull-down menu, or use the Viewports tool from the Viewports toolbar. Figure 3.20 shows the Viewports dialog box.

It is always best to give a name to a viewport configuration first, then click the desired configuration from the standard viewport list. Note that the Setup section can be set to 2D or 3D. When working on 3D models, it should be set to 3D; this way the viewports automatically have their viewpoints set. Once you have chosen your settings, click the OK button to apply them.

If you change Display to Current Viewport in the Apply to section, you will be able to subdivide the currently active viewport.

Once you have named the viewports, you can restore them by using the Named Viewport tab on the Viewports dialog box.

Note: Some of the tools on the Viewports toolbar work only in paper space and do not function in model space.

Viewport Control

Once viewports are displayed, you need only set the various viewpoints in each viewport. This can be achieved in a variety of ways, depending on the user, but one constant is that you need to activate the viewport first. This is accomplished simply by

Figure 3.20
Viewports dialog box

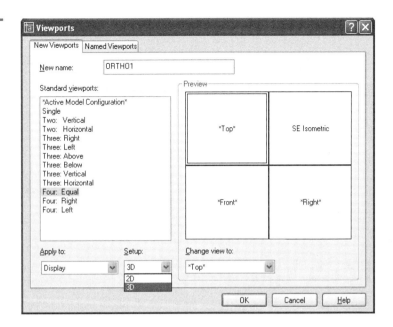

moving the cursor into the particular viewport. If a cursor is displayed, then the viewport is already activated. If an arrow is displayed, the viewport has not been activated yet, and you'll need to use the click button to change the arrow to a cursor. Once activated, you can use the VPOINT, PLAN, or VIEW command to set the viewpoint. If a similar scale is desired in each viewport, then the ZOOM scale command can be used. To set the scale to 1, enter the following command in each activated viewport:

Command: **ZOOM**
Specify corner of window, enter a scale factor (nX or nXP), or
All/Center/Dynamic/Extents/Previous/Scale/Window/real time: **1X**

With this feature, any common scale can be displayed in any viewport when the Model tab is active. With a Layout tab active, and the MODEL button displayed, 1XP would be used to set the scale in a viewport. Refer to Chapter 16.

3D VIEWPOINT

Viewports

Remember that when you save the viewport configuration, it is saved inside the current drawing only. You cannot pass viewport configurations to other drawing files through insertion. If you begin a new drawing, and the prototype template drawing contains viewports, those viewports will be passed to the new drawing.

Like views, viewport configurations can be saved and recalled in the model. This is accomplished by using the VPORTS command. The layout of the viewport is saved, as are the current viewpoints. If you have a combination of viewpoints that are associated with each other, you can group them into a viewport configuration for easy redisplay. To redisplay the combination of viewpoints, you simply recall that particular viewport.

Note also that it is possible to display layers independently in different viewports. But this technique is used when tilemode is set to 0 and is explained in detail in Chapter 16.

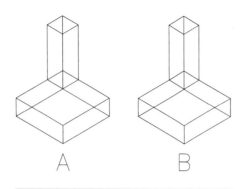

Figure 3.21
Two seemingly identical wireframe models

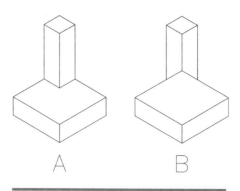

Figure 3.22
Using HIDE to distinguish differences

3.7 Hidden Line Removal (temporary)

The HIDE command displays an enhanced view by temporarily removing edges that would be obstructed by other features. This command works only if surfaces or solids are present. If the model is composed solely of wireframe, evoking the HIDE command will have no effect. Using this command periodically during construction of the model helps you to check the behavior of edges. With the HIDE command, you can tell whether objects are actually intersecting the model or running behind it. Let's look at a wireframe display. Note that Parts A and B in Figure 3.21 appear to be identical. Figure 3.22 is the same model but with hidden lines removed. You now can easily see that the two boxes intersect each other in Part A and that one box is in front of the other in Part B. It is also helpful to use the HIDE command when you cannot tell whether viewing is from above or below the model.

When using hidden line removal on complicated models, generating the final view can take a significant amount of time. The easiest way to speed up the process is to break the model into different layers. This is a good practice in any drawing. But in the case of a complicated model, using different layers allows you to freeze those layers that are not important to the HIDE command. AutoCAD's HIDE command ignores any object that is on a frozen layer. However, the HIDE command still factors in objects that are on a turned-off layer. (Turning off layers can create some interesting effects; for instance, you can blank out a portion of the model in order to accent text.) After using the HIDE command, use Regen to restore the previously displayed state.

3.8 Shade Mode (semipermanent)

The shade mode controls the manner in which the model is displayed on the screen in a semipermanent manner. This means that unlike the HIDE command, the shade mode stays on until you set it otherwise. Depending on the mode selected, the

44

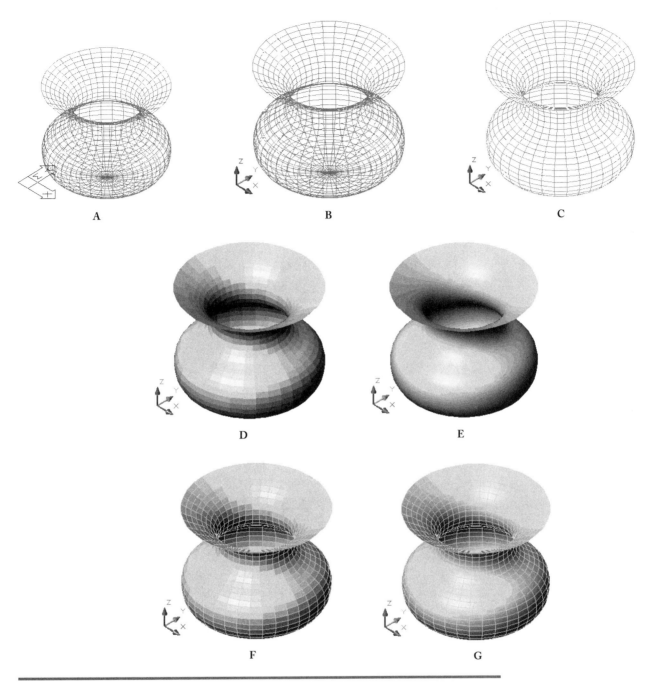

Figure 3.23
Illustration of the shade modes

model's surfaces are shaded or colored in to give a more attractive and realistic view of a 3D model. Figure 3.23 shows the various shade modes. The following is a description of the various modes.

2D Wireframe (A)	Displays objects using lines and curves to represent edges. Raster objects, linetypes, and lineweights are visible. Displays the standard UCS icon as an L or as a 3D axis. This depends on the UCSICON properties, discussed later in the text.

Figure 3.24
Shade toolbar

2D Wireframe / Hidden / Gouraud \ Gouraud, Edges On
3D Wireframe   Flat   Flat, Edges On

3D Wireframe (B)	Displays objects using lines and curves to represent edges. Raster objects, linetypes, and lineweights are not visible. Displays the standard UCS icon as shaded 3-axis arrows.
Hidden (C)	Displays objects using 3D wireframe and hides lines of hidden edges.
Flat Shaded (D)	Displays objects as shaded surfaces. Each surface is discernible. Materials applied to the surfaces are shown.
Gouraud Shaded (E)	Displays objects as shaded surfaces but blends edges to give smoother surfaces. Materials applied to the surfaces are shown.
Flat Shaded, Edges On (F)	Displays objects as shaded surfaces with wireframe overlap.
Gouraud Shaded, Edges On (G)	Combines Gouraud shading and wireframe overlap.

Figure 3.24 shows the Shade toolbar from which you can change the shade mode. You can also use the View/Shade pull-down menu or type **SHADE-MODE** on the command line.

Toolbars are displayed using the View/Toolbars pull-down menu or by right-clicking on a currently displayed toolbar.

3D VIEWPOINT

Shade Modes and Viewing

The use of the SHADE mode is a good way to test surface coverage of a model. You can tell if a surface covers a complete area by studying its shading. However, sometimes the shade modes, (other than 2D wireframe) do not function properly. This can happen when working with paper space floating viewports and the creation of perspective views for plotting. It is best to switch to 2D wireframe to create the viewports and set the perspective views and then switch to a different shade mode.

3.9 Saving and Restoring Views

You can save any view displayed in a viewport. Once a view is saved, it can be restored. In this way you can keep track of various viewpoints and then display them as required. Figure 3.25 shows the View dialog box. It is divided into two main sections: Named Views and Orthographic & Isometric Views. The Named Views section is used to save and restore a view in a viewport. The New button is used to save the view, and the Set Current button is used to display a highlighted, named view.

When you save a view, indicate the name, the location (viewpoint), the UCS (explained in Chapter 4), and whether the view is a perspective. You can also store the current state of the layer settings with the view. When you recall the view, the

Figure 3.25
View dialog box

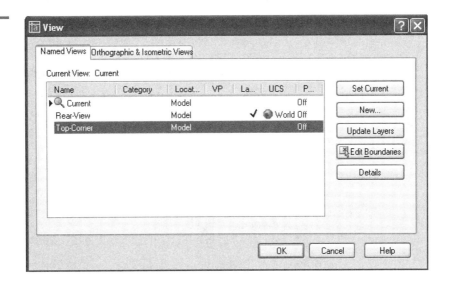

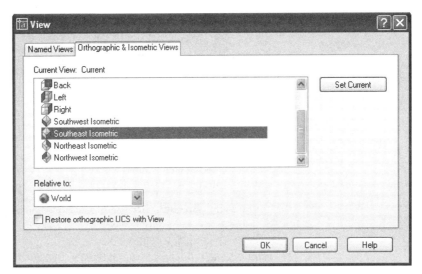

layers will be turned on or off/frozen or thawed, depending or their state when the view was saved.

The Orthographic & Isometric Views section of the View dialog box allows you to click from preset viewpoints, such as top and front.

Lab 3.A   Using 3D Orbit and Shade Modes

Purpose

Lab 3.A introduces you to the 3DORBIT command and the various shade modes.

Objectives

You will be able to rotate the view of your model dynamically so that you can see your model as you change your view of it. You will also be able to display the model in various shade modes to help visualize your model.

Primary Commands

3DORBIT

SHADEMODE

47

Procedure

1. Open the L-shape.dwg file from the a3d2005 folder. Refer to Appendix A on how to use the CD-ROM that is enclosed with the textbook, if needed.

    Display the View and 3D Orbit toolbars. You may want to dock them at the side or top of the graphics screen so that they don't overlap your model.

2. Make sure the UCSVP is set to 0 by typing **UCSVP** on the command line. This makes sure the working plane does not keep changing every time you change a viewport.

    Type **UCSICON** on the command line and enter **ON.** Repeat the command and enter **ORIGIN.** This displays the UCS orientation icon to help identify the *X, Y,* and *Z* axes.

3. Display the top view using the PLAN command.

Command: **PLAN**
Enter an option [Current ucs/Ucs/World] <Current>: **W**

4. Using the VPOINT command or the SE Isometric View tool, display the isometric view using the coordinates 1, −1, 1.

Displaying Various Shades Using the SHADEMODE Command

5. Using the SHADEMODE command, display the following shade modes one after another and observe how the model changes:
    2D wireframe
    3D wireframe
    Hidden
    Flat
    Gouraud
    Flat with edges displayed
    Gouraud with edges displayed

Command: **SHADEMODE**
Current mode: 2D wireframe
Enter option [2D wireframe/3D
wireframe/Hidden/Flat/Gouraud/fLat+edges/gOuraud+edges] <Hidden>: **3D**

6. Set the shade mode to Hidden as shown in Figure 3.26.

Rotating the View Using the 3DORBIT Command

7. Display a top view of the L-shape using the PLAN command. Use Zoom Realtime to reduce the size of the L-shape on the screen. This will help with viewpoint manipulation.

Figure 3.26
Model displayed with link hidden

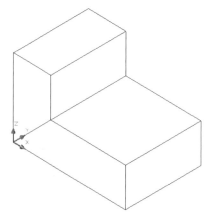

8. Display the 3D Orbit arc ball by using the 3DORBIT command or the 3D Orbit tool.

Command: **3DORBIT**
Press ESC or ENTER to exit, or right-click to display the shortcut menu.

The arc ball circle should appear over your model. Note the four small circles at the quadrants of the larger circle. These are used to restrict the view rotation to a particular axis. Move your cursor over each one and pause. Observe how the cursor changes to depict the type of view rotation.

Move your cursor outside the arc ball circle and observe the cursor icon. It depicts a circle with a ball in the middle. This rotation is in the axis perpendicular to the current viewing plane (screen).

Move your cursor inside the arc ball. The cursor changes to a combination of two ellipses. This allows rotation in all axes depending on the direction you drag the cursor.

Move your cursor so that it is outside the arc ball, click and drag around the outside of the arc ball, and observe the view of the L-shape. The view rotates around the axis perpendicular to the screen. Move the cursor until the view is similar to Figure 3.27 and release the click button to lock the view position.

9. Move your cursor into the small circle at the top of the arc ball; click and drag slowly up and down, observing the view of the L-shape. The view rotates around the horizontal axis parallel to the screen (viewing plane). Move the cursor until the view is similar to Figure 3.28 and release the click button to lock the view position.

10. Move the cursor into the small circle on the right quadrant of the arc ball. Click and drag slowly left and right, observing the movement of the L-shape. This view is rotating around the vertical axis. Move the cursor until you achieve a view similar to Figure 3.29.

11. Move the cursor inside the arc ball, click, and drag. Note how the view rotates in all the axes, allowing virtually any view position. Release the click button at any time to lock the position.

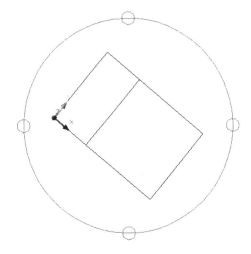

Figure 3.27
View rotation around the perpendicular axis

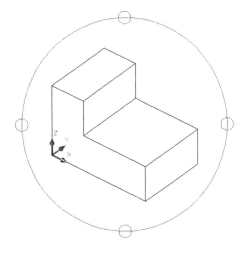

Figure 3.28
View rotation around the horizontal axis

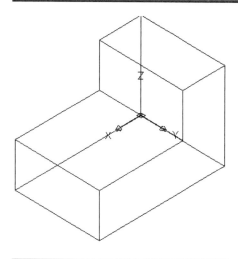

Figure 3.32
Rear-right view from above

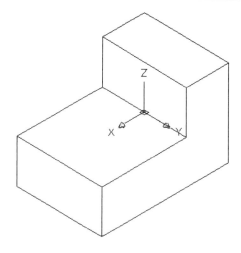

Figure 3.33
Hidden line removed display

Command: **VPOINT**
Current view direction: VIEWDIR= [current viewpoint coordinates]
Specify a view point or [Rotate] <display compass and tripod>: **0, –1,0**

> The display shows the front orthographic view.

9. Using the Named Views tool, save the currently displayed front view as FRONT. Use the New button and enter **FRONT** as the view name. Turn off the Save UCS with View box. Click OK to complete. The new view name should appear in the View dialog box.

> Not only does this save the current view, but it also saves the viewpoint.

10. Use the View toolbar to display the other five viewpoints: top, right side, left side, rear, and bottom.

> Save the model at this point as L-shape.

Recalling a Previous Viewpoint

11. Using the Name Views tool, restore the previously saved view called FRONT. The front viewpoint should now be displayed on the screen. Experiment saving and recalling different viewpoints.
12. Display the top view, using the PLAN command.

Command: **PLAN**
Enter an option [Current ucs/Ucs/World] <Current>: **W**

Moving the Viewpoint Through Rotation

13. Using the VPOINT ROTATE command, display an isometric view.

Command: **VPOINT**
Current view direction: VIEWDIR= [current viewpoint coordinates]
Specify a view point or [Rotate] <display compass and tripod>: **R**
Enter angle in XY plane from X axis <270>: **–45**
Enter angle from XY plane <90>: **45**

Figure 3.34
Viewpoint through rotation

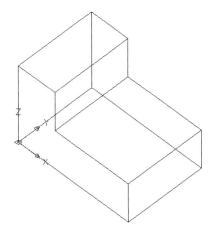

The display should look similar to that shown in Figure 3.34.
Use the HIDE command to display the model.

Moving the Viewpoint Through Compass

14. Using the VPOINT compass command, rotate the object to display the lower-left rear.

Command: **VPOINT**
Current view direction: VIEWDIR= [current viewpoint coordinates]
Specify a view point or [Rotate] <display compass and tripod>: **<Enter>**

The display should switch to show the compass input screen. Place the cursor as shown in Figure 3.35.

Once the cursor has been digitized in the compass area, the display should look similar to Figure 3.36.

Figure 3.35
Compass input screen

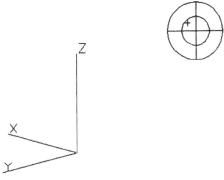

Figure 3.36
Viewpoint through the compass input screen

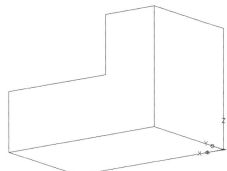

53

Now use the HIDE command to see the effect. Experiment at this point: Use the compass and HIDE command to move around the model.

Using the Preset Viewpoints

15. Select the pull-down menu View/3DViews/Viewpoint Presets to select a preset view of the front of the model. The dialog box should appear as shown in Figure 3.37.

    Use the graphics window in the Viewpoint Presets dialog box to set 270 for the angle from the X axis and 0 degrees for the angle from the X–Y plane. The display should look similar to Figure 3.38.

16. Now tilt the model using a preset view of the front (270 degrees) and an angle other than 0. Enter an angle of 45 degrees from the X–Y plane.

    Use the HIDE command. The display should look similar to Figure 3.39.

17. Experiment with preset views that automatically set the viewpoint, such as Top, Front, and NE Isometric. These can be found under the View/3D Views pull-down menu or on the View toolbar.

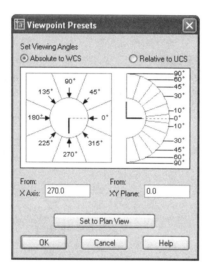

Figure 3.37
Viewpoint Presets dialog box

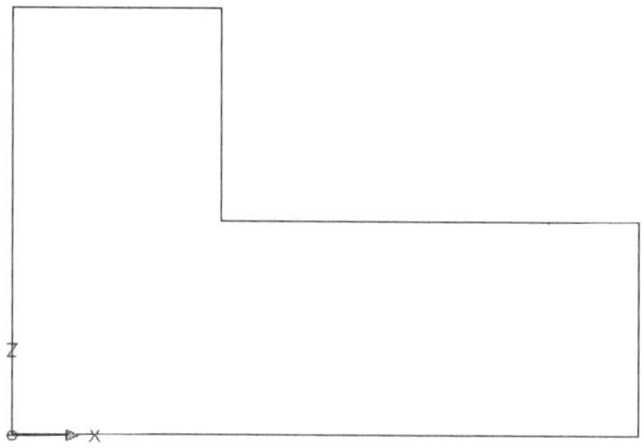

Figure 3.38
Viewpoint through dialog box

Figure 3.39
Hidden line removed display

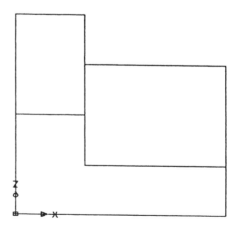

Lab 3.C   Multiple Viewports

Purpose

Lab 3.C familiarizes you with multiple viewports used in conjunction with 3D modeling when TILEMODE is set to 1.

Objectives

You will be able to:

- Configure multiple viewports
- Display multiple viewpoints
- Save multiple viewport configurations

Primary Commands

VPORTS
VPOINT
HIDE

Procedure

1. Open the L-shape.dwg file from the a3d2005 folder. Refer to Appendix A on how to use the CD-ROM that's enclosed with the textbook, if needed.

    Display the View and 3D Orbit toolbars. You may want to dock them at the side or top of the graphics screen so that they don't overlap your model.

    Make sure that the Model tab (at the bottom of the graphics screen) is active. This sets TILEMODE to 1.

2. Display the bottom viewpoint.

Displaying a Multiple Viewport Display

3. Using the VPORTS command or the Display Viewports Dialog tool from the Viewports toolbar, display the Viewports dialog box as shown in Figure 3.40. Name the viewport configuration ORTHO1.

    Click on Four: Equal to highlight it. This divides the screen into four equal-sized viewports.

    Make sure Setup is set to 3D. Note how the Preview shows the various views, such as Top and Front. This is set automatically when 3D is the setup.

Figure 3.40
Viewports dialog box with proper settings

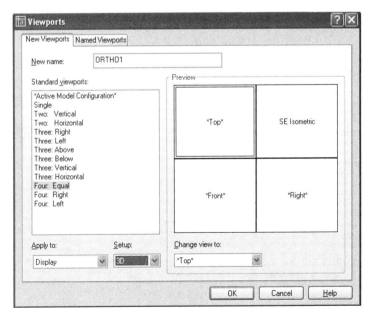

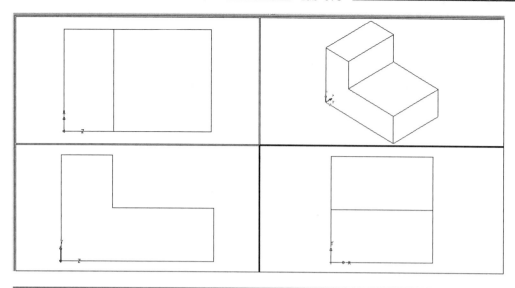

Figure 3.41
Four viewports displayed showing top, front, right, and isometric views.

Refer to Figure 3.40 to confirm all the proper settings. Once you're satisfied, click the OK button. The screen should change to display the four viewports, as shown in Figure 3.41.

4. Make the isometric viewport active by clicking inside it. Change the shade mode in that viewport to Hidden.

Drawing Between Viewports

5. Activate the top view viewport and enter UCS on the command line. Enter WCS as the option. This makes sure that you're drawing on a working plane that's paralllel to the top view.

6. Draw a circle in the top view similar to Figure 3.42. The size of the circle is not important.

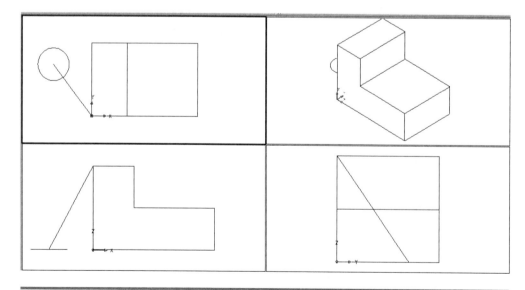

Figure 3.42
Line shown in all viewports

7. Start to draw a line from the center of the circle (use object snap) in the top view.

8. While still in the LINE command, right-click in the isometric viewport to activate it and object snap onto the top corner of the L-shaped object. Refer to Figure 3.42.

 This demonstrates how you can draw from one viewport to another.

9. Save your file as L-shape**. Replace ** with your initials.

Questions

1. What is the advantage of displaying an axonometric view of a model?

2. What two crucial components must be considered in generating a proper view?

3. Is the VPOINT command used to generate an axonometric or a perspective view?

4. Does VPOINT use UCS or WCS for reference?

5. Explain the four ways of setting a viewpoint.

6. What do the terms *isometric, dimetric,* and *trimetric* mean?

7. Draw a diagram to indicate the compass position that would display a left-front view looking underneath a model.

8. What is the function of the PLAN command?

9. Explain the procedure for controlling the orientation of an orthographic view generated by VPOINT.

10. In what way are viewports independent and in what way are they linked?

11. Why is it useful to use the HIDE command during construction?

12. What is the effect of freezing a layer before accessing the HIDE command? How does this compare to the effect of turning a layer off?

13. How does using the VPOINT command affect the size of the displayed model?

14. Explain the procedure for maintaining multiple viewports. How can they all be displayed on the screen at one time?

15. Identify the four different 3D Orbit cursor icons by name and briefly describe the function of the four 3D Orbit modes.

16. What is the difference between the Gouraud shade mode and the Gouraud, Edges On shade mode?

Assignment

Read the complete assignment before beginning.

1. Set up a prototype drawing that has the following preset:

 ■ Set the UCSVP system variable to 0 by entering **UCSVP** on the command line. This should be done before creating any viewports.

Figure 3.43
Four-viewport configuration:
ORTHO1

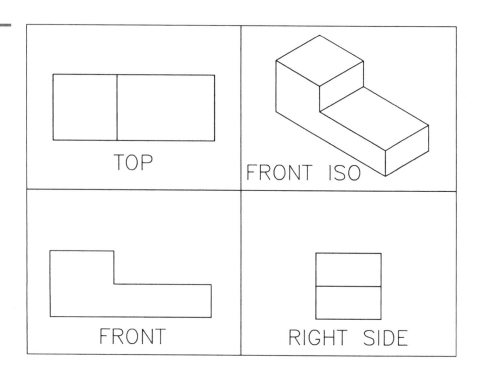

- A configuration of four equal viewports that contains the top, front, and right-side views plus the SE Isometric view. Save the configuration as ORTHO1 using the VPORTS command (see Figure 3.43).
- A configuration of four equal viewports that contains the bottom, rear, and left-side views plus the NW Isometric view. Save the configuration as ORTHO2 using the VPORTS command (see Figure 3.44). (*Hint:* Use the *Change View To* setting in the Viewports dialog box to change a view in a viewport.)

Figure 3.44
Four-viewport configuration:
ORTHO2.

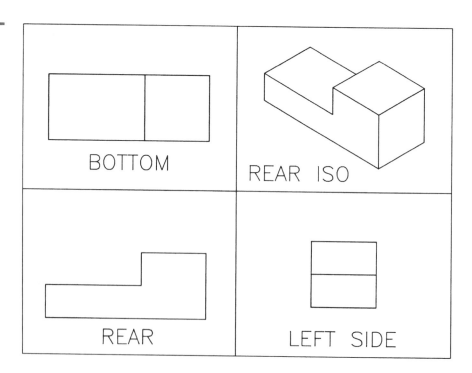

■ A single viewport that contains the SE Isometric view. Save it as ISO1 using the VPORTS command (see Figure 3.45).

Name all the various viewpoints as well as the viewports. Call the file 3DSET. This prototype drawing now can be utilized anytime you start a project in 3D.

Note: In Figures 3.43, 3.44, and 3.45, the L-shape is used as an example, but any model can be used to test the configurations. However, the final file 3DSET should not contain any geometry.

2. Recall the L-shape model created during the labs in this chapter. Using the Vpoint rotation option, display the following viewpoints in a four-viewport configuration: Viewport 1 is an isometric view, 2 is a dimetric view, 3 is a trimetric view, and 4 is a bottom view (see Figure 3.46).

Figure 3.45
Single-viewport configuration: ISO1

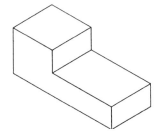

Figure 3.46
Different viewpoints using rotation

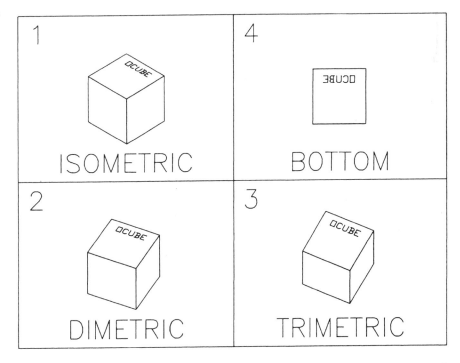

59

3. After recalling the L-shape model created during the labs, display four identical views of the model using the four Vpoint options in a four-viewport configuration: Viewport 1 is displayed using the Coordinate option, 2 uses the Rotation option, 3 uses the Compass option, and 4 uses the Viewpoint Preset dialog box option (see Figure 3.47).

4. With the L-shape model recalled, use the Coordinate option of the VPOINT command to display the four different orientations of the top view (see Figure 3.48). Try using the 3DORBIT command to perform the same function.

Figure 3.47
Different methods for displaying the same view

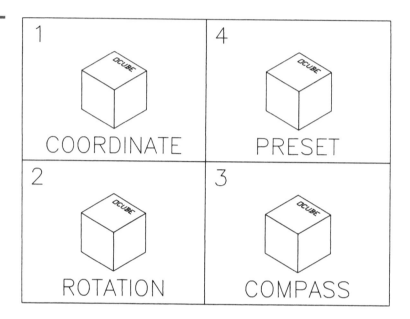

Figure 3.48
Different orientations of the same view

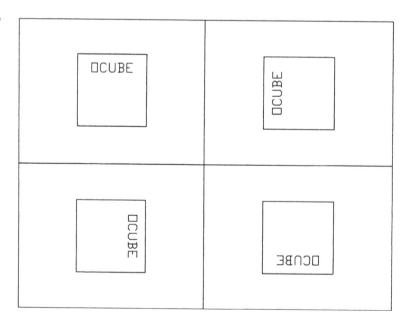

Working in 3D Space

Overview

In Chapter 4, you will learn how to break a model into working planes and define these planes for retrieval in order to simplify the construction and modification of the model itself. The techniques discussed here range from the easy-to-learn ones for beginners to the more exotic techniques (which can, in fact, be made simpler under specific circumstances). When you have mastered these procedures, you will be ready to construct your own 3D models.

Concepts Explored

- The purpose of the working plane
- How the World Coordinate System and the User Coordinate System are related
- The different forms of the UCS icon
- How to set elevated working planes
- How to manipulate the UCS icon
- How to create working planes

4.1   Introduction

When creating three-dimensional models, almost all PC-based CAD systems construct their geometry out of flat surfaces (see Figure 4.1). To perform this construction, the systems need a flat plane base. These planes, which we call *working planes*, are the bases on which all 3D construction takes place. Even when the CAD user is only drawing a view in two dimensions, the constructing geometry still uses a working plane. Because the geometry being drawn is simply a flat outline of the object, the use of a working plane is not apparent. It is only when 3D construction takes place that the various working planes become evident.

The working plane can be thought of as a flat surface similar to a sheet of paper. As can be said of a sheet of paper, you can draw on the working plane no matter where it is placed or at what angle.

When working in three dimensions, the user must align the working plane to the surface where creation of the model is to take place. This alignment (making parallel) is the key to all three-dimensional modeling. Figure 4.2 shows a hand holding a cube. If that were your hand holding the cube and you wanted to draw on it with a pencil, all you would need to do is pick the side to draw on, get a pencil, and proceed to draw. The procedure is similar in AutoCAD. You must tell the program on

Figure 4.1
Models created with flat surfaces

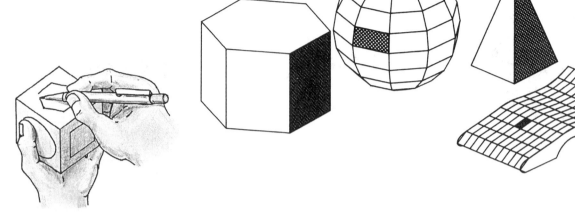

Figure 4.2
Manually drawing on a cube

which surface (side) the drawing or construction is going to take place. This is done using two systems of coordinates—the World Coordinate System (WCS) and the User Coordinate System (UCS).

4.2 World Coordinate System

The WCS is AutoCAD's master coordinate system. This system has X, Y, and Z coordinates with origin points of $0x$, $0y$, $0z$. However, the orientation of these axes cannot be changed or moved in any way. Using this system of coordinates, Auto-CAD keeps track of all geometry, whether 2D or 3D. All dimensional information is related back to the WCS. This guarantees that the user cannot get "lost" in 3D space. The WCS can always be used as a frame of reference.

4.3 User Coordinate System

The UCS is the means by which AutoCAD allows the user to create and save the various working planes required to generate any complex 3D model (see Figure 4.3). Like the WCS, this system of coordinates has X, Y, and Z axes. The difference is that the UCS axes can be rotated, moved, or aligned to any location on the 3D model. Think of the UCS as telling the program which side of the cube you want to draw on and which point is going to be used as the origin point $0x$, $0y$, $0z$.

When a user initially draws in 2D, the UCS, by default, is aligned to the WCS, thereby matching the coordinates of the two systems. This working plane is customarily referred to as the *top* or *plan* view.

3D VIEWPOINT

Working Planes

You can create and save as many UCS working planes as you desire, but only one can be active at any one time. UCS working planes are saved with the UCS command, and are retained in the drawing.

Figure 4.3
3D object illustrating working planes

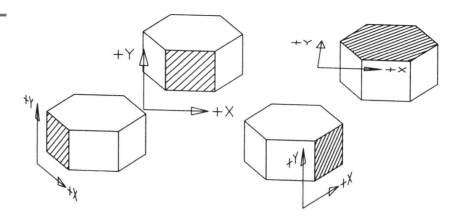

UCS Command

In 3D, the working plane can be created in a number of ways, all requiring the alignment of the UCS to a set of WCS coordinates. Thankfully, doing the alignment with AutoCAD is easy because most of its options use existing geometry.

Command: **UCS**
Current ucs name: *WORLD*
Enter an option [New/Move/orthoGraphic/Prev/Restore/Save/Del/Apply/?/World]
<World>: **enter option**

The following lists alignments and the UCS options that achieve them:

UCS OPTION SUBOPTION	DESCRIPTION OF ALIGNMENT OR OPTION
New	
Specify origin	Moves only the origin point; the alignment stays the same.
Zaxis	Defines the new direction of the positive Z axis.
3Point	Defines the UCS by entering three points to define a plane; these points are origin, positive X-axis direction, and the positive Y-axis direction.
OBject	Aligns the UCS to an existing object.
Face	Aligns the UCS to the face of a 3D solid.
View	Aligns the UCS to the plane of the current view.
X or Y or Z	Rotates the UCS about the selected axis.
Move	
Specify origin	Moves only the origin point; the alignment stays the same.
Zdepth	Moves the UCS along the Z axis.
orthoGraphic	Aligns the UCS to preset planes such as Top and Front.
Prev	Returns UCS alignment to last UCS.
Restore	Restores a saved UCS by name.
Save	Saves the current UCS under a name.
Del	Removes a named UCS.
Apply	Applies current UCS to a viewport.
World	Aligns the UCS to the WCS.

The UCS options can be accessed by typing **UCS** on the command line, looking under the Tools pull-down menu, or using the UCS or UCS II toolbars. Figure 4.4 shows the two toolbars.

Toolbars are displayed using the View/Toolbars pull-down menu or by right-clicking on a currently displayed toolbar. The Standard toolbar contains a flyout for UCS tools.

63

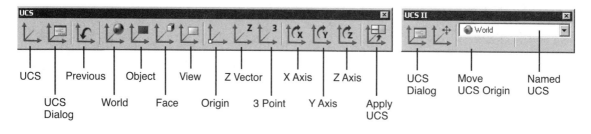

Figure 4.4
The UCS and UCS II toolbars

Saving and Restoring UCS Working Planes

You should get into the habit of naming the UCS working planes you create. By doing this you will find that you can restore them at a later time, making the process of establishing the working plane that much more efficient. You can use the UCS command to save and restore a UCS or you can use the UCS dialog box. To display the UCS dialog box, as shown in Figure 4.5, type **UCSMAN** on the command line or use the UCS or UCS II toolbars. Refer to Figure 4.4 for the proper tool.

Assigning a UCS to Each Viewport

It is possible to assign a different UCS working plane to each viewport. Whenever the viewport is activated, that UCS is then activated. This is controlled by the UCSVP system variable.

Figure 4.5
UCS dialog box showing named UCSs

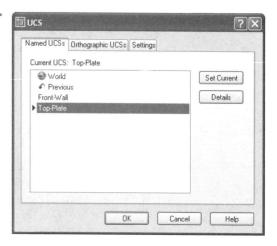

If the UCSVP variable is set to 0, only one UCS is active no matter which viewport is active. This is often easier to use for the beginner. This way you can set the UCS in one viewport, such as the isometric view, and then make use of the same UCS in another viewport.

If the UCSVP variable is set to 1, each viewport can contain a different UCS. This can be useful if you are constantly switching from viewport to viewport and you want the UCS to change as well. This method is best left until you are more practiced with the UCS. Sometimes the beginner can forget which UCS is active in which viewport. This can lead to confusion and frustration.

UCS Icon

The UCS icon is used to help the user keep track of the X, Y, and Z axes of the current UCS. The UCS icon is a directional beacon, telling you in what direction the axes of your UCS are pointing. The icon's display can be turned off or on, and it normally appears in the lower-left corner of the screen's graphics display (refer to the next section and Lab 4.A). Remember, because any number of UCS working planes can be created, it is essential to know which one is currently active. The UCS icon aids in identifying which working plane is active by letting the user know where the UCS origin point 0,0,0 is located and in which directions the X, Y, and Z axes are pointing.

There are different forms of the UCS icon. There is the standard 2D wire version and the 3D wire version. Both of these are set by the Properties option of the UCSICON command.

Figure 4.6A shows the standard 2D wire UCS icon. Note the W. When the W is visible, the UCS and WCS are in alignment; when a cross (+) is visible, it means that the icon is sitting directly on the UCS origin point (0,0,0).

Figure 4.6B shows the 3D wire UCS icon. With this form of the icon, the appearance of the box represents the alignment of the UCS with the WCS.

We prefer the use of the 2D wire version because it makes it easier to see that the icon is flat against the surface upon which you want to work. We use this representation of the icon in most of the figures in this text.

For ease of reference, we will refer to the flat, L shape for the descriptions. The behavior of the two icons is the same. Only their physical appearance is different.

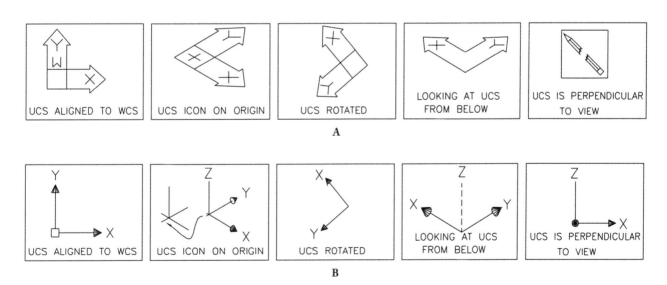

Figure 4.6
(A) 2D wire UCS icon: different orientations; (B) 3D wire UCS icon: different orientations

Refer to the flat UCS icon shown in Figure 4.6A. The icon is formed in the shape of an "L," with arrowheads on the ends of the *X* and *Y* axes pointing in the positive direction of the axes. In addition, each arrowhead is labeled with the appropriate axis letter.

Note the "W" below the *Y*-axis letter. The "W" on the icon indicates that the UCS is aligned to the WCS; that is, the coordinates used when constructing with the UCS match those of the master WCS coordinates.

3D VIEWPOINT

UCS Icon

The UCS icon will only appear on the origin point (0,0,0) if it is set to do so and if there is room on the screen to display the entire icon. If some of the icon would be cut off by an edge of the display screen, the icon jumps to the lower-left corner of the screen. Only the icon, **not** *the current UCS, moves.*

Figure 4.7
Warning! The working plane is not visible to the viewer

Figure 4.8
Shaded 3D UCS icon

By observing the direction of the icon arrowheads, you can easily tell which way the *X* and *Y* axes are pointing. To identify the *Z* axis for you, AutoCAD forms a box at the base of the icon, as shown in Figure 4.6A. Note that the box is formed by the extension of the two lines indicated by arrows in the figure. When those lines are displayed, it means that the *Z* axis is going in a positive direction toward the viewer. To help identify the directions in which the axes are pointing, refer to the right-hand rule explained in Section 3.2.

When the lines on the *X* and *Y* axes do not form a box, it means that the *Z* axis is going in a positive direction away from the viewer, as shown in Figure 4.6A. The object is usually viewed from the bottom in this situation.

It is possible to rotate the displayed view so that the UCS icon is displayed completely flat. When this happens, the icon is replaced by a broken pencil symbol, as illustrated in Figure 4.7. The broken pencil is a warning that using the pointing device to locate coordinates will be virtually useless or, worse, disastrous. When this symbol appears, the cursor can move in only one axis, and thus it is impossible to be certain which coordinate is going to be used for the other immobile axis.

The UCS icon also changes depending on the shade modes. If the shade mode is set to 2D wireframe, the icon will be shown in 2D wire or 3D wire depending on the Properties option of the UCSICON command. If the shade mode is set to anything else, the UCS icon will be displayed as a shaded 3D axis icon as shown in Figure 4.8.

UCSICON Command

The commands used to manipulate the UCS icon are as follows:

UCS ICON COMMAND	DESCRIPTION
UCSICON ON	Displays the icon.
UCSICON OFF	Turns the icon off.
UCSICON All	Displays the icon in all the viewports.
UCSICON No origin	Shows the icon is not on the origin.
UCSICON OR	Displays the icon at the origin of the UCS.
UCSICON Properties	Displays the UCS Icon dialog box used to control the appearance of the 2D and 3D wire UCS icons. It will display a dialog box similar to Figure 4.9A.

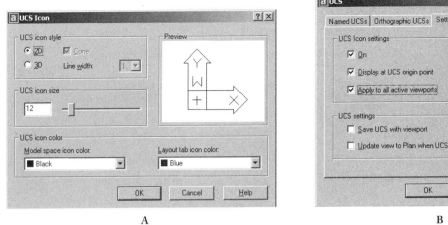
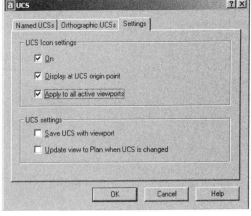

A   B

Figure 4.9
(A) UCS Icon dialog box and (B) the UCS dialog box showing Settings tab for UCS icon settings

You can also control the UCS icon settings by using the UCS dialog box. To display the box, enter **UCSMAN** on the command line. Click the Settings tab and a display similar to Figure 4.9B appears. Pay close attention to the behavior of the UCS icon. When switching from one viewport to another, the UCS can change. This is indicated by a change in the orientation of the UCS icon. Always note the orientation of the UCS icon before you start creating objects in a viewport.

4.4 Elevated Working Planes

It is possible to draw above or below the current working plane by using the ELEVATION command. When you need to insert geometry above or below an already set working plane, the ELEVATION command allows you to do so. Consider, for example, one design situation: An AutoCAD user is laying out a kitchen plan. If the user sets the working plane to the floor level of the kitchen plan, then, to insert cabinetry at the desired distance above the floor, the user must use the ELEVATION command.

When using the ELEVATION command, entering positive distances causes the working plane to be temporarily elevated in the positive Z direction. Entering negative distances causes the working plane to be lowered in the negative Z direction. Figure 4.10 illustrates these effects. If the ELEVATION command is activated from the command line, it has an effect on the extrusion thickness of the geometry. This is explained in the next chapter. At this point, it is enough to note that the extrusion thickness starts from the elevation point.

ELEVATION Command

The ELEVATION command is activated by typing **ELEV** at the command prompt.

Command: **ELEV**
Specify new default
elevation <current>: **Enter positive or negative distances**
Specify new default
thickness <current>: **Enter the desired positive or negative object thickness**

67

Figure 4.10
Elevated working planes—
positive and negative

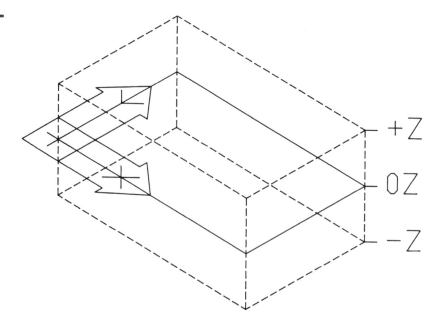

Always remember to refer to the coordinate readout at the bottom of the screen. The Z coordinate is displayed as well as the X and Y coordinates. When you change the Z elevation, the value is displayed as the Z coordinate. The UCS icon does not move to the new elevation point.

3D VIEWPOINT

The ELEVATION Command

Always remember to return the elevation setting back to 0 when completed. If you forget, when you try to draw on a UCS working plane, you will instead draw above or below the plane by the previously set elevation distance. This can give annoying results.

 Lab 4.A   The UCS Icon

Purpose

Lab 4.A familiarizes you with the UCS icon and its functions.

Objectives

You will be able to:

■ Activate and deactivate the UCS icon
■ Align the UCS icon to the origin of the UCS

Primary Command

UCSICON

Procedure

Activating the UCS Icon

1. Open the L-shape.dwg file from the a3d2005 folder. Refer to Appendix A on how to use the CD-ROM that's enclosed with the textbook, if needed. Set the shade mode to 2D wireframe.

Set the UCSVP system variable to 0 and display the UCS and View toolbars. To match the figures, set the UCS icon to 2D using the Properties option of the UCSICON command.

2. Set the display to show the plan view of the OCUBE.

Command: **PLAN**
Enter an option [Current ucs/Ucs/World] <Current>: **W**

This displays the plan view of the World Coordinate System.
Use ZOOM 0.5X to reduce the displayed view.

3. Activate the UCS icon. Use the View/Display/UCS Icon/On pull-down menu item.

Command: **UCSICON**
Enter an option [ON/OFF/All/Noorigin/ORigin/Properties] <current ON/OFF state>: **ON**
Command: **UCSICON**
Enter an option [ON/OFF/All/Noorigin/ORigin/Properties] <ON>: **N**

This turns on the UCS icon, displaying it in the lower-left corner of the graphics screen. At this point, the display should look similar to Figure 4.11.

Deactivating the UCS Icon

4. Select the UCSICON command.

Command: **UCSICON**
Enter an option [ON/OFF/All/Noorigin/ORigin/Properties] <current ON/OFF state>: **OFF**

This turns off the display of the UCS icon. At this point, the display should look similar to Figure 4.12.

Turn the icon back on now and change the shade mode to 3D Wireframe. Note how the UCS icon changed to a 3D shaded version (see Figure 4.13).

This can be useful when you are performing a number of viewpoint changes. However, when you are changing the UCS working plane, you may find that the flat, L-shaped UCS icon is easier to see and relate to.

Change the shade mode back to 2D Wireframe for the rest of the lab.

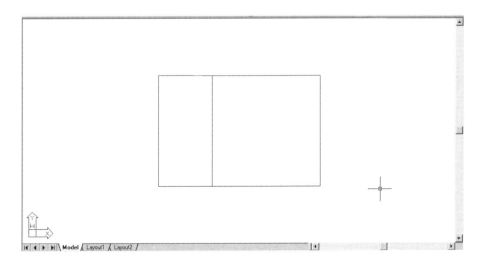

Figure 4.11
The activated UCS icon

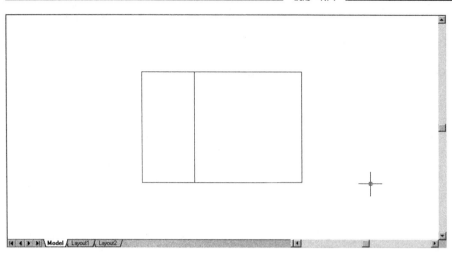

Figure 4.12
Turning the UCS icon off

Aligning the UCS Icon to the UCS Origin

5. Select the UCSICON command.

Command: **UCSICON**
Enter an option [ON/OFF/All/Noorigin/ORigin/Properties] <current ON/OFF state>: OR

This displays the icon at the 0,0,0 location of the current UCS. At this point, the display should look similar to Figure 4.14.

If the UCS is changed, then the icon moves with it. Remember, the icon only displays at the 0,0,0 location if there is enough room for the entire icon to be displayed. If some of the icon would be cut off, the icon is displayed in the lower-left corner of the screen, regardless of the 0,0,0 point (see Figure 4.15).

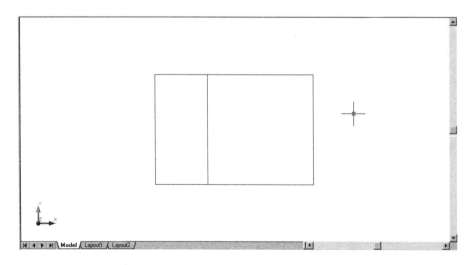

Figure 4.13
Display showing 3D shaded UCS icon

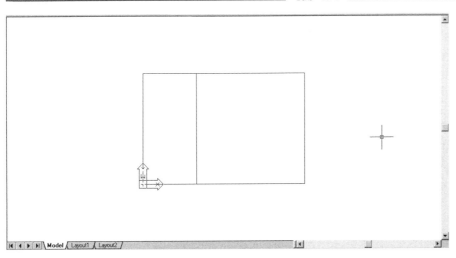

Figure 4.14
Displaying the UCS icon on
the origin

6. Use the ZOOM Window and PAN commands to manipulate the view of the orientation OCUBE so that the icon either displays at the 0,0,0 point or is forced to be displayed in the lower-left corner.
7. Use the Noorigin option of the UCSICON so that the icon does not align itself with the origin of the UCS.
8. Use the ZOOM command to move about the screen and observe the UCS icon.
9. Use the VPOINT command to look at the cube from below using a negative value for the Z axis as in 1,1,–1. Note what happens to the UCS icon. Refer back to Figure 4.6A if you are unsure.

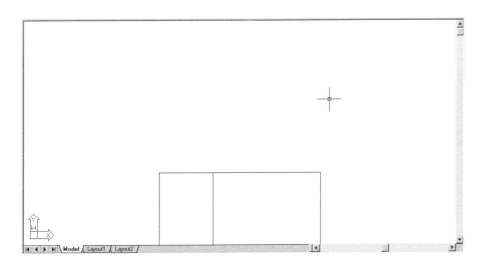

Figure 4.15
The UCS icon forced off the
origin

71

Lab 4.B

Creating Working Planes Using the 3Point Method

Purpose

Lab 4.B shows you how to create a working plane using the 3-point method. This method of aligning the UCS to create a working plane is the most useful, the simplest, and hence the most commonly used. The 3-point method normally uses existing geometry, but it can align to the UCS using coordinates alone. This lab demonstrates the method using existing geometry.

Objectives

You will be able to:

- Create a working plane (UCS)
- Name and retrieve a working plane (UCS)
- Draw on a working plane

Primary Commands

UCS 3Point
UCS Save
UCS Restore
UCS Tools

Procedure

Activating the UCS Icon

1. Open the L-shape.dwg file from the a3d2005 folder.
   Set the UCSVP system variable to 0 and display the UCS and View toolbars. To match the figures, set the UCS icon to 2D using the Properties option of the UCSICON command.

2. Set the display to show an isometric view of the cube using the VPOINT command or the SE Isometric View tool.

Command: **VPOINT**
Rotate/<View point><current>: **1,−1,1**

> This displays the iso view of the orientation cube looking from above-right front.

3. Activate the UCS icon.

Command: **UCSICON**
Enter an option [ON/OFF/All/Noorigin/ORigin/Properties] <current ON/OFF state>: **ON**

> This turns on the UCS icon, displaying it in the lower-left corner of the graphics screen.

4. Align the icon to the current working plane (UCS).

Command: **UCSICON**
Enter an option [ON/OFF/All/Noorigin/ORigin/Properties] <current ON/OFF state>: **OR**

> If the icon is not aligned (showing the plus sign), use the ZOOM command to scale down the displayed view of the orientation cube.

Command: **ZOOM**
Specify corner of window, enter a scale factor (nX or nXP), or
    [All/Center/Dynamic/Extents/Previous/Scale/ Window] <real time>: **0.5X**

> This reduces the display view by half. Experiment with this command to achieve the best view. At this point, the display should look similar to Figure 4.16.

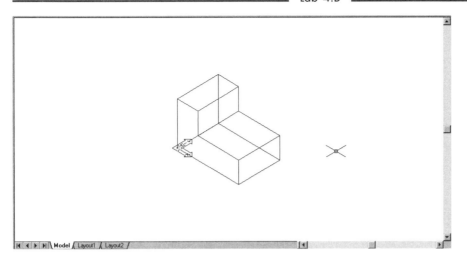

Figure 4.16
The activated UCS icon

Figure 4.17
Defining a new working plane

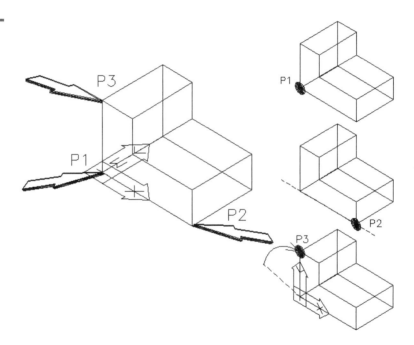

Creating a New Working Plane

5. Align the working plane to the front side of the orientation cube. Looking at Figure 4.17, the front side is the side facing toward the left. You can use the UCS command or the 3Point UCS tool.

Command: **UCS**
Current ucs name: *WORLD*
Enter an option [New/Move/orthoGraphic/Prev/Restore/Save/Del/Apply/?/World]
    <World>: **New** (You can skip the New option if you enter 3 to go immediately to the 3-point method.)
Specify origin of new UCS or [ZAxis/3point/OBject/Face/View/X/Y/Z] <0,0,0>: **3**
Specify new origin point <0,0,0>: **refer to following text**

73

At this point, the command is asking you where the new origin point would be located (see Figure 4.17). Click P1. Remember to use the object snap endpoint to lock the cursor at the correct location. The use of object snaps is extremely important when performing operations in 3D.

Specify point on positive portion of X-axis <default>: **refer to following text**

Here, the program needs to know which direction the positive X axis will be pointing. An imaginary line is calculated from the new origin to the point checked for the positive direction of the X axis (refer to Figure 4.17). Click P2. (Use object snap endpoint.)

Specify point on positive-Y portion of the UCS XY plane <default>: **refer to following text**

This is where the program needs a point to calculate where the working plane is going to be. It pivots the plane around the new X axis based on the point aligned for the positive Y (refer to Figure 4.17). Click P3. (Use object snap endpoint.)

Note that the UCS icon has moved to indicate the new working plane. This indicator can be invaluable when performing 3D modeling on complex models.

Giving the Current Working Plane a Name

6. Use the UCS command to give a name to the current working plane. This allows quick retrieval (aligning) of previous working planes whenever necessary.

Command: **UCS**
Current ucs name: *NO NAME*
Enter an option [New/Move/orthoGraphic/Prev/Restore/Save/Del/Apply/?/World]
    <World>: **Save**
Enter name to save current UCS or [?]: **FRONT**

The name "FRONT" is used uniquely to describe that working plane. If you enter a question mark instead of a name, the previously named working planes (UCS) will be listed.

Aligning the Screen to the Current Working Plane

7. To facilitate the creation of objects in the X–Y plane, it is often desirable to have the display screen parallel to the working plane. This is accomplished by using the PLAN command.

Command: **PLAN**
Enter an option [Current ucs/Ucs/World] <Current>: **press the Enter key**

When you press Enter at this point, you instruct the screen to align itself to the current UCS or working plane, which should be similar to Figure 4.18. Use the ZOOM command to reduce the view of the L-shape.

Drawing on the Working Plane

8. Using either the MTEXT or DTEXT command, add the word "FRONT" to the upper left of the L-shape, as shown in Figure 4.19. It's important to note that you should turn off OSNAP when placing the text.
9. Add a 5-sided polygon to the front face and observe the results with Step 10.

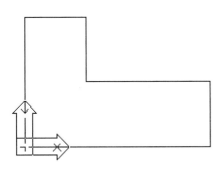

Figure 4.18
Displaying a plan view of the current
working plane

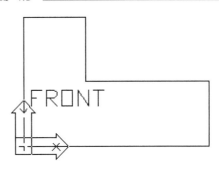

Figure 4.19
Adding text to the new working plane

 10. Use the VPOINT command or the SE Isometric View tool to display the ISO (1,–1,1) view again, and switch to Hidden shade mode. The view should be similar to Figure 4.20. Note the location of the UCS icon, the polygon, and the text.

 11. Using the 3Point option of the UCS command, repeat Steps 5 to 10 for each of the remaining sides of the orientation cube. The final rendering should look similar to Figure 4.21.

At this point, the working plane should be on one of the five sides other than the front. If it is not, set it to one of the other sides.

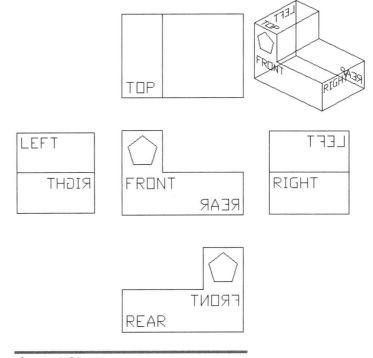

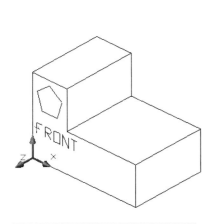

Figure 4.20
Displaying an isometric view

Figure 4.21
Text to be added to the sides of the cube

75

Restoring a Previously Saved Working Plane

12. Restore the working plane named FRONT.

Command: **UCS**
Current ucs name: *current*
Enter an option [New/Move/orthoGraphic/Prev/Restore/Save/Del/Apply/?/World]
   <World>: **R**
Enter name of UCS to restore or [?]: **FRONT**

> Note how the UCS icon switched to the front working plane. It is important to save working planes so that you can align them quickly for construction. If you name planes as you create them, then you do not have to repeat several commands to realign a plane. Instead, you simply restore the previously named plane.

13. Display on the screen a list of the newly created working planes. Use the UCS-MAN command or the Display UCS Dialog tool.

Command: **UCSMAN**

> The UCS dialog box appears and the Named UCS's tab should be visible. You should be able to see the FRONT UCS in the list.
> If you wanted to set the UCS to a named one contained in the list, you would highlight the name and then pick the Set Current button. Try it now by highlighting World, clicking the Set Current button, and then clicking the OK button to exit from the dialog box. You should see the W appear on the flat, L-shaped UCS icon. This signifies that you have aligned the UCS to the WCS.

14. Save the model as L-shape2** (replace ** with your initials).

Lab 4.C — Creating Working Planes Using the Axes

Purpose

Lab 4.C demonstrates how to create various working planes quickly by revolving the UCS about the *X, Y,* and *Z* axes. The lab is straightforward and easy to perform. However, this method of creating working planes is very useful to master early.

Objective

You will be able to rotate the UCS about the *X, Y,* and *Z* axes.

Primary Commands

UCS X
UCS Y
UCS Z
UCS Tools

Procedure

Activating the UCS Icon

1. Open the L-shape that was modified in Lab 4.B. The file name is L-shape2**.
   Set the UCSVP system variable to 0 and display the UCS and View toolbars. To match the figures, set the UCS icon to 2D using the Properties option of the UCSICON command.

2. Set the display to show an isometric view of the cube. Use the VPOINT command or the SE Isometric View tool.

Command: **VPOINT**
Current view direction: VIEWDIR = [current viewpoint coordinates]
Specify a view point or [Rotate] <display compass and tripod>: **1, −1, 1**

This displays the isoview of the orientation cube looking from above-right front.

3. Reduce the displayed view of the cube using the ZOOM command to see the UCS icon better when it is on.

Command: **ZOOM**
Specify corner of window, enter a scale factor (nX or nXP), or
[All/Center/Dynamic/Extents/Previous/Scale/Window] <real time>: **.8X**

This reduces the displayed view to 80% of its current size.

4. Use the UCS command or the World UCS tool to ensure that the working plane is set to the World Coordinate System (WCS).

Command: **UCS**
Current ucs name: *current*
Enter an option [New/Move/orthoGraphic/Prev/Restore/Save/Del/Apply/?/World]
<World>: **press Enter to accept the default of World**

5. Activate the UCS icon if it is not displayed.

Command: **UCSICON**
Enter an option [ON/OFF/All/Noorigin/ORigin] <current ON/OFF state>: **ON**

6. Align the icon to the current working plane (UCS).

Command: **UCSICON**
Enter an option [ON/OFF/All/Noorigin/ORigin] <current ON/OFF state>: **OR**

The UCS icon should now be displayed on the origin of 0,0,0 at the lower-left corner of the cube (see Figure 4.22).

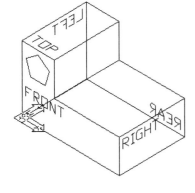

Figure 4.22
UCS icon displayed at lower-left corner

Moving the Origin Point

7. Using the Move option of the UCS command or the Origin UCS tool, move the origin point to the lower-right corner of the cube. The Move option allows you to move the origin point of the working plane but maintains the orientation of the X–Y plane.

Command: **UCS**
Current ucs name: *WORLD*
Enter an option [New/Move/orthoGraphic/Prev/Restore/Save/Del/Apply/?/World]
<World>: **Move**
Specify new origin point or [Zdepth]<0,0,0>: **endpoint** (endpoint object snap)
of **click the lower-right corner of the cube**

Note how the UCS icon moved to indicate the new origin point (see Figure 4.23).

Rotating the UCS About the X Axis

8. Repeat the UCS command, except use the X option to rotate the UCS 90 degrees about the X axis.

Command: **UCS**
Current ucs name: *NO NAME*
Enter an option [New/Move/orthoGraphic/Prev/Restore/Save/Del/Apply/?/World]
<World>: **N**
Specify origin of new UCS or [ZAxis/3point/OBject/Face/View/X/Y/Z] <0,0,0>: **X**
Specify rotation angle about X axis <default>: **90**

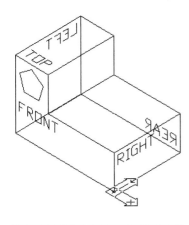

Figure 4.23
The new origin point

77

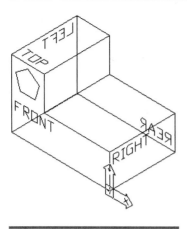

Figure 4.24
Rotating the UCS using the
X axis as the pivot

Note the UCS icon has now rotated to show the movement of the UCS working plane (see Figure 4.24).

Rotating the UCS About the Y Axis

9. Repeat the UCS command, except use the Y option to rotate the UCS 90 degrees about the *Y* axis.

Command: **UCS**
Current ucs name: ***NO NAME***
Enter an option [New/Move/orthoGraphic/Prev/Restore/Save/Del/Apply/?/World] <World>: **N**
Specify origin of new UCS or [ZAxis/3point/OBject/Face/View/X/Y/Z] <0,0,0>: **Y**
Specify rotation angle about Y axis <default>: **90**

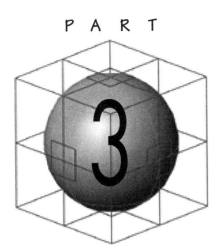

Construction of 3D Surface Models

In this part, you will learn the commands required to create and modify a 3D model on the screen. Chapter by chapter, you'll progress from the simplest processes to the most complex models allowed within the confines of the software (and these are impressive models by anyone's standards). As in previous chapters, you'll follow a step-by-step approach and be provided with many illustrative training activities.

5 Thickness Extrusion

Overview

Even with very little experience in the method, any user will find thickness extrusion to be simple, fast, and visually effective. For this reason, it is a good stepping stone to 3D modeling. With more experience in 3D modeling, you will use more advanced methods for model creation. Using thickness can allow for quick temporary construction to build from.

Concepts Explored

- How extruded forms are commonplace
- How the thickness extrusion process works and the way objects behave under thickness extrusion
- How to manipulate extruded forms using the thickness property
- How to create models through extrusion

5.1 Introduction

Most objects have their basis in extrusion techniques. Figure 5.1 shows some familiar items that can be created easily with thickness extrusion methods: walls, tables,

Figure 5.1
Familiar items created through extrusion

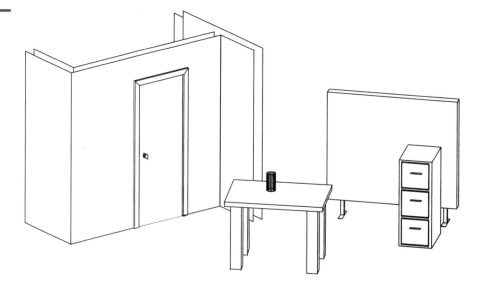

Figure 5.2
Mechanical objects created
through extrusion

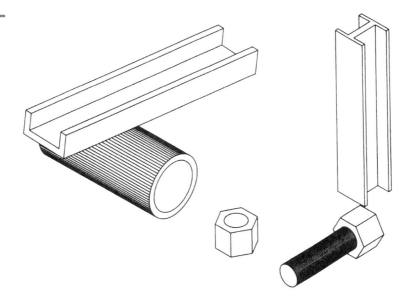

glasses, file cabinets, wall dividers, and many more. Figure 5.2 displays ordinary mechanical objects: a pipe, structural shapes, and a nut and bolt. What all of these shapes have in common is that, in each object, the outline or profile controls its final shape.

To be extruded, the profile does not have to be as simple as that of a file cabinet; it can be as complex as the outline of a floor plan or an I-beam. What is important to note is that the surfaces are parallel in the direction the profile is going to be extruded. The first step in the construction of any model should always be an analysis to determine which portion of the model can be constructed through extrusion. The method of extrusion is perhaps the easiest and fastest way to generate a model. You need make only three commands to turn a flat 2D floor plan into a three-dimensional model.

5.2   Thickness Concepts

Thickness is the result of taking an object—perhaps a line—and pushing its shape along an axis to form a 3D object—such as a sheet. AutoCAD assigns a thickness property to each object, thus allowing the operator to transform it from a two-dimensional shape into a three-dimensional shape. This property should be considered like any other property, such as color or linetype. The thickness of an object can be added, removed, or altered at any time, just like any other property of an object. The thickness property operates only in the Z direction. The object is drawn along an X–Y plane and is extruded along the Z axis.

Access to the thickness setting can be gained through the ELEVATION command or the Properties dialog box. Here, the thickness can be entered as a positive or negative distance, and the distance will go either in the positive direction or negative direction along the Z axis. The elevation of the object also can be added here. Elevation is not a property but a location in 3D space along the Z axis. The elevation can be different at the start of the object than at its finish. The thickness, on the other hand, applies to the entire length of the object because it is a property. Think of an object with the color red. The color property covers the whole object. You couldn't have a line half red and half green without breaking the object into two separate pieces.

Note that AutoCAD's Thickness option not only forms a three-dimensional shape, but also creates a surface over the thickness area. A covered surface is a requirement for the display of a hidden line removed or shaded picture. So the Thickness option actually performs two functions. This way, a user new to 3D can display an interesting 3D model using relatively few commands.

5.3   **Thickness Behavior**

The act of extruding objects through the thickness property has different effects on different object types. Also, the orientation of the object can alter the extrusion process. The following figures illustrate the effects of the thickness property on different objects.

Figure 5.3 shows the line object. If the UCS is aligned with the object, the extrusion takes place in a normal fashion, as shown in part A of the figure. However, as part B shows, if the UCS is not aligned with the line, the extrusion takes place along the Z axis, regardless of the inclination of the line. This type of extrusion is useful when a certain effect is desired.

Figure 5.4A shows a circle extruded. A circle drawn with the thickness property has a surface over its top and bottom, forming an enclosed shape. If you use the HIDE or RENDER commands, the top/bottom surface will be visible. If you use a shade mode, the top/bottom will not be displayed. The arc shown in Figure 5.4B does not have a surface on either its top or bottom. Two arcs can be used to create an open cylinder.

Figure 5.5A shows a polyline with no width (2D). In Figure 5.5B, width has been added to the polyline, and its possible graphic uses increase. Finally, in Figure 5.5C, a polyline with curves and width has been given thickness. When width is given to a polyline, the surface covering the area is defined by the width.

Figure 5.6A displays a polyline donut that behaves like a regular polyline. Figure 5.6B shows a polygon that does not have a surface covering its area, either at the top or bottom.

Figure 5.7 shows an object created with the SOLID command. This is a 2D command, not to be confused with 3D solids. An irregular shape created by the SOLID command has a top and bottom surface when given a thickness.

Figure 5.3
Extruded lines

Figure 5.4
Extruded arcs

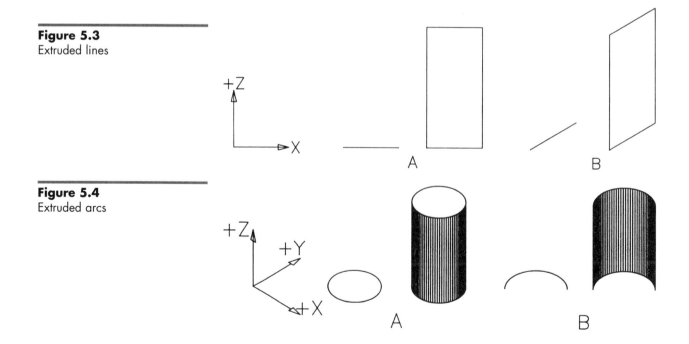

Figure 5.5
Extruded polylines

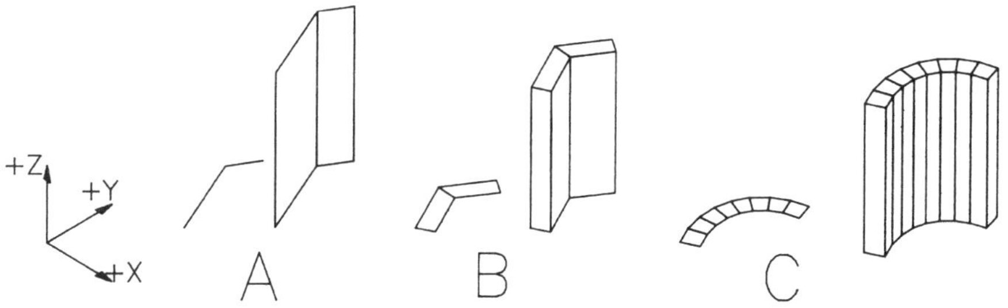

Figure 5.6
Extruded polylines: donut and polygon

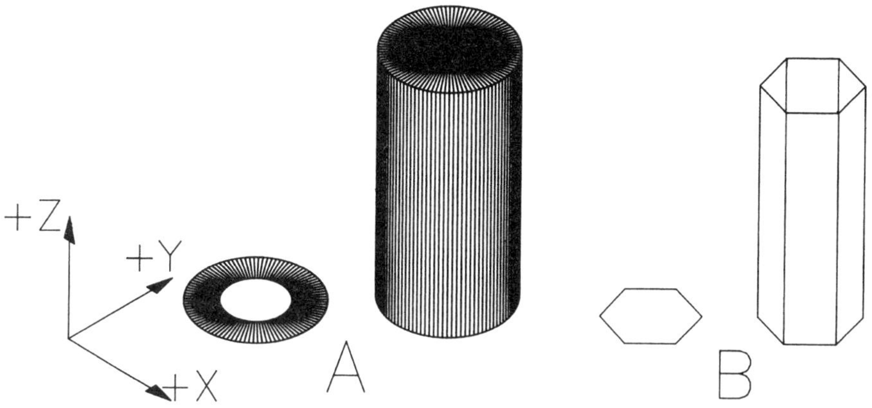

Figure 5.7
Extruded 2D solid (not a 3D solid)

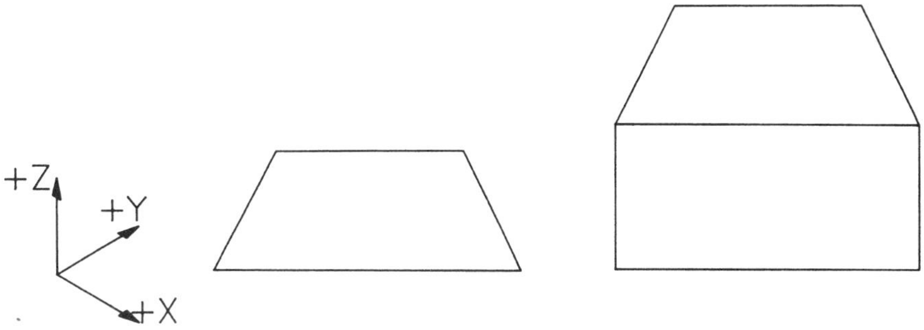

5.4   Thickness Property

Normally, the best practice is to set the thickness property before drawing an object. As mentioned earlier, to access the Thickness option, the ELEV, or THICKNESS, command is used. This command sets the thickness and sets the elevation above or below the current working plane, as described in Section 4.4. The Thickness option also can be accessed through a pull-down menu, as shown in Figure 5.8.

3D VIEWPOINT

Thickness Property

Remember to return the thickness setting to 0 when you are finished. If left at some value and forgotten, it can result in some unpredicted results— namely, numerous objects with unwanted three-dimensional thickness.

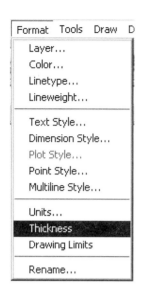

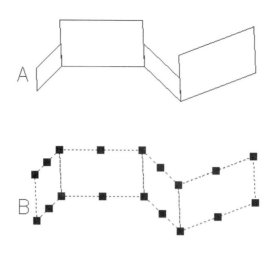

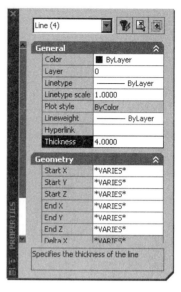

Figure 5.8
Pull-down menu to access thickness setting

Figure 5.9
Using the Properties dialog box to change the thickness

5.5 Thickness Modification

The thickness of any object can be altered through the Properties dialog box, as shown in Figure 5.9. This box is displayed using the Properties tool, by entering PROPERTIES on the command line, or selecting Properties from the Modify pull-down menu. Part A shows several lines with different thicknesses. By selecting all the objects to change, the Properties dialog box is used to set them to the same thickness, in this case a value of 1, as shown in part B.

A quick way to get access to an object's properties to adjust thickness is to click on the object to highlight it and then right-click to bring up the context menu. From the menu you can select Properties.

5.6 Thickness Effect on Object Snap

Because a form with thickness is bound by the originating object, the snap locations on the extruded form reflect the original object snap points. Figure 5.10 shows common objects and the various snap points on their extruded forms: A is a line, B is a polyline, C is a circle, and D is a polygon. Remember that polylines that have a width are bound by the original "no-width" start and stop points (vertices). This means that there are no snap points around the corners of a polyline with a width, but you can snap to the midpoint of the vertical thickness.

Figure 5.10
Snap points on extruded objects

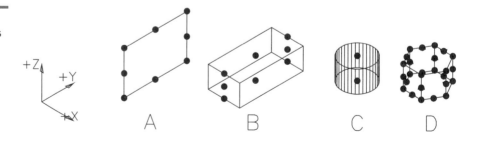

Lab 5.A   Bolt Thickness Extrusion

Purpose

Lab 5.A will show you how thickness extrusion methods are used to create the model of a bolt. This model will be used again in Assignment 1 in Chapter 7.

Objectives

You will be able to:

- Set the Elevation and Thickness options
- Display multiple viewpoints
- Create a 3D model through thickness extrusion

Primary Commands

ELEV–Elevation/Thickness
VPORTS
VPOINT
HIDE

Final Model

Figure 5.11 shows the completed extruded bolt model.

Procedure

1. Start a new drawing called BOLT, using the following settings or open file a3dex5a from the a3d2005 folder. This file has most of the settings already set. All you should need to do is display the UCS, View, and 3D Orbit toolbars.

Units = decimal
Limits = −1, −1 to 1,1
Grid = 0.25
Snap Incr = 0.125
Current Layer = 0
Viewport Configuration = single/plan viewpoint
UCSICON = On and set to 2D display properties
UCSVP = 0 (always set before creation of viewports)
UCS toolbar = displayed
View toolbar = displayed

Creating the Bolt Head

2. Select the ELEV command and enter 0 for the elevation and 0.25 for the thickness. This will give thickness to the bolt head.
3. Using the POLYGON command, draw the bolt head as shown in Figure 5.12. The center of the polygon should have the coordinates 0, 0.

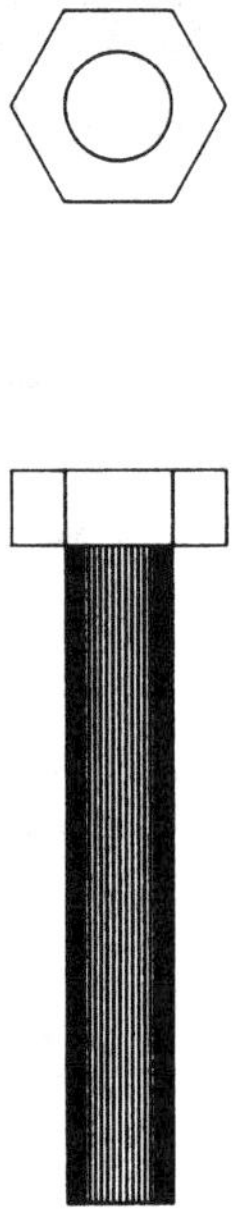

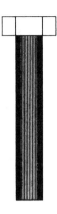

Figure 5.11
Extruded bolt model

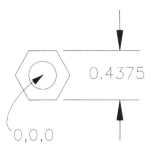

Figure 5.12
Top view of bolt head hexagon

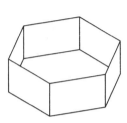

Figure 5.13
Isometric view of bolt head

4. Display an isometric view (1, −1, 1) and use the HIDE command. The results should be similar to Figure 5.13. Note that there is no top to the polygon. This will be added in Chapter 7, after surfaces are explained.

Displaying Multiple Viewports

5. Using the VPORTS command, create a new configuration using the Four: Equal, 3D setup. You should be able to see the top, front, side, and isometric views of your model. Save the viewport configuration as ORTHO1.

Creating the Bolt Shaft

6. Select the ELEV command and enter 0 for the elevation and −1.5 for the thickness. This will give thickness to the bolt shaft along the negative Z axis.
7. Activate the top viewpoint viewport. Using the CIRCLE command, draw the shaft as shown in Figure 5.14. Do *not* use object snap. Object snap will override the elevation settings.
8. Experiment with the ZOOM CENTER command to display all three orthographic views at the same scale. (Try a factor of 2.)
9. Save the model as BOLT.

Figure 5.14
Top view showing circle placement and size

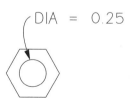

Lab 5.B   Table Thickness Extrusion

Purpose

Lab 5.B shows you how thickness extrusion methods can be used to create a model of a table. This model will be used again in Assignment 1 in Chapter 13.

Objectives

You will be able to:

- Set the Elevation and Thickness options
- Display multiple viewpoints
- Create a 3D model through thickness extrusion

Primary Commands

ELEV–Elevation/Thickness
VPORTS
VPOINT
HIDE
View tools and Shade modes

Final Model

Figure 5.15 shows the finished extruded table model.

Procedure

1. Start a new drawing called TABLE with the following settings or you can open file a3dex5b from the a3d2005 folder. This file has most of the settings already set. All you should need to do is display the UCS, View, and 3D Orbit toolbars.

    Units = architectural
    Limits = −1′,−1′ to 6′,4′
    Grid = 6″
    Snap Incr = 1″
    Current Layer = 0
    Viewport Configuration = single/plan viewpoint
    Fill = OFF
    UCSICON = On and set to 2D display properties
    UCSVP = 0 (always set before creation of viewports)

Figure 5.15
Extruded table model

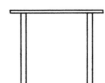

UCS toolbar = displayed
View toolbar = displayed

Creating the Table Top

2. Select the ELEV command and enter 2'5″ for the elevation and −1″ for the thickness. This places the table top at an elevation of 2'5″ and gives it a thickness of 1″. You may have to periodically use the ZOOM Extents command to see all the geometry.

3. Using the PLINE (polyline) command, draw the table top as shown in Figure 5.16. (*Note:* The polyline should have a width of 3'.) The polyline was used because of its simplicity to create and its characteristic of allowing surfaces on its top, bottom, and sides.

Displaying Multiple Viewports

4. Using the VPORTS command, create a new configuration using the Four: Equal, 3D setup. You should be able to see the top, front, side, and isometric views of your model. Save the viewport configuration as ORTHO1.

Creating the Table Legs

5. Select the ELEV command and enter 0 for the elevation and 2' 4″ for the thickness. This places the legs on the ground and gives a thickness that extrudes to meet the top. Do *not* use object snap. Object snap will override the elevation settings.

6. Activate the top viewpoint viewport. Using the LINE command, draw the legs as shown in Figure 5.17.

Displaying a Hidden Line Removed Model

7. Use the ZOOM CENTER command in each viewport to set a matching scale. Try a scale factor of 4'.

8. Activate each viewport and use the HIDE command (see Figure 5.18). Note that the table top has a surface covering it.

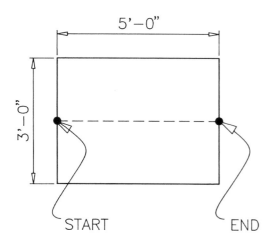

Figure 5.16
Top view showing polyline size

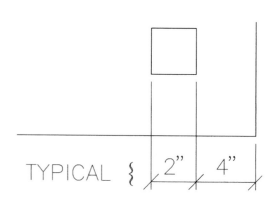

Figure 5.17
Top view showing leg size and placement

Figure 5.18
Viewports showing final model

Setting the Base Point

9. Because this model will be used later in Chapter 13, a new base point needs to be set. The base point is the cursor handle point when the block (the table) is inserted into another model. It is used to identify where the block will be placed. This base point should have an elevation of 0Z, and the X and Y location should be in the center of the table (see Figure 5.19). To set the new base point:

■ Activate the top viewpoint viewport.
■ Select the BASE command.
■ Select the .*XY* point filter by entering .*xy* on the command line when prompted to enter the coordinates of the base point (if desired, more can be learned about filters in Section 6.2).
■ Select the object snap midpoint option.
■ Select the top width of the polyline of the table top.
■ Enter 0 for the request of the Z coordinate.

A new base point has now been set.

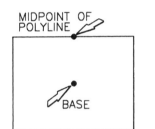

Figure 5.19
Top view showing base point

10. Save the model as TABLE.
11. Experiment with moving around the model using the VPOINT or View tools and Hide or Shade modes commands.

 ## Lab 5.C   Chair Thickness Extrusion

Purpose

Lab 5.C shows you how thickness extrusion methods can be used to create a model of a chair. This model will be used again in Assignment 1 in Chapter 13.

89

Objectives

You will be able to:

- Set the Elevation and Thickness options
- Display multiple viewpoints
- Create a 3D model through thickness extrusion

Primary Commands

ELEV–Elevation/Thickness
VPORTS
VPOINT
HIDE
View tools and Shade modes

Final Model

Figure 5.20 shows the final extruded chair model.

Procedure

1. Start a new drawing called CHAIR with the following settings or you can open file a3dex5c from the a3d2005 folder. This file has most of the settings already set. All you should need to do is display the UCS, View, and 3D Orbit toolbars.

   Units = architectural
   Limits = −1″,−1″ to 2′,2′
   Grid = 2″
   Snap Incr = 0.5″
   Current Layer = 0
   Viewport Configuration = single/plan viewpoint
   Fill = OFF
   UCSICON = On and set to 2D display properties
   UCSVP = 0 (always set before creation of viewports)

Figure 5.20
Extruded chair model

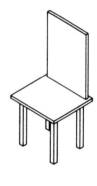
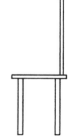

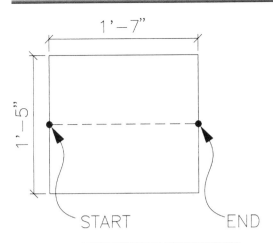

Figure 5.21
Top view of polyline chair seat

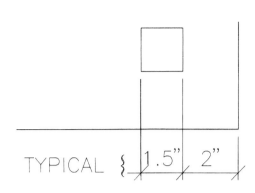

Figure 5.22
Top view of chair legs

UCS toolbar = displayed
View toolbar = displayed

Creating the Chair Seat

2. Select the ELEV command and enter 1′6″ for the elevation and −1″ for the thickness. This places the chair seat at an elevation of 1′6″ and gives it a thickness of 1″.
3. Using the PLINE command, draw the chair seat as shown in Figure 5.21. (*Note:* Set the width of the polyline to 1′5″.) As in Lab 5.A, the polyline was used because of its simplicity to create and its allowance of surfaces on its top, bottom, and sides.

Displaying Multiple Viewports

4. Using the VPORTS command, create a new configuration using the Four: Equal, 3D setup. You should be able to see the top, front, side, and isometric views of your model. Save the viewport configuration as ORTHO1. You may have to periodically use the ZOOM Extents command to see all the geometry.

Creating the Chair Legs

5. Select the ELEV command and enter 0 for the elevation and 1′6″ for the thickness. This places the legs on the ground and gives a thickness that extrudes to meet the seat. Do *not* use object snap. Object snap will override the elevation settings.
6. Activate the top viewpoint viewport. Using the LINE command, draw the legs as shown in Figure 5.22.

Creating the Chair Back

7. Select the ELEV command and enter 1′5″ for the elevation and 2′ for the thickness. This is used to place the back on the seat and to give a thickness that extrudes above the seat. Do *not* use object snap. Object snap will override the elevation settings.

91

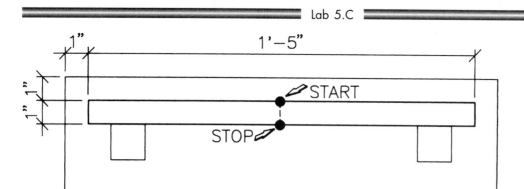

Figure 5.23
Top view of polyline chair back

8. Activate the top viewpoint viewport. Using the PLINE command, draw the back as shown in Figure 5.23. (*Note:* Set the width of the polyline to 1'5".)

Displaying a Hidden Line Removed Model

9. Use the ZOOM Center command in each viewport to set a matching scale. Try a scale factor of 5'.
10. Activate each viewport and use the HIDE command (see Figure 5.24). Note that the seat and the back have surfaces.

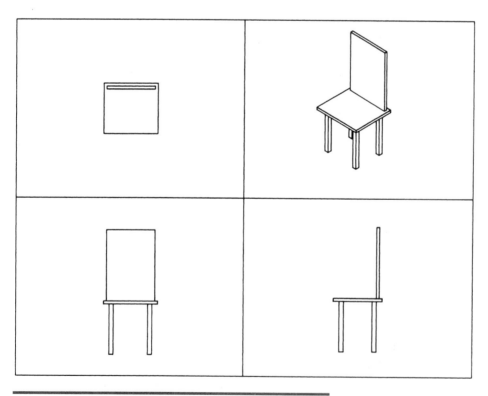

Figure 5.24
Viewports showing final model

Figure 5.25
Top view showing base point

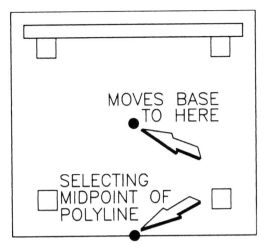

Setting the Base Point

11. Because this model will be used later in Chapter 13, a new base point needs to be set. This base point should have an elevation of 0Z, and the X and Y location should be in the center of the chair (see Figure 5.25). To set a new base point:

   ■ Activate the top viewpoint viewport.
   ■ Select the BASE command.
   ■ Select the *.XY* filter by entering *.xy* on the command line when prompted to enter the coordinates of the base point. (Refer to Section 6.2 if you are unsure how to do this.)
   ■ Select the object snap midpoint option.
   ■ Select the bottom width of the polyline of the seat.
   ■ Enter 0 for the request of the Z coordinate.

   A new base point has now been set.

12. Save the model as CHAIR.
13. Experiment with moving around the model using the VPOINT or View tools and the HIDE or Shade modes commands.

Questions

1. What two elements define the shape of an extrusion?

2. Explain the process of generating an extrusion.

3. Explain the process for altering the thickness of an object that has already been created.

4. What is the significance of AutoCAD's thickness property compared to other CAD programs' extrusion capabilities?

5. How can the inclination of a line affect its extrusion?

6. What is the difference between a circle and an arc thickness?

7. What is the difference between the thickness of a polygon and the thickness of a solid?

8. What are the two methods for accessing the Thickness option?

93

Assignments

Note: The prototype drawing 3DSET created in Assignment 1 of Chapter 3 is used in the following assignments, or you can use the VPORTS command and set it to Four: Equal 3D.

1. Create a 3D model of a file cabinet using only thickness extrusion (see Figure 5.26). Save it as FCAB. (*Hint:* Use different elevations for the drawers or draw one and copy in a *Z* direction.) Use 3DSET for the prototype drawing. Use the HIDE command when finished to determine if any surfaces are missing. This model will be used again in Chapter 16, Assignment 2.

2. Generate a 3D model of a bookshelf using only thickness extrusion (see Figure 5.27). Save it as BSHEL. Use 3DSET for the prototype drawing. Use the HIDE command when finished and observe the results. This model will be used again in Chapter 16, Assignment 2.

3. Draw a length of an I-beam (structural member) using only thickness extrusion (see Figure 5.28). Use 3DSET for the prototype drawing. Use the HIDE command when finished and depending on whether lines, polylines, or solids are used, note where there are no surfaces.

4. Referring to Figure 5.29, create an architectural floor plan. Use 3DSET for the prototype drawing. Experiment with the VPOINT or View tools and the Hide

Figure 5.26
File cabinet extruded model

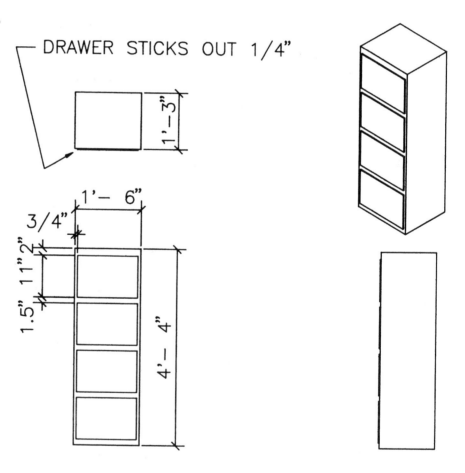

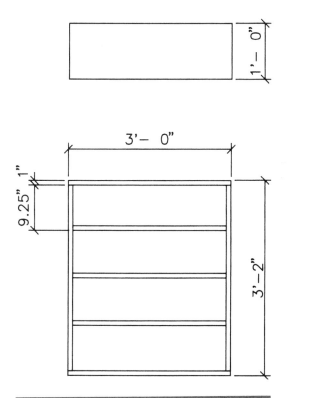
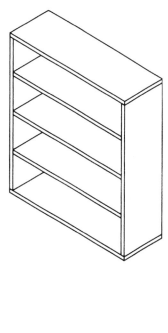

3'– 0"

1'– 0"

1"

9.25"

3'–2"

Figure 5.27
Bookshelf extruded model

Figure 5.28
I-beam extruded model

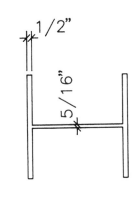

1/2"

5/16"

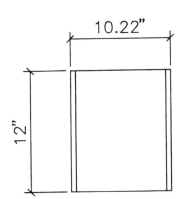
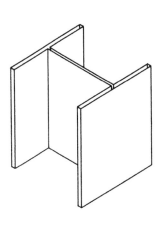

10.22"

12"

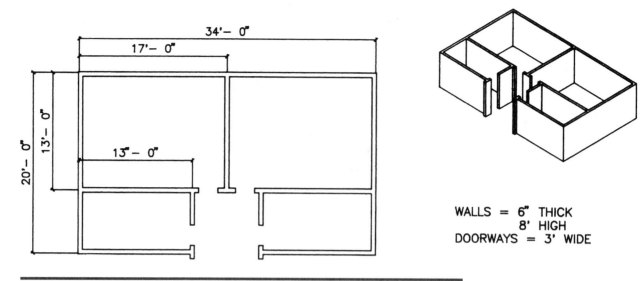

WALLS = 6" THICK
8' HIGH
DOORWAYS = 3' WIDE

Figure 5.29
Floor plan extruded model

Wireframe

Overview

This chapter explains the basic concepts you'll need to understand in order to generate true 3D models. Methods and applications mentioned in Chapters 3 and 4 are utilized here. For instance, in this chapter you will use working planes.

Concepts Explored

- What wireframe models represent
- The application of nodes
- The significance of coordinate filters
- The projection techniques required to solve model problems
- The behavior of true 3D objects
- The construction of wireframe models

6.1 Introduction

The concept behind true three-dimensional modeling is that the start point and the finish point of any piece of geometry can have completely independent sets of coordinates. Because AutoCAD's line object can start and stop at any location in three-dimensional space, it is considered a true three-dimensional object (see Figure 6.1).

The initial method of model building using the concept of 3D modeling is wireframe construction. *Wireframe* means that lines are used to represent the boundary edge of any shape or model. Wireframes often serve as the skeleton of models. With some complex models, wireframes need to be constructed before surfaces can be formed. And surfaces are required before hidden line removal can be performed. Some of the AutoCAD automatic surface commands require that wireframe profiles be created before the surfaces are generated.

Node points control the shape of the wireframe. Nodes are the intersection points of the various lines, or the vertices of polylines. Sometimes in the initial stages of model creation, the node points are the first objects to be added, followed by lines or surfaces defined by the node points. Figure 6.2 illustrates a model showing node points. Node points are further utilized in Chapter 23.

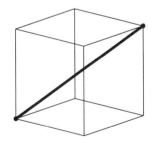

Figure 6.1
A cube showing a true 3D line

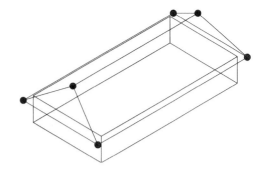

Figure 6.2
A model of a house showing
node points for a hip roof

6.2 **Coordinate Point Filters**

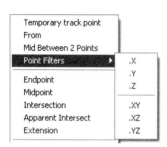

When entering node points, it is often necessary to make use of geometry that has
already been created, such as object endsnap, or mid- or intersection points. Sometimes it is necessary to use only part of the coordinates at the snap point instead of
all three *X, Y, Z* axis points. Consider this typical scenario: A user needs the *X* and
Y location of a point but wants the *Z* point at a different elevation. AutoCAD has
foreseen this situation and has incorporated the Filters tool into the program. This
option allows the user to extract any combination of points from a digitized (clicked)
location on a model and then to type in the missing coordinate. Two of the six fil-
tering combinations (*.X, .Y, .Z, .XY, .XZ, .YZ*) are as follows. The other four combinations follow the same pattern.

FILTER	MEANING
.X	The user selects a point on the model. AutoCAD extracts the *X* coordinate and asks the user to enter the *Y* and *Z* coordinates.
.XY	The user selects a point on the model. AutoCAD extracts the *X* and *Y* coordinates and asks the user to enter the *Z* coordinate.

Figure 6.3 illustrates the use of the Filters option to enter 3D lines. Part A of the
figure shows the original line drawn in 3D space. Part B shows the extraction of the
XY coordinate from one end of the original line and the input of 1.5 for the *Z*
coordinate. Finally, part C shows the extraction of the *XY* coordinate from the other
end of the original line and the input of 1.5 for the *Z* coordinate. The result is a
new line whose *X* and *Y* coordinates match the first line but whose *Z* location is different. The following is the command procedure to create the new line from the
original:

Command: **LINE**
Specify first point: **.XY**
of **ENDPOINT**
of **click one end of the original line**

Figure 6.3
Using the Filters option to draw
a line

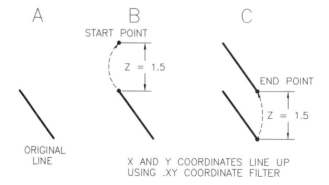

(need Z): 1.5
Specify next point or [Undo]: **.XY**
of **ENDPOINT**
of click the other end of the original line
(need Z): **1.5**
Specify next point or [Close/Undo]: **press Enter to quit the command**

Coordinate Point Filters can be accessed by typing on the command line, or using the shift-right-click context menu when drawing or moving objects.

3D VIEWPOINT

UCS Working Plane and Object Snaps

It's very important to note that if OSNAPS are turned on, they will override the current location of the UCS working plane. This means that you may have set the UCS working plane at one level and drawn on another level with object snap by mistake. Take care to watch out for this. You may want to turn OSNAP off when not snapping to an actual object.

6.3 Projection Techniques

Projection is a very useful method of locating node points on a complex model. *Projection* refers to the technique of projecting lines along an axis until they intersect with lines projected along a different axis, resulting in a node point. A series of node points can then be used to generate a "line of intersection" outline where one object intersects another. Figures 6.4 to 6.7 illustrate how this technique is used for arc intersection. *Note:* The more node points, the smoother the line of intersection.

FIGURE	DESCRIPTION
6.4A	Finished model of two arcs intersecting
6.4B	Initially created two planes
6.4C	Addition of arcs subdivided
6.4D	Projection of lines perpendicular to arcs
6.4E	Identification of intersection nodes
6.4F	Addition of 3D polyline through node points
6.5	Final model displayed in four viewports

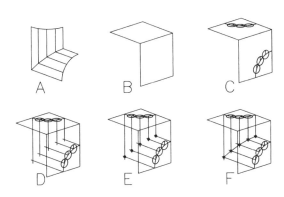

Figure 6.4
Creating a line of intersection

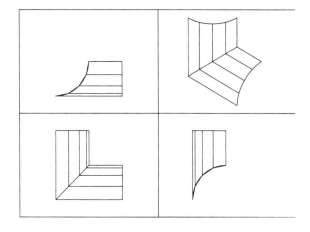

Figure 6.5
The final model in four viewports

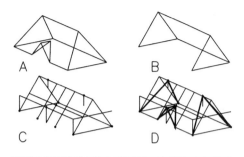

Figure 6.6
Creating intersecting roofs

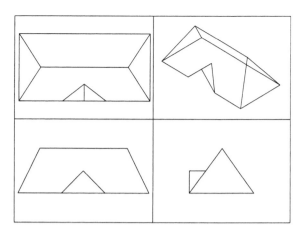

Figure 6.7
The final roof model in four viewports

Figures 6.6 and 6.7 illustrate how this technique is used for roof intersection:

FIGURE	DESCRIPTION
6.6A	Finished model of the two roofs intersecting
6.6B	Initially created planes
6.6C	Identification of intersection nodes
6.6D	Addition of lines through node points
6.7	Final model displayed in four viewports

6.4   2D Polyline versus 3D Polyline

Although lines can be drawn along any axis at any time just by object snapping or by entering the 3D coordinates, the regular polyline is restricted to being aligned to wherever the working plane is currently set. The regular polyline can be thought of as a planar object. Even if a user entered coordinates in an attempt to make the polyline nonplanar, the polyline would project the coordinates onto the working plane until the polyline became flat. To overcome this limitation, AutoCAD has established the 3D polyline. The 3DPOLY command creates a polyline that can run along any axis at any time, just like a line. Currently however—and this is the only negative aspect—no width or thickness can be given to a 3D polyline. Figure 6.8 illustrates a 2D polyline in the shape of a circle aligned to a plane. Figure 6.9 shows a 3D polyline in the form of a helical coil, illustrating that a polyline is indeed not limited to one plane.

Figure 6.8
A flat 2D polyline

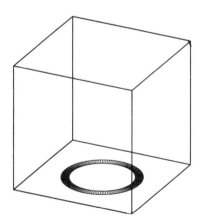

Figure 6.9
A helical 3D polyline

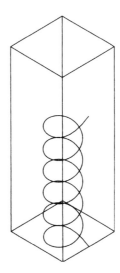

Refer back to the 3D polyline shown in Figure 6.4F. There, the polyline follows the intersecting curve regardless of the coordinates. When creating models with irregular curves that lie in no particular plane, you'll find the 3D polyline extremely useful.

 # Lab 6.A Angle Block

Purpose

Lab 6.A familiarizes you with wireframe methods of model construction. You will create a wireframe model of an angle plate, emphasizing angular lines. The methods you'll be using demonstrate AutoCAD's true 3D capabilities. This model will be used again in Chapter 7, where you will learn how to apply a surface to the wireframe skeleton. It should be noted that this model could easily be constructed using 3D solid modeling. However, it's used here so that you're prepared for the complexity of wireframe construction.

Objectives

You will be able to:

■ Construct a wireframe model
■ Display multiple viewpoints

Primary Commands

ELEV—Elevation/Thickness
VPORTS
HIDE
View tools and Shade modes

Final Model

Figure 6.10 shows the final wireframe model you'll be constructing.

Procedure

1. Start a new drawing called ANGPLT (ANGle PLaTe) with the following settings or you can open file a3dex6a from the a3d2005 folder. This file has most of the settings already set. All you should need to do is display the UCS, View, and 3D Orbit toolbars.

   Units = decimal
   Limits = −1, −1 to 8,8
   Grid = 1
   Snap Incr = 0.5
   Current Layer = WIRE

Figure 6.10
Angle plate wireframe model

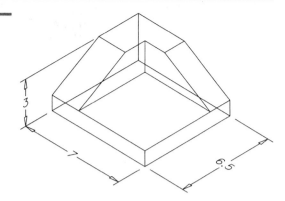

UCSICON = On and set to 2D display properties
UCSVP = 0 (always set before creation of viewports)
UCS toolbar = displayed
View toolbar = displayed
Viewport Configuration = New viewport, Four: Equal, 3D setup

Creating an Orientation 3D Box

When starting construction, it is useful to create a 3D box for initial orientation. This gives you some overall perspective while you're constructing, and lets you know if construction exceeds the boundary of the 3D box during the building process.

2. Using the ELEV command, set the elevation to 0 and the thickness to 3.
3. Activate the top view viewport, and draw the box as shown in Figure 6.11. Observe the results in the other viewports.

Creating Working Planes

Three working planes are going to be created at this stage: the front, right side, and top. Another working plane will be created later.

4. Following Figure 6.12, create a working plane using the UCS command on the front of the cube. Make sure you use object snaps. Save the UCS as FRONT. You may have to use the ZOOM Extents periodically to see all the geometry.
5. Using the same procedure as you did to create the front UCS working plane, create the working planes for the top and right side, and save each UCS with the names TOP and RSIDE. Make sure to use object snaps. Stop and save the model as ANGPLT.

Figure 6.11
Creating the orientation 3D box

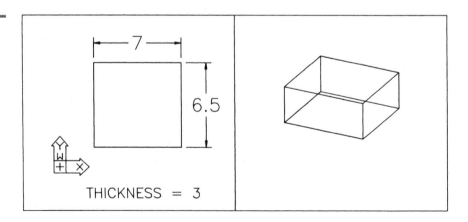

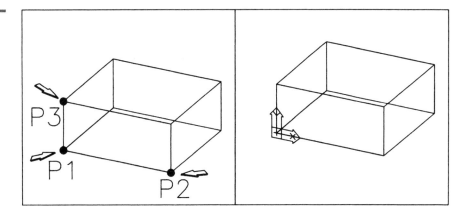

Figure 6.12
Creating the FRONT working plane

Drawing on the Front Plane

6. Set the FRONT UCS working plane as current.
7. Using the ELEV command, set the elevation to 0 and the thickness to 0.
8. Activate the front-view viewport, and draw the line shown in Figure 6.13. Observe the isometric viewport. It's very important to note that if OSNAPs are turned on, they'll override the current location of the UCS working plane. This means that you may have set the UCS working plane at one level and drawn on another level using object snapping by mistake. This is particularly true when drawing in an orthographic viewport such as a front view. Take care to watch out for this. Turn OSNAP off when not snapping to an actual object.

Drawing on the Right-Side Plane

9. Set the RSIDE UCS working plane as current.
10. Activate the right-side-view viewport, and draw the line shown in Figure 6.14.

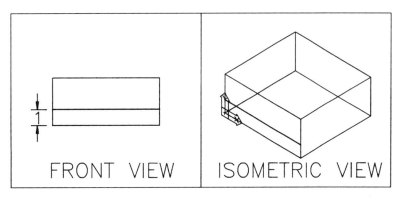

Figure 6.13
Adding a line on the FRONT working plane

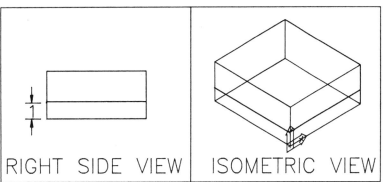

Figure 6.14
Adding a line on the RSIDE working plane

Figure 6.15
Creating on the TOP working plane

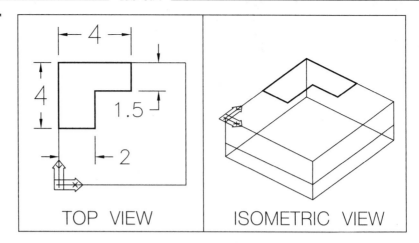

TOP VIEW | ISOMETRIC VIEW

Drawing on the Top Plane

11. Set the TOP UCS working plane as current.
12. Activate the top-view viewport, and draw the profile (six lines in all) shown in Figure 6.15. Estimate the remaining dimensions. Stop and save the model as ANGPLT.

Drawing on an Incline

13. Activate the isometric viewport, and draw the lines indicated in Figure 6.16. It is very important to use object snap endpoint to ensure the lines are in the correct position.
14. With the use of the COPY command, create parallel line B using line A, and then create line D using line C (see Figure 6.17).

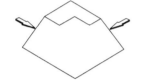

Figure 6.16
Adding sloped lines using object endpoint snap

Creating a New Working Plane

15. Referring to Figure 6.18, create a new working plane. Make sure you use object snaps. Save the UCS as TPLATE (Top of PLATE).
16. Keep the isometric viewport active, and add lines E and F, as shown in Figure 6.19.

Figure 6.17
Adding sloped lines with COPY

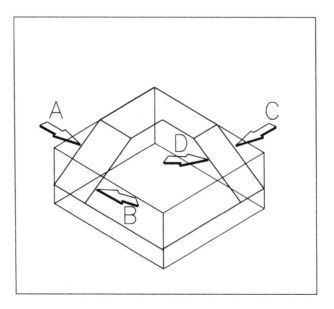

Figure 6.18
Creating a new working plane

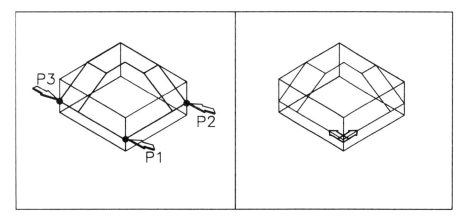

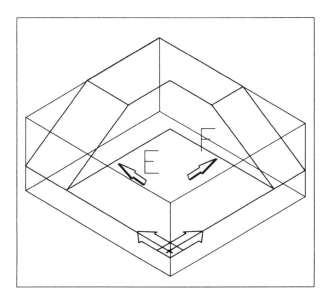

Figure 6.19
Adding lines to the top plate

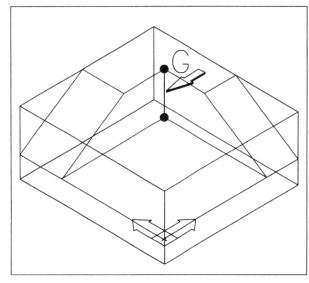

Figure 6.20
Adding a vertical line

17. Using object snap endpoint, draw in line G, as shown in Figure 6.20. Stop and save the model as ANGPLT.

Returning the Orientation Cube to Zero Thickness

18. Using the PROPERTIES command, set the original orientation cube lines back to 0 thickness, as shown in Figure 6.21. These lines will be used as part of the wireframe. Remember you can change the properties of an object by clicking on the object and right-clicking to bring up the context menu. From the menu, select Properties.

19. After observing the model in all the viewports, add the missing lines to finish the model. Refer back to Figure 6.10. (*Note:* Make sure to use object snap endpoint for this construction.)

20. Use the HIDE command or Hide shade mode and observe the results. Hidden line removal only works with surfaces. Surfaces will be added to this model in the next chapter.

21. Save the model as ANGPLT.

105

Figure 6.21
Returning lines to zero thickness

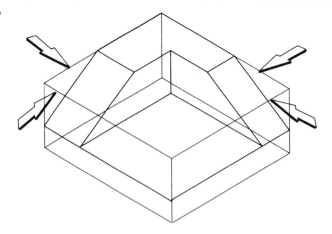

Lab 6.B — Inca Structure

Purpose

Lab 6.B familiarizes you with wireframe methods of model construction. You will create a wireframe model of an ancient Inca structure, emphasizing inclined lines. The methods you will be using will demonstrate AutoCAD's true 3D capability.

Objectives

You will be able to:

- Construct a wireframe model
- Display multiple viewpoints

Primary Commands

ELEV—Elevation/Thickness
VPORTS
VPOINT
HIDE
View tools and Shade modes

Final Model

Figure 6.22 shows the final wireframe model you'll be constructing.

Procedure

1. Start a new drawing called INCA (INCA structure) with the following settings or you can open file a3dex6b from the a3d2005 folder. This file has most of the settings already set. All you should need to do is display the UCS, View, and 3D Orbit toolbars.

   Units = architectural
   Limits = −10′, −10′ to 260′, 240′
   Grid = 10′
   Snap Incr = 10′
   Current Layer = WIRE
   UCSICON = On and set to 2D display properties
   UCSVP = 0 (always set before creation of viewports)
   UCS toolbar = displayed
   View toolbar = displayed
   Viewport configuration = New viewport, Four: Equal,
       3D setup

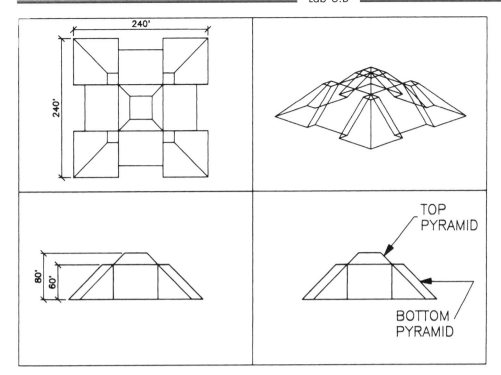

Figure 6.22
Inca structure wireframe model

Creating an Orientation 3D Box

When starting construction, it is useful to create a 3D box for initial orientation. This gives you some overall perspective while you're constructing, and it lets you know if construction exceeds the boundary of the 3D box during the building process.

For this model, two orientation cubes will be constructed: one for the bottom pyramid shape and another for the top pyramid shape.

2. Using the ELEV command, set the elevation to 0 and the thickness to 60′.
3. Activate the top-view viewport, and draw the 240′ square box as shown in Figure 6.23. Observe the results in the other viewports.
4. Using the ELEV command, set the elevation to 60′ and the thickness to 20′. This sets the second cube on top of the first.
5. Activate the top-view viewport, and draw the 80′ square box as shown in Figure 6.23. Observe the results in the other viewports. It's very important to note that if OSNAPS are turned on, they'll override the current location of the UCS working plane. This means that you may have set the UCS working plane at one level and drawn on another level by object snapping accidentally. This is particularly true when drawing in an orthographic viewport such as a front view. Take care to watch out for this. Turn OSNAP off when not snapping to an actual object.

Creating Working Planes

Three working planes (one for each elevation point) are going to be created at this stage: Level 1, Level 2, and Level 3.

6. Following Figure 6.24, create the three working planes using the UCS command. Save each working plane so that they may be restored any time. Call them LEVEL1, LEVEL2, and LEVEL3. Stop and save the model as INCA.

107

Figure 6.23
Creating two orientation boxes

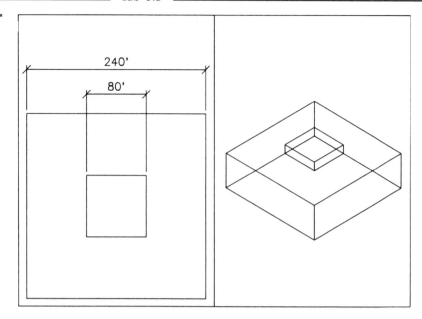

Figure 6.24
Creating three working planes

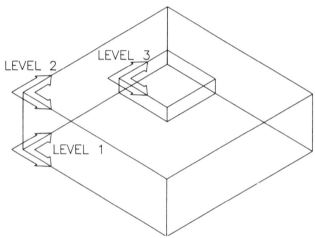

Drawing on the LEVEL1 Plane

7. Set the LEVEL1 UCS working plane as current.
8. Using the ELEV command, set the elevation to 0 and the thickness to 0.
9. Activate the top-view viewport, and draw the lines shown in Figure 6.25. Observe the isometric viewport.

Drawing on the LEVEL2 Plane

10. Set the LEVEL2 UCS working plane as current.
11. With the top-view viewport still activated, draw the lines shown in Figure 6.26. Observe the isometric viewport.

Adding the Inclined Lines to the First Pyramid

The inclined lines from Level 1 to Level 2 will now be added.

12. Activate the isometric viewport. Using object snap endpoint, add lines connecting the node points on Level 1 with those on Level 2. You need to alter the viewpoint as lines are added around the model (see Figure 6.27).

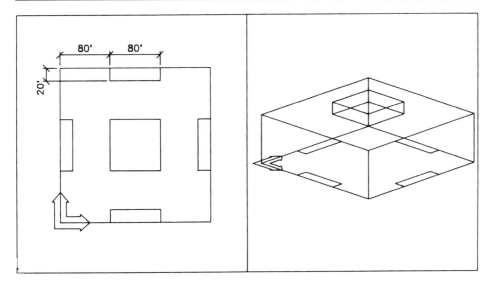

Figure 6.25
Creating on LEVEL1

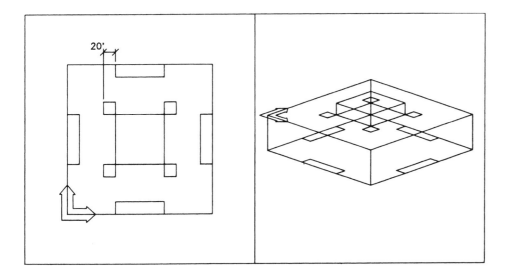

Figure 6.26
Creating on LEVEL2

Figure 6.27
Adding sloped lines using object
snap endpoint

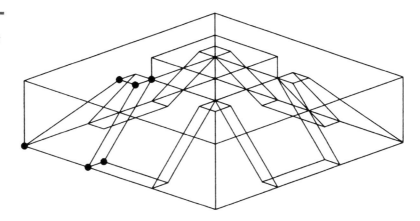

109

Figure 6.28
Returning lines to zero thickness

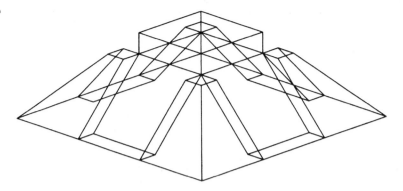

13. Using the PROPERTIES command, return the thickness of the bottom orientation cube to 0, as shown in Figure 6.28. Remember, you can change the properties of an object by clicking the object and right-clicking to bring up the context menu. From the menu select Properties. Stop and save the model as INCA.

Drawing on the LEVEL3 Plane

14. Set the LEVEL3 UCS working plane as current.
15. Make sure the elevation and the thickness are set to 0.
16. Activate the top-view viewport, and draw the lines shown in Figure 6.29. Observe the isometric viewport.

Adding the Inclined Lines to the Second Pyramid

The inclined lines from Level 2 to Level 3 are now added.

17. Activate the isometric viewport. Using object snap endpoint, add lines connecting the node points on Level 2 with those on Level 3. You may need to alter the viewpoint as lines are added around the model (see Figure 6.30).

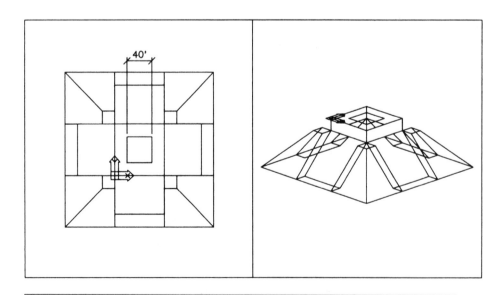

Figure 6.29
Creating on LEVEL3

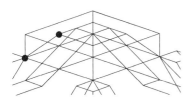

Figure 6.30
Adding sloped lines

18. Using the PROPERTIES command, return the thickness of the top orientation cube to 0 and use the TRIM command to remove lines at the base of the structure, as shown in Figure 6.31. Stop and save the model as INCA.

Altering the Viewpoint to Achieve a Better View

19. Activate the isometric viewport.
20. Using the VPOINT command, enter the coordinates (1,−2,3). This should generate a trimetric view, as shown in Figure 6.32. The trimetric view of this model should be more pleasing.
21. Use the HIDE command and observe the results. Because this is only a wire-frame model and it has no surfaces, the HIDE command has no effect.

Figure 6.31
Trimming the model

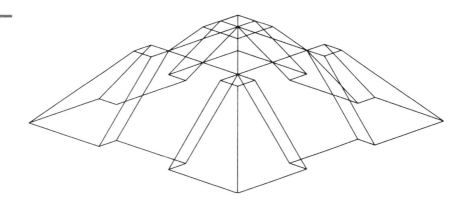

Figure 6.32
Trimetric view of the model

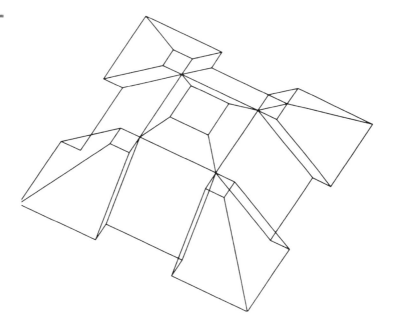

Lab 6.C Using Projection to Solve a Problem

Purpose

Lab 6.C demonstrates how to use projection to determine the line of intersection between a sloped surface and an intersecting rectangular box. In this case, the sloped surface is a roof and the rectangular box is a chimney.

Objective

You will be able to use projection to solve a problem.

Primary Commands

UCS
LINE

Procedure

Problem

1. Figure 6.33 represents a rectangular chimney that intersects a sloped roof. You need to create the line of intersection that represents the point at which the chimney and the roof surfaces meet. To solve this problem, use the projection techniques discussed in Section 6.3.

Initial Settings

2. Start a new drawing called INTERS (INTERSection) with the following settings or you can open file a3dex6c from the a3d2005 folder. This file has most of the settings already set. All you should need to do is display the UCS, View, and 3D Orbit toolbars.

Units = Architecture
Limits = −1′, −1′ to 10′, 11′
Grid = 1′
Snap Inc = 1′
UCS = WCS
UCSICON = On, Origin, and set to 2D display properties
UCSVP = 0 (always set before creation of viewports)
UCS toolbar = displayed
View toolbar = displayed

Create the following layers:

LAYER NAME	DESCRIPTION
OCUBE	Orientation cube
ROOF	Roof surface
CHIM	Chimney surface
PROJ	Projection lines
INTERS	Line of intersection
PROF	Chimney profile

You may want to give a different color to each layer to help differentiate the geometry being shown at any time.

Figure 6.33
Chimney meets roof

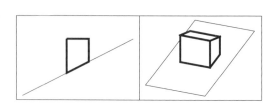

Creating an Orientation Cube

3. Make the OCUBE layer current and use ZOOM Extents to display the limits of the model.
4. Using the ELEV command, set the elevation to 0, and the thickness to 5′, the height of the roof for this project.
5. Refer to Figure 6.34 and use the LINE command to draw the outline of the orientation cube. The geometry is 8′ along the X axis, 10′ along the Y axis, and 5′ along the Z axis. The lower-left corner should start at 0,0,0. (As with the previous labs, the orientation cube is not necessarily a cube. The term *cube* is used as a standard name.)

Creating the Chimney Surfaces

6. Set CHIM as the current layer.
7. With the elevation still set to 0 and the thickness to 5′, use the LINE command to draw the outline of the chimney as shown in Figure 6.35. Because the chimney is drawn using lines with thickness, there are surfaces that represent the perimeter of the chimney.

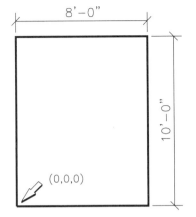

Figure 6.34
Orientation cube

Creating a Working Plane

You are going to create a working plane along the right side of the OCUBE. This requires that you display a trimetric view of the OCUBE.

8. Using the VPOINT command, set the view to 2, −3, 1. It should look similar to Figure 6.36.
9. Using the 3Point option of the UCS command, create the new working plane by using the points indicated in Figure 6.36.

Creating Multiple Viewports

10. To allow better viewing, create two viewports side by side using the VPORTS command. The left viewport should display a plan view of the current UCS and the right viewport should display a trimetric view (2, −3, 1).
11. Use the ZOOM command in each viewport with a scale setting of 0.8×. This will reduce the displayed geometry to 80% so that you can see the UCS icon better.

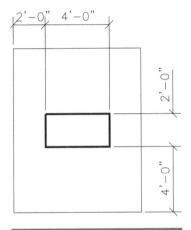

Figure 6.35
Chimney outline

Creating the Sloped Roof

12. Set the current layer to ROOF.
13. Set the elevation to 0 and the thickness to −8′. This gives thickness that stretches from the right to left side of the orientation cube.

Figure 6.36
Creating the side working plane

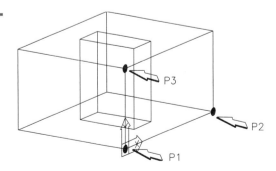

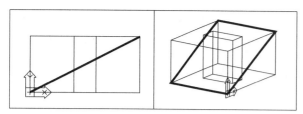

Figure 6.37
Sloped roof line

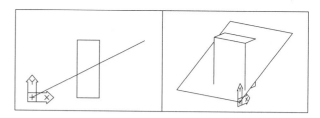

Figure 6.38
Results of the HIDE command

14. Activate the right viewport and, using the LINE command, draw the sloped line as shown in Figure 6.37.

Observing the Results of the HIDE Command

15. Freeze the OCUBE layer.
16. Now use the HIDE command and observe the results. They should look similar to Figure 6.38. Note that some of the chimney surfaces disappeared and you cannot tell where the chimney penetrates the roof. Unfortunately, the HIDE command does not work well on surfaces that pass through each other. Determining the line of intersection corrects the problem.
17. Thaw the OCUBE layer again.

Creating Projection Lines

Creating various projection lines produces intersection nodes so that you can create the line of intersection that represents where the chimney penetrates the roof.

18. Set elevation to 0, thickness to 0, and the current layer to PROJ.
19. Activate the left viewport that displays the plan view of the current UCS, as shown in Figure 6.39. Draw the two vertical lines by lining the cursor up with the chimney bottom. (Do not use object snap; instead use increment snap.) The vertical lines should extend so that they pass the slope of the roof.
20. Activate the right viewport that displays the trimetric view. This time use object snap endpoint to draw a line over the top of the roof line, as shown in Figure 6.39.
21. Use the COPY command to copy all three lines to the left side of the roof, as shown in Figure 6.40.
22. Using the 3Point option of the UCS command, create a working plane along the slope of the roof. Refer to Figure 6.41 for the three points.

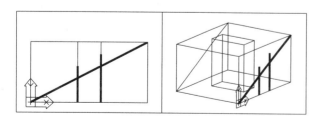

Figure 6.39
Two vertical lines and one sloped line

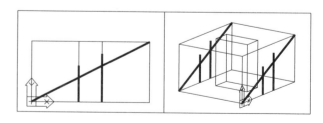

Figure 6.40
Copying the three lines from the right to the left side

114

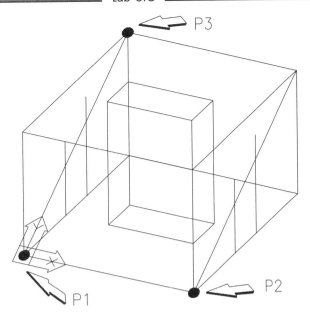

Figure 6.41
Creating a sloped UCS working plane

23. Activate the left viewport and use the PLAN command to display the plan view of the current UCS.
24. In the left viewport, use the LINE command to draw two vertical lines that overlap the chimney lines. Refer to Figure 6.42 for their approximate lengths.
25. Activate the right viewport and use the VPOINT command to set the viewpoint to 3, −4, 1. Once this is done use the ZOOM command and set the scale to 0.8×. This should give you a view similar to Figure 6.43 but without the extra lines.
26. Using intersect object snap, draw lines that extend across the roof, as shown in Figure 6.43.

Generating the Lines of Intersection

You should now have the four main projection lines that lie on the roof surface and surround the chimney. You are going to use these lines that intersect at the four corners of the chimney to generate the line of intersection.

27. Set the current layer to INTERS. This contains the lines of intersection. Freeze the OCUBE layer.
28. Using the intersect object snap, draw around the perimeter of the chimney where it penetrates the roof. Use the intersection nodes of the projection lines as your intersection snap points (see Figure 6.44).

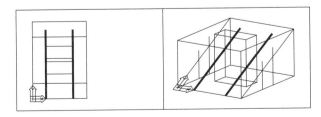

Figure 6.42
Adding lines to sloped surface

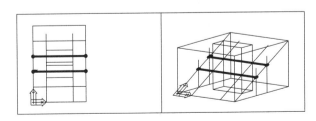

Figure 6.43
Adding horizontal lines across the roof surface

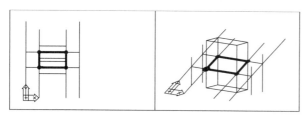

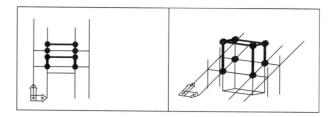

Figure 6.44
Adding the lines of intersection

Figure 6.45
Adding wireframe lines to represent the chimney profile

Creating a Wireframe Profile of the Chimney

You are now going to create a wireframe profile of the chimney portion that extends upward past the chimney.

29. Set the current layer to PROF.
30. Use the VPOINT command to set the viewpoint to 4, −5, 1. This makes it easier to click points on the chimney. Your view should look similar to Figure 6.45.
31. Using object snap, create lines that overlap the edges of the chimney surfaces, as shown in Figure 6.45.

Simulating the Hidden View

You are going to simulate what the hidden view of the extended chimney would be even though it will be shown in wireframe.

32. Freeze all layers, except for ROOF, CHIM, INTERS, PROF. Those layers should be thawed and visible.
33. Using the VPOINT command set the viewpoint to 2, −3, 1.
34. Use the HIDE command. Because the CHIM surface layer is still visible, AutoCAD used it in the hidden line calculations.
35. Freeze the CHIM layer. With the CHIM layer not visible you should only see the roof surface and the wireframe of the chimney and its penetration of the roof. The display should look similar to Figure 6.46.
36. Save your model.

Now, you have practiced one application of using intersections to solve a three-dimensional problem. Later, when you are able to create 3D faces, you may add them to represent the sides of the chimney.

Figure 6.46
Simulated hidden chimney lines

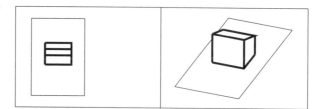

Lab 6.D   Piping Run

Purpose

Lab 6.D adds to your skill in wireframe construction. When creating industrial piping runs, initially a wireframe centerline is created along the length of piping. Once this is done, a pipe profile can be created along the run. In this exercise you'll create the initial wireframe centerline and pipe profile. In the next chapter, in Lab 7.D, you'll generate the pipe surface using the centerline and profile.

Objectives

You will be able to:

- Construct a wireframe model
- Work on several UCS planes

Primary Commands

Thickness
VPORTS
UCS

Final Model

Figure 6.47 shows the final wireframe model you'll be constructing and the final piping model you'll create in the next chapter. Review the centerline and pipe, noticing the various planes they travel along.

Procedure

1. Start a new drawing called PIPERUN with the following settings, or open file a3dex6d from the a3d2005 folder. This file has most of the settings already set. All you should need to do is display the UCS, View, and 3D Orbit toolbars.

Units = decimal
Limits = −1, −1 to 10, 6
Grid = 1
Snap Inc = 0.5
Current Layer = OCUBE
UCSICON = On and set to 2D display properties
UCSVP = 0 (always set before creation of viewports)
UCS toolbar = displayed
View toolbar = displayed
Viewport Configuration = Single

Creating the Orientation Planes

When starting construction, it's useful to create three-dimensional orientation planes that can help with the location of UCS working planes. Because the

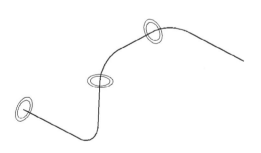
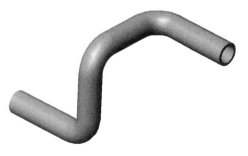

Figure 6.47
Pipe run centerline and surfaced model

117

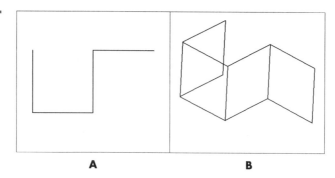

Figure 6.48
Lines in plan view, shown in adjusted isometric view

A   B

centerline of the pipe run travels on several planes, the orientation planes are a necessity.

2. Select Thickness from the Format pull-down menu and set it to 4.
3. Draw four lines as shown in Figure 6.48A. Each line is 4″ long.

4. Display an isometric view using the SE Isometric View tool and then use the 3D Orbit tool to rotate the view slightly to see all the wires (see Figure 6.48B).

Creating Working Planes

There will be four UCS working planes created at this stage. You'll need to create more later on.

5. Refer to Figure 6.49 to create the four working planes: Left Side, Front, Right Side, and Top. Use the 3Point option of the UCS command. Save each UCS so that you can recall them as you work.

Drawing on Front Plane

The first length of pipe run is created on the Front UCS working plane. Polylines (2D) are required to generate the centerline. Because the polyline is 2D in nature, the pipe run needs to be created in stages on different 2D planes. The 3Dpoly object won't work because it can't be filleted.

6. Set the Front UCS to current. Create a layer called WIRE and make it current.
7. Draw an L-shaped polyline as shown in Figure 6.50A and use the FILLET command to add a 1.0 radius fillet to the corner of the polyline (see Figure 6.50B).

Figure 6.49
Creating four UCS working planes

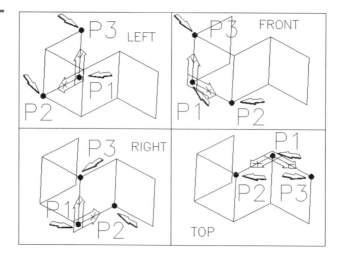

Figure 6.50
Polyline on Front plane

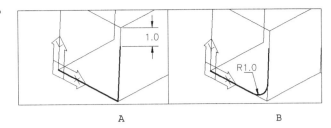

Figure 6.50
Polyline on Front plane

Drawing on Right Plane

The second length of pipe run is created on the Right Side UCS working plane.

8. Set the RightSide UCS to current.
9. Draw an L-shaped polyline as shown in Figure 6.51A and use the FILLET command to add a 1.0 radius fillet to the corner of the polyline (see Figure 6.51B).

Drawing on Top Plane

The third length of pipe run is created on the Top UCS working plane.

10. Set the Top UCS to current.
11. Draw an L-shaped polyline as shown in Figure 6.52A and use the FILLET command to add a 1.0 radius fillet to the corner of the polyline (see Figure 6.52B).

Drawing on Left Plane

The initial profile of the pipe run is created on the Left UCS working plane. This profile is placed perpendicular at the start of the first pipe run.

12. Set the Left UCS to current.
13. Draw two circles as shown in Figure 6.53, with diameters of 1.0 and 0.75, respectively.

Figure 6.51
Polyline on Right plane

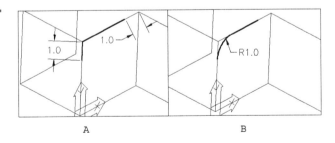

Figure 6.52
Polyline on Top plane

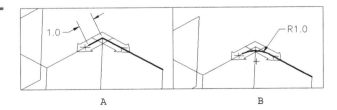

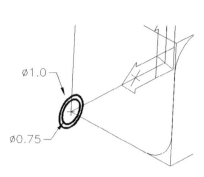

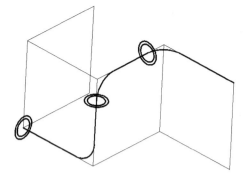

Figure 6.53
Circle profiles on Left plane

Figure 6.54
The addition of two other pipe profiles

Working on Other Planes

You need to create two other pipe profiles that are the start of the two other pipe runs. These also need to be perpendicular.

14. Figure 6.54 shows the two other pipe profiles.

For the first profile, set the UCS to WCS and then use the UCS Origin option to move the UCS to the start of the second pipe run. Draw the two circles as before.

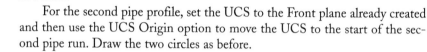
For the second pipe profile, set the UCS to the Front plane already created and then use the UCS Origin option to move the UCS to the start of the second pipe run. Draw the two circles as before.

15. Display the entire polyline pipe centerline and pipe profile circles and freeze the OCUBE layer. The screen should look similar to Figure 6.47A.

Questions

1. What defines the true three-dimensionality of an object?

2. Why are wireframe models constructed?

3. Explain the use of filters in the entering of 3D coordinates.

4. Define *node* in the context of 3D modeling.

5. What advantage does a 3D polyline have over the regular 2D polyline? What disadvantage does it have?

6. Explain the projection technique of finding node points.

7. Explain the effect of the HIDE command on wireframe models.

8. What purposes does the orientation cube serve in the construction of models?

9. Basing your opinion on your experience with the labs so far, what might be the possible advantages of using multiple viewports? What disadvantages might there be?

Assignment

1. Produce the wireframe model illustrated in Figure 6.3. This requires the application of filters. The size of the model is not important. Save the model as SLOPE.

2. Draw the wireframe model illustrated in Figure 6.5.

3. Move on to the wireframe model illustrated in Figure 6.7. Can you produce this one? Save it as ROOF.

4. Generate the wireframe model of the structure shown in Figure 6.55. Save it as STRUC.

5. Keeping in mind that extrusion can be used for the circular base and the cylindrical center column, produce the wireframe model of the part shown in Figure 6.56. Use wireframe on the base and the four ribs. Save it as BPLATE.

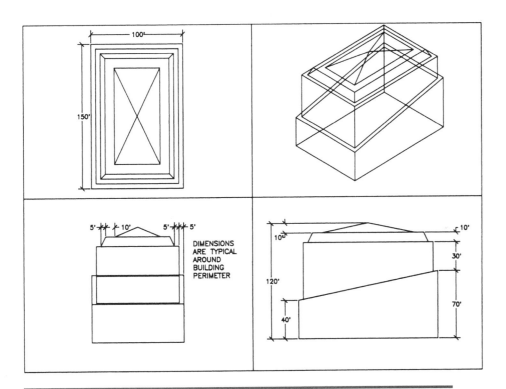

Figure 6.55
Wireframe building

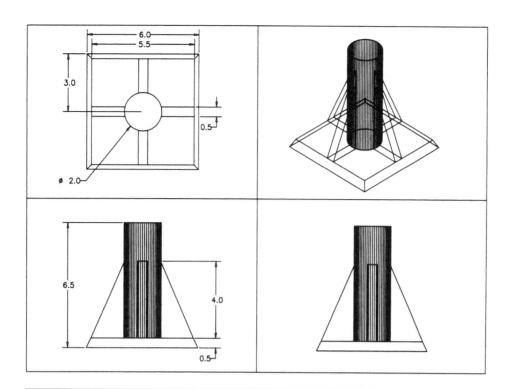

Figure 6.56
Wireframe baseplate

7 Creating a Shell

Overview

Now we're coming to the exciting stuff. In this chapter, for the first time, you will create a covered surface, add the possibility of texture and shade, and hide lines and entire objects. Your models will start having a truly 3D appearance. Most users, after reaching this point, begin to feel really accomplished. As the visual feedback becomes more satisfying, you'll begin to feel more confident in your use of 3D.

Concepts Explored

- The implications of adding surfaces to a model
- The area definition technique of creating surfaces
- How to create planar surfaces
- How to apply surface techniques to solve problems
- The creation of surface models

7.1 Introduction

In Chapter 6, we explored the concept behind wireframe modeling. For construction purposes, wireframe is extremely important. However, trying to study a complex wireframe model can be quite confusing. But add a shell to cover the wireframe, and the model becomes much easier to perceive. And if you add shading, then the overall three-dimensionality of the model becomes obvious. Figure 7.1 illustrates how covering and shading a wireframe creates a more effective 3D model: Part A is a wireframe display, Part B shows the same model with a shell, and Part C shows the shell shaded.

Each planar area of a shell is referred to as a *surface*. To display a model with hidden lines removed or shaded, surfaces must be present. To create a surface, you can use object thickness, which was explained in Chapter 5. As you will recall, thickness was cited as the easiest way to build a three-dimensional model. Another method used to create a surface is area definition, which is simply the defining of an area to be covered by a planar surface.

Sometimes area definition and extrusion can be combined. The three objects that make use of area definition are 2D polylines, 2D solids, and 3D faces. The first two objects use a combination of area definition and extrusion, but 3D faces use area definitions exclusively.

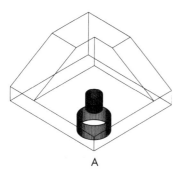

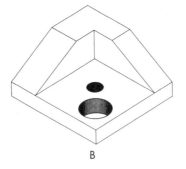

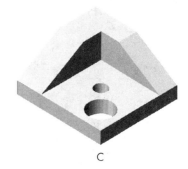

A   B   C

Figure 7.1

Wireframe model, with hidden lines removed and shaded

A fourth type of object, called a region, can be used to cover an area with a surface. Its formation makes use of solid modeling commands, which are explained in more detail in Chapter 9. However, the region is mentioned here so that you may be aware, earlier in your creation, of its capabilities.

Surfaces Toolbar

The Surfaces toolbar can be used to access the commands to create most surfaces. Toolbars are displayed using the View/Toolbars pull-down menu or by right-clicking on a currently displayed toolbar.

You can also use the Draw/Surfaces pull-down menu.

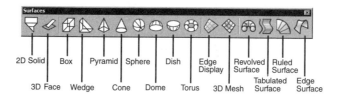

7.2   Polylines and Solids Revisited

We have already discussed how polylines and 2D solids (not to be confused with solid modeling) are relevant to 3D construction. We know that each object allows extrusion of its respective form to create a 3D shape. But because both polylines and solids can acquire width or area, they also can form a surface over that area, regardless of their shapes. The polyline tool is found on the Draw toolbar or the Draw pull-down menu. The 2D Solid tool is found on the Surfaces toolbar. These aren't necessarily the best way to draw covered surfaces but they're sometimes the quickest.

Figure 7.2 shows some of the various forms that a 2D polyline with width can describe. Note that each time the polyline changes direction, an edge bisects the width and separates the polyline into segments. Now look at Figure 7.3. Part A shows an area defined using the SOLID command. Whenever a new area is defined here, a line divides the two segmented areas, just like in the polyline. These dividing lines in both polylines and solids can be quite numerous, depending on the complexity of the area defined, and sometimes they result in a distracting surface. (Later, you will see how this problem can be overcome by using 3D Faces.)

Solids are defined through a triangular process. Look at Figure 7.3B and note the order of definition (or the order in which each area to be covered by a solid is defined). Figure 7.3C shows what happens if the wrong order is used.

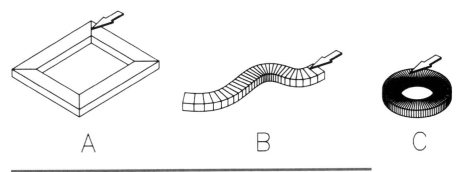

Figure 7.2
Polylines with width and thickness

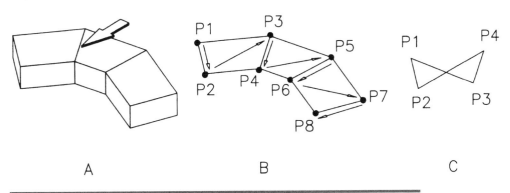

Figure 7.3
Solids showing order of creation

7.3 **3D Faces**

 The 3D face uses area definition to form its shape by simply specifying the node points that define the perimeter of the desired area, and using 3D face forms to cover it. The 3D face in Figure 7.4 is a true 3D object because it is not bound by the current UCS working plane. You can click node points at any 3D coordinates to form the face (see Figure 7.5). Part A shows the four click points used to create a 2D solid. Even though the points clicked should create a sloped edge, the 2D solid is bound by the current UCS. Part B shows the creation of a 3D face. It is not bound by the current UCS. However, a 3D face is still a planar (flat) object that uses only coordinates that will form a flat plane. Without these coordinates, the 3D face becomes

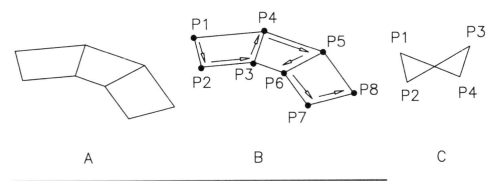

Figure 7.4
3DFACE command showing order of creation

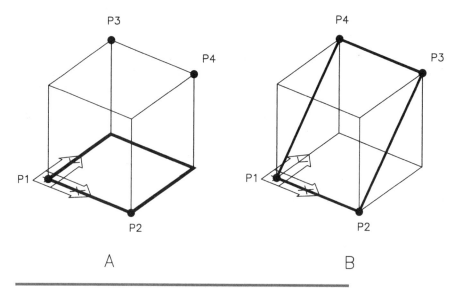

Figure 7.5
Defining a 2D solid versus a 3D face using 3D coordinates

nonplanar and you may get unexpected results when hiding edges or rendering. In addition to this, remember *not* to add thickness to a 3D face. Its purpose is to cover an area, not to be extruded.

3D VIEWPOINT

The HIDE Command and 3D Faces

Sometimes the HIDE command does not perform perfectly. It will leave behind dots on the screen where 3D faces meet or where objects intersect surfaces such as 3D faces. There is no immediate remedy to this; instead, you must use regions rather than 3D faces.

3D Face Definition

The act of defining a 3D face is similar to that of defining a 2D solid: You specify node points around its perimeter. Looking back to Figure 7.3, note that the definition of 2D solids requires a triangular pattern. Now refer to Figure 7.4 for the 3D face definition, which is a rectangular definition. If you specify the node points of a 3D face in a triangular pattern for four points, you produce the bow-tie shape shown in Figure 7.4C.

The following is the command to form the shape illustrated in Figure 7.4B:

Command: **3DFACE**
Specify first point or [Invisible]: **click P1**
Specify second point or [Invisible]: **click P2**
Specify third point or [Invisible] <exit>: **click P3**
Specify fourth point or [Invisible] <create three-sided face>: **click P4**

(If you press Enter instead of clicking a fourth point, a triangular 3D face is created.)

Specify third point or [Invisible] <exit>: **click P5**

(The third and fourth click points are repeated, allowing connected faces. Pressing Enter at this point stops the command.)

Specify fourth point or [Invisible] <create three-sided face>: **click P6**
Specify third point or [Invisible] <exit>: **click P7**
Specify fourth point or [Invisible] <create three-sided face>: **click P8**
Specify third point or [Invisible] <exit>: **press Enter to exit the command**

3D VIEWPOINT

Order of Clicking 3D Face Points
When you click the points to define a 3D face, you click in a rectangular order; when you click points to define a 2D solid, you click in a triangular order.

7.4 Invisible 3D Face Edges

Unlike 3D polylines with width or 2D solids, the 3D face object can have some or all invisible edges. Figure 7.6 shows a polyline and a solid in contrast to the same shape using 3D faces. By using invisible edges, an open, uncluttered area can be formed.

The procedure for making 3D face edges invisible can occur during the 3D face-creation stage. Just before clicking the point that will start the invisible edge, select the Invisible option. Figure 7.7A shows the desired outcome and Figure 7.7B shows the click points. Just before clicking P3, enter I for invisible and click P3 and P4. Then, before clicking P5, again enter I, and click P5 through P8. The edges between P3 and P4 as well as P5 and P6 would be invisible, as illustrated in Figure 7.7C. If you need to see the invisible edges temporarily, you can set the system variable SPLFRAME to 1 and REGEN the screen. All invisible edges are displayed as shown in Figure 7.7D. To return to invisibility, set the variable back to 0 and REGEN.

Figure 7.6
A polyline and a solid compared to a 3D face with invisible edges

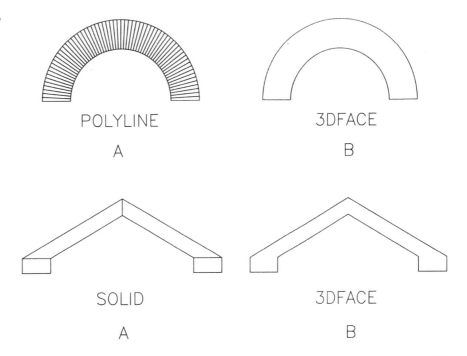

POLYLINE

A

3DFACE

B

SOLID

A

3DFACE

B

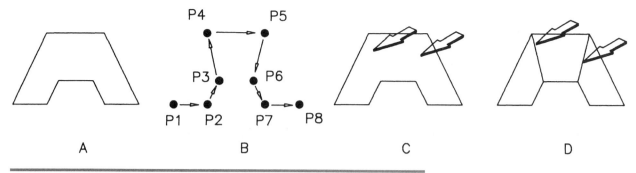

Figure 7.7
Creating a 3D face with invisible edges

Often it's easier to modify the edges of an already created 3D face by using the PROPERTIES command. You can move the node points and change the visibility of any edge.

In addition, the EDGE command is available to allow the user to selectively change the visibility of 3D face edges. To use the command, simply type **EDGE** on the command line or use the Edge tool found on the Surfaces toolbar. You can select visible edges to be turned invisible. You can also display the invisible edges to allow you to click them and turn them visible.

7.5 Creating Surfaces with Regions

Regions are two-dimensional enclosed areas that you create from a closed form such as a polyline or circle or lines that form a complete loop. Regions can be used in place of 3D faces to cover complex areas. You can find the REGION command in the Draw pull-down menu or the Draw toolbar. The command converts a closed object such as a polyline into a region.

Regions and 3D solids are similar in behavior. The only difference is that regions are two-dimensional with no thickness and 3D solids are three-dimensional. The same commands that are used to create complex composite 3D solids are used to create complex composite regions. Detailed explanations on the use of regions and 3D solids are explained in Chapters 9 through 12.

At this point, let's take a look at the basics of region creation (see Figure 7.8). Figure 7.8C shows the final desired model—a hole in an irregular shape. Figure 7.8A shows the creation of a closed polyline, and Figure 7.8B shows the creation of a circle to represent the hole. Now the REGION command is used to turn the polyline and the circle into separate regions. Once you generate regions, you can use the SUBTRACT command from solid modeling. It can also be used to subtract one region from another. In this case, click the polyline region and then subtract the circle region

Figure 7.8
Creating a hole in a surface by subtracting one region from another

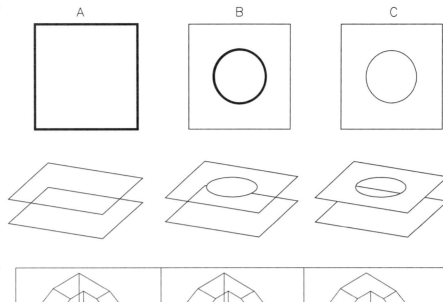

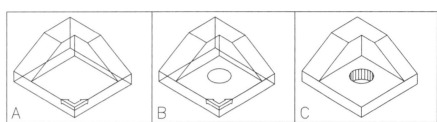

Figure 7.9
Application of two regions to create a hole

from it. The result is a composite region that is a surface with a hole through it. If you want the hole to appear to extend into the model, you need to add arcs with thickness, as you would with the 3D face method.

It is very important to note that regions are side dependent when rendering or using shaded shade modes. What this means is that a rendered or shaded region is only visible when viewed from the side it was created on (the positive *Z* axis of the UCS during creation). If you view a region from the other side, it will appear as if it is gone. You may want to experiment with this by creating a region, turning on Gouraud shading, and then using 3DORBIT to rotate around the region. On one side you will see the region shaded, on the other side it will disappear.

Figure 7.9 shows applications of using regions to create a hole.

To manipulate regions or 3D solids, boolean operations are used. These are: union, subtract, and intersection. *Union* allows you to join two or more regions together. *Subtract* allows you to click the parent region and then subtract another region from it. *Intersection* creates a new region from the overlaping surfaces of two regions. They can be found in the Modify/Solids Editing pull-down menu or the Solids Editing toolbar.

 Lab 7.A   Creating 3D Faces and Regions

Purposes

Lab 7.A shows you how to create simple and complex surfaces. Once you are comfortable with these new methods, continue with Labs 7.B and 7.C.

Objectives

You will be able to:

- Construct simple surfaces using 3D faces
- Make use of the Invisible Edge option of the 3DFACE command
- Construct complex surfaces using regions

Primary Command

3DFACE–Invisible Edge
REGION
SUBTRACT

Procedure

1. Start a new drawing called SURF with the following settings or you can open file a3dex7a from the a3d2005 folder. This file has most of the settings already set. All you should need to do is display the Surfaces, View, and 3D Orbit toolbars.

Units = decimal
Limits = −1,−1 to 10,9
Grid = 0.5 (ON)
Snap Incr = 0.5 (ON)
Elevation = 0
Thickness = 0
Current Layer = Surface
UCS = WCS

Creating 3D Faces

2. To start, create the simple 3D face shown in Figure 7.10. The size is not important. Remember that you create 3D faces in a rectangular pattern and you need to press Enter to complete the command when you have defined your corners of the 3D face. The following illustrates the command:

Command: **3DFACE**
Specify first point or [Invisible]: **click P1**
Specify second point or [Invisible]: **click P2**
Specify third point or [Invisible] <exit>: **click P3**
Specify fourth point or [Invisible] <create three-sided face>: **click P4**
Specify third point or [Invisible] <exit>: **press Enter to finish**

3. Now create the 3D face shown in Figure 7.11. Note that it is only a triangle. When creating 3D faces, you can press the Enter key after defining only three edges; a triangular shape is created. Refer to the following showing the command steps:

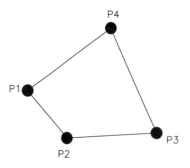

Figure 7.10
Simple 3D face

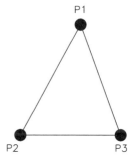

Figure 7.11
Triangular 3D face

Command: **3DFACE**
Specify first point or [Invisible]: **click P1**
Specify second point or [Invisible]: **click P2**
Specify third point or [Invisible] <exit>: **click P3**
Specify fourth point or [Invisible] <create three-sided face>: **press Enter**
Specify third point or [Invisible] <exit>: **press Enter to finish**

4. Create the more complex shape in Figure 7.12 with the continued use of the 3DFACE command. When creating 3D faces, you can continue specifying the third and fourth points; new 3D faces will be created next to the last until you press Enter to finish the command. Refer to the following procedure:

Command: **3DFACE**
Specify first point or [Invisible]: **click P1**
Specify second point or [Invisible]: **click P2**
Specify third point or [Invisible] <exit>: **click P3**
Specify fourth point or [Invisible] <create three-sided face>: **click P4**
Specify third point or [Invisible] <exit>: **click P5**
Specify fourth point or [Invisible] <create three-sided face>: **click P6**
Specify third point or [Invisible] <exit>: **press Enter to finish**

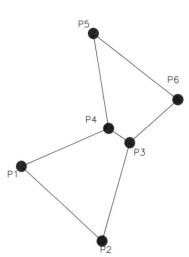

Figure 7.12
Complex 3D faces

Changing the Visibility of 3D Faces

5. Select the simple 3D face you created in Step 2 so that it's highlighted and right-click it to bring up the context menu. From this menu, select Properties. The Properties dialog box appears with information about the 3D face.

6. Look down the Properties dialog box until you see the Geometry section. Under this section, you should see a listing of Edge 1, Edge 2, Edge 3, and Edge 4. These are used to control visibility of the 3D face edges (see Figure 7.13).

   Experiment turning edges on and off until you are comfortable; then press the Esc key several times until the 3D face is no longer highlighted.

Figure 7.13
Properties dialog box showing 3D face properties

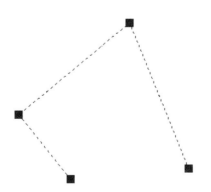

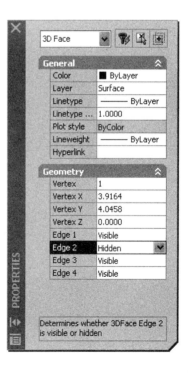

132 Lab 7.A
Creating 3D Faces
and Regions

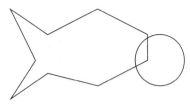

Figure 7.14
Creating regions

7. Try to change the visibility of the complex 3D faces that are touching from Step 4. You will have to change the visibility of the edges of both 3D faces. Even though it appears that the 3D faces are joined, they are really separate objects.

Using Regions

8. You are now going to create some regions. Remember you can create regions out of closed polylines or circles.

Create the closed polyline and the circle shown in Figure 7.14. Note how the circle overlaps the closed polyline.

9. Using the REGION command, turn the closed polyline and the circle into two separate regions as follows:

Command: **REGION**
1 found Select objects: **select the closed polyline**
1 found, 2 total Select objects: **select the circle**
Select objects: **press Enter to continue**
2 loops extracted
2 Regions created

The closed polyline and circle are now two region objects.

10. Subtract the circle from the closed polyline by using the SUBTRACT command as follows:

Command: **SUBTRACT**
Select solids and regions to subtract from . . .
Select objects: **select the region created from the closed polyline**
1 found
Select objects: **press Enter to continue**
Select solids and regions to subtract ..
1 found Select objects: **select the circle region**
Select objects: **press Enter to finish the command**

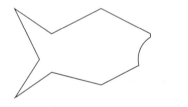

Figure 7.15
Results of using the SUBTRACT
command

Observe the results, as shown in Figure 7.15. What remains is a new region that has a piece subtracted from it. Another command you may want to try is the UNION command. It adds two or more regions together. Figure 7.16 shows some figures before and after unions. Remember, you need to use the REGION command to turn closed polylines or circles into regions before you can use the UNION command.

11. Save your drawing as SURF.

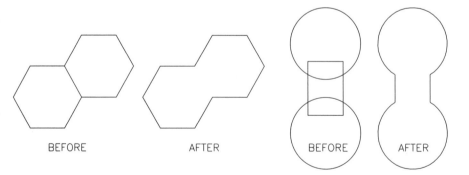

BEFORE   AFTER   BEFORE   AFTER

Figure 7.16
Before and after the use of the UNION command

Lab 7.B   Surfaced Angle Plate

Purpose

Lab 7.B shows you how to use surface modeling techniques to add surfaces to the wireframe model created in Lab 6.A in Chapter 6. It should be noted that this model could be created using solid modeling techniques but at this stage of the learning process it is a good application of surface creation.

Objectives

You will be able to:

■ Create 3D faces or use regions
■ Make use of the Invisible Edge option of the 3DFACE command

Primary Commands

3DFACE–Invisible Edge
REGION
SUBTRACT

Final Model

Figure 7.17 shows the angle plate model with the surfaces you'll be adding.

Procedure

1. Open the model ANGPLT that was created in Lab 6.A. Use these settings:

```
Units = decimal
Limits = −1, −1 to 8, 8
Grid = 0.25
Snap Incr = 0.25
Elevation = 0
Thickness = 0
Current Layer = SURFACE
UCS = WCS
UCSICON = On, Origin, and set to 2D display properties
UCSVP = 0 (always set before creation of viewports)
UCS toolbar = displayed
View toolbar = displayed
Viewport Configuration = New viewport, Four: Equal, 3D setup
```

Adding 3D Faces

2. Using the 3DFACE command, add faces to the areas shown in Figures 7.18, 7.19, and 7.20. (*Note:* The Invisible option must be used just before P3 on

Figure 7.17
Angle plate model with surfaces

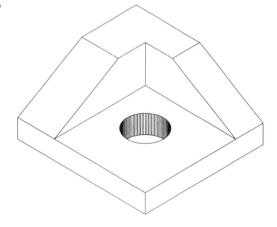

133

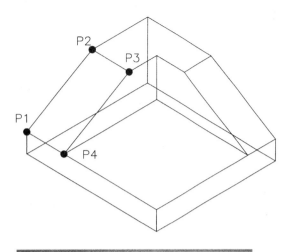

Figure 7.18
Sloped 3D face

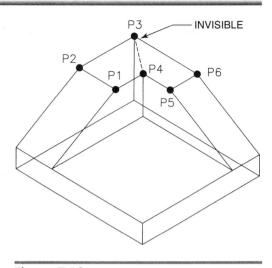

Figure 7.19
Top 3D face

 Figure 7.19 is entered.) If desired, you can use regions instead of 3D faces. To use regions, set the UCS to each working plane and draw a closed polyline around the desired perimeter. Then use the REGION command to turn the closed polyline into a region. When you use regions you will not need to use the Invisible option.

Changing the Viewpoint

3. Using the VPOINT coordinated command, enter the following coordinates: −2, −2, 1.
4. Using the 3DFACE command, add a face as shown in Figure 7.21. (*Note:* The Invisible option must be used just before P3 is entered.) As in Step 2, you can use regions instead of 3D faces. Remember to set the UCS to each working plane prior to creating the closed polyline around the desired perimeter. When you use regions, you will not need to use the Invisible option.

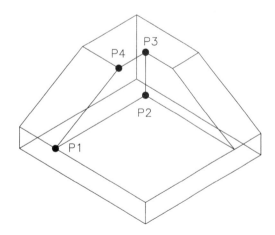

Figure 7.20
Upright 3D face

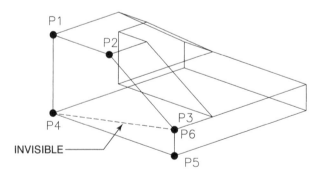

Figure 7.21
Side 3D face

Figure 7.22
Working plane set to TPLATE and regions added.

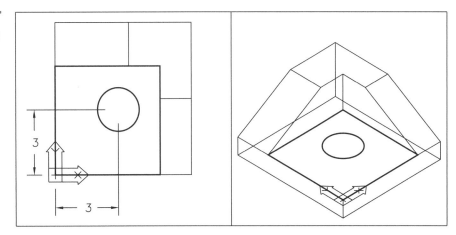

Add 3D faces to other surfaces around the model except for the top and bottom where the hole is to be placed in Step 5. Use the HIDE command or shade modes periodically to determine missing faces.

Adding the Hole Model

Now is the time to add a hole to the plate. First you need to create a rectangular region surface and then a circle to represent the hole.

5. Restore the working plane called TPLATE (created in Lab 6.A). Observe the placement of the UCS in Figure 7.22.
6. Split the screen into two equal viewports similar to Figure 7.22.
7. Activate the left viewport. Use the PLAN <UCS> command to display the top view of the plate.
8. Create a layer called REGION, and make it current.
9. Keeping the top viewport active, create a rectangular, closed polyline and a circle, as shown in Figure 7.22. The circle has a diameter of 2.
10. Use the REGION command to turn the rectangle and the circle into regions. Then, use the SUBTRACT command to subtract the hole from the rectangle.
11. To check the results, shade the model. You should be able to see the hole in the plate's surface, as shown in Figure 7.23.

Figure 7.23
Shade model showing hole

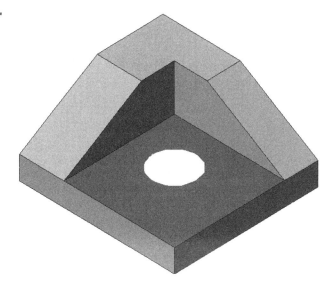

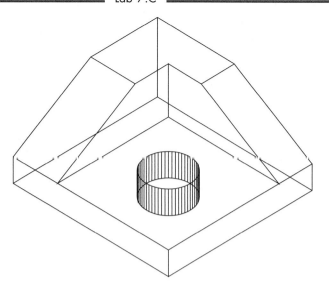

Figure 7.24
Adding two arcs that have thickness

Adding the Arcs

Two arcs need to be added that will give an inside surface to the hole. The two arcs will have a negative thickness that goes from the top of the plate to the bottom. Create the arcs using the Center, Start, and End options.

12. Using the ELEV command, set the elevation to 0 and the thickness to −1.
13. Add the two arcs as shown in Figure 7.24. Both arcs should have a diameter of 2 to match the hole model.
14. Use the HIDE command or different shade modes. The display should look similar to Figure 7.17.

    There are times when the HIDE command does not perform perfectly. It will leave behind dots on the screen. These usually are pieces of objects that show through surface joints. In the case of this model, some of the arcs with thickness may show through the 3D face joints. Use the Hidden shade mode. This should alleviate the problem.
15. Save the model as ANGPLT.

 ## Lab 7.C — Surfaced Coffeemaker Model

Purpose

Lab 7.C shows you how to use surface modeling techniques to create a surfaced model of a coffeemaker. This model will be used again in Chapter 9.

Objectives

You will be able to:

- Construct a surfaced model
- Create 3D faces or use regions
- Make use of the Invisible Edge option of the 3DFACE command

Primary Commands

3DFACE–Invisible Edge
REGION

Final Model

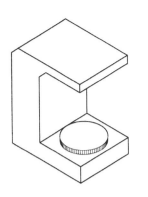

Figure 7.25
Coffeemaker model with surfaces

Figure 7.25 shows the surfaced coffeemaker model you'll be creating.

Procedure

1. Start a new drawing called COFMK (COFfeeMaKer) with the following settings or you can open file a3dex7c from the a3d2005 folder. This file has most of the settings already set. All you should need to do is display the Surfaces, View, and 3D Orbit toolbars.

Units = decimal
Limits = −1,−1 to 11,8
Grid = 1
Snap Incr = 1
Elevation = 0
Thickness = 12
Current Layer = OCUBE
UCS = WCS
UCSICON = On, Origin, and set to 2D display properties
UCSVP = 0 (always set before creation of viewports)
UCS toolbar = displayed
View toolbar = displayed

Creating an Orientation Cube

2. Split the screen into two equal viewports, as shown in Figure 7.26.
3. Activate the left viewport, and use the PLAN command to display a top view of WCS.
4. With the thickness set to 12, use the LINE command to draw the box, as shown in Figure 7.26.

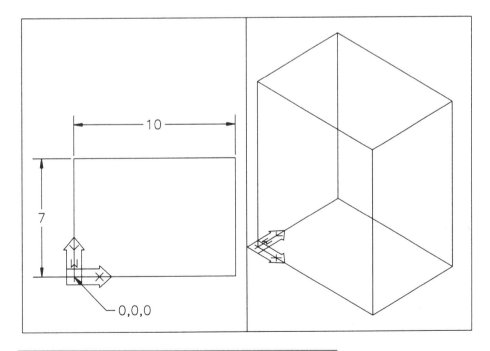

Figure 7.26
Orientation cube

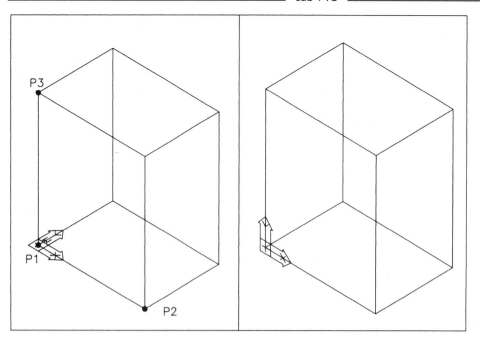

Figure 7.27
Defining the FRONT working plane

Creating a Side Working Plane

5. Activate the right viewport, and use the VPOINT command to set the coordinates, 1, −1, 1, or use the SE Isometric View tool from the View toolbar.
6. Use the 3Point option of the UCS command and create a working plane, as shown in Figure 7.27. Name it FRONT. Display the plan view of the current UCS.

Adding Extruded Lines

7. Use the ELEV command to set the thickness to −7. Keep the elevation set to 0. Create a layer called SURF, and make it current.
8. Using lines, draw around the perimeter to create the profile shown in Figure 7.28. (Use increment snap, or relative or polar coordinates, but *not* object snap.)

Adding the 3D Faces or Regions

9. Using the 3DFACE command, create faces, as shown in Figure 7.29. Follow the specific order shown. Use the Invisible option just before entering P3, P5, and P7. (Use increment snap, or relative or polar coordinates, but *not* object snap.) *Note:* If desired, you can use regions instead of 3D faces. To use regions, set the UCS to each working plane and draw a closed polyline around the desired perimeter. Then use the REGION command to turn the closed polyline into a region. When you use regions, you do not need to use the Invisible option.
10. Activate the isometric viewport and make the invisible 3D face edge visible by setting the SPLFRAME variable to 1. REGEN the screen. If you created a region instead of a 3D face, you can skip this step.
11. Copy the newly created 3D face to the other side of the profile, and then return the 3D face edges back to invisibility. If you created a region instead of a 3D

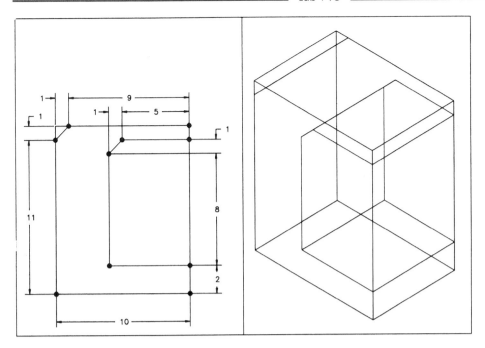

Figure 7.28
Adding extruded lines to create the profile

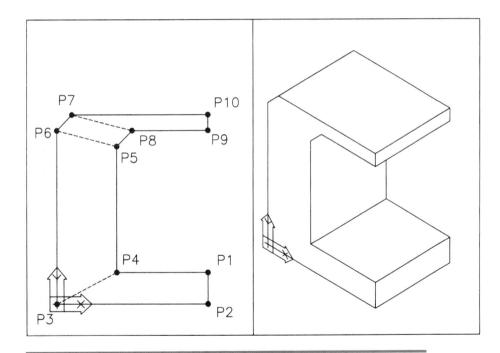

Figure 7.29
Adding the side 3D face

face, you will need to set the UCS working plane to the other side and create a new region. Remember that regions are side dependent. This means that they are visible from one side and invisible on the other when shaded or rendered. Make sure you create the region on the outside of the coffeemaker and not on the inside. Freeze layer OCUBE.

Creating a Lower Working Plane

12. Using the UCS command, create a working plane, as shown in Figure 7.30.

Adding the Warmer Plate

13. Using the ELEV command, set the thickness property to 0.5 and elevation to 0.
14. Activate the top-view viewport and add a circle, as shown in Figure 7.31.
15. Activate the isometric view, and use the HIDE command or use a shade mode. It should be noted that with some shade modes, the top surface of a circle with thickness will disappear. To get around this, you can add another circle to the top and turn it into a region to create a surface.
16. Save the model as COFMK.

Figure 7.30
Creating the lower working plane

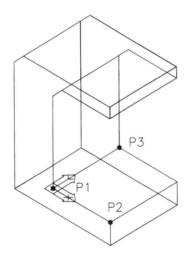

Figure 7.31
Adding the warmer plate

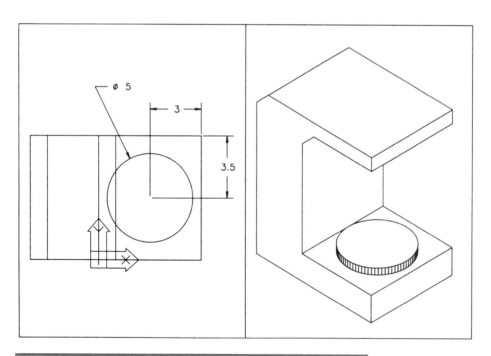

Lab 7.D   Surfaced Piping Run

Purpose

Lab 7.D shows you how to apply surface modeling and a preview of solid modeling. Using the pipe run wireframe model you created in Lab 6.D in Chapter 6, you're going to turn the pipe profiles into region surfaces and then extrude them into 3D solids.

Objectives

You will be able to:

■ Create regions and subtract from one another
■ Create 3D solids and union to one another

Primary Commands

REGION
SUBTRACT
EXTRUDE
JOIN

Final Model

Figure 7.32 shows the final piping model.

Procedure

1. Open the model PIPERUN that was created in Lab 6.D.

Units = decimal
Limits = −1,−1 to 10,6
Grid = 1
Snap Inc = 0.5
Current Layer = SOLID
UCSICON = On and set to 2D display properties
UCSVP = 0 (always set before creation of viewports)
Solids toolbar = displayed
Solids Editing toolbar = displayed
View toolbar = displayed
Viewport Configuration = Single

Creating Regions

In Lab 6.D you set all the ground work with the wireframe construction. You'll find that to create the solid pipe run is very simple now. The first step is to convert the circles into regions and subtract the inside circle from the outside circle. This creates a surface area in the form of a donut. This represents the cross-sectional area of the pipe.

Figure 7.32
Pipe run solid model

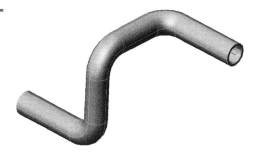

141

2. Select the Region tool from the command line and click all six circles. They'll all be turned into regions.

3. The next step is to subtract the inside circle from the outside circle. This needs to be done one at a time.

Select the Subtract tool from the Solids editing toolbar and click an outside circle, press Enter, and then click the corresponding inside circle.

If the command was used properly, a new single region was created. To test this, temporarily turn on the Gouraud with edges on shade mode. You should be able to see the first donut surface region. Note how only the edges are visible. This is because regions are view dependent. This means you can only see the surface from the side it was created on. It will be invisible from the other. If you use 3DORBIT to revolve the model, you'll see the region from the other side.

Repeat the use of the Subtract tool to create the other two donut regions. The results should look similar to Figure 7.33 with Gouraud with edges on and shade mode on. This has no effect on the creation of the solids in the next stage.

Creating Three Solids

In the next stage you're going to create a solid using a combination of a region and polyline. The region is extruded along the polyline, which is used as the path.

4. Select the Extrude tool from the Solids toolbar (*not* the Solids Editing toolbar) and use the following procedure:

Command: **EXTRUDE**
Current wireframe density: ISOLINES = 4
Select objects: **click the first region**
Select objects: **press Enter**
Specify height of extrusion or [Path]: **P** (enter P for path)
Select extrusion path or [Taper angle]: **click the first polyline centerline**

The first solid pipe has now been created. Figure 7.34 shows the results. Your screen should be similar.

Figure 7.33
Regions created and subtracted

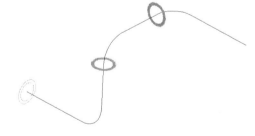

Figure 7.34
Creation of first pipe section

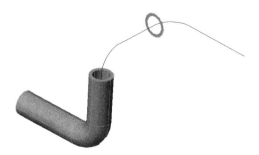

5. Repeat using the Extrude tool to create the other two pipe runs.
6. Use the Union tool from the Solids Editing toolbar to join all three sections of pipe into one. The results should look like Figure 7.32.
7. Use the 3D Orbit tool to rotate the pipe to see it from various angles.
8. Save your model as PIPERUN.

Questions

1. What function does surfaces perform?
2. How can surfaces be created out of the properties of an object?
3. What is the drawback of using 2D polylines and 2D solids to create surfaces?
4. What is the difference between the order of entering nodes for solids and the order of entering nodes for 3D faces?
5. What is the limitation of 3D faces?
6. How does the current UCS (working plane) control the creation of a 3D face?
7. Explain the procedure for creating invisible edges on 3D faces.
8. Describe the procedure for showing the invisible edges of 3D faces.
9. Why would regions be used in place of 3D faces?

Assignments

1. Restore the BOLT model from Lab 5.A. Add a surface to the top of the bolt head. Invisible edges are required. Once the head has a surface on it, use the HIDE command or different shade modes and note how different the model looks.

2. After restoring the INCA model from Lab 6.B, add surfaces over the wireframe. Once that is done, use the HIDE command or different shade modes on the surfaced model.

3. Restore the model ROOF from Assignment 3 in Chapter 6 and add surfaces. Once that is done, use the HIDE command or different shade modes on the surfaced model.

4. Restore the model STRUC from Assignment 4 in Chapter 6 and add the missing surfaces. Once that is done, use the HIDE command or different shade modes on the surfaced model.

5. Create a NUT that will match the BOLT surfaced in Assignment 1. Refer to Lab 5.A for the size of the head of the bolt and use the same size for the nut. (*Hint:* Use regions to create a hole in the nut.)

Elaborate Surfaces

Overview

In this final chapter of Part 3, you will create covered surfaces that either intersect or run parallel to each other, further enhancing the modeling you have been doing. What you learn in this chapter are the ideas and skills behind the ultimate in 3D modeling. The techniques presented here are used to model, for example, an automobile chassis, a 3D terrain for training simulations, a production for a commercial video presentation, and a cinematic special effect. Also included in this chapter are simple 3D geometric constructs that can be used as building blocks to create 3D models quickly.

Concepts Explored

■ The time-saving methods that create elaborate surfaces through automatic means
■ The creation and manipulation of 3D geometric constructs
■ The various methods of generating 3D polygon meshes and how these methods are specialized
■ How to construct surfaced models using polygon meshes

8.1 Introduction

With the information that has been presented up to this point, you could, given time and patience, create any complex surface. However, you'll find the job of creating complex shapes much easier after you learn more of AutoCAD's commands. The commands presented here allow you to create, in only a few steps, multiple planar surfaces to form meshes that can cover any type of area. These commands link together many or few polygons to create convoluted, meshed shapes automatically. This ability to generate multiple surfaces makes the creation of irregular surfaces much less arduous and time consuming. All you need to do is create a wireframe or series of nodes to control the formation of the multiple polygons. Figure 8.1A shows the wireframe model used to generate the surface-covered form pictured in Figure 8.1B.

Some of AutoCAD's commands are more automatic than others, depending on the type of area to be covered. The area type also controls the number of wires or nodes that may be required to achieve the desired shape. Area types may be cylindrical, conical, parallel, wave, or totally irregular, like terrain. Each multiple surface command has its own area of specialty, which we'll explain later.

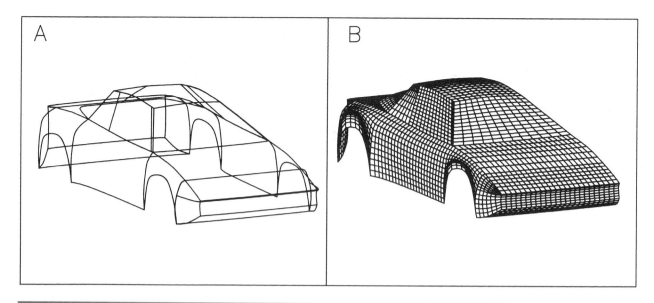

Figure 8.1
Wireframe model automatically covered with surfaces

3D VIEWPOINT

Surfaces versus 3D Solids

Sometimes a model's surface is too complex for the use of a 3D solid. For example, terrain modeling can be quite convoluted and usually you don't need to see what is under the terrain. In this case, surfaces are used to represent the terrain.

Surfaces Toolbar

The Surfaces toolbar can be used to access the commands to create most surfaces. Toolbars are displayed using the View/Toolbars pull-down menu or by right-clicking on a currently displayed toolbar.

You can also use the Draw/Surfaces pull-down menu.

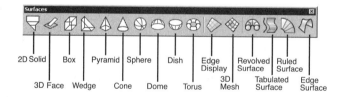

8.2 **3D Objects**

Before we begin our exploration of mesh generation, we need to discuss an even simpler method of model creation. In the ways they are used and manipulated, 3D objects can be likened to building blocks. The constructs also are very similar in usage to their two-dimensional cousins; whereas the 2D user creates complex drawings by manipulating lines, circles, rectangles, polygons, and the like, the 3D user pieces

146

together objects such as boxes, cones, and domes to form more complicated models. These 3D primitives, which can serve as the first step in the generation of complex shapes for the beginner or as a supplement for the advanced user, are really parts of a formulated program that AutoCAD uses to create a desired shape out of a series of 3D faces held together as a block (or mesh, as described by the software itself). With this program, the user simply fills in the missing data, such as length, height, or radius, and AutoCAD combines 3D faces to create a shape to the user's specifications. Once created, the new form is treated like a single object, even though it might be made of many separate 3D faces.

Figure 8.2 lists the different 3D primitive objects and illustrates some of the shapes that can be made from them. The input data that these various 3D objects require from the user are given in the following list.

3D OBJECTS	REQUIRED INPUT
Box 3D	Corner/length/width or cube/height/rotation
Pyramid	1st base point/2nd base/3rd base/tetrahedron or fourth base/ridge (1st and 2nd) or top or apex point
Wedge	Corner/length/width/height/rotation

Figure 8.2
3D primitive objects

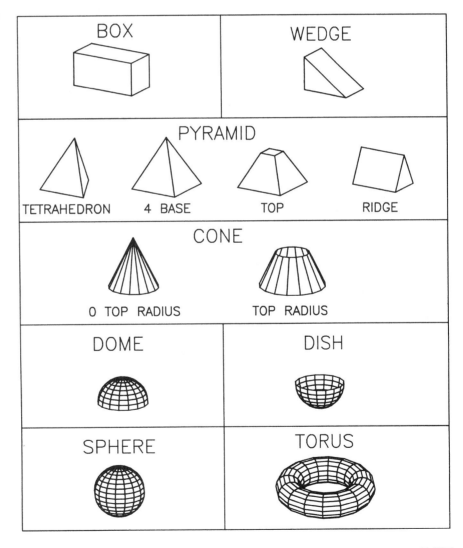

Mesh	1st corner/2nd corner/3rd corner/4th corner/mesh msize (2 to 256)/mesh nsize
Cone	Base center/base diameter/top diameter/height/ number of segments
Sphere	Center/diameter/number of longitudinal segments/ number of latitudinal segments
Dome	Center/diameter/number of longitudinal segments/ number of latitudinal segments
Dish	Center/diameter/number of longitudinal segments/ number of latitudinal segments
Torus	Center/torus diameter/tube diameter

When using the cone, sphere, dome, dish, and torus, entering a limited number of segments can produce some interesting shapes. For example, if 16 segments are used with a sphere, the final curved shape will look moderately smooth, but if only four segments for the longitude and two for latitude are used, a crystal will be formed (see Figure 8.3).

The 3D objects can be accessed using the Surfaces toolbar or the Draw/Surfaces pull-down menu. They can also be used as commands if they are proceeded by AI_ (for example, AI_BOX). The purpose of the AI_ prefix is to differentiate the surface commands from the solid commands of the same name.

3D VIEWPOINT

Exploding a 3D Object

It is possible to take 3D objects apart in order to delete or distort some of the surfaces. To take the objects apart, first explode the object using the EXPLODE command. Then you can manipulate each individual piece.

Figure 8.3

Generating a sphere with only eight surfaces

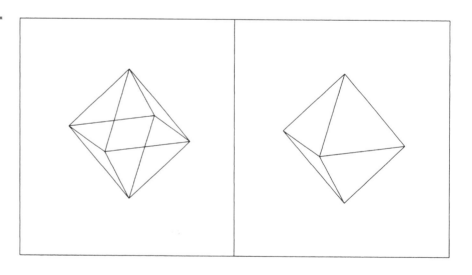

8.3 **3D Polygon Meshes**

To cover an area with a number of linked surfaces, AutoCAD uses what is called a *polygon mesh*. This mesh can form a flat surface or approximate a curved one. It is defined by the number of segments in an *M* and *N* direction. (These letters are used to ensure that there will be no confusion with the axis directions *X, Y,* and *Z.*) The number of mesh segments in any one direction controls the smoothness or roughness of the surface. AutoCAD uses two variables for this control: SURFTAB1 and SURFTAB2.

The SURFTAB variables control the number of faces created along each axis of the final form. The higher the number, the more faces created along the axis. Refer to Figure 8.6, shown later, for a demonstration of how the TABSURF command works. When using this command, faces are created around one axis. The SURFTAB1 variable controls the number of faces created. Refer to Figure 8.7, also shown later, for a demonstration of the REVSURF command. In that figure, faces are created in two axes and as a result both SURFTAB1 and SURFTAB2 variables are used. Try to limit the number of faces using the SURFTAB variable to the number necessary for your particular model. Using large values can create a large model and slow down some operations, such as hidden line removal and rendering. A value of 12 is sufficient in most cases.

When rendering using the RENDER command, there is an option called Smooth Shade. This option smooths the intersecting edges of 3D objects. Because of this, you can reduce the number of facets or sides on an object and still achieve a smooth curve.

When applying shade modes, the Gouraud shade mode automatically smooths the intersecting edges of 3D objects.

3D Mesh

The 3DMESH command constructs the most irregularly covered surface. It is used predominantly by outside programs to generate an irregular terrain. AutoCAD refers to the meshes generated as topologically rectangular polygon meshes. Basically, the area to be covered is divided into a number of nodes or vertices in the *M* and *N* directions. The minimum number of divisions in the *M* and *N* directions is 2, and the maximum is 256. Then, each vertex of the array is given a three-dimensional coordinate. After all the coordinates have been entered, AutoCAD constructs a mesh of polygons. The corners of the polygons are the coordinates that were just entered (see Figure 8.4).

3D VIEWPOINT

SURFTAB1 and SURFTAB2 Variable Values

Because these variables control the number of surfaces created using commands such as REVSURF and EDGESURF, the best way to determine the number is to ascertain how close the viewer will be to the object. If the view is very close, a large number will give a smooth effect. If objects will be in the distance, then a lower number will suffice. A median starting value is 12 for each. When using REVSURF with polylines, each polyline segment will be divided by the SURFTAB1 or SURFTAB2 value, requiring a smaller SURFTAB value for polylines.

Figure 8.4
3DMESH command

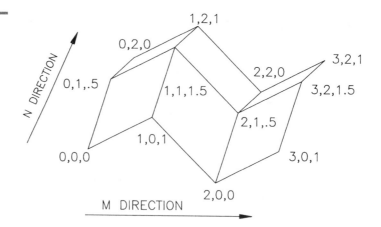

The required input for the 3DMESH command is as follows.

Command: **3DMESH**
Mesh M size: **enter an integer from 2 to 256**
Mesh N size: **enter an integer from 2 to 256**
Vertex (m,n): **a three-dimensional coordinate is required input**

The Vertex input request is repeated until all the vertices have been given coordinates.

For a detailed application of 3DMESH, see Chapter 23.

Ruled Surfaces

The RULESURF command is useful for generating a surface between two defining curves or lines. Each curve or line is divided based on the SURFTAB1 variable, and connecting polygon faces are formed along the divisions. The same number of divisions is used on both defining objects. However, since the size and shape of each defining object may be different, each created polygon face twists and turns to accommodate both objects—starting on one defining object and stretching to the other. The most common application of the RULESURF command is for radial development of conical or semiconical shapes. Examine Figure 8.5 for the creation of a semiconical form referred to as a transition piece (square to round). The required input for the RULESURF command follows:

Command: **RULESURF**
Select first defining curve: **even though a curve is requested, other objects can be selected**
Select second defining curve: **as above, lines, points, arcs, circles, and 2D or 3D polylines can be selected**

Tabulated Surfaces

The TABSURF command is used to create a series of parallel polygon faces extruded over a desired area. A path for the polygons to follow and a direction/extrusion vector are required input. The number of faces is controlled by the SURFTAB1 variable. One common application of the TABSURF command is to produce a curve that defines the path of the faces to be generated and a line that travels obliquely to the curve that controls the length of the faces. Figure 8.6 shows such an application in the creation of an offset duct or pipe. The pipe is traveling along one axis but must be offset to avoid some obstacle. Both the starting and ending diameters are the same, but each has a different center location. Because each face created is parallel

Figure 8.5
RULESURF command

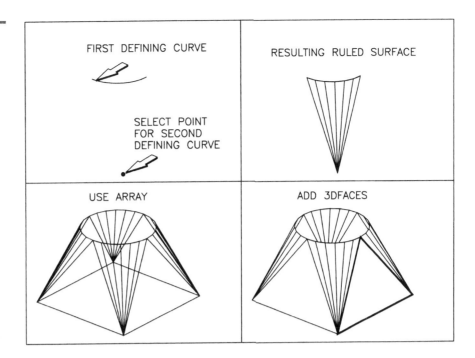

Figure 8.5
RULESURF command

Figure 8.6
TABSURF command

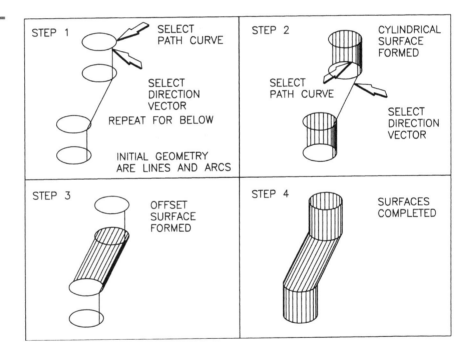

Figure 8.6
TABSURF command

to the next, this method of surface creation is referred to as *parallel development*. Refer to Figure 8.6 for the method of creation, and see the next description of the TABSURF command's required input.

Command: **TABSURF**

Select path curve: **a line, arc, circle, or 2D or 3D polyline can be selected to control the path the polygons will follow**

Select direction vector: **the object selected now will control the length of the polygons and the direction they will be pointing; only a line or open 2D or 3D polyline is acceptable as a direction vector**

151

Revolved Surfaces

The REVSURF command is used to generate surfaces that create circular forms such as light bulbs and soda bottles. A complete 360-degree form or a semicircular form can be created. Any type of profile can be swept around an axis to create the final shape; the only restriction is that the profile must be a single object. To have a convoluted profile, a polyline is required. Depending on the application, it can be useful to apply the Spline option of the PEDIT command to the polyline to smooth the sharp edges. The variables SURFTAB1 and SURFTAB2 are required for the REVSURF command. SURFTAB1 controls the number of surfaces around the axis, whereas SURFTAB2 controls the number of surfaces along the profile. Refer to Figure 8.7 for the application of the REVSURF command and note the following required input:

Command: **REVSURF**
Select path curve: **the object selected now is the profile to be swept around an axis**
Select axis of revolution: **the object selected now must be either a line or an open polyline; it controls the center axis of the final shape**
Start angle <0>: **this locates the position of the start of the surfaces**
Included angle (+=ccw −=cw)<Full circle>: **this sets the size of the surface in degrees**

Edge Surfaces

The EDGESURF command is used to create a surface that is controlled by a boundary of four curves. A surface is interpolated between these four curves. The technical term for the surface is a *Coons surface patch*. The variable SURFTAB1 controls the number of divisions along the first curve picked and SURFTAB2 controls the density of the mesh in the other direction. *Note:* When creating the controlling curves, it is important to remember that they must form a completely enclosed area. If one of the corners is not closed, an error results and AutoCAD informs the user as to which edge is not touching.

Figure 8.7
REVSURF command

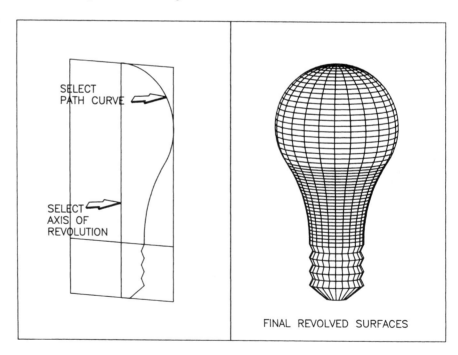

Figure 8.8
EDGESURF command

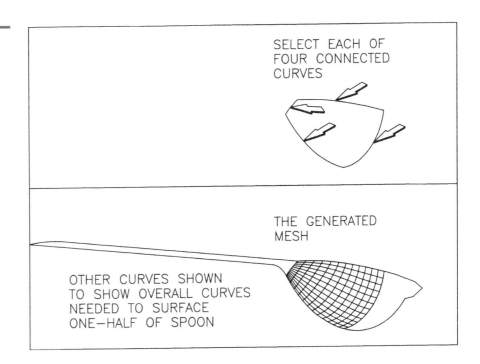

Refer to Figure 8.8 for the application of the EDGESURF command. Its required input is listed next:

Command: **EDGESURF**
Select edge 1: **select the first of the four connected curves (lines, arcs, polylines can be used)**
Select edge 2: **select the second of the four connected curves (lines, arcs, polylines can be used)**
Select edge 3: **select the third of the four connected curves (lines, arcs, polylines can be used)**
Select edge 4: **select the fourth of the four connected curves (lines, arcs, polylines can be used)**

Modifying Meshes

Once a mesh has been created with any of the commands we have just discussed, it then can be modified to any desired shape. This is accomplished by using the PEDIT command. The Edit Polyline tool is found on the Modify II toolbar. This command, normally used to edit polylines, can also edit meshes. When you use PEDIT, after you have identified the mesh you wish to modify, you are presented with various options that can be performed on the mesh, including vertex modification and mesh smoothing.

Note: You must be careful when modifying meshes because it is possible to distort the surface mesh so much that it will affect hidden line removal and rendering.

Lab 8.A   Coffeepot Surfaced Model

Purpose

Lab 8.A shows you how to use the REVSURF command to create a surfaced model of a coffeepot. This model will be used again in Assignment 1 in Chapter 13.

153

Objectives

You will be able to:

- Construct a surfaced model using the REVSURF command
- Create 3D faces
- Make use of the Invisible Edge option of the 3DFACE command

Primary Commands

REVSURF
3DFACE–Invisible Edge

Final Model

Figure 8.9 shows the coffeepot model you'll be creating.

Procedure

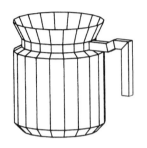

Figure 8.9
Coffeepot model

1. Start a new drawing called COFPT (COFfeePoT) with the following settings or you can open file a3dex8a from the a3d2005 folder. This file has most of the settings already set. All you should need to do is display the Surfaces, View, and 3D Orbit toolbars.

Units = decimal
Limits = −3,−3 to 3,3
Grid = 1
Snap Incr = 0.25
Elevation = 0
Thickness = 0
Current Layer = PROFILE
UCS = WCS
UCSICON = On, Origin, and set to 2D display properties
UCSVP = 0 (always set before creation of viewports)
UCS toolbar = displayed
View toolbar = displayed
Viewport Configuration = New viewport, Four: Equal, 3D setup

Creating an Orientation Plane

With this model, it is better to use a single plane rather than a cube for orientation. The plane represents the surface on which the profile to be swept is drawn.

2. Use the ELEV command to set the thickness to 6.5.
3. Activate the top-view viewport, and draw a line 5.5 units long, as shown in Figure 8.10. The start point should be at −2.75,0,0.

Creating a Working Plane

4. Use the 3Point option of the UCS command to create a working plane that is aligned to the newly created orientation plane (see Figure 8.11).

Drawing the Profile and Axis Line

5. Set the thickness back to 0.
6. Activate the front-view viewport.
7. Using PLINE, draw a profile to represent the edge of the pot. Figure 8.12 shows the node points and the final profile.
8. Using the LINE command, draw a center axis line, as shown in Figure 8.13. The length of this line is insignificant. Only its direction is important.

Creating the Surface of Revolution

9. Create a layer called SURF, and make it current.

Figure 8.10
Creating an orientation plane

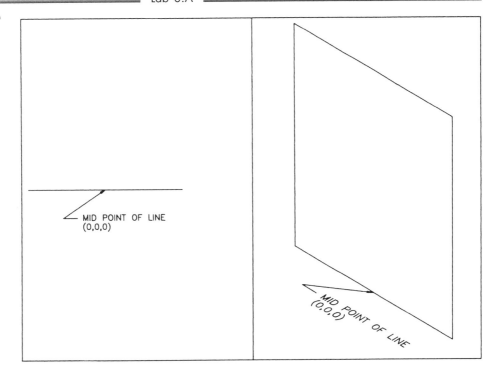

Figure 8.11
Creating a working plane

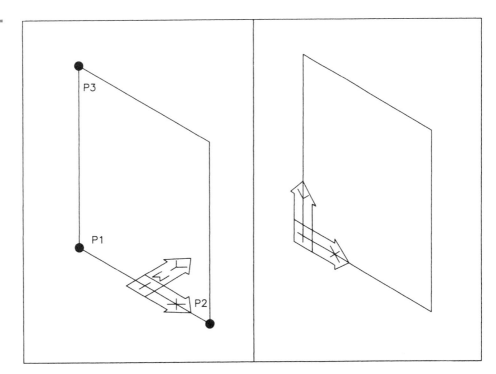

10. Delete the orientation line, and turn FILL off.
11. Set the variables SURFTAB1 and SURFTAB2 to 20.

12. Use the REVSURF command to create a revolved surface.

Command: **REVSURF**
Select path curve: **select the profile as shown in Figure 8.14 (P1)**
Select axis of revolution: **select the center axis line as shown in Figure 8.14 (P2)**
Start angle <0>: **press Enter to start the surfaces at 0 degrees**

155

Figure 8.12
Nodes and profile

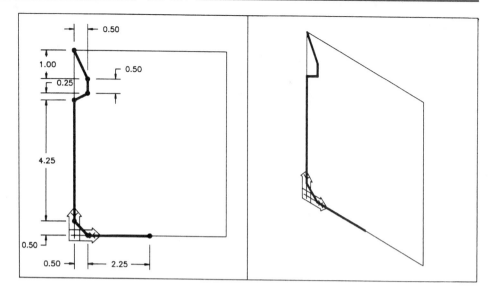

Figure 8.13
Center axis line

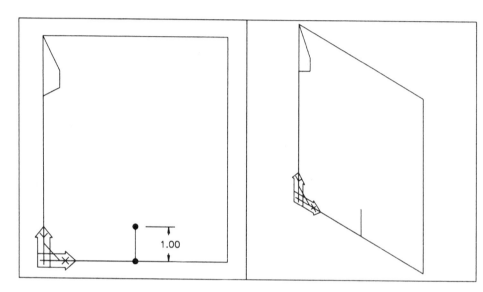

Figure 8.14
Creating a surface of
revolution

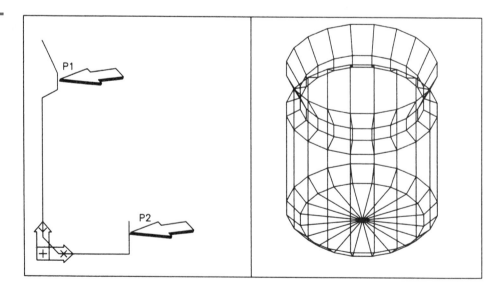

Figure 8.15
The handle with node
points

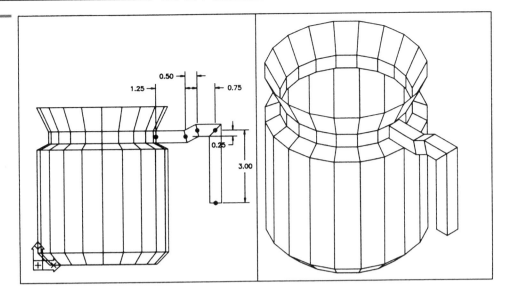

Included angle (+=ccw −=cw)<Full circle>: **press Enter for a complete circle**

Creating the Handle

13. Turn off the PROFILE layer.
14. Activate the front-view viewport.
15. Set the elevation to 0.25 and the thickness to −0.5. These settings place the handle in the center of the orientation plane.
16. With the PLINE command, draw the handle using the points shown in Figure 8.15. The polyline should have a width of 0.5.
17. Save the model as COFPT.
18. Use the HIDE command or use different shade modes in the isometric view and observe the results.

 ## Lab 8.B   Surfaced House Model

Purpose

Lab 8.B shows you how to use predefined 3D blocks to create a surfaced model of a house. This model will be completed in Lab 13.B in Chapter 13.

Objective

You will be able to construct a surfaced model using 3D objects.

Primary Commands

AI_BOX, AI_PYRAMID, and AI_CONE
CIRCLE–Extruded

Final Model

Figure 8.16 shows the house model you'll be creating.

Procedure

1. Start a new drawing called BDWELL (Basic DWELLing) with the following settings or you can open file a3dex8b from the a3d2005 folder. This file has most of the settings already set. All you should need to do is display the Surfaces, View, and 3D Orbit toolbars.

157

Figure 8.16
House model

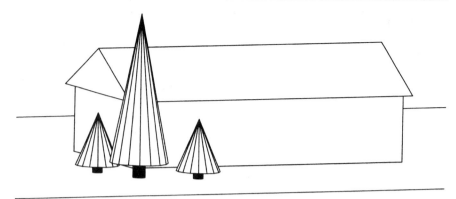

Units = architectural
Limits = −1′,−1′ to 137′, 89′
Grid = 10′
Snap Incr = 1′
Elevation = 0
Thickness = 0
Current Layer = GROUND
UCS = WCS
UCSICON = On, Origin, and set to 2D display properties
UCSVP = 0 (always set before creation of viewports)
UCS toolbar = displayed
View toolbar = displayed
Viewport Configuration = New viewport, Four: Equal, 3D setup

Creating the Ground

2. Using the 3DFACE command, draw a surface with the following coordinates.

P1 = 0, 0   P2 = 136′, 0
P3 = 136′, 88′   P4 = 0, 88′

This will be used as the ground plane.

Creating the Building

3. Create a layer called BUILDING, and make it current.
4. Using the 3D Objects AI_BOX command, draw the shape shown in Figure 8.17. (*Note:* The 3D Objects option needs to be loaded first; see Section 8.2.)

Command: **AI_BOX**
Corner of box: **40′, 30′, 0′**
Length: **40′** (distance along the *X* axis)
Cube/<Width>: **20′** (distance along the *Y* axis)
Height: **9′** (distance along the *Z* axis)
Rotation angle about Z axis: **0**

Creating the Roof

5. Create a layer called ROOF, and make it current.
6. Using the 3D Objects AI_PYRAMID command, draw the shape shown in Figure 8.18.

Command: **AI_PYRAMID**
First base point: **39′, 29′, 9′**

Figure 8.17
Creating the building with a box

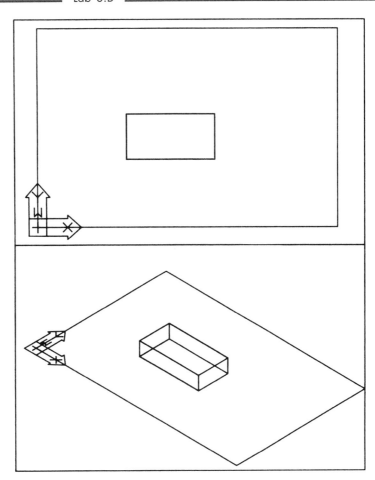

Figure 8.18
Creating the roof with a pyramid

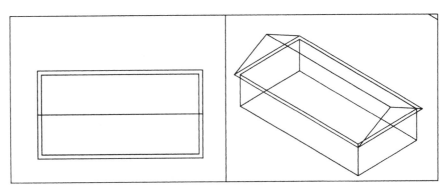

Second base point: **81′, 29′, 9′**
Third base point: **81′, 51′, 9′**
Tetrahedron/<Fourth base point>: **39′, 51′, 9′**
Ridge/Top/<Apex point>: **R**
First ridge point: **39′, 40′, 15′**
Second ridge point: **81′, 40′, 15′**

7. Save the model as BDWELL. Try the HIDE command and observe the results.

Creating the Trees

8. Create a layer called TREE, and make it current.
9. Using the ELEV command, set the thickness to 1′.

10. Using the CIRCLE command, draw the trunks of the small trees. They have a radius of 8″ and are at the following coordinates.

1st tree: 33′2″, 26′6″, 0′
2nd tree: 44′2″, 17′4″, 0′

11. Using the ELEV command, set the thickness to 2′.
12. Using the CIRCLE command, draw the trunk of the large tree. It has a radius of 10″ and is at the coordinates 36′6″, 20′0″, 0′.

13. Use the 3D Objects AI_CONE command to draw each tree (see Figure 8.19).

    FIRST TREE
Command: **AI_CONE**
Base center point: **33′2″, 26′6″, 1′**
Diameter/<radius> of base: **3′**
Diameter/<radius> of top <0>: **0**
Height: **7′**
Number of segments <16>: **16**
    SECOND TREE
Command: **AI_CONE**
Base center point: **44′2″, 17′4″, 1′**
Diameter/<radius> of base: **3′**
Diameter/<radius> of top <0>: **0**
Height: **7′**
Number of segments <16>: **16**
    THIRD TREE
Command: **AI_CONE**
Base center point: **36′6″, 20′, 2′**
Diameter/<radius> of base: **4′**
Diameter/<radius> of top <0>: **0**
Height: **20′**
Number of segments <16>: **16**

14. Save the model as BDWELL.

Setting the Viewpoint

15. Use VPOINT or View tools to display the model (which should be similar to Figure 8.16), and use the HIDE command or different shade modes.
16. If desired, use hatching to cover the walls with brick or siding and the roof with shingles. First, explode the 3D objects into 3D faces and set the UCS working plane to each surface to hatch.
17. Save the model as BDWELL.

Figure 8.19
Adding the trees

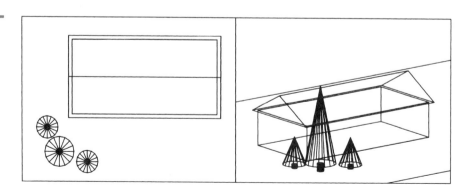

Lab 8.C   Surfaced Automobile Hood Model

Purpose

Lab 8.C shows you how to use the EDGESURF command to create a surfaced model of an automobile hood.

Objective

You will be able to construct a surfaced model using the surface mesh commands.

Primary Commands

EDGESURF
SURFTAB1, SURFTAB2
PLINE

Final Model

Figure 8.20 shows the final surfaced model of the automobile hood.

Procedure

1. Start a new drawing called CARH (CAR Hood) with the following settings or you can open file a3dex8c from the a3d2005 folder. This file has most of the settings already set. All you should need to do is display the Surfaces, View, and 3D Orbit toolbars.

Units = architectural
Limits = −1′,−1′ to 5′,5′
Grid = 3″
Snap Incr = 3″
Elevation = 0
Thickness = 0
Current Layer = OCUBE
UCS = WCS
UCSICON = On, Origin, and set to 2D display properties
UCSVP = 0 (always set before creation of viewports)
UCS toolbar = displayed
View toolbar = displayed
Viewport Configuration = New viewport, Four: Equal, 3D setup

Creating the Orientation Cube

2. Activate the top-view viewport.
3. Set the thickness to 6″.
4. Using the LINE control, draw a 4′ square rectangle, as shown in Figure 8.21.

 **Figure 8.20**
Surfaced model of automobile hood

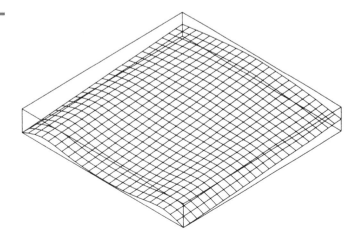

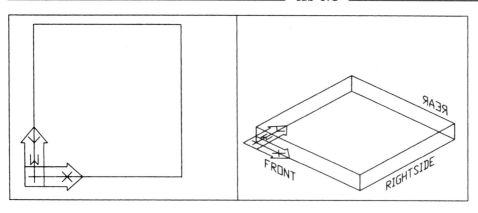

Figure 8.21
Orientation cube and working planes

Creating the Working Planes

5. Using the UCS command, create three working planes: Front, Rear, and Right-side. Save the working planes so that they may be restored by name.

Drawing the Front Profile

When you use EDGESURF, it is most important that the profiles you create touch at all four corners. If they do not meet, the surface will not be generated.

6. Create a layer called PROFILES, and make it current. Return the Thickness variable to 0.
7. Restore the Front working plane, and activate the front-view viewport.
8. Using the PLINE command, draw a polyline as shown in Figure 8.22A.
9. Use PEDIT to change the polyline into a spline, as shown in Figures 8.22B and C.

Drawing the Rear Profile

10. Restore the Rear working plane, activate the front-view viewport, and display the PLAN UCS in that viewport.
11. Using the PLINE command, draw a polyline as shown in Figure 8.23A.
12. Use PEDIT to change the polyline into a spline, as shown in Figures 8.23B and C.

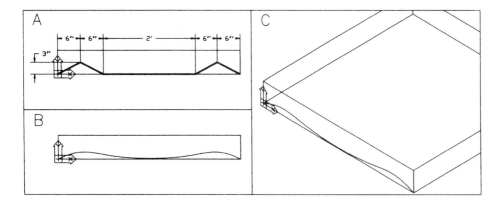

Figure 8.22
Front polyline

162

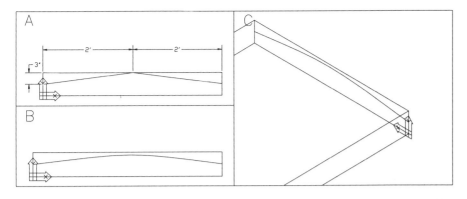

Figure 8.23
Rear polyline

Drawing the Side Profile

13. Restore the Rightside working plane and activate the right-side-view viewport.
14. Using the PLINE command, draw a polyline, as shown in Figure 8.24A.
15. Use PEDIT to change the polyline into a spline, as shown in Figures 8.24B and C.
16. Activate the isometric viewport, and copy the newly created polyline to the left side of the orientation cube.

Creating a Surface Mesh

17. Turn the OCUBE layer off.
18. Set variables SURFTAB1 and SURFTAB2 to 24.
19. Create a layer called SURF, and make it current.
20. Use the EDGESURF command and click each profile. A surface should now be covering the defined area and the model should look similar to the one shown in Figure 8.20.
21. Save the model as CARH.

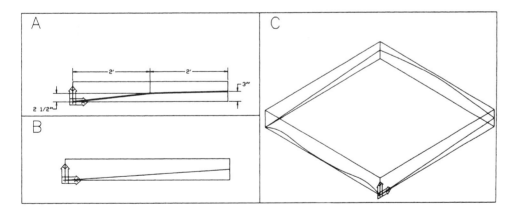

Figure 8.24
Right-side polyline

Questions

1. What previously constructed geometry (for instance, curves, lines, profiles, or points) is required to apply each of the following polygon mesh commands? What do you suppose the command names stand for?
   a. 3DMESH
   b. RULESURF
   c. TABSURF
   d. REVSURF
   e. EDGESURF

2. What functions do the variables SURFTAB1 and SURFTAB2 serve?

3. In the creation of meshes, what do the letters *M* and *N* stand for?

4. Of what objects are AutoCAD's 3D objects comprised?

5. Explain the process for constructing AutoCAD's 3D objects.

6. List and describe the eight 3D objects.

7. What is a polygon mesh?

8. Of AutoCAD's six commands for generating a mesh-covered area, which would you use to create a wine glass?

9. Which command would you use to create a wavy sheet of metal?

10. Identify the surface-generating command that would be used to create a topographical map.

Assignments

1. Create a surfaced model of a coffee mug using REVSURF and PLINE (see Figure 8.25). (*Note:* This model will be used in Assignment 1 in Chapters 13 and 14.)

MUG STATISTICS
Model Name = COFMUG

Figure 8.25
Coffee mug surfaced model

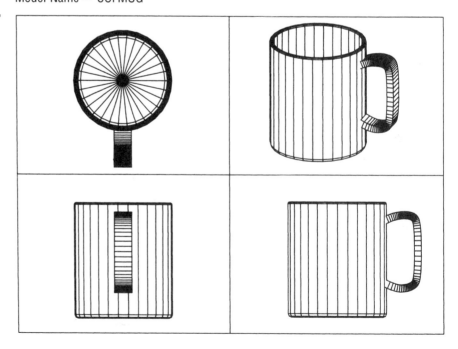

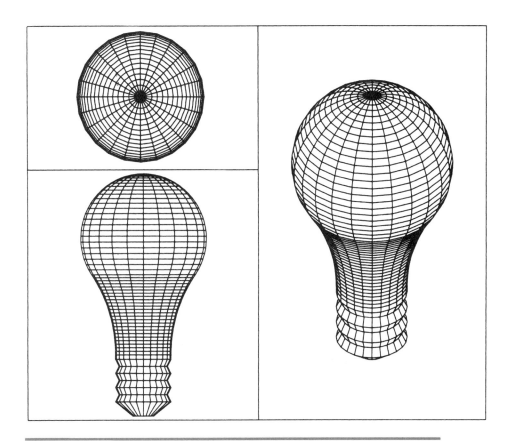

Figure 8.26
Lightbulb surfaced model

Diameter = 3-1/2''
Height = 4''
Wall Thickness = 1/8''
Handle Width = 5/8''
Handle Thickness = 1/4''
BASE POINT = 0,0,0 (mug bottom/center)

2. Generate a surfaced model of a lightbulb using REVSURF (see Figures 8.26 and 8.7).

LIGHTBULB STATISTICS
Model Name = LBULB
Bulb Diameter = 2-1/4''
Bulb Height = 3-1/4''
Base Diameter = 1''
Base Height = 1''
Overall Height = 4-1/4''

3. Using the RULESURF command, draw a surfaced model of a transition duct (see Figures 8.27 and 8.5).

TRANSITION DUCT STATISTICS
Model Name = TDUCT
Top Diameter = 4''
Base Square = 6''
Height = 4''

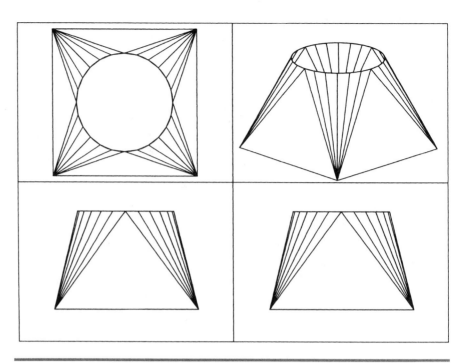

Figure 8.27
Transition duct surfaced model

4. Create a surfaced model of an offset duct using TABSURF (see Figures 8.28 and 8.6).

OFFSET DUCT STATISTICS
Model Name = ODUCT
Duct Diameter = 4''
Offset Distance = 4''
Length of Duct = 4''

5. Using EDGESURF, generate a surfaced model of a spoon (see Figures 8.29 and 8.8). (*Note:* This model will be used in Assignment 1 in Chapter 13.)

SPOON STATISTICS
Model Name = SPOON
Overall Length = 6''
Dish Length = 2''
Dish Width = 1-1/4''
Dish Depth = 1/4''
Handle Width = 1/2''
BASE POINT = 0,0,0 (dish bottom)

6. Create a surfaced model of an automobile (see Figure 8.30). The top part of the figure illustrates the wireframe that is used to create the surfaced model in the lower part. The entire body and window surfaces should be created using the EDGESURF command. The tires should be created using the REVSURF command. Save the model as CAR. It will be plotted in Assignment 4 of Chapter 16.

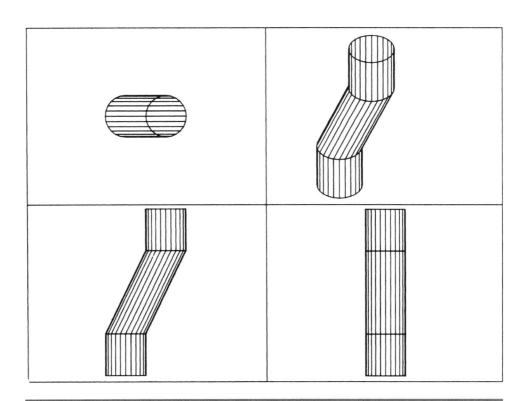

Figure 8.28
Offset duct surfaced model

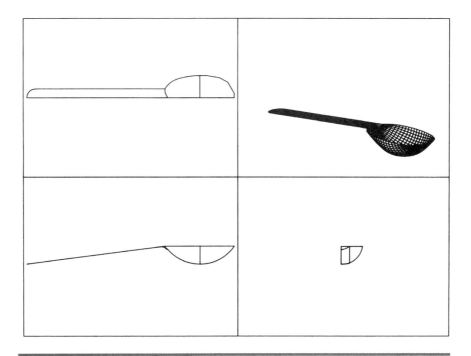

Figure 8.29
Spoon surfaced model

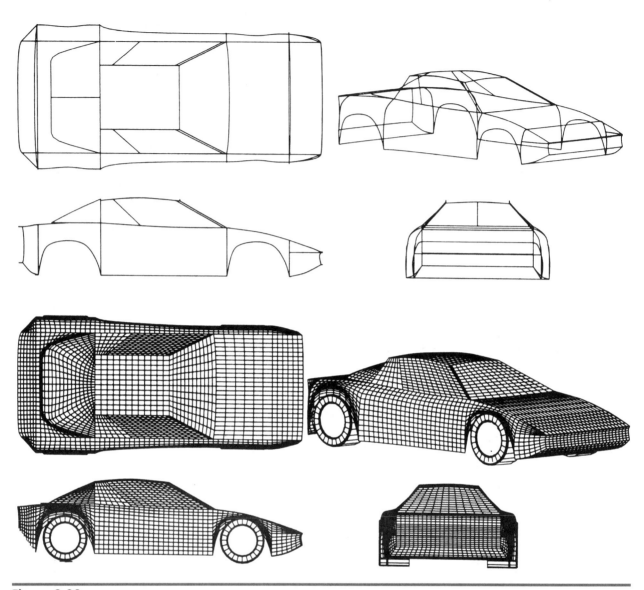

Figure 8.30
Automobile surfaced model

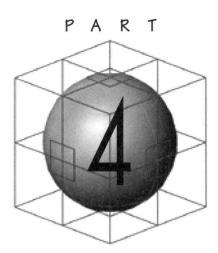

Solid Modeling

This part introduces AutoCAD's integrated solid modeling. Here you will learn how to create actual solid models rather than surface-covered models. The concepts and basic techniques of solid modeling are explored as you learn about solid primitive creation, how to build complex composite solids from these primitives, and how to display the models. The final chapter supplies advanced solid editing techniques. The integration of solid modeling into AutoCAD is an exciting and new area, one that is becoming the focus of mechanical engineering.

Concepts Behind Solid Modeling

9.1 Introduction

Solid modeling creates three-dimensional (3D) models with database properties, giving the models mass and density. The computer "believes" the model is a solid form, from the outside through to its inner core (see Figure 9.1), so capabilities that are unavailable with wireframe or surfaced modeling can be accessed with solid modeling. Think of yourself as a sculptor or a modeler of clay when you approach solid modeling. You start with a solid block, carve away a piece here, bore a hole there, or add a protrusion. This is how solid modeling works—by addition and subtraction. That is the basic process that you, as the user, need to understand. However, in the background, complex mathematical operations are taking place to accomplish the seemingly simple additions and subtractions. As more and more of these subtractions and additions are made, the mathematical intricacies and convolutions increase, which means, of course, that there is a price to pay. But the benefits in the model definition—especially in prototype generation and modification—can outweigh the disadvantage of extra calculation time.

It is important to note that the benefits of wireframe and surfaced modeling are not lost by adding solid modeling. Each method has its own place and uses. There

Figure 9.1
Solid model of an apple

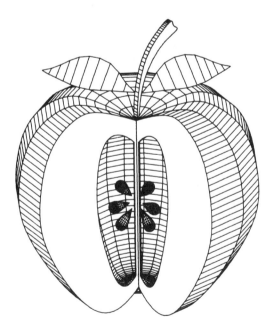

are, in fact, many situations in which solid modeling does not perform well, such as in terrain modeling. Solid modeling was not intended for that application; it is much more useful in the design of a mechanical component.

In addition, the techniques of model creation mastered up to this point were not learned in vain. They will remain as important in the creation of solid models as they were in the creation of wireframe and surfaced models. Solid modeling complements, rather than usurps, the other modeling methods. After some exploration of its techniques, you will soon locate the niche in which to place it.

9.2   Solids Toolbar

The Solids toolbar can be used to create primitive solid shapes and modify solids. The solid commands can be accessed under the Draw/Solids pull-down menu or the Solids toolbar.

Toolbars are displayed using the View/Toolbars pull-down menu or by right-clicking on a currently displayed toolbar.

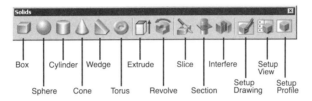

| Box | Cylinder | Wedge | Extrude | Slice | Interfere | Setup View |
| Sphere | Cone | Torus | Revolve | Section | Setup Drawing | Setup Profile |

3D VIEWPOINT

Advanced Modeling Extension

Before Release 13, AutoCAD made use of an extension program to create solid models; this was referred to as Advanced Modeling Extension, or AME. Objects created with AME were AME blocks. Solid modeling has now been totally integrated into the AutoCAD program and the objects created are now referred to as 3D solids. AME solids and 3D solids are totally different entities. Because of this, you must convert AME solids from previous releases to 3D solids. This can be accomplished with the AMECONVERT command. Because the new 3D solids are more accurate than the previous AME solids, you may see some differences in the converted AME model. This is important to note, especially if you attempt to import solids that you or someone else created before Release 13 of AutoCAD.

9.3   Solids and Regions

Two types of objects make use of solid modeling commands: 3D solids and regions. Three-dimensional solids are 3D objects that have solid properties. Regions can be thought of as flat solids (see Figure 9.2); they have physical and material properties, but they have no thickness and are two-dimensional (2D).

Complex 3D solids and regions can be created using the same commands, except that solids use 3D primitives, such as boxes and cylinders, and regions use 2D primitives, such as circles and polygons. Regions are composed of totally enclosed

Figure 9.2
A region

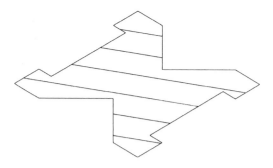

areas called *loops.* Loops can be combinations of lines, polylines, circles, arcs, ellipses, elliptical arcs, splines, 3D faces, traces, and solids (2D). These objects must form closed loops and be planar (on a flat plane) in nature.

To turn the basic objects into a region, use the REGION command. Once you have created region loops, you can make use of the solid modeling commands such as UNION or SUBTRACT to make more complex regions, or use the EXTRUDE command to generate complex profiled 3D solids. In either case, you can use the MASSPROP command to extract information such as the calculated area and the perimeter of the region.

Note that even though the same commands are used to form the complex shapes, 3D solids and regions *cannot* be combined. Because 3D solids are three-dimensional and regions are two-dimensional, 3D solids can combine with 3D solids and regions can combine with regions. The two can never be mixed; however, a region can be made three-dimensional and a 3D solid two-dimensional by means of a process that is explained later.

Note: For the sake of simplicity, and because solids and regions use similar techniques for creation, the discussion here focuses on 3D solids.

Construction and Display of 3D Solids

The primitives used by solid modeling to create final, complex forms can be viewed as building blocks that are added to or subtracted from each other to create the final form. (Note that 3D solids can also be created by extruding or revolving 2D objects.) The building blocks for 3D solids are boxes, wedges, cylinders, spheres, cones, and tori. Solid modeling can create these basic forms.

Once created, primitives can be combined in a number of ways to form what is called a *composite model.* A composite model is the final desired result of any combination of primitives or other composites. There are two types of composite models: composite 3D solids and composite regions. As is true of primitive 3D solids and regions, composite 3D solids and regions cannot be directly combined.

The composite model can be enhanced by special editing. Chamfering, filleting, slicing, and sectioning are types of 3D solid editing.

Like surface models, 3D solids can be displayed in four ways: wireframe, hidden line removed, shaded, and rendered. To control the display, 3D solids have some system variables that are particular to them; 3D solids also can provide graphic information to aid in the creation of 2D drafting drawings. These capabilities are explained in greater detail later.

Solid modeling keeps track of the material properties of 3D solids for use within AutoCAD in mass property calculations or outside AutoCAD for finite element analysis.

9.4 Primitive Creation

Six commands will create the six basic 3D solid primitives: BOX, WEDGE, CYLINDER, CONE, SPHERE, and TORUS. These commands have different options, to be used according to the primitive being created. However, their similarities allow for easy mastery. These primitives are very similar to the surfaced primitives discussed earlier. Figure 9.3 illustrates their various forms. The Solid tools are found under the Solids toolbar. The following explains each primitive creation command and its options:

BOX	Creates a 3D solid box by defining its diagonal corners, by defining its base and height, or by indicating its center and overall dimensions. A rubber band technique is used to visually determine sizes. It has two options: the Center option allows the user to define the center of the box and the Corner of Box option allows the user to define the corners of the box.
WEDGE	Creates a 3D solid wedge. Its parameters are identical to that of the BOX command. The base is parallel to the current working plane and the sloped face tapers along the X axis.
CYLINDER	Creates a 3D solid cylinder by defining its base and height. CYLINDER has two options: the Elliptical option allows the user to define the axis of the ellipse and the Center Point option allows the user to define the center of the cylinder.
CONE	Creates a 3D solid cone. Its parameters are identical to that of the CYLINDER command, except for references to the apex of the cone.
SPHERE	Creates a 3D solid sphere by defining its radius or diameter and its center.
TORUS	Creates a 3D solid torus, which is a donut shape, by defining two radii: one for the tube shape and one from the center of the torus to the center of the tube. If the radius of the tube is greater than the torus radius, a self-intersecting torus, resembling a football in shape, is formed.

Figure 9.3
Primitive solids

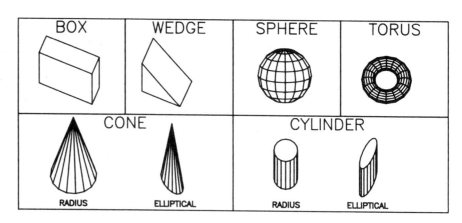

Primitives from 2D Objects

Two commands are used to create 3D solid primitives from 2D objects or regions: EXTRUDE and REVOLVE. The primitive 3D solids created by these commands are shown in Figure 9.4. The following subsections explain each command.

EXTRUDE Command

The EXTRUDE command creates a 3D solid by extruding existing 2D objects or regions. You can select multiple objects on which to perform the extrusion. The extrusion always takes place perpendicular to the base of the object, and it can have parallel or tapered sides. If you wish to create a sloped extrusion, base the taper on the angle measured in from the perpendicular sides of the extrusion. It must be greater than 0 and less than 90 degrees. It is also possible to extrude a profile along a 2D polyline path simply by clicking the profile and the path. It should be noted that the Extruded Faces tool on the Solids Editing toolbar look almost identical to the Extrude tool on the Solids toolbar. Take care not to confuse the two.

3D VIEWPOINT

Extruding 3D Solids

You cannot extrude 3D solids; the EXTRUDE command will work only on closed curves such as polylines, polygons, rectangles, circles, ellipses, closed splines, donuts, and regions.

EXTRUDE

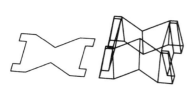

2D PROFILE EXTRUDED INTO A SOLID

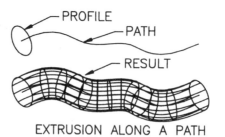

EXTRUSION ALONG A PATH

REVOLVE

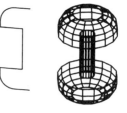

2D PROFILE REVOLVED INTO A SOLID

Figure 9.4
Primitive solids from 2D objects

REVOLVE Command

The REVOLVE command creates a 3D solid by revolving a profile around an axis. This command is similar to the AutoCAD surface command REVSURF. Only one profile can be selected at a time, and only circles, polylines, polygons, ellipses, and region objects can be revolved. Blocks or 3D objects *cannot* be revolved.

 ## Lab 9.A   Introduction to Primitive Solids

Purpose

This lab introduces you to the basic commands for solid model creation. These commands generate simple primitive solids. Further use will be made of this model in later labs.

Objective

You will be able to create primitive solids.

Primary Commands

BOX
WEDGE
ISOLINES

Procedure

Initial Settings

1. Start a model called PSOL1 (Primitive SOLids 1) with the following settings or you can open file a3dex9a from the a3d2005 folder. This file has most of the settings already set. All you should need to do is display the UCS, Solids, View, and 3D Orbit toolbars.

Units = decimal
Limits = −1,−1 to 6,6
Grid = 0.5
Snap Incr. = 0.5
Elevation = 0
Thickness = 0
UCS = WCS
UCSICON = On, Origin, and set to 2D display properties
UCSVP = 0 (always set before creation of viewports)
UCS toolbar = displayed
View toolbar = displayed
Solids toolbar = displayed
Current Layer = SOLID
Display an axonometric view (VPOINT 0.5,−1,1)

Setting the Appearance of 3D Solids

2. The method used to control the appearance of 3D solids on the screen uses the ISOLINES command. This command is explained in more detail in Chapter 11, and its use is illustrated in labs in that chapter. However, it is desirable to set this variable now:

Command: **ISOLINES**
Enter new value for ISOLINES <4>: **4**

Figure 9.5
Creating two primitive solids

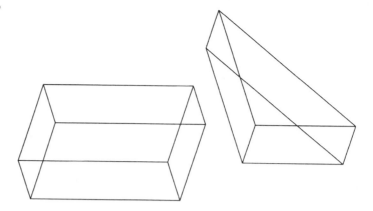

Creating a Solid Box

3. The procedure for creating solid primitives is very similar to the procedure for creating 3D surfaced objects. To create a solid box shape, use the following command:

Command: **BOX**
Specify corner of box or [CEnter] <0, 0, 0>: **0, 0, 0**
Specify corner or [Cube/Length]: **L**
Specify length: **3**
Specify width: **2**
Specify height: **1**

You have created a solid box; the command is that simple.

Creating a Wedge

4. You will now create a solid wedge. In this step you will see that the different solid primitive creation commands are very similar.

Command: **WEDGE**
Specify first corner of wedge or [CEnter] <0, 0, 0>: **4, 1, 0**
Specify corner or [Cube/Length]: **L**
Specify length: **2**
Specify width: **1**
Specify height: **3**

Note how the slope of the wedge lies along the *X* axis. This is always the case. To align the wedge to a different orientation during creation, change the orientation of the UCS before creating the wedge.

The creation of the two primitives is illustrated in Figure 9.5.

5. Save the model as PSOL1.
6. Use the LIST command and click the two solids. Refer to the displayed data about the objects. Note their object names.

Lab 9.B

Creating Primitive Solids Through Extrusion and Revolution

Purpose

In this lab, you use basic solid model creation commands to create solids from the extrusion and revolution of a 2D profile. Further use is made of this model in later labs.

Objective

You will be able to create primitive solids from 2D profiles.

Primary Commands

ISOLINES
EXTRUDE
REVOLVE

Procedure

Initial Settings

1. Start a model called PSOL2 (Primitive SOLids 2) with the following settings or you can open file a3dex9b from the a3d2005 folder. This file has most of the settings already set. All you should need to do is display the Solids, View, and 3D Orbit toolbars.

Units = decimal
Limits = −1, −1 to 10, 10
Grid = 0.5
Snap Incr. = 0.5
Elevation = 0
Thickness = 0
UCS = WCS
UCSICON = On, Origin, and set to 2D display properties
UCSVP = 0 (always set before creation of viewports)
UCS toolbar = displayed
View toolbar = displayed
Solids toolbar = displayed
Current Layer = SOLID
Display a plan view
ISOLINES = 15

Creating the 2D Star Profile

2. Using the PLINE command, create the profile that is shown in Figure 9.6. Make sure you use the CLOSE command so that the profile is completely enclosed.
3. Copy the star profile 5″ to the right.

Extruding the Profile into a Solid

4. Display an axonometric view using a VPOINT setting of 1,−1,1, or use the SE Isometric View tool.
5. Using the EXTRUDE command, select the profile of the first star. It will be extruded to a height of 3″.

Command: **EXTRUDE**
Current wire frame density: ISOLINES = 15
Select objects: **click the first star**

Figure 9.6
2D polyline profile

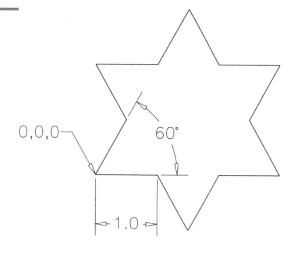

1 found
Select objects: **press Enter**
Specify height of extrusion or [Path]: **3**
Specify angle of taper for extrusion <0>: **0**

> The first star has been turned into a solid.

6. Using the EXTRUDE command, select the second profile of the second star. It also will be extruded to a height of 3″, but this time a taper is added.

Command: **EXTRUDE**
Current wire frame density: ISOLINES = 15
Select objects: **click the second star**
1 found
Select objects: **press Enter**
Specify height of extrusion or [Path]: **3**
Specify angle of taper for extrusion <0>: **5**

> Setting the extrusion taper angle to 5 causes the sides of the star to taper inward, toward the top. Now the second star has been turned into a solid, but with sloped sides. The two stars created in Steps 5 and 6 are illustrated in Figure 9.7.

7. Save the model as PSOL2.

Figure 9.7
Solids created through extrusion

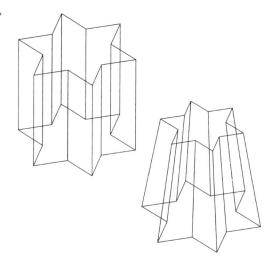

Figure 9.8
Polyline profile

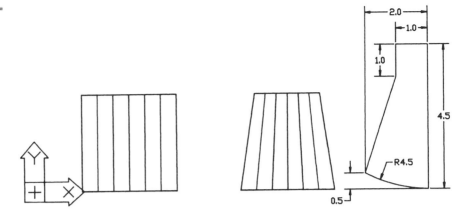

Creating a 2D Profile for Revolution

8. Revolve the UCS about the *X* axis so that the *Y* axis of the UCS matches the *Z* axis of the WCS:

Command: **UCS**
Current ucs name: *WORLD*
Enter an option [New/Move/orthoGraphic/Prev/Restore/Save/Del/Apply/?/World]
<World>: **N**
Specify origin of new UCS or [ZAxis/3point/OBject/Face/View/X/Y/Z] <0, 0, 0>: **X**
Specify rotation angle about X axis <90>: **90**

9. Display the plan view of the new UCS.
10. Create the profile shown in Figure 9.8 using the PLINE command. You could also use lines and arcs and turn them into a polyline loop using the PEDIT command. Remember that the polyline must be closed.

Creating the Revolved Solid

11. Display the axonometric view using the VPOINT −1, −1, 1.

12. Using the REVOLVE command, select the polyline profile to turn it into a revolved solid. Use the endpoints of the vertical line for the start and end axis endpoints.

Command: **REVOLVE**
Current wire frame density: ISOLINES = 15
Select objects: **click the polyline profile**
1 found
Select objects: **press Enter**
Specify start point for axis of revolution or
define axis by [Object/X (axis)/Y (axis)]: **click the top of the vertical line using end-point object snap**
Specify endpoint of axis: **click the bottom of the vertical line using endpoint object snap**
Specify angle of revolution <360>: **press Enter to create a 360-degree revolved solid**

A solid in the shape of the revolved profile has now been created. Your model should look like the one shown in Figure 9.9.

13. Save the model as PSOL2.

179

Figure 9.9
Revolved solid with extruded
solid stars with the addition of
the solid object on the far sight

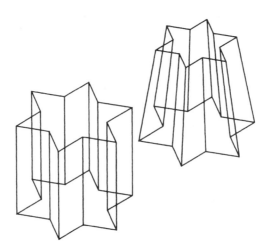
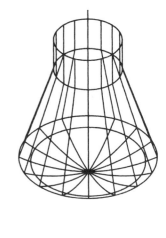

Questions

1. What is solid modeling?

2. What does AME stand for?

3. What is the difference between solids and regions?

4. Identify the six commands for creating solid primitives. What are the similar commands for creating surfaced objects?

5. Explain the purposes of the EXTRUDE and REVOLVE commands.

6. What AutoCAD surface command is similar to the REVOLVE command?

Assignments

1. Create each of the following primitive solids: cone, sphere, and torus.

2. Create a circular cylinder and an elliptical cylinder solid.

3. Create a torus with a tube radius that is greater than the torus radius. What is the outcome?

4. Come up with an interesting 2D profile that could be extruded into a solid using the Taper option of the EXTRUDE command.

5. Generate a solid primitive of a soft drink bottle using the REVOLVE command.

6. Create a region from a closed polyline in the shape of a triangle by using the REGION command. Use the area command to determine the area of the triangle. Now draw a closed polyline of a more complex perimeter, turn it into a region, and calculate its area.

C H A P T E R

Composite Solids: Creation and Modification

10.1 Introduction

Chapter 9 introduced you to solid modeling and its method of creating simple primitive solids. Learning about those methods gave you a good beginning for learning about creating truly functional solid models. To learn this, you need to know how to create composites.

A complex form, known as a composite, is created through the interrelationship of two primitives (solids with solids or regions with regions). Once the relationship is determined, a composite is formed. The process is very simple.

For example, to insert a hole through a rectangular plate, where the plate is a box solid and the hole is a cylinder solid, identify the relationship between the box and the cylinder by subtracting the volume of the cylinder from the volume of the box. The final result is a plate with a hole through it, or a *composite* (see Figure 10.1).

Figure 10.1
Creating a hole in a solid plane

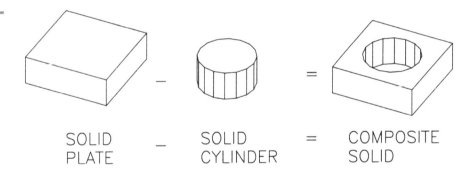

```
SOLID          _     SOLID         =    COMPOSITE
PLATE                CYLINDER           SOLID
```

10.2 Solids Editing Toolbar

The Solids Editing toolbar contains various tools for performing modifications on solids.

Toolbars are displayed using the View/Toolbars pull-down menu or by right-clicking on a currently displayed toolbar.

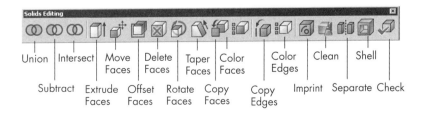

10.3 Relation Commands

Three commands are used to relate primitives to each other: UNION, SUBTRACT, and INTERSECT. The UNION command is used to add solids to each other; SUBTRACT is used to subtract solids from one another; and INTERSECT is used to create a composite from the intersection of two solids. Figure 10.2 illustrates the relationships between solids created by these three commands. You can repeat the relationship commands with any two solids, composite or primitive, to create as complex a solid object as desired. The tools for relating solids can be found under the Solids Editing toolbar.

3D VIEWPOINT

Combining Solids That Do Not Overlap

It is possible to use the UNION command to combine solids that do not overlap. The solids that are combined are then treated as one solid and can be moved or acted on as one solid.

10.4 Modifying Composites

To further enhance your composite model, use the standard modify commands, CHAMFER and FILLET, and the 3D solid command, SLICE. Because you are modifying 3D solids, the CHAMFER and FILLET commands behave slightly differently than they do when used on 2D objects. The following is an explanation of the three commands.

Figure 10.2
Relationships between solids

	TWO SOLIDS WITH SOME COMMON VOLUME ↓	TWO SOLIDS WITH NO COMMON VOLUME ↓	TWO SOLIDS WITH IDENTICAL VOLUME ↓
BOOLEAN OPERATION ↓			
UNION →			
SUBTRACTION →			NO ACTION TAKEN
INTERSECTION →		NO ACTION TAKEN	

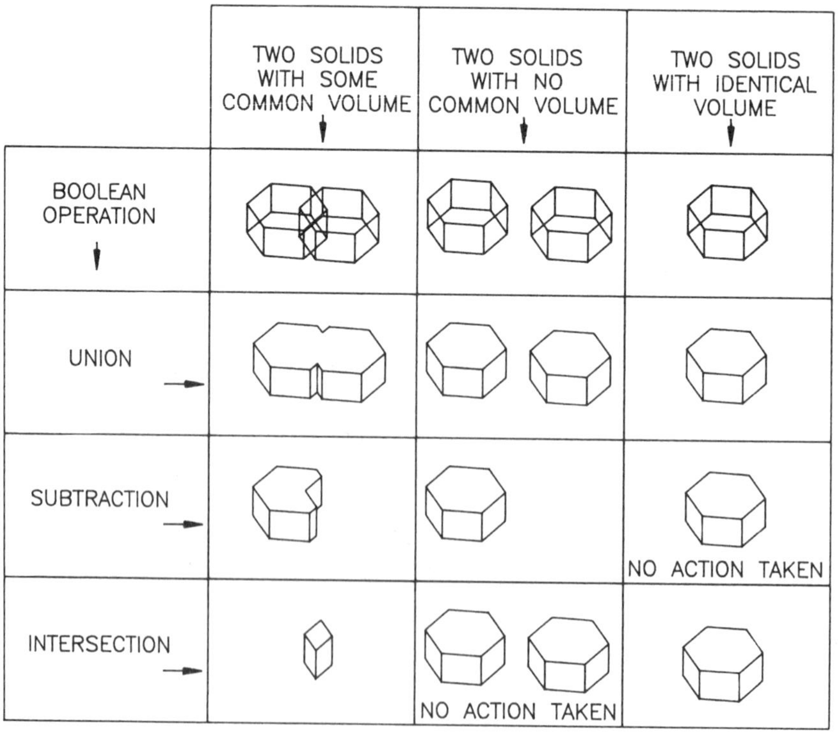

CHAMFER Command

To produce a chamfer of a solid, use the CHAMFER command. It will automatically subtract the solid area defined by the CHAMFER settings. To use the command, refer to Figure 10.3 and follow this procedure:

Command: **CHAMFER**
(TRIM mode) Current chamfer Dist1 = 0.5000, Dist2 = 0.5000
Select first line or [Polyline/Distance/Angle/Trim/ Method]: **click edge on solid**
Base surface selection . . .
Enter surface selection option [Next/OK (current)] <OK>: **one of the two surfaces adjoining the selected edge is highlighted; either OK it to be used as the base surface or use the Next option to move to the next surface**
Specify base surface chamfer distance <0.5000>: **enter the distance from the edge of the base surface**
Specify other surface chamfer distance <0.5000>: **enter the distance from the edge of the adjoining surface**
Select an edge or [Loop]: Select an edge or [Loop]: **click as many edges that surround (are adjacent to) the base surface**

FILLET Command

To create a fillet along the edge of a solid, use the FILLET command. It creates an internal or external arc (concave or convex) along selected edges of a solid. Refer to Figure 10.4 and the following procedure:

Command: **FILLET**
Current settings: Mode = TRIM, Radius = 0.5000
Select first object or [Polyline/Radius/Trim]: **click an edge of the solid to fillet**
Enter fillet radius <0.5000>: **enter the desired radius of the fillet**
Select an edge or [Chain/Radius]: **press Enter or click additional edges**
1 edge(s) selected for fillet

Figure 10.3
The CHAMFER command

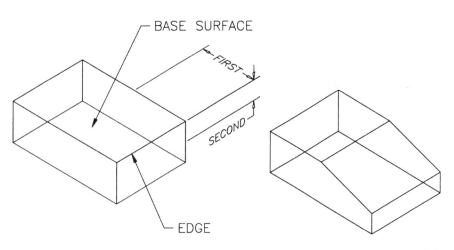

Figure 10.4
The FILLET command

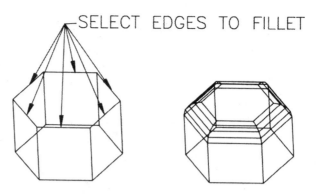

SELECT EDGES TO FILLET

3D VIEWPOINT

Filleting a Series of Solid Edges

The Chain option of the FILLET command can be used to fillet a series of connected edges that lie on the same plane. By specifying the Chain option, you can click a single edge, and all the edges that are connected on the same plane will be clicked automatically to be filleted.

Slicing a Solid in Two

AutoCAD has the ability to take a solid and slice it into two pieces along a user-defined plane. This ability is accessed with the SLICE command. You can find the SLICE tool in the Solids toolbar. Once the slice has been made, both new solids or only one may be retained. The options for defining the slicing plane are Object, ZAxis, View, XY, YZ, ZX, and 3Points. Refer to Figure 10.5 and the following procedure:

Command: **SLICE**
Select objects: **click the solid to be sliced**
1 found
Select objects: **press Enter to continue**
Specify first point on slicing plane by [Object/Zaxis/View/XY/YZ/ZX/3points]
<3points>: **enter the desired method for specifying the slicing plane**

Figure 10.5
The SLICE command

CUTTING PLANE

Specify a point on desired side of the plane or [keep Both sides]: **press Enter to keep both sides or click on the desired side to retain**

The following are descriptions of the slicing plane options:

Object   Aligns the slicing plane with an object such as a circle, ellipse, circular or elliptical arc, 2D spline, or 2D polyline segment.

Zaxis   Defines the slicing plane by a specified point on the *Z* axis of the *X-Y* plane.

View   Aligns the slicing plane with the current viewport's viewing plane.

XY   Aligns the slicing plane with the current UCS *X-Y* plane.

YZ   Aligns the slicing plane with the current UCS *Y-Z* plane.

ZX   Aligns the slicing plane with the current UCS *Z-X* plane.

3Points   Defines the slicing plane by identifying three points on the plane.

Lab 10.A   Relating Solids to One Another

Purpose

This lab uses actual models to illustrate how solids relate to each other. The relationships formed will serve as building blocks for the creation of complex composite solids. In later labs you will apply this knowledge to create more complex models.

Objectives

You will be able to:

- Create primitive solids
- Form relationships between solids to create composite solids

Primary Commands

ISOLINES
CYLINDER
UNION
SUBTRACT
INTERSECT

Procedure

Initial Settings

1. Start the model called RELSOL (RELation of SOLids) and enter the following settings or you can open file a3dex10a from the a3d2005 folder. This file has most of the settings already set. All you should need to do is display the Solids, Solids Editing, View, and 3D Orbit toolbars.

Units = decimal
Limits = −1,−1 to 4,4
Grid = 0.5
Snap Incr. = 0.5
Elevation = 0
Thickness = 0
UCS = WCS
UCSICON = On, Origin, and set to 2D display properties
UCSVP = 0 (always set before creation of viewports)
UCS toolbar = displayed
View toolbar = displayed
Solids toolbar = displayed
Solids Editing toolbar = displayed

Display an axonometric view (VPOINT 0,−1,1)
Current layer = SOLID
ISOLINES = 15

Creating Solid Primitives

2. Using the CYLINDER command, create two cylinders (see Figure 10.6A).

Command: **CYLINDER**
Current wire frame density: ISOLINES = 15
Specify center point for base of cylinder or [Elliptical] <0,0,0>: **0,0,0**
Specify radius for base of cylinder or [Diameter]: **0.5**
Specify height of cylinder or [Center of other end]: **0.5**
Command: **CYLINDER**
Current wire frame density: ISOLINES = 15
Specify center point for base of cylinder or [Elliptical] <0,0,0>: **0.75,0,0**
Specify radius for base of cylinder or [Diameter]: **0.5**
Specify height of cylinder or [Center of other end]: **0.5**

Relating Solids by Union

3. Relate the two solids by uniting them with the UNION command. This adds the mass of the two solids to create the final composite solid.

Command: **UNION**
Select objects: **click the two solids**

> AutoCAD calculates the union of the two cylinders and then displays the results. The screen should look similar to Figure 10.6B. Note that the composite solid is a single object and that the geometry does not overlap. AutoCAD calculated what was unique mass and what was identical mass and produced the composite solid.

Separating Solids

4. There is no special command for separating solids. The AME utility does have a command called SOLSEP to separate solids, but this command is not part of the integrated solid modeling. To separate solids that have just been related, use the UNDO command, or U. Proceed to undo the UNION command, so that the two distinct solids are visible.

Relating Solids by Subtraction

5. Relate the two solids by subtraction with the SUBTRACT command. This command subtracts the mass of one of the solids from the mass of the other solid to create the final composite.

Figure 10.6
Relating solids by union

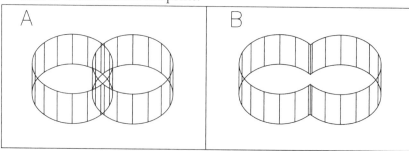

Figure 10.7
Relating solids by subtraction

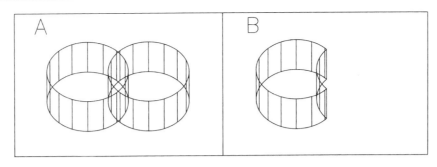

Command: **SUBTRACT**
Select solids and regions to subtract from . . .
Select objects: **click the left cylinder**
1 found
Select objects: **press Enter to continue**
Select solids and regions to subtract . . .
Select objects: **click the right cylinder**
1 found
Select objects: **press Enter to finish**

> AutoCAD calculates the subtraction of the right cylinder from the left cylinder and then displays the results. The screen should look similar to Figure 10.7B. Note how the composite solid has a piece subtracted from it. AutoCAD calculated the overlapping mass of the right cylinder and produced the composite solid.

Separating Solids

6. Use the UNDO command to undo the SUBTRACT command, so that the two distinct solids are visible.

Relating Solids by Intersection

7. Relate the two solids by intersection by using the INTERSECTION command. This command takes the overlapping masses of the two solids to create the composite.

Command: **INTERSECT**
Select objects: **click the two cylinders**

> AutoCAD calculates the intersection and then displays the results. The screen should look similar to Figure 10.8B. Note how only the overlapping mass of the two cylinders remains.

Figure 10.8
Relating solids by intersection

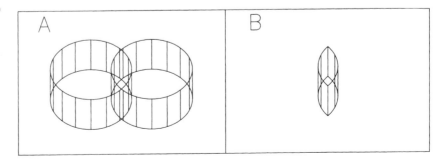

Separating Solids

8. Use the UNDO command to undo the INTERSECT command, so that the two distinct solids are visible.
9. Save the model as RELSOL.

You have now created composite solids from primitives. Remember that you can relate composite solids to each other in the same ways you related primitives in this lab. Thus, the possible final complex solids you can create are unlimited. You will be creating more complex composites in the labs in Chapters 11 and 12.

Lab 10.B   Modifying Solids

Purpose

This lab introduces you to the use of modify commands to alter the shape of solids.

Objectives

You will be able to:

- Fillet and chamfer solids
- Slice solids in two

Primary Commands

FILLET
CHAMFER
SLICE

Procedure

1. Open model PSOL1 from Lab 9.A.
2. Use the SAVEAS command to save it as MODSOL (MODifying SOLids).
3. Set the VPOINT to 0.75,−1,1.

Filleting a Solid

4. Using the FILLET command, round the top edge of the wedge, as shown in Figure 10.9.

Command: **FILLET**
Current settings: Mode = TRIM, Radius = 0.5000
Select first object or [Polyline/Radius/Trim]: **click top edge**
Enter fillet radius <0.5000>: **0.25**
Select an edge or [Chain/Radius]: **press Enter to accept edge clicked earlier**
1 edge(s) selected for fillet

The top edge should now be filleted with a 0.25 radius.
The first time you clicked the edge, you identified the solid object; the second time, you identified the edge to fillet. You could have clicked more edges at this point if you wanted to add more fillets at the same time.

Figure 10.9
Modifying solids

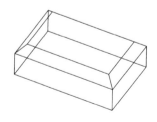

Chamfering a Solid

5. Using the CHAMFER command, add a 45-degree bevel to the top edges of the solid box:

Command: **CHAMFER**
(TRIM mode) Current chamfer Dist1 = 0.5000, Dist2 = 0.5000
Select first line or [Polyline/Distance/Angle/Trim/ Method]: **click a top edge**
Base surface selection . . .
Enter surface selection option [Next/OK (current)] <OK>: **enter OK if top surface is highlighted or enter NEXT until top surface is highlighted, then enter OK**
Specify base surface chamfer distance <0.5000>: **0.25**
Specify other surface chamfer distance <0.5000>: **0.25**
Select an edge or [Loop]: Select an edge or [Loop]: **click each edge around the top of the box and press Enter to finish**

All the top edges of the box should now have a 45-degree bevel.

Slicing a Solid in Two

6. Set VPOINT to 0.5, −1,0.75.
7. Using the CYLINDER command, create two solid cylinders, one inside the other. The top surface of the inside cylinder will coincide with the top surface of the outside cylinder.

Command: **CYLINDER**
Current wire frame density: ISOLINES = 15
Specify center point for base of cylinder or [Elliptical] <0,0,0>:**1.5,4.5,0**
Specify radius for base of cylinder or [Diameter]: **2**
Specify height of cylinder or [Center of other end]: **2**
Command: **CYLINDER**
Current wire frame density: ISOLINES = 15
Specify center point for base of cylinder or [Elliptical] <0,0,0>: **1.5,4.5,1**
Specify radius for base of cylinder or [Diameter]: **1**
Specify height of cylinder or [Center of other end]: **1**

8. Using the SUBTRACT command, subtract the inside cylinder from the outside cylinder. You should now have a composite cylinder with a hole in its top.

9. Using the SLICE command, slice the composite cylinder into two halves (Figure 10.10):

Figure 10.10
Slicing a solid in half

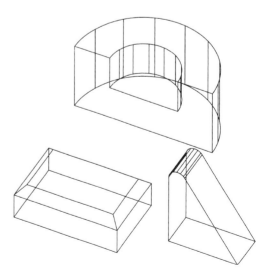

Command: **SLICE**
Select objects: **click the composite cylinder**
1 found
Select objects: **press Enter to continue**
Specify first point on slicing plane by [Object/Zaxis/View/XY/YZ/ZX/3points] <3points>: **ZX**
Specify a point on the ZX-plane <0,0,0>: **0,4.5,0** (4.5 is the center of the cylinder)
Specify a point on desired side of the plane or [keep both sides]: **0,5,0**

The composite cylinder has now been sliced into two halves, and only one half has been retained.

10. Save the model as PSOL1.

Lab 10.C Solid Model of a Socket Head Cap Screw

Purpose

This lab introduces you to more basic solid model creation commands during the modeling of a socket head cap screw. You will use the commands to extrude 2D profiles, generate simple primitive solids, and form complex composite solids by interrelating primitives.

Objectives

You will be able to:

- Create primitive solids
- Create composite solids
- Create solids for 2D profiles
- Perform modifications to solids

Primary Commands

ISOLINES
EXTRUDE
CYLINDER
SUBTRACT
UNION
CHAMFER

Final Model

Figure 10.11 is the final solid model of the socket head cap screw.

Procedure

Initial Settings

1. Start the model called SOCSOL (SOCket head cap screw SOLid) and enter the following settings or you can open file a3dex10c from the a3d2005 folder. This file has most of the settings already set. All you should need to do is display the Solids, Solids Editing, View, and 3D Orbit toolbars.

Units = decimal
Limits = −1,−1 to 2,2
Grid = 0.5
Snap Incr. = 0.5
Elevation = 0
Thickness = 0
UCS = WCS

Figure 10.11
Solid model of socket head cap screw

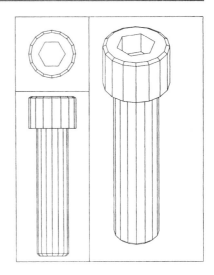

UCSICON = On, Origin, and set to 2D display properties
UCSVP = 0 (always set before creation of viewports)
UCS toolbar = displayed
View toolbar = displayed
Solids toolbar = displayed
Solids Editing toolbar = displayed
Display an axonometric view (VPOINT 1, −1,1)
Current layer = SOLID
ISOLINES = 15

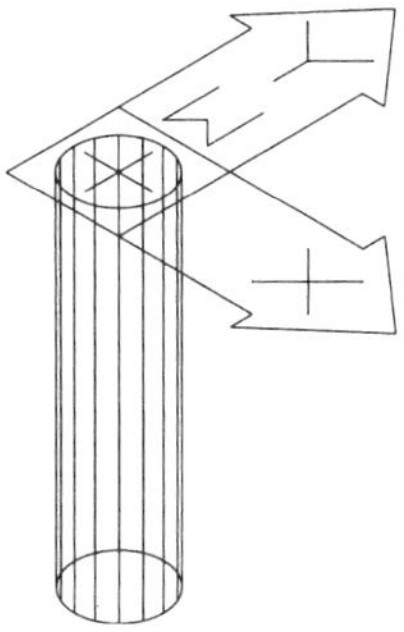

Creating a Solid Cylinder

The body and the head of the screw are created first, using the CYLINDER command. The top of the body is at 0,0,0 and the rest of the body extends in a negative Z direction. The head sits on top of the body and extends in the positive Z direction.

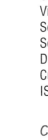

Figure 10.12
Solid model of cylinder body

2. Using the CYLINDER command, create the body of the screw as shown in Figure 10.12.

Command: **CYLINDER**
Current wire frame density: ISOLINES = 15
Specify center point for base of cylinder or [Elliptical] <0,0,0>: **press Enter**
Specify radius for base of cylinder or [Diameter]: **0.125**
Specify height of cylinder or [Center of other end]: −**1**

3. Using the CYLINDER command, create the head of the screw, as shown in Figure 10.13.

Command: **CYLINDER**
Current wire frame density: ISOLINES = 15
Specify center point for base of cylinder or [Elliptical] <0,0,0>: **press Enter**
Specify radius for base of cylinder or [Diameter]: **0.1875**
Specify height of cylinder or [Center of other end]: **0.25**

Creating a 2D Profile and Extruding It

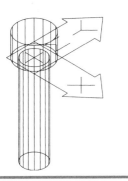

Figure 10.13
Adding the head to the body

4. Using the POLYGON command, draw a hexagon that will represent the socket in the head of the screw (Figure 10.14).

191

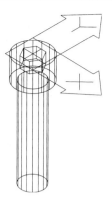

Figure 10.14
Adding the hexagon socket

Figure 10.15
Chamfer of the head

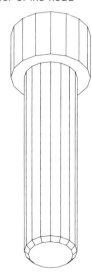

Figure 10.16
Chamfer of the body

192

Command: **POLYGON**
Enter number of sides <4>: **6**
Specify center of polygon or [Edge]: **0,0,0.25**
Enter an option [Inscribed in circle/Circumscribed about circle] <I>: **C**
Specify radius of circle: **0.09375**

5. Using the EXTRUDE command, select the hexagon and give it a height of −0.120 with no taper angle.

Command: **EXTRUDE**
Current wire frame density: ISOLINES = 15
Select objects: **click hexagon**
Specify height of extrusion or [Path]: −**0.120**
Specify angle of taper for extrusion <0>: **press Enter**

The final results should look similar to Figure 10.14.

Chamfering Solids

The top of the head and the bottom of the body each have a different chamfer. Both make use of the CHAMFER command.

6. Using the CHAMFER command, create a chamfer along the top edge of the head of the screw, as shown in Figure 10.15.

Command: **CHAMFER**
(TRIM mode) Current chamfer Dist1 = 0.5000, Dist2 = 0.5000
Select first line or [Polyline/Distance/Angle/Trim/ Method]: **click one top edge of the head**
Base surface selection . . .
Enter surface selection option [Next/OK (current)] <OK>: **press Enter if top surface is highlighted or Next until top surface is highlighted, then press Enter**
Specify base surface chamfer distance <0.5000>: **0.019**
Specify other surface chamfer distance <0.5000>: **0.019**
Select an edge or [Loop]: **click each edge around the top of the head and press Enter**

7. Repeat the CHAMFER command for the bottom of the body, as shown in Figure 10.16.

Command: **CHAMFER**
(TRIM mode) Current chamfer Dist1 = 0.5000, Dist2 = 0.5000
Select first line or [Polyline/Distance/Angle/Trim/ Method]: **click one bottom edge of the body**
Base surface selection...
Enter surface selection option [Next/OK (current)] <OK>: **press Enter if bottom surface is highlighted or Next until bottom surface is highlighted, then press Enter**
Specify base surface chamfer distance <0.5000>: **0.019**
Specify other surface chamfer distance <0.5000>: **0.010**
Select an edge or [Loop]: **click each edge around the bottom of the body and press Enter**

Relating the Primitives to Each Other

At this point, the head, body, and hexagon are all separate solids. Now they will be related to each other to create the complex composite solid illustrated in Figure 10.17.

8. Using the SUBTRACT command, subtract the solid hexagon from the solid head.

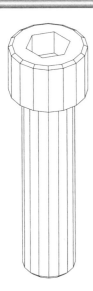

Figure 10.17
The final composite model

Command: **SUBTRACT**
Select solids and regions to subtract from . . .
Select objects: **click the head solid**
Select solids and regions to subtract ...
Select objects: **click the hexagon solid**

9. Using the UNION command, add the body and the head.

Command: **UNION**
Select objects: **click the body and the head**

10. Save the model as SOCSOL.
11. Use the HIDE command and observe the results. Try different FACETRES variable values and the HIDE command to see the effect on the model.

Questions

1. Identify and explain the commands used to create solid relationships.

2. Explain the command that is used to cut a solid in two.

3. Explain the two commands used to bevel and round edges of a solid.

Assignments

1. Create a solid of the 1/4″ machine nut shown in Figure 10.18. (*Hint:* To achieve the chamfer on the edge of the nut, relate a chamfered solid cylinder to a hexagon solid by intersection.)

Figure 10.18
Solid model of a machine nut

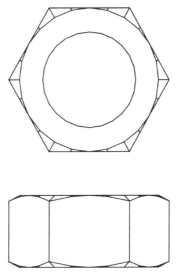

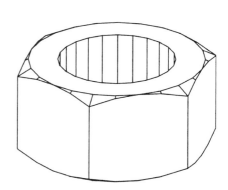

2. Generate a solid model of the 1/4″ wrench socket shown in Figure 10.19.

3. Examine the chess piece illustrated in Figure 10.20. Produce a model of this solid.

4. Create a solid model of a wooden pencil. This is a composite, so use cones, an extruded hexagon, and a revolved profile of the eraser end.

5. Create an apple shape. Now, take a bite out of it, graphically speaking.

Figure 10.19
Solid model of a wrench socket

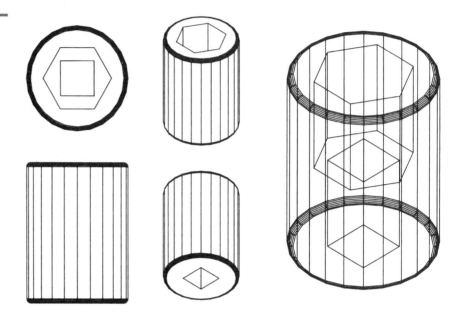

Figure 10.20
Solid model of a rook chess piece

Solid Display and Inquiry

11.1 Introduction

The solid model utilities of AutoCAD are powerful—not only can you construct a composite model quickly and accurately, but you can also utilize a variety of methods to display it, in both 3D and 2D, and extract information about its properties. This chapter explores these abilities, discussing the various methods of representing a solid model and the methods of inquiring about the model's characteristics.

11.2 3D Representation

A solid model can be displayed as wireframe, hidden lines removed, shaded, and rendered. However, there are two variables that have a direct effect on those types of displays: the ISOLINES and FACETRES variables. The ISOLINES variable controls the number of tessellation lines that are used to define the curved features of the model in wireframe. Tessellation lines are the parallel lines used to define the curve of a surface for easier visualization. The FACETRES variable controls the resolution of the facets that are created when you perform a hidden line removed, shaded, or rendered display of a solid. You may enter an integer value from 0 to 2047 for the number of isolines per surface of a solid. The higher the value, the greater the number of isolines. You may enter a value from 0.01 to 10.0 for the facet resolution. The higher the value, the more facets that are created and the smoother the resultant figure.

It should be noted that ISOLINES have no effect on objects when displayed using shade modes other than 2D wireframe. The FACETRES variable controls how smooth the perimeter of a curved object will be when using shade modes.

Effect of ISOLINES and FACETRES Settings on a Sphere

Look at the sphere shown in Figure 11.1A. This sphere was created with an ISOLINES value of 4. Only a few lines are used to define the curved surfaces. Now refer to Parts B, C, and D of Figure 11.1. The sphere in Part B is shown in wireframe with an ISOLINES setting of 10. Because of the higher number, more isolines are drawn, giving a clearer view of the sphere. However, it takes longer to manipulate the view of the model with a higher ISOLINES setting. Finally, refer to the next two spheres, hidden lines removed and with FACETRES settings of 0.2 and 0.5. You can see that the ISOLINES and FACETRES variables are independent of each other.

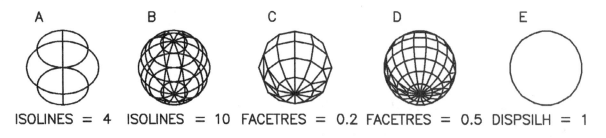

Figure 11.1
Wireframe and hidden displays

You can change the ISOLINES and FACETRES variables at any time to increase or decrease the number of lines and facets when representing the solid model. Use the least number of isolines that you can and still be able to manipulate the solid. Use the least number of facets possible when creating initial settings for rendering and then increase the number for the final render.

If you don't want to see all the various facet faces on the 3D solid when you hide it, you can set the variable DISPSILH to 1. This setting shows only the silhouette of the solid when using the HIDE command or hiding when plotting. Figure 11.1E shows the results of hiding with DISPSILH = 1. To see the faces again, set DISPSILH to 0. *Note:* You usually need to use the REGEN command after changing the FACETRES or ISOLINES variables to recalculate the solid objects.

3D VIEWPOINT

Rendering Solids

If you are going to use the Smooth option of the RENDER command, you may not need to have as many facets on a solid. The Smooth option blends edges together to give a smooth curve. You can then reduce the FACETRES variable before rendering and consequently reduce the rendering time.

11.3 2D Representation

You can create 2D objects from a 3D solid model using several commands: SECTION, SOLPROF, SOLVIEW, and SOLDRAW. Using these commands you can create 2D drawings that can be dimensioned. SECTION works with TILEMODE set to 1 (Model tab active) or 0 (Layout tab active). The others require you to have TILEMODE set to 0 and be working in paper space. Section 16.4 of Chapter 16 explains the details of paper space.

You can also lay out 2D drawings using Mechanical Desktop (MDT); this is explained in Chapter 24.

Creating Sections with SECTION

The SECTION command creates section view objects automatically by specifying the cutting plane. It works very much like the SLICE command. But instead of slicing the model, it creates a profile outline of the cut area. Refer to Figure 11.2 and the following procedure:

196

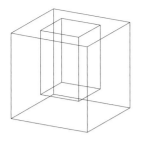 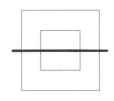 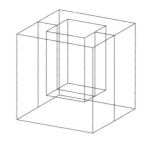 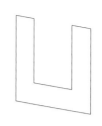

MOVED FOR CLARITY

ORIGINAL
SOLID MODEL

DEFINE CUTTING PLANE
USING SECTION COMMAND

RESULTING SECTION PROFILE

Figure 11.2
Creating a section view

Command: **SECTION**
Select objects: **click the solid to be sectioned**
1 found
Select objects: **press Enter to continue**
Specify first point on Section plane by [Object/Zaxis/View/XY/YZ/ZX/3points]
<3points>: **enter the desired method for specifying the section plane**

Solid Profiles Using SOLPROF

The SOLPROF command is used to create a projected 2D profile view of a solid. This works only from a floating viewport created in PAPERSPACE (Section 16.4).

The following is the procedure for using the command:

1. Create the 3D solid.
2. Set TILEMODE to 0 (Layout tab active).
3. Make sure you are in paper space by using the PS alias command for PAPERSPACE.
4. Create a floating viewport using the MVIEW command.
5. Enter into MODELSPACE using the MS alias.
6. Click in the floating viewport to activate it.
7. Using a VIEW command set the desired view, either orthographic or axonometric.
8. Use the SOLPROF command. You will be asked to:

   Click the objects to project;
   Display hidden profile lines of separate layers;
   Project profile lines onto a plane;
   Delete tangential edges.

   You normally answer *yes* to the previous requests. The profile objects are then created. They are created on new layers with the prefixes PV and PH. The layer name is followed by the handle name of the viewport itself. PV stands for Profile Visible (visible lines) and Profile Hidden stands for hidden lines. You may have to load the Hidden linetype and assign it to the proper layer.

9. To see the profile, you need to freeze the original 3D solid in that viewport only.
10. These profiles are designed to be seen from paper space. If you switch back to TILEMODE 1 (Model tab active), you will see the profile objects in 3D space. The profiles are actual objects added to your drawing.

197

Solid Profiles Using SOLVIEW and SOLDRAW

The SOLVIEW and SOLDRAW commands are used together to create 2D views of a 3D solid. As with the SOLPROF command, these commands work only with TILEMODE set to 0 (Layout tab active) and in PAPERSPACE. The SOLVIEW command sets up the floating viewports and views based on a primary view. The SOLDRAW command updates the viewports created using SOLVIEW with the proper visible and hidden profiles.

3D VIEWPOINT

Exploding a Solid

When you explode a solid, it breaks down into individual regions (and sometimes an object called a body). If you explode the region, you end up with polylines or lines. You can then extract as many of the resulting objects as you need.

The following is the procedure for using the SOLVIEW and SOLDRAW commands:

1. Create the 3D solid.
2. Set TILEMODE to 0 (Layout tab active).
3. Make sure you are in paper space by using the PS alias command for PAPERSPACE.
4. Create a primary floating viewport using the MVIEW command. This viewport is used to create and position the other viewports.
5. Enter into MODELSPACE using the MS alias.
6. Click in the floating viewport to activate it.
7. Using a VIEW command, set the desired orthographic view, such as the top view.
8. Switch back to PAPERSPACE using PS.

9. Use the SOLVIEW command. You will be asked to:

   Set the type of view, such as orthographic or auxiliary;
   Click the side of the primary viewport to project;
   Click the location of the view's center and press Enter;
   Click the corners that set the size of the floating viewport;
   Enter the unique name of the view.

   The viewport and profile are created. Special layers are created with the prefix of the unique name of the view and followed by VIS, HID, and DIM. As with SOLPROJ, these layers are used to store the separate profiles for visible and hidden lines as well as dimensions you add. You may have to load the Hidden linetype and assign it to the proper layers.

10. Once you have created the views, use the SOLDRAW command to update each viewport you click. If you use the All option to select objects, you can update all the SOLVIEW viewports at once.

11. These profiles are designed to be seen from paper space. If you switch back to TILEMODE 1 (Model tab active), you will see the profile objects in 3D space. The profiles are actual objects added to your drawing.

12. If you modify your 3D solid, use the SOLDRAW command to update the viewports to reflect the changes.

Figure 11.3
Extracting a 2D profile view

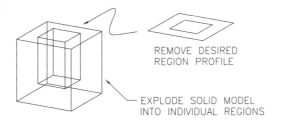

REMOVE DESIRED
REGION PROFILE

EXPLODE SOLID MODEL
INTO INDIVIDUAL REGIONS

Exploding a Solid

If you explode a solid, it breaks down into individual region and body objects. From these objects, you can extract the surface area profiles to help create a 2D drawing (Figure 11.3).

Using a DXB Plot File

You can create a projected view of your model by plotting a view to a DXB file and then importing the resultant DXB file back into your drawing. This allows you to assemble a 2D view of any view of a model. However, the DXB plot file converts all arcs into lines.

To plot a DXB file, you must use the CONFIG command to add a DXB plotter. You can plot to the DXB plotter as you would any plotter. To insert the DXB file into a drawing, type **DXBIN** on the command line.

11.4   Extracting Solid Model Information

As with regular AutoCAD objects, you can inquire and receive information about the model you are constructing. You can inquire about area as well as mass properties.

Area Calculations

The AREA command displays the calculated surface areas of selected solids and regions. You can use the Add option of the AREA command to total the areas of several individual solids.

Mass Property Calculations

You can extract mass properties from solids and regions. This is accomplished with the MASSPROP command by selecting the solid model from which you wish to extract the mass property information. The MASSPROP tool is found in the Inquiry toolbar under the List flyout. Refer to the following data for the sample mass properties of a 2″ cube:

SOLIDS

Mass:		8.0000
Volume:		8.0000
Bounding box:	X:	0.0000 − 2.0000
	Y:	0.0000 − 2.0000
	Z:	0.0000 − 2.0000
Centroid:	X:	1.0000
	Y:	1.0000
	Z:	1.0000
Moments of inertia:	X:	21.3333
	Y:	21.3333
	Z:	21.3333

Products of inertia:	XY: 8.0000
	YZ: 8.0000
	ZX: 8.0000
Radii of gyration:	X: 1.6330
	Y: 1.6330
	Z: 1.6330

Principal moments and X-Y-Z directions about centroid:

I: 5.333 along [1.0000 0.0000 0.0000]
J: 5.333 along [0.0000 1.0000 0.0000]
K: 5.333 along [0.0000 0.0000 1.0000]

Definitions of Mass Property Terms

Here are brief definitions of the terms used for the solid modeling mass property calculations as given by AutoCAD:

Mass	The measure of inertia of a body. Because AutoCAD uses a density of 1, mass and volume have the same value.
Volume	Amount of space occupied by the selected object.
Bounding box	A 2D or 3D rectangular box that encloses the object and upon which the calculations are performed.
Centroid	Center of the selected object.
Moments of inertia	Amount of force required to rotate the selected object about its various axes.
Products of inertia	Values used in determining the forces causing the motion of an object.
Radii of gyration	Radial distance from the point of rotation at which the total mass must be concentrated.
Principal moments	*X-Y-Z* directions about centroid values derived from products of inertia; the first value is the axis through which the moment of inertia is the highest, the second is the axis through which the moment of inertia is the lowest, and the third lies between the highest and the lowest.

Indication of Solid Interferences

It is possible to exhibit the interferences between solids with overlapping masses. The INTERFERE command finds the interference of two or more solids and highlights the pairs that interfere. You can turn the interference volume into a separate solid if you desire. The command allows you to create two selection sets and compare the first set to the second. However, if you only select the first set, the solids in that set will be compared to one another.

 Lab 11.A

Displaying a Solid and Extracting the Solid's Information

Purpose

This lab demonstrates the different methods for controlling the display of a solid model. You will alter the variables that control the display and observe the results. You will also learn how to extract solid property information about your model.

Objectives

You will be able to:

- Change the representation of a solid in wireframe
- Change the representation of a solid in hidden line removal
- Extract solid property information

Primary Commands

ISOLINES
FACETRES
CYLINDER
MASSPROP

Procedure

Initial Settings

1. Start the model called DISSOL (DISplay of SOLids) and enter the following settings or you can open file a3dex11a from the a3d2005 folder. This file has most of the settings already set. All you should need to do is display the View and 3D Orbit toolbars.

Units = decimal
Limits = −3,−3 to 3,3
Grid = 0.5
Snap Incr. = 0.5
Elevation = 0
Thickness = 0
UCS = WCS
Display an axonometric view (VPOINT 0.5,−1,0.5)
Current layer = SOLID

2. Set the ISOLINES variable to 4.

Creating a Solid Cylinder

3. Using the CYLINDER command, create a cylinder with a center at 0,0,0, a radius of 2, and a height of 3. The resulting model should look similar to Figure 11.4A.

Figure 11.4
Altering the display of a cylinder

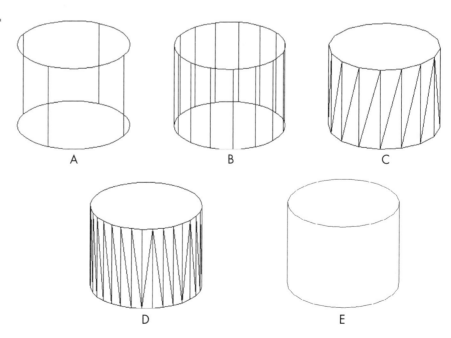

201

202 Lab 11.A
Displaying a Solid and
Extracting the Solid's
Information

Increasing the Number of Tessellation Lines

4. Increase the value of the ISOLINES variable to 15 and then REGEN the screen. The screen should look similar to Figure 11.4B. Note the greater number of lines defining the curves. This helps with visualization but slows down the display of AutoCAD. You will have to decide on a "happy medium" between speed and number of lines.

Setting the Resolution of Solid Facets

5. Set the FACETRES variable to 0.5 and then use the HIDE command (see Figure 11.4C). The cylinder is shown with hidden lines removed, but it is slightly rough looking along the curves.

Smoothing a Surface

6. Increase the FACETRES variable to 1 and then use the HIDE command (see Figure 11.4D). Note how there are now more facets than before and that the curved edge is smoother. Similar to the ISOLINES variable, you need to decide how many facets you require to display a model. The more facets, the more time needed to display the model.

    Now set the variable DISPSILH to 1 and try the HIDE command again (see Figure 11.4D). Remember that DISPSILH does *not* work with the Hidden shade mode for screen display, but will work when plotted. This variable controls whether you see the faces of a solid or just the silhouette. Return the variable to 0 if you want to see the faces.

Performing Mass Property Calculations

7. Using the MASSPROP command, select the cylinder to display the mass properties of the cylinder. Note three items:

   ■ volume of the cylinder
   ■ bounding box
   ■ centroid

   You can easily identify the volume of a cylinder of these proportions, the rectangular bounding box the cylinder fits within, and where the center of the mass of the cylinder is located.

Questions

1. What is the purpose of the ISOLINES variable?

2. What is the purpose of the FACETRES variable?

3. How can you extract a sectional view from a solid?

4. How can you extract mass property information from a solid?

Assignments

1. Experiment with the solid models created in Labs 9.A, 10.A, and 10.B using the ISOLINES and FACETRES variables.

2. Use the MASSPROP command on the solid models created in Labs 9.A, 10.A, and 10.B. Note the results.

C H A P T E R

Advanced Solid Editing

12.1 Introduction

The purpose of this chapter is to introduce you to additional advanced editing commands that you can apply to your solid models. These commands are used to modify the edges, faces, and bodies of solid models. You can perform some advanced functions such as extrude, move, and offset faces or create a shell out of a solid body.

12.2 Solidedit

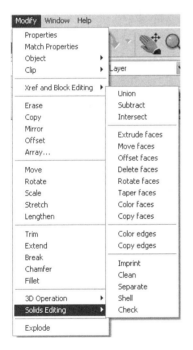

A singular command called SOLIDEDIT is used to perform the advanced solid editing. It has various options, which can be separated into three areas: face editing, edge editing, and body editing. You can find the solid editing commands under the Modify/Solids pull-down menu or in the Solids Modify toolbar. Refer to the following showing the command and its basic options:

Command: **SOLIDEDIT**
Solids editing automatic checking: SOLIDCHECK = 1
Enter a solids editing option [Face/Edge/Body/Undo/eXit] <eXit>:

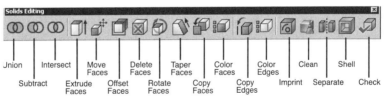

Selection Options

When you are modifying a solid, you must select the correct face, edge, or body. This ensures that the command will function properly. If you select more features than required, the command will usually return an error. To aid in this, there are four options during the selection mode: Undo, Remove, All, and Add. Note that Remove and Add are alternately accessible or inaccessible, depending on your selection.

Undo is used to cancel the most recent selection. Remove is used to remove unwanted features such as faces or edges from the current selection. Add is used to add features. The All option adds all the features to the selection.

12.3 Face Editing

The Face option of the SOLIDEDIT command is used to edit surfaces on the 3D solid object. It contains the following suboptions:

[Extrude/Move/Rotate/Offset/Taper/Delete/Copy/coLor/Undo/eXit] <eXit>:

Each suboption performs a particular change to a selected surface or selected surfaces. The following describes each suboption.

Extrude

The Extrude option extrudes selected planar faces of a solid object to a specified height or along a specified path. More than one face can be selected at a time. As does the standard solid EXTRUDE command, the Face Extrude option allows you to taper the extrusion. Figure 12.1 shows an example of the Face Extrude option. It should be noted that the Extruded Faces tool on the Solids Editing toolbar look identical to the Extrude tool on the Solids toolbar. Take care not to confuse the two.

Move

The Move option moves selected faces of a solid object to a specified height or distance. More than one face can be selected at a time. Similar to the standard MOVE command, you specify a base point as the origin point and a second point as the destination location. Figure 12.1 shows an example of the Face Move option.

Rotate

The Rotate option rotates selected faces or a collection of features on a solid object about a specified axis. It behaves in a similar manner to the standard ROTATION command except that it contains the following suboptions to give you choices of alignment for the rotation axis:

2Points	Aligns the axis of rotation to two points.
Axis by objects	Aligns the axis of rotation with an existing object.
View	Aligns the axis of rotation with the viewing direction of the current viewport that passes through the selected point.
Xaxis, Yaxis, Zaxis	Aligns the axis of rotation with the X, Y, or Z axis that passes through the selected point.

Once you have specified the axis of rotation, the option proceeds as would the standard ROTATION command by asking for a rotation angle or a reference angle. Figure 12.2 shows an example of the Face Rotate option.

Figure 12.1
Application of Face Extrude and Face Move options

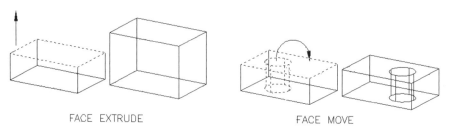

FACE EXTRUDE   FACE MOVE

Figure 12.2
Application of Face Rotate and
Face Offset options

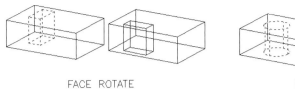

Offset

The Offset option offsets faces equally by a specified distance. It operates similar to the standard OFFSET command except that the faces are moved and not copied. Entering a positive distance increases the size or volume of the solid, whereas a negative distance decreases the size or volume of the solid. Figure 12.2 shows an example of the Face Offset option.

Taper

The Taper option tapers faces to a specified angle. The angle is taken from an axis you specify by clicking two points: the base point and a second point along the selected vector. Figure 12.3 shows an example of the Face Taper option.

Delete

The Delete option deletes or removes selected faces, including fillets and chamfers. Figure 12.3 shows an example of the Face Delete option.

Copy

The Copy option copies selected faces such as a region or a body, similar to the standard COPY command. Figure 12.4 shows an example of the Face Copy option.

Color

The Color option changes the color of selected faces.

Figure 12.3
Application of Face Taper and
Face Delete options

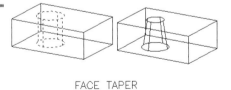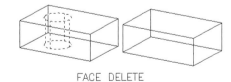

Figure 12.4
Application of Face Copy option

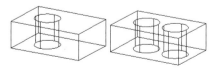

Figure 12.5
Application of Edge Copy option

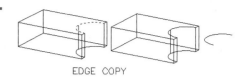

EDGE COPY

12.4 Edge Editing

The Edge option of the SOLIDEDIT command is used to edit individual edges on a 3D solid object. There are only two suboptions to the Edge option: copy and color.

Copy

The Copy option copies 3D edges and creates a line, arc, circle, ellipse, or spline, depending on the shape of the edge copies, and operates in the same manner as the standard COPY command. Figure 12.5 shows an example of the Edge Copy option.

Color

Color changes the color of selected edges.

12.5 Body Editing

The Body option of the SOLIDEDIT command edits the entire solid object. There are several suboptions:

[Imprint/seParate solids/Shell/cLean/Check/Undo/eXit] <eXit>:

The following describes the five main options.

Imprint

The Imprint option imprints an object onto the selected solid. The object must intersect one or more faces on the solid. The following objects are allowed as imprints: arcs, circles, lines, 2D and 3D polylines, ellipses, splines, regions, bodies, and 3D solids. Figure 12.6 shows an example of the Body Imprint option.

Separate

The Separate option separates a solid object with disconnected volumes into independent solid objects.

Shell

The Shell suboption creates a hollow, thin wall with a specified thickness. If you specify a positive thickness, the shell is created outside the solid. If the thickness is negative, the shell is created on the inside of the solid. A solid can have only one shell applied to it. Figure 12.6 shows an example of the Body Shell option.

Clean

The Clean option removes shared edges or vertices having the same surface or curve definition. It also removes imprints.

Figure 12.6
Application of the Body Imprint
and Body Shell options

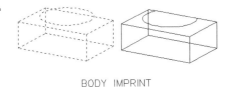

BODY IMPRINT

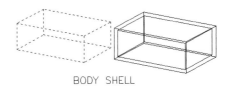

BODY SHELL

Check

The Check option validates that the solid object is a valid ACIS solid.

Lab 12.A   Advanced Solid Editing

Purpose

This lab introduces you to the advanced solid editing commands. This knowledge guarantees more control over the 3D solid models you create.

Objectives

You will be able to:

- Extrude and move a face
- Create a body imprint and extrude it
- Create a body shell

Primary Commands

SOLIDEDIT
Face Extrude
Face Move
Body Imprint
Body Shell

Procedure

1. Start a model called SOLAED (SOLid Advanced EDiting) with the following settings or you can open file a3dex12a from the a3d2005 folder. This file has most of the settings already set. All you should need to do is display the Solids, Solids Editing, View, and 3D Orbit toolbars.

Units = decimal
Limits = −2,−2 to 3,3
Grid = 0.5
Snap Incr. = 0.5
Elevation = 0
Thickness = 0
UCS = WCS
UCSICON = On, Origin, and set to 2D display properties
UCSVP = 0 (always set before creation of viewports)
Solids toolbar = displayed
Solids Editing toolbar = displayed
Current Layer = SOLID
Display a plan view

Creating Regions

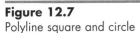

Figure 12.7
Polyline square and circle

2. Draw a rectangular, closed polyline, 2 inches square. Place a 1-inch-diameter circle in the center of the square (see Figure 12.7).

3. Using the REGION command, turn both the square and the circle into regions.

4. Using the SUBTRACT command, subtract the circle from the square.

Configuring the Viewports

5. Using the VPORTS command, configure the viewports for Three: Right with a 3D setup. Using ZOOM and PAN, set up the viewports to look similar to Figure 12.8.

Creating a 3D Solid

6. Using the EXTRUDE command, select the composite region and extrude it 3 inches. The results should be similar to Figure 12.9.

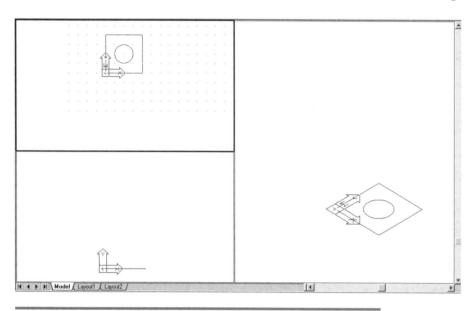

Figure 12.8
Viewport configuration

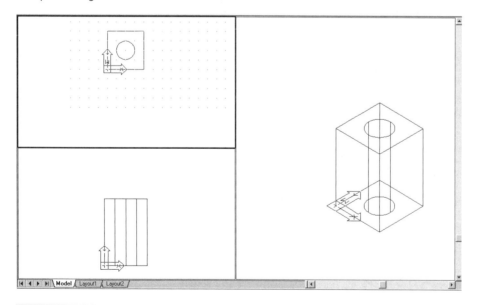

Figure 12.9
Extruded region to create a 3D solid

Face Extrusion

The first advanced solid editing you will perform is to extrude the front face of the 3D solid to make it longer.

7. Make sure the SNAP increment is off and activate the front viewport (lower left).
8. *Note:* If you use Solid Editing tools, some command steps are skipped. Select the SOLIDEDIT command and proceed with the following:

Command: **SOLIDEDIT**
Solids editing automatic checking: SOLIDCHECK = 1
Enter a solids editing option [Face/Edge/Body/Undo/eXit] <eXit>: **F**
Enter a face editing option
[Extrude/Move/Rotate/Offset/Taper/Delete/Copy/coLor/Undo/eXit] <eXit>: **E**
Select faces or [Undo/Remove]: **click the front face in the front viewport**

Figure 12.10 shows the correct highlighted face. If you click the incorrect face, use Undo and click again.

1 face found
Select faces or [Undo/Remove/ALL]: **press Enter to continue**
Specify height of extrusion or [Path]: **2**
Specify angle of taper for extrusion <0>: **press Enter**
Solid validation started. Solid validation completed.
Enter a face editing option
[Extrude/Move/Rotate/Offset/Taper/Delete/Copy/coLor/Undo/eXit] <eXit>:
    press Enter
Solids editing automatic checking: SOLIDCHECK = 1
Enter a solids editing option [Face/Edge/Body/Undo/eXit] <eXit>: **press Enter**

The screen should now look similar to Figure 12.11.

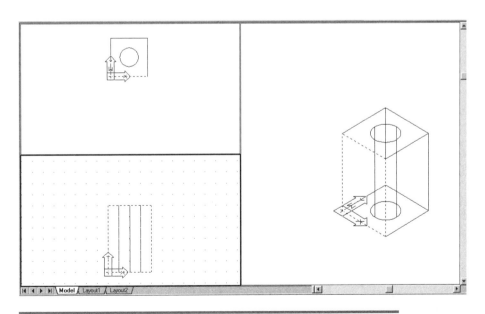

Figure 12.10
Correct face highlighted

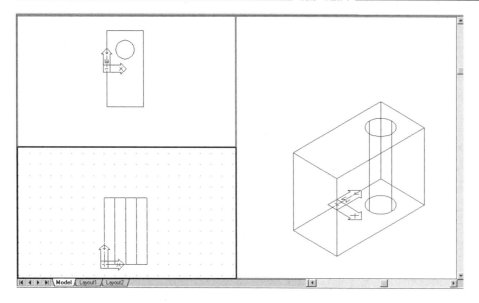

Figure 12.11
3D solid with front face extruded

Face Move

The second advanced solid editing you will perform is to move the circular feature to the center of the newly enlarged surface.

9. Activate the top viewport and make sure the SNAP increment is now on.
10. Select the SOLIDEDIT command and proceed with the following:

Command: **SOLIDEDIT**
Solids editing automatic checking: SOLIDCHECK = 1
Enter a solids editing option [Face/Edge/Body/Undo/eXit] <eXit>: **F**
Enter a face editing option
[Extrude/Move/Rotate/Offset/Taper/Delete/Copy/coLor/Undo/eXit] <eXit>: **M**
Select faces or [Undo/Remove]: **click the edge of the circle in the top viewport**

Figure 12.12 shows the correct highlighted faces.

2 faces found
Select faces or [Undo/Remove/ALL]: **press Enter to continue**
Specify a base point or displacement: **click the center of the circle using snap increment**
Specify a second point of displacement: **click the center of the rectangular face using snap increment**
Solid validation started. Solid validation completed.
Enter a face editing option
[Extrude/Move/Rotate/Offset/Taper/Delete/Copy/coLor/Undo/eXit] <eXit>: **press Enter**
Solids editing automatic checking: SOLIDCHECK = 1
Enter a solids editing option [Face/Edge/Body/Undo/eXit] <eXit>: **press Enter**

The screen should look similar to Figure 12.13.

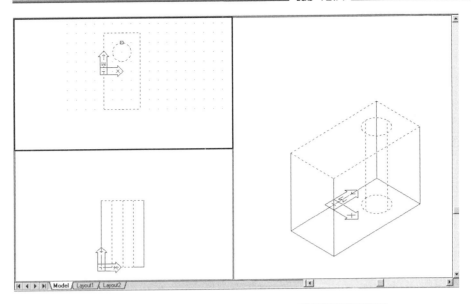

Figure 12.12
Correct faces highlighted

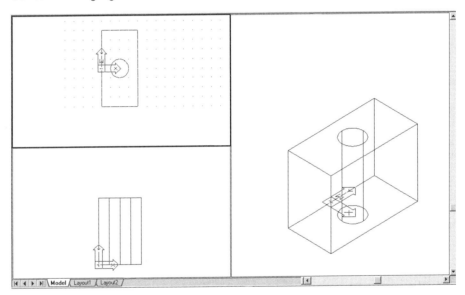

Figure 12.13
Move circular feature

Imprinting a Circle on the Body

The third advanced solid editing you will perform is to imprint a circle onto the body of the solid. This will be used later to extrude a face.

11. Using the ELEVATION command, set the elevation to 3. This should place the working plane at the top face of the solid.
12. Using the CIRCLE command, draw a circle with a diameter of 3 inches in the center of the original circle. Use increment snap to place the circle (see Figure 12.14).
13. Select the SOLIDEDIT command and proceed with the following:

Command: **SOLIDEDIT**
Solids editing automatic checking: SOLIDCHECK = 1
Enter a solids editing option [Face/Edge/Body/Undo/eXit] <eXit>: **B**

211

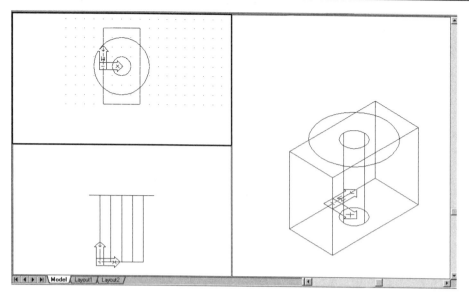

Figure 12.14
Placement of circle

Enter a body editing option
[Imprint/seParate solids/Shell/cLean/Check/Undo/eXit] <eXit>: **I**
Select a 3D solid: **click the 3D solid**
Select an object to imprint: **click the 3 inch circle**
Delete the source object <N>: **Y**
Select an object to imprint: **press Enter to continue**
Enter a body editing option
[Imprint/seParate solids/Shell/cLean/Check/Undo/eXit] <eXit>: **press Enter**
Solids editing automatic checking: SOLIDCHECK = 1
Enter a solids editing option [Face/Edge/Body/Undo/eXit] <eXit>: **press Enter**

The screen should look similar to Figure 12.15.

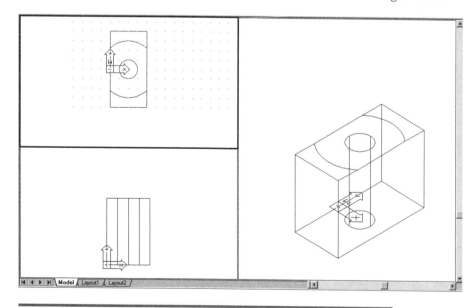

Figure 12.15
The imprinted circle on the solid

Face Extrusion

You are now going to extrude the newly imprinted circle to create new faces.

14. Select the SOLIDEDIT command and proceed with the following:

Command: **SOLIDEDIT**
Solids editing automatic checking: SOLIDCHECK = 1
Enter a solids editing option [Face/Edge/Body/Undo/eXit] <eXit>: **F**
Enter a face editing option
[Extrude/Move/Rotate/Offset/Taper/Delete/Copy/coLor/Undo/eXit] <eXit>: **E**
Select faces or [Undo/Remove]: **click the top arc in the top viewport**

Figure 12.16 shows the correct highlighted face. If you click the incorrect face, use Undo and click again.

1 face found
Select faces or [Undo/Remove/ALL]: **press Enter to continue**
Specify height of extrusion or [Path]: **1**
Specify angle of taper for extrusion <0>: **press Enter**
Solid validation started. Solid validation completed.
Enter a face editing option
[Extrude/Move/Rotate/Offset/Taper/Delete/Copy/coLor/Undo/eXit] <eXit>: **press Enter**
Solids editing automatic checking: SOLIDCHECK = 1
Enter a solids editing option [Face/Edge/Body/Undo/eXit] <eXit>: **press Enter**

The screen should now look similar to Figure 12.17.

Body Shell

You're now going to create a shell on the inside of the 3D solid.

15. Select the SOLIDEDIT command and proceed with the following:

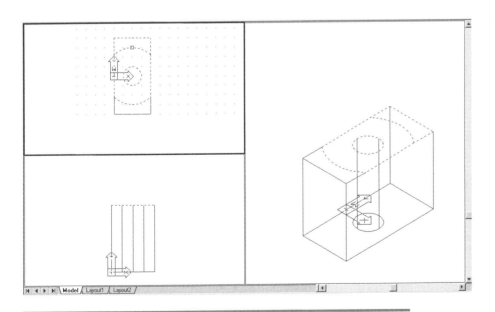

Figure 12.16
Correct face highlighted

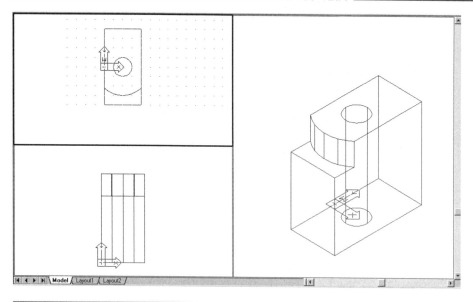

Figure 12.17
3D solid with top face extruded

Command: **SOLIDEDIT**
Solids editing automatic checking: SOLIDCHECK = 1
Enter a solids editing option [Face/Edge/Body/Undo/eXit] <eXit>: **B**
Enter a body editing option
[Imprint/seParate solids/Shell/cLean/Check/Undo/eXit] <eXit>: **S**
Select a 3D solid: **click the solid in the top viewport**
Remove faces or [Undo/Add/ALL]: **press Enter**
Enter the shell offset distance: **0.125**
Solid validation started. Solid validation completed.
Enter a body editing option
[Imprint/seParate solids/Shell/cLean/Check/Undo/eXit] <eXit>: **press Enter**
Solids editing automatic checking: SOLIDCHECK = 1
Enter a solids editing option [Face/Edge/Body/Undo/eXit] <eXit>: **press Enter**

Your screen should appear similar to Figure 12.18. It's hard to tell that there is a shell inside the 3D solid. The following lets you see that there is a shell.

Slicing the Solid

You're going to slice the solid in half to see the shell.

16. Using the View/Shade pull-down menu, set the isometric view to Hidden.
17. Select the SLICE command and proceed with the following:

Command: **SLICE**
Select objects: **click the solid in the top viewport**
1 found
Select objects: **press Enter to continue**
Specify first point on slicing plane by [Object/Zaxis/View/XY/YZ/ZX/3points]
<3points>: **YZ**
Specify a point on the YZ-plane <0,0,0>: **click the center of the circle using snap increment (in the top viewport)**

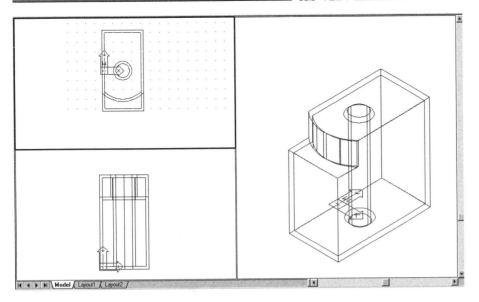

Figure 12.18
A solid with a shell

Specify a point on desired side of the plane or [keep Both sides]: **click the left side of the solid in the top viewport**

The screen should be similar to Figure 12.19.

18. Using the View/Shade pull-down menu, set the isometric viewport to Gouraud shaded with edges on. The viewport should look like Figure 12.20. You can easily see that a shell was created all around the inside of the solid body.
19. Save your model as SOLAED.

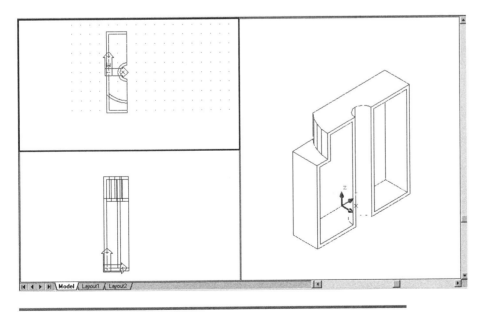

Figure 12.19
The solid sliced in half.

215

Figure 12.20
Shaded, sliced solid

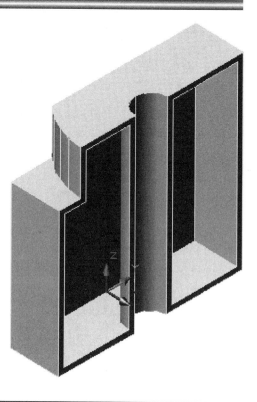

Questions

1. Why is it important to select the correct features to perform a modification?

2. List and briefly explain the eight face editing options.

3. What two options are available to modify an edge?

4. List and briefly explain the five body editing options.

Assignments

1. Create the solid model of a strap clamp shown in Figure 12.21.

2. Create the solid model of a die base shown in Figure 12.22.

3. Examine the solid model of a miniature pneumatic cylinder body, as shown in Figure 12.23. Generate it.

4. Research the works of the British sculptor Henry Moore. Create a solid model that is similar in style to one of his sculptures.

Figure 12.21
Solid model of a strap clamp

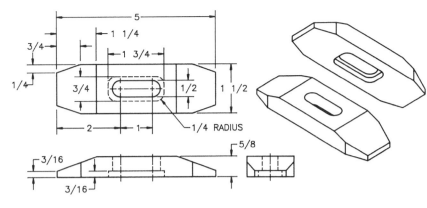

Figure 12.22
Solid model of a die base

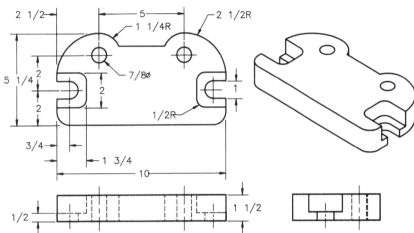

Figure 12.23
Solid model of a miniature pneumatic cylinder

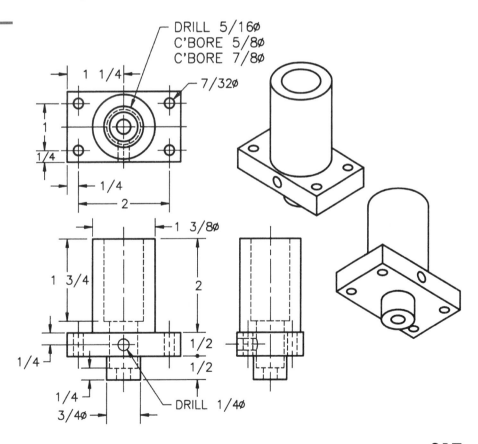

Enhancing the Use of 3D

The chapters in this part will give you some helpful tips, tricks, shortcuts, and timesaving hints for generating 3D models. Experienced users eventually discover these helpers on their own, but they are usually unknown and inaccessible to beginners. Too frequently left out of manuals, these helpful tips will add to your growing experience with 3D CAD. This "wisdom" is incorporated in two chapters: Chapter 13, which focuses on the creation of three-dimensional libraries, and Chapter 14, which covers parametric design.

C H A P T E R

Three-Dimensional Libraries

Overview

This chapter provides instruction on the creation of repetitious libraries of models. It also explains how to modify the elements within these libraries. For the architect, these elements might be window or door styles; for the mechanical engineer, they might be various nuts, bolts, or structural members. Thus, the elements contained within libraries differ from discipline to discipline, but the time-saving nature of the libraries themselves is a constant. This chapter also describes three movement commands that aid in the orientation of 3D objects.

Concepts Explored

- The process of creating 3D symbols and the factors that control their creation
- The scaling characteristics of 3D symbols
- Time-saving techniques in the use of 3D symbols
- The proper orientation for the insertion of 3D symbols
- Differences between blocks and external reference files

13.1 Introduction

As you probably know, 2D users employ blocks to speed up the drawing process. Blocks are of no less importance to 3D users. In fact, blocks have new applications in the 3D realm. Not only can 3D users scale, rotate, and position 3D blocks to suit the models being constructed, but they can also extrude the forms—stretch the blocks three-dimensionally—to make connections, such as those needed in piping, structural, or wood construction.

Because it is now possible to add external files to drawings by either inserting blocks or attaching external reference files (Xrefs), we'll refer to the original term *block* by a new term, *symbol*. A symbol is any group or association of objects that creates a single object, whether it is a block or an Xref. The differences between blocks and Xrefs are explained in Section 13.6, which also explains how Xrefs can be substituted for blocks. Before we do that, however, let's consider how symbols are created and used.

220

13.2 Creation Considerations

The 3D symbol is much the same as the 2D symbol, except of course for the obvious third dimension. The process of constructing a 3D symbol is virtually the same as that of constructing any three-dimensional model. But when a model is being constructed to be used as a symbol, some construction factors become especially important. The addition of the third dimension affects not only the shape of an object, giving it a three-dimensional form, but also the base point and the insertion process.

The orientation of the model during construction has a direct bearing on how it can be oriented when it is inserted into another model. Currently, AutoCAD allows insertion rotation in the *X* and *Y* directions only. A model cannot be rotated in the *Z* axis during the insertion process. Thus, during initial construction, the orientation of the model in the *Z* direction must be considered.

The positioning of the base point in the application of 2D symbols is an easy task. But with three-dimensional models, the *Z* location must be considered because the new location of the base point has an effect on its placement when inserted. When a base point is moved from the 0*Z* location on a model, AutoCAD informs the user, "Warning, *Z* insertion base is not zero." This is nothing to be worried about, only something to note. When entering the base point, the *Z* axis can be entered as a third coordinate (as in 34,21,8) or it can be set automatically by object snapping onto an existing three-dimensional object.

13.3 Insertion and Working Planes

When inserting a 3D model, it is (obviously) important to orient the model. This orientation usually is controlled by the current model's presently active UCS working plane. The user simply activates the working plane on which the 3D symbol is to be inserted. When inserting a 3D symbol, however, orientation is affected by the alignment of the WCS and UCS during the creation of that symbol.

Symbols can be created in two ways—as an original model file or with the use of the BLOCK command inside another model file. Each creation method affects the orientation of the model during insertion differently.

If the model is a separate external file that is to be inserted into a target model, the external file's WCS aligns itself with the target model's active UCS (see Figure 13.1). Therefore, the user must choose the desired alignment based on the WCS *before* the symbol model is created. During symbol creation the user must realize that whichever plane on the symbol model is aligned to the WCS will also be aligned to the UCS of the current model when the symbol is inserted. If you've created a 3D

Figure 13.1
WCS of an external file aligns itself to the active UCS of the current model upon insertion

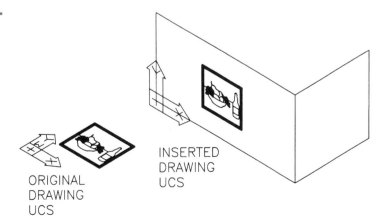

ORIGINAL
DRAWING
UCS

INSERTED
DRAWING
UCS

221

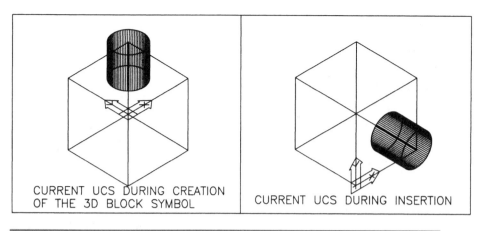

Figure 13.2
UCS of block aligns itself to the active UCS of the current model upon insertion

object and realize that it's in the wrong orientation to the WCS, you can use the ROTATE3D and MIRROR3D commands to change the object's orientation. These are discussed at the end of this chapter before the first lab.

3D VIEWPOINT

Inserting Blocks and the UCS
Always remember to set the UCS to the correct working plane before insertion takes place to ensure proper alignment of the symbol.

If the 3D symbol is created using the BLOCK command, then the UCS working plane that was active during the block creation aligns itself to the current model's active UCS working plane during insertion (see Figure 13.2). In this case, during creation the user must realize that whichever plane on the symbol model is aligned to the UCS when the block is made will be aligned to the current UCS on insertion.

13.4 **Scaling the 3D Symbol**

A 3D symbol can be scaled upon insertion in the same manner as a 2D symbol, with the additional option of scaling in the Z direction.

Figure 13.3 shows the Insert dialog box and the following text. Whether using the dialog box or the command line, you can enter the scaling in all three axes. If you type INSERT on the command line, the dialog box appears. However, if you add the minus prefix, as in −INSERT, you can enter values directly on the command line, as shown next.

Command: **−INSERT**
Enter block name or [?] <cube>: **LSHAPE**
Specify insertion point or [Scale/X/Y/Z/Rotate/PScale/PX/PY/PZ/PRotate]: **3,11,4**
Enter X scale factor, specify opposite corner, or [Corner/XYZ] <1>: **XYZ**
Specify X scale factor or [Corner] <1>: **1**
Enter Y scale factor <use X scale factor>: **1**
Specify Z scale factor or <use X scale factor>: **2**
Specify rotation angle <0>: **0**

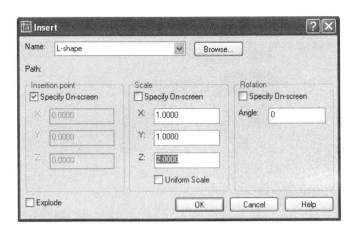

Figure 13.3
Insert dialog box

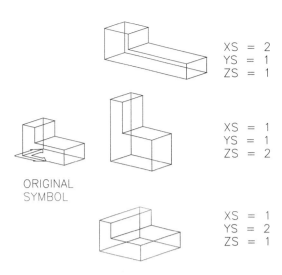

Figure 13.4
Scaling a 3D symbol in any axis

You can scale the 3D symbol independently in all three axes, as shown in Figure 13.4. Independent scaling is explained further in Chapter 14.

13.5 Simple versus Complex Symbol Models

We all know that three-dimensional models can get quite complex in form. A complex model that is going to be used as a symbol can become cumbersome to manipulate on the screen. And, depending on the model's complexity, it can significantly slow the computer's processing speed. To overcome both of these problems at once, we can use the technique of 3D symbol replacement, which uses a complex symbol or series of symbols to define a whole model. The 3D symbol replacement technique simply involves having two definitions of a symbol type—a simple symbol and a complex symbol. The complex symbol is the completed, fully detailed model. The simple symbol is constructed of rectangular forms that outline the area of the symbol and is used for insertion and manipulation in the model. Both symbols should be created as individual drawing files.

The entire model is then laid out using the simple symbols. Once the planning and placement are accomplished and the overall model is complete, the simple symbols in the current workfile are quickly replaced with the complex, fully detailed ones from external files. This is accomplished using AutoCAD's ability to update symbols with the use of the equal (=) sign during the command line insert process (−INSERT). Figure 13.5 illustrates the use of 3D symbol replacement. It shows a layout for a grocery store checkout counter. During the initial construction phase, a simple symbol called CHECKS (CHECKout counter Simple) is inserted into the desired locations. Once construction is complete, the −INSERT command is used to replace the simple symbol with the completed complex symbol called CHECKC (CHECKout counter Complex):

Command: **−INSERT** (Note the use of the minus prefix.)
Enter block name or [?] <cube>: **CHECKS=CHECKC**
Block "checks" already exists. Redefine it? [Yes/No] <N>: **Y**
Block "checks" redefined
Regenerating model
Specify insertion point or [Scale/X/Y/Z/Rotate/PScale/ PX/PY/PZ/PRotate]: **press ESC**
Cancel

223

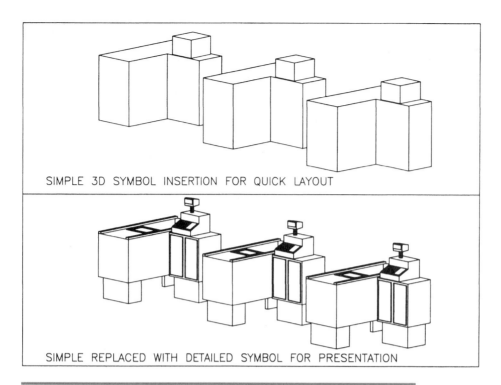

SIMPLE 3D SYMBOL INSERTION FOR QUICK LAYOUT

SIMPLE REPLACED WITH DETAILED SYMBOL FOR PRESENTATION

Figure 13.5
Replacing a simple symbol with a complex one

Now all occurrences of CHECKS in the current workfile are replaced (redefined) by the external file CHECKC. (*Note:* The name of the symbol in the model remains CHECKS, but the symbol itself is redefined as CHECKC.)

Using simple symbols first can save time and make the manipulation process easier. Because a simple symbol does not have as many objects as a complex one, the computer does not have to process as much information. Therefore, movement of the symbols—simply zooming in—is accomplished much more easily and quickly.

Remember that both symbols must be in their own separate files for this type of insertion to work. The files should also be contained in the working subdirectory so that AutoCAD can find them for insertion.

If you want to return to the simple symbol after you redefined the complex symbol, use the −INSERT command again and use CHECKS=CHECKS instead of CHECKS=CHECKC.

13.6 **Xrefs and Blocks**

As mentioned earlier, objects that are grouped or associated into a single object are known as blocks. The process that allows many objects to be manipulated as one in a variety of applications, which has always been and continues to be useful and efficient, now relates both to blocks and external referenced files (Xrefs). Blocks and Xrefs behave in a similar fashion; they both can be attached (inserted), scaled, and rotated. But there are differences, too. Once blocks are created or inserted from external files, the objects are stored in a library inside the drawing file from which they can be recalled at any time. This internal library retains the original form of the block, regardless of what happens to the original external file. This is an important facet of blocks, and it is the main difference between them and Xrefs.

224

Xrefs differ from blocks in another, related way: in their referenced form; Xrefs are not physically part of the drawing. They are like a projection of the external file onto the current workfile (referencing file). The Xref objects are not added to an internal library, only the name and path of the referenced file are kept in the current workfile. The Xrefs can be seen but not modified directly. However, when the original external file is changed, these changes automatically appear in the Xrefs. When a change is made to the referenced files, then that same change is made to the referencing file. Whenever the referencing file is opened in the drawing editor or if the XREF/RELOAD command is used, that file is automatically updated to match the external file.

Because the Xrefs are not actually part of the workfile, they can handicap the workfile in one respect. Although it saves disk space when a workfile storing only the names and not the objects of referenced files is saved, what happens when that disk is given to someone who does not have access to the referenced files? Either the external files have to be given as well or they have to be permanently attached to the referencing file.

You'll need to determine which symbol best suits the needs of each of your models. Use a block symbol when you do not want the block symbol to be altered if the original external file is modified. For example, you would not want the parts (symbols) of a completed design to suddenly change when the external file is updated in some way, so you would use blocks as the symbols in that design. (Should you need to insert revised block symbols in a completed design, you can do so manually by reinserting the block symbols as outlined in Section 13.5.) Use Xrefs when symbols are constantly changing and you want the model to reflect those changes automatically. When you so desire, you can permanently attach an entire external referenced file to a model by using the XREF/BIND command. The XBIND command allows you to partially attach an Xref to a model. Basically, these commands turn Xrefs into blocks.

Automatic Revisions

What makes the Xref so valuable is its ability to affect automatic revisions in the drawing that references it. Whenever a drawing is opened, it automatically recalls the external drawing information from the Xrefs. If one of the externally referenced drawings has been revised, the revision is automatically shown in the newly opened drawing. In this way, you can assemble a complex drawing from individual external referenced drawings and have the main drawing automatically updated whenever changes are made to the individual drawings. A drawing of a mechanical assembly can have its parts updated whenever a change is made to an individual part. A complex building drawing, which might contain architectural, electrical, and mechanical systems, can have each discipline's drawing externally referenced. Whenever a change is made to one of the discipline's drawings, the main drawing reflects the change.

Xref Do's and Don'ts

As mentioned earlier, Xrefs are very similar to blocks but there are some differences. Here are some things they can do, as well as some things they can't:

- You can manipulate the layers of an Xref, but you cannot draw on an Xref layer. Layers added using Xref have the name of the Xref added to the layer name, separated by a vertical bar (|). The Xref layer name is usually grayed out, signifying that it's inaccessible.
- You can object snap to Xref objects but cannot directly change the Xref objects. You can edit Xref objects if you use the REFEDIT command. It opens the Xref objects and allows editing. You must close the Xref objects by using

the REFCLOSE command. This saves the changes to the original Xref drawing.

■ You can see Xref blocks that have been inserted in the Xref drawing, but you cannot use the Xref blocks directly. Blocks of an Xref drawing are called dependent blocks because they are dependent on the Xref drawing of which they are a part.

3D VIEWPOINT

Blocks and Xrefs

You cannot Xref a file into a drawing where the file has already been inserted as a block. You must erase all occurrences of the block and purge the drawing of the block before you can Xref the file.

Attaching and Detaching

To reference a drawing externally, use the Attach option of the XREF command and select the name of the file to attach. If it was already attached, then all occurrences of the Xref in the drawing are updated and another copy is made to be placed in the drawing. If a block of the same name has already been inserted into the drawing, the command is aborted and an error message is displayed. Note that you cannot attach a drawing that is already a block. An example of the command follows:

The following is the procedure to attach an Xref to a drawing:

1. Command: XREF (The External Reference tool can be found in the Insert toolbar or under the Insert Block flyout in the Draw toolbar.)
2. The Xref Manager dialog box appears as shown in Figure 13.6A.
3. Click the Attach button, and the Select Reference File dialog appears as shown in Figure 13.6B. This allows you to click the file to be referenced.
4. Select the file and open.
5. The External Reference dialog box appears, allowing you to place the Xref in the same manner as with a block (see Figure 13.6C). Use the Browse button if you want to select a different file.

You can use the minus prefix with XREF, as in −XREF, to insert manually an Xref. To remove all occurrences of an Xref in a drawing, use the Detach option of the XREF command.

Updating an Xref

To update the definition of an Xref in a currently open drawing, use the Reload option of the XREF command and highlight the files. This command is useful if you suspect that an Xref drawing was modified while you were working on the current drawing.

Binding and the XBIND Command

You may want to attach Xrefs permanently to the master drawing when giving the complete drawing to someone outside the drawing network or to prevent automatic, and perhaps unintentional, revisions. There are two ways to go about this. If you use the Bind option of the XREF command, the entire Xref drawing is then changed

Figure 13.6
Dialog boxes used to attach
and Xref

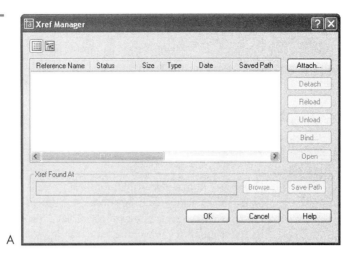

A

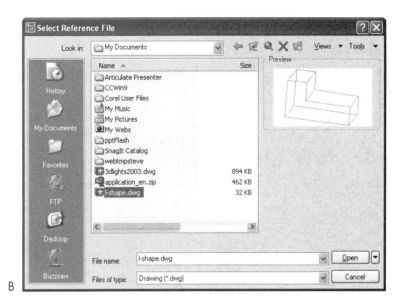

B

C

into a block and added permanently to the drawing (you can still erase the block and purge). If you would like to add part of an Xref drawing, use the XBIND command. In the case of XBIND, you can add blocks, dimension styles, layers, linetypes, and text styles from an Xref without adding the entire Xref drawing. Any part of an Xref that is added to the current drawing is named with the Xref drawing name, except now the name is separated by a number sandwiched between two dollar signs (0). If the name already exists, the number is increased (1).

Path Names

When you attach a drawing, the location of the file (or path) is also stored with the name so that when loading the master drawing, the program knows where to find the Xref drawings. If you change the location of an Xref drawing, you must change its referenced path in the master drawing with the Browse/SavePath options of the XREF command.

Using the Overlay Option

The Overlay option references a drawing into the current drawing. If the current drawing is Xref'ed into an additional drawing, the overlay will not appear. Title blocks commonly use the overlay.

13.7 3D Movement Commands Useful for Moving Blocks

There are three 3D movement commands, ALIGN, ROTATE3D, and MIRROR3D, that can be invaluable in the manipulation of 3D symbols as well as any three-dimensional geometry.

ALIGN Command

The ALIGN command is used to align existing objects to specified 2D or 3D planes. The command performs a rotation and a movement in one command. Refer to Figure 13.7A and the following demonstration of the command:

Command: **ALIGN**
Select Objects: **click the objects you want to move**
Specify 1st source point: **click a point on the objects (P1)**
Specify 1st destination point: **click the point to which you want the first point to travel (P2)**
Specify 2nd source point: **click a second point on the objects (P3)** (This point, in combination with the first point, defines a source axis on the objects.)
Specify 2nd destination point: **click a second destination point (P4)** (This point, in combination with the first destination point, defines the destination axis.)
Specify 3rd source point or <continue>: **click a third source point (P5)** (This point is used with the first and second source points to form a source plane.)
Specify 3rd destination point: **click a third destination point (P6)** (This point is used with the first and second destination points to form a destination plane.)
Scale objects to alignment points?[yes/no]<no>:

The source plane is aligned with the destination plane, causing the objects to move and rotate in 3D space, into the new position as shown in Figure 13.7B.

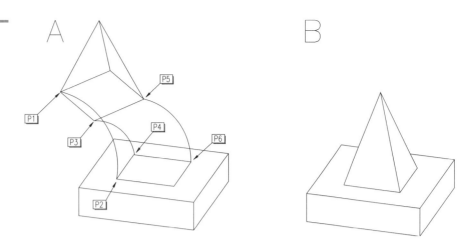

Figure 13.7
Using the ALIGN command

ROTATE3D Command

The ROTATE3D command is used to rotate existing objects about a three-dimensional axis that you define with the Object, Last, View, Xaxis, Yaxis, Zaxis, or 2Point options. Figure 13.8 illustrates the use of the ROTATE3D command using the Entity option:

Command: **ROTATE3D**
Current positive angle: ANGDIR=counterclockwise ANGBASE = 0
Select objects: **click object to rotate**
1 found
Select objects: **press Enter to continue**
Specify first point on axis or define axis by
[Object/Last/View/Xaxis/Yaxis/Zaxis/2points]: **Object**
Select a line, circle, arc, or 2D-polyline segment: **click object to use as the rotation axis**
Specify rotation angle or [Reference]: **enter the desired rotation angle**

OPTION	DEFINITION
Object	Aligns the axis of rotation with an existing object
Last	Uses the last specified axis of rotation
View	Aligns the axis of rotation with the viewing direction of the current viewpoint and a specified point

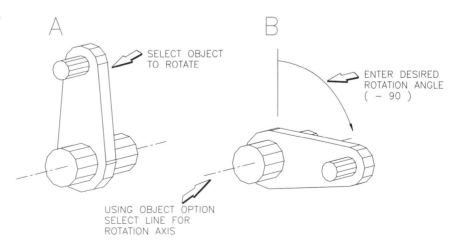

Figure 13.8
Using the ROTATE3D command

SELECT OBJECT TO ROTATE

USING OBJECT OPTION SELECT LINE FOR ROTATION AXIS

ENTER DESIRED ROTATION ANGLE (– 90)

Figure 13.9
Using the MIRROR3D command
with various options

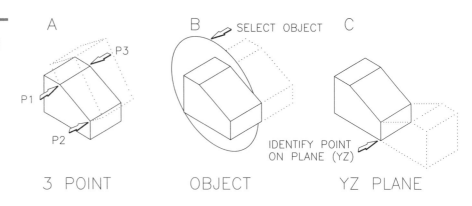

3 POINT   OBJECT   YZ PLANE

Xaxis, Yaxis, Zaxis	Aligns the axis of rotation with one of the X, Y, or Z axes and a specified point
2Point	Aligns the axis of rotation through two specified points

MIRROR3D Command

The MIRROR3D command allows the user to mirror an object about an arbitrary three-dimensional plane defined with the Object, Last, Zaxis, View, XY, YZ, ZX, or 3Point options. Refer to Figure 13.9 and the following for a demonstration of the command:

Command: **MIRROR3D**
Select objects: **click object to mirror**
1 found
Select objects: **press Enter to continue**
Specify first point of mirror plane (3 points) or
[Object/Last/Zaxis/View/XY/YZ/ZX/3points] <3points>: **3P**
Specify first point on mirror plane: **enter or click a point (P1)**
Specify second point on mirror plane: **enter or click a point (P2)**
Specify third point on mirror plane: **enter or click a point (P3)**
Delete source objects? [Yes/No] <N>: **enter N to keep original or Y to erase**

The MIRROR3D command works similarly to the MIRROR command, except that the former requires a mirror plane defined in three dimensions.

 Lab 13.A   House Symbols

Purpose

Lab 13.A familiarizes you with the creation of 3D symbols. In this lab, you will create a symbol of a window, a door, and a fence section. These symbols will be used again in Lab 13.B.

Objective

You will be able to construct 3D symbols.

Primary Commands

PLINE
BASE

Final Model

Figure 13.10 shows the 3D symbols you'll be creating.

Figure 13.10
3D symbols of a window, a
door, and a fence section

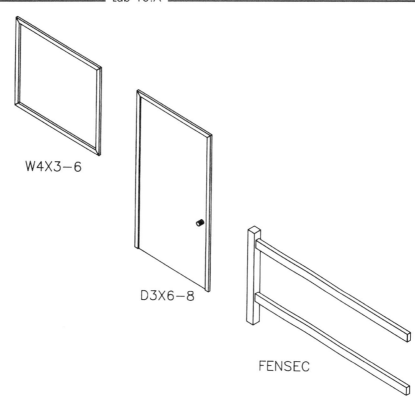

W4X3−6

D3X6−8

FENSEC

Procedure

1. Start a new drawing called W4X3-6 (Window 4′ by 3′6″) with the following settings or you can open file a3dex13a from the a3d2005 folder. This file has most of the settings already set. All you should need to do is display the View and 3D Orbit toolbars.

Units = Architectural
Limits = −1″,−1″ to 5′,10′
Grid = 1′
Snap Incr. = 1″
Elevation = 0
Thickness = 1″
Current Layer = 0
UCS = WCS
UCSICON = On, Origin, and set to 2D display properties
UCSVP = 0 (always set before creation of viewports)
Viewport Configuration = New viewport, Four: Equal, 3D setup
Fill = off

Creating the Window

2. Activate the plan view viewport.
3. Using the PLINE command, draw the window frame as shown in Figure 13.11. Use a width of 2″ for the polyline. The coordinates for the polyline are

P1 = 0,0,0   P2 = 0,3′8″
P3 = 4′2″,3′8″   P4 = 4′2″,0

Close the polyline.

4. Use the BASE command to set the base insertion point of P5. Enter the coordinate 2′1″,3′9″,0. This places the base insertion point at the top rear of the window frame.

Figure 13.11
Window symbol

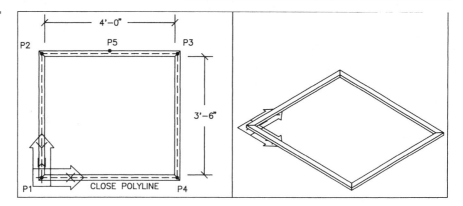

If desired, other features can be added to the model before it is saved.

5. Save the model as W4X3-6.

Creating the Door

6. Erase the window object.
7. Using the PLINE command, draw the door frame as shown in Figure 13.12. Use a width of 2″ for the polyline. The coordinates for the polyline are

   P1 = 0,0,0   P2 = 0,6′9″
   P3 = 3′8″,6′9″   P4 = 3′8″,0

   Do not close the polyline.

8. Set Thickness to 0.5″.
9. Using the PLINE command, draw the door as shown in Figure 13.13. The polyline has a width of 3′6″. The coordinates for the polyline are

   P1 = 1′10″,0,0   P2 = 1′10″,6′8″

10. Draw a circle with a thickness of 2.5″ and a diameter of 2″ at the coordinate 3′4″,2′10″,0.5″. Refer to Figure 13.13 for P3.

Figure 13.12
Door frame symbol

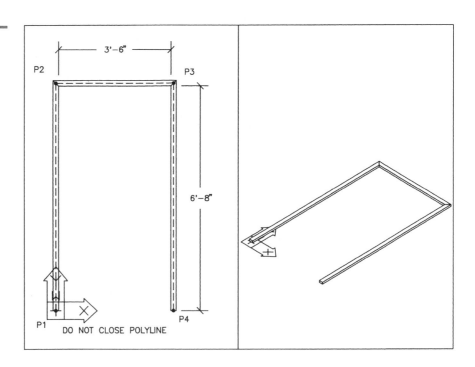

232

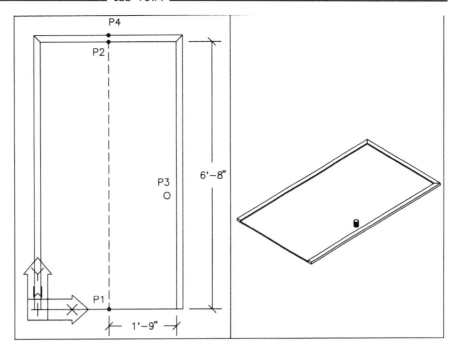

Figure 13.13
Door symbol

11. Use the BASE command to set the base insertion point of P4. Enter the coordinate 1'10",6'10",0. This places the base insertion point at the top rear of the door frame.
12. Save the model as D3X6-8.

Creating the Fence Section

13. Erase the door objects.
14. Use the PLINE command to draw the post (see Figure 13.14). The polyline has a width of 4", a thickness of 4', and an elevation of 0. Draw the polyline from 0,0 to 4",0.

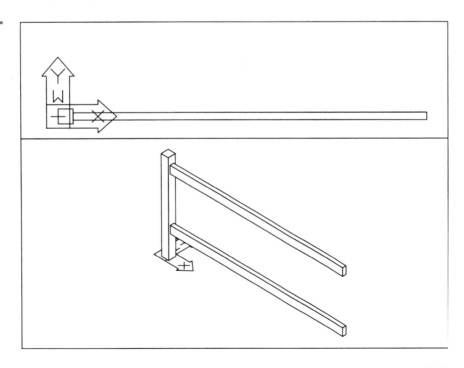

Figure 13.14
Fence section symbol

15. Use the PLINE command to draw the fence boards as shown in Figure 13.14. The polyline has a width of 2″, a thickness of 4″, and a length of 8′. The bottom elevation of the board is 3′4″.
16. Use the COPY command to copy the top board to the lower location. The bottom elevation of the lower board is 1′.
17. Use the BASE command to set the insertion point on the fence section to the coordinate 0,0,0.
18. Save the model as FENSEC (FENce SECtion).

● Lab 13.B   Symbol Insertion

Purpose

Lab 13.B shows you how to manipulate 3D symbols. In this lab, you will insert the symbols of the window, door, and fence section you created in Lab 13.A into the BDWELL model you created in Lab 8.B in Chapter 8.

Objective

You will be able to insert and manipulate 3D symbols.

Primary Commands

UCS
INSERT

Final Model

Figure 13.15 shows the 3D house model you'll be creating.

Procedure

1. Restore the BDWELL model created in Lab 8.B. Use these settings:

Grid = 1′
Snap Incr. = 1″
Elevation = 0
Thickness = 0
Current Layer = 0
UCS = WCS
UCSICON = On, Origin, and set to 2D display properties
UCSVP = 0 (always set before creation of viewports)
Viewport Configuration = New viewport, Four: Equal, 3D setup
TREE layer = frozen
Fill = off

Inserting the Door

2. Create a layer called DOOR, and make it current.
3. Using the UCS command, create a working plane on the front of the building, as shown in Figure 13.16.

Figure 13.15
3D house model

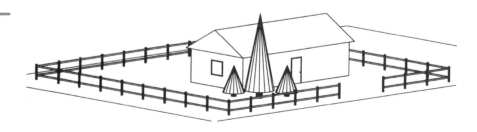

Rendering of 3D model with materials added — day scene
(IMAGE COURTESY OF TED WHITE)

Rendering of 3D model with materials added — night scene
(IMAGE COURTESY OF ERIC ALLARD)

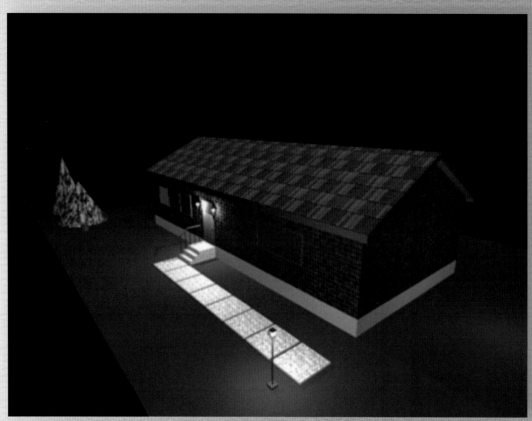

Chapter 18 — Rendering of 3D house model with materials added

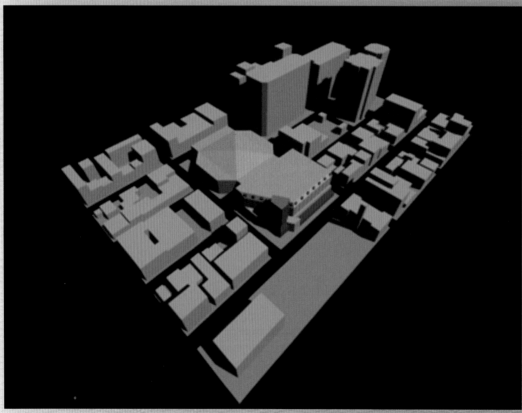

Chapter 19 — Rendering of 3D city model

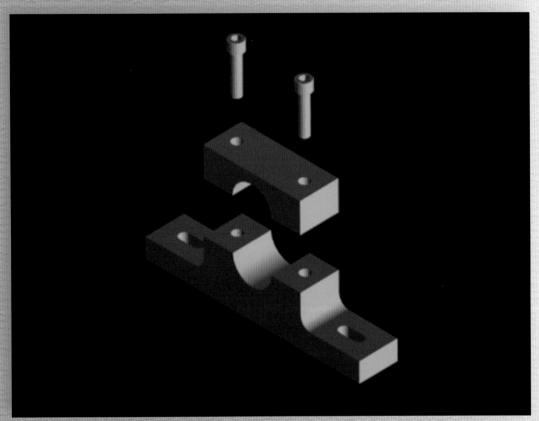

Chapter 20 — Rendering of 3D mechanical model

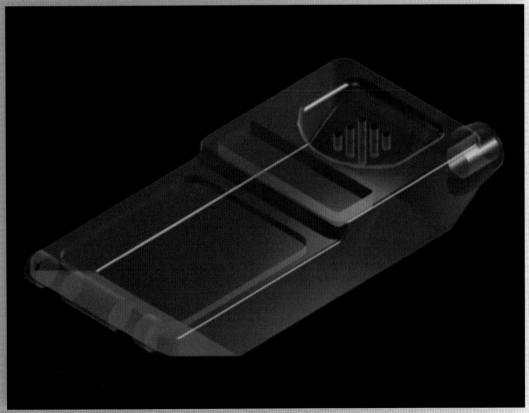

Chapter 21 — Rendering of 3D phone model with glass material added

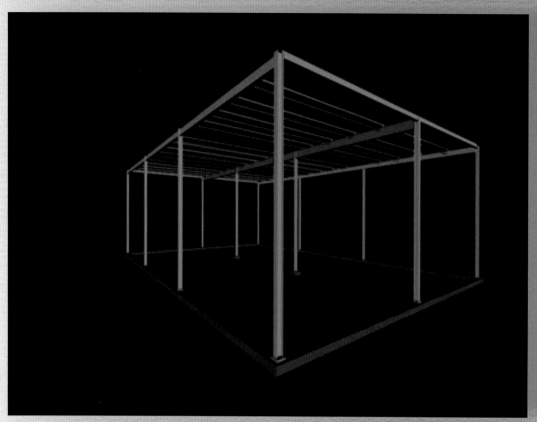

Chapter 22 — Rendering of 3D structural model

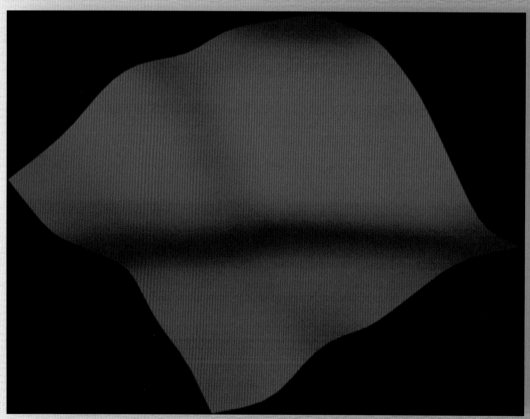

Chapter 23 — Rendering of 3D terrain model

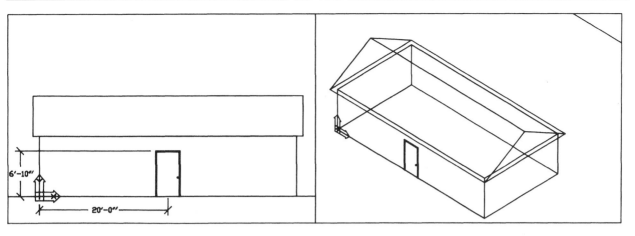

Figure 13.16
Inserting the door

4. Activate the front view viewport.
5. Use the INSERT command to insert the door (D3X6-8), as shown in Figure 13.16. The scale is kept at 1 (full size). Note how the door is aligned to the wall.

Inserting the Window

6. Create a layer called WINDOW, and make it current.
7. Using the UCS command, create a working plane on the left side of the building, as shown in Figure 13.17.
8. Activate the right-side viewport and use the PLAN/UCS command to display the left-side view.

9. Use the INSERT command to insert the window (W4X3-6), as shown in Figure 13.17. The scale is kept at 1 (full size). Note how the window is aligned to the wall.

Inserting the Fence Section

10. Create a layer called FENCE, and make it current.
11. Using the UCS command, set the UCS to the WCS.
12. Activate the plan view viewport.

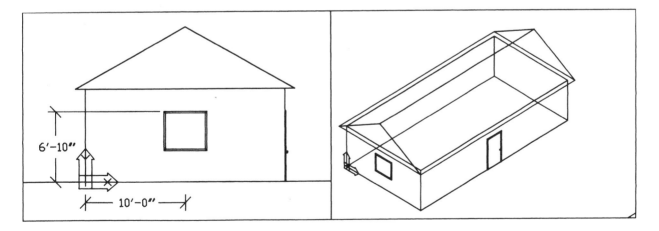

Figure 13.17
Inserting the window

235

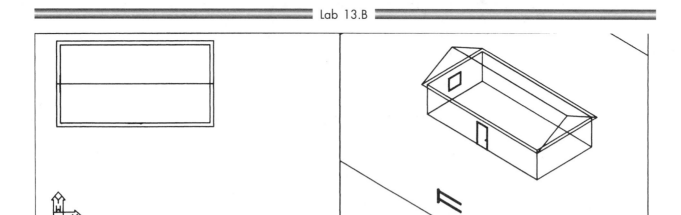

Figure 13.18
Inserting the fence section

13. Use the INSERT command to insert the fence section (FENSEC) at the coordinate 68′8″,5′2″,0 (see Figure 13.18).

Copying the Symbol

14. Use the ARRAY command to copy the fence section along the front to the left, as shown in Figure 13.19. The distance between the posts is 8′4″. The array has one row and three columns.
15. Repeat the insert and copy procedures to form the fence around the lot perimeter (see Figure 13.20).

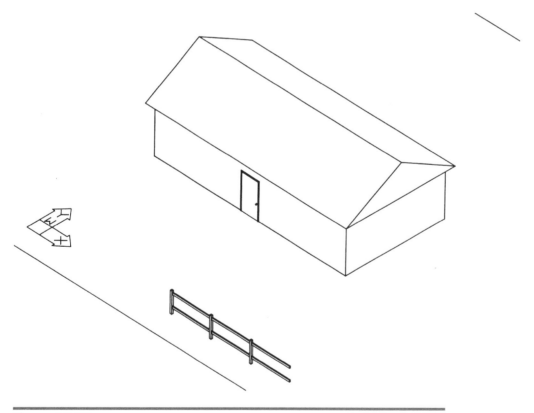

Figure 13.19
Copying the fence along the front

Figure 13.20
Layout of the fence perimeter

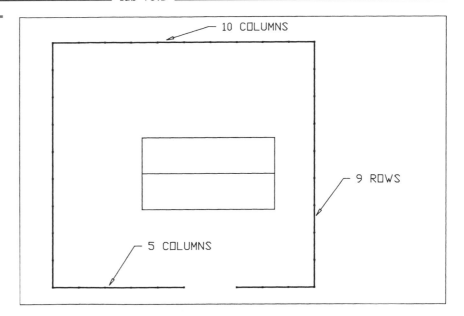

16. Use PLINE to add the missing fence post.
17. Thaw the TREE layer and use the VPOINT command to display a view similar to that shown in Figure 13.15. Use the HIDE command and observe the results.
18. Save the model as BDWELL.

Lab 13.C   Simple versus Complex Blocks and Xrefs

Purpose

Lab 13.C demonstrates how to insert simple blocks in a model and then replace them with complex blocks when the layout is complete. You will also practice the application of Xrefs to revise a model automatically. This lab makes use of the models created in Chapter 5, Labs 5.B and 5.C, the table and chair models. It will also make use of the 3D floor plan from Assignment 4 in Chapter 5.

Objectives

You will be able to

■ Use simple and complex blocks
■ Use Xrefs to revise a model automatically

Primary Commands

INSERT
XREF

Procedure

Part A: Simple and Complex Blocks—Simple Table

1. Start a new drawing called TBSIM (TaBle SIMple) with the following settings or you can open file a3dex13c from the a3d2005 folder. This file has most of the settings already set. All you should need to do is display the View and 3D Orbit toolbars.

Units = Architectural
Limits = −1′,−1′ to 6′,4′
Grid = 1′
Snap Incr. = 1′

237

UCS = WCS
UCSICON = ON, ORIGIN

2. Refer to Figure 13.21 and create the 3D rectangle using the AI_BOX command. This represents a simplified version of the TABLE model.

Command: **AI_BOX**
Corner of box: **0,0,0**
Length of box: **5′**
Cube/<width>: **3′**
Height: **2′5″**
Rotation angle about Z axis: **0**

3. Using the BASE command, set the base insertion point to 2′6″,1′6″,0. This is the center of the box in the *X* and *Y* axes. This point must match the complex TABLE model.
4. Save the drawing as TBSIM.

Simple Chair

5. Start a new drawing called CHSIM (CHair SIMple) with the following settings:

Units = Architectural
Limits = −1′,−1′ to 3′,2′
Grid = 1″
Snap Incr. = 1″
UCS = WCS
UCSICON = ON, ORIGIN

6. Refer to Figure 13.22 and create the model using a line and an arc with a 3′5″ thickness. This represents the simplified version of the CHAIR model.
7. Using the BASE command, set the base insertion point to 9-1/2″,8-1/2″,0. This is the center of the model in the *X* and *Y* axes. This must match the complex CHAIR model.
8. Save the drawing as CHSIM.

Simple Layout

9. Start a new drawing called BHALL (Banquet HALL) with the following settings:

Units = Architectural

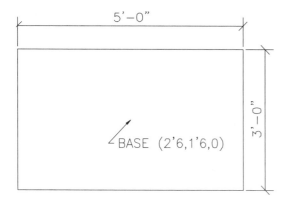

Figure 13.21
TBSIM model

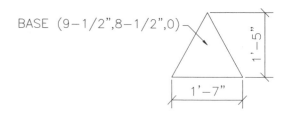

Figure 13.22
CHSIM model

Figure 13.23
Simple layout

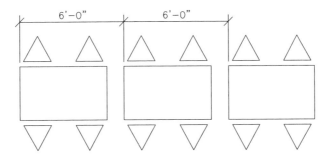

Limits = −1′,−1′ to 19′,7′
Grid = 1′
Snap Incr. = 6″
UCS = WCS
UCSICON = ON, ORIGIN

10. Insert the simple blocks of the table (TBSIM) and the chair (CHSIM) to create the layout shown in Figure 13.23. Remember to rotate the chair when required.
11. Save the model as BHALL.

Replacing the Simple with the Complex

12. Display an axonometric view (1,−1,1).
13. Using the INSERT command, replace the simple table with the complex one:

Command: **−INSERT** (Note the use of the minus prefix.)
Enter block name or [?] <cube>: **TBSIM=TABLE** (The TABLE model was created in Lab 5.B.)
Block "tbsim" already exists. Redefine it? [Yes/No] <N>: **Y**
Block "tbsim" redefined
Regenerating model
Specify insertion point or [Scale/X/Y/Z/Rotate/PScale/PX/PY/PZ/PRotate]: **ESC**
Cancel

The complex table should now be displayed in the scene, as shown in Figure 13.24.

14. Repeat the INSERT command, now replacing the simple chair with the complex one:

Figure 13.24
Model with complex tables and simple chairs

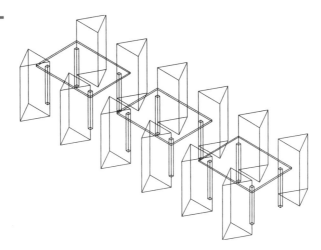

239

Figure 13.25
Complete replacement

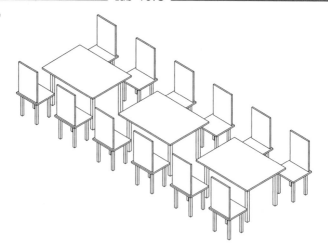

Command: **−INSERT** (Note the use of the minus prefix.)
Enter block name or [?] <cube>: **CHSIM=CHAIR** (The CHAIR model was created in Lab 5.C.)
Block "chsim" already exists. Redefine it? [Yes/No] <N>: **Y**
Block "chsim" redefined
Regenerating model
Specify insertion point or [Scale/X/Y/Z/Rotate/ PScale/PX/PY/PZ/PRotate]: **press ESC**
Cancel

The scene now shows the complex tables and chairs illustrated in Figure 13.25.

15. Save the model as BHALL.

Reversal

16. Using the INSERT command once more, return the tables and chairs to their simple forms. Use the following commands:

Command: −INSERT
CHSIM=CHSIM

and

Command: −INSERT
TBSIM=TBSIM

It is that easy to switch from simple to complex blocks and back again.
Quit this drawing.

Part B: Using Xrefs

17. Make a copy of the complex table and chair models. Name the copies TBOFF (TaBle OFFice) and CHOFF (CHair OFFice), respectively.
18. Open the 3D floor plan from Assignment 4 in Chapter 5. Turn the FILL variable off.
19. Display a plan view, as shown in Figure 13.26.
20. Using the XREF command, attach the TBOFF model, as shown in Figure 13.27. The table should have a scale of 1 and a rotation of 180 degrees.

21. Using the XREF command, attach the CHOFF model, as shown in Figure 13.28. The chair should have a scale of 1 and a rotation of 180 degrees.
22. Repeat to fill the office as shown in Figure 13.29.
23. Save the model as OFFICE.

240

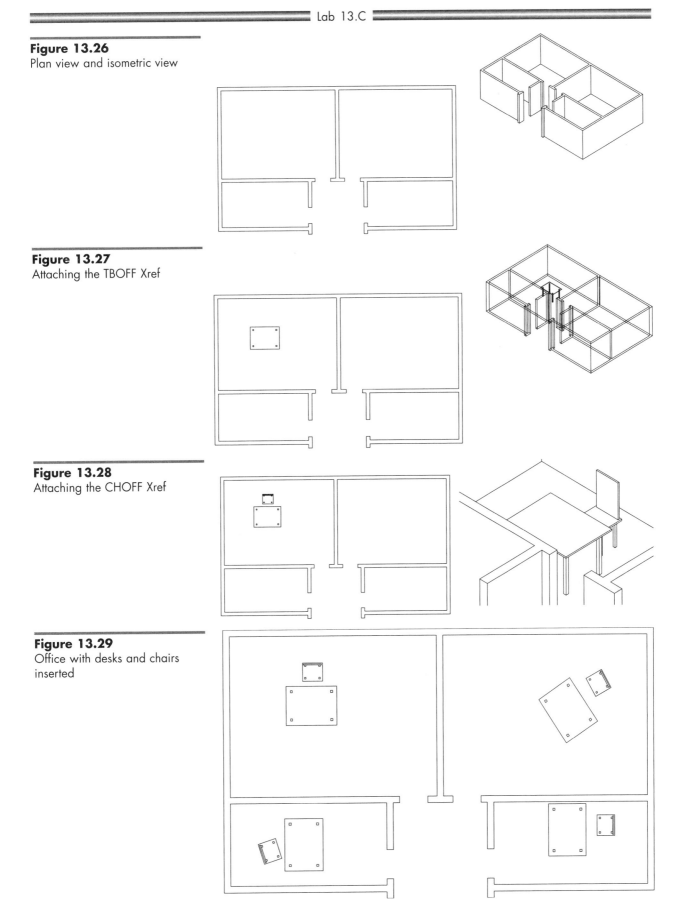

Figure 13.26
Plan view and isometric view

Figure 13.27
Attaching the TBOFF Xref

Figure 13.28
Attaching the CHOFF Xref

Figure 13.29
Office with desks and chairs inserted

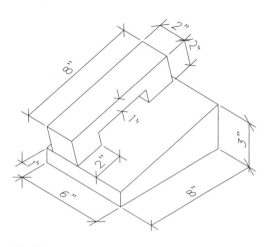

Figure 13.30
PHONE drawing

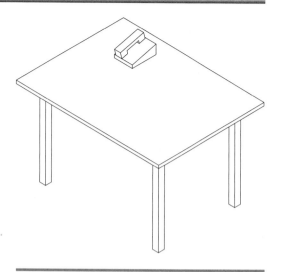

Figure 13.31
Inserting the PHONE on the table

24. Start a new drawing called PHONE with the following settings:

Units = Architectural
Limits = −1″,−1″ to 7″,9″
Grid = 1″
Snap Incr. = 0.5″
UCS = WCS
UCSICON = ON, ORIGIN

25. Create the model shown in Figure 13.30 using lines and 3D faces.
26. Set the BASE point to one of the corners of the phone.
27. Save the model as PHONE.
28. Open the TBOFF model.
29. Using the INSERT command, place the PHONE model on the table, as shown in Figure 13.31.

Figure 13.32
The final outcome of the Xrefs

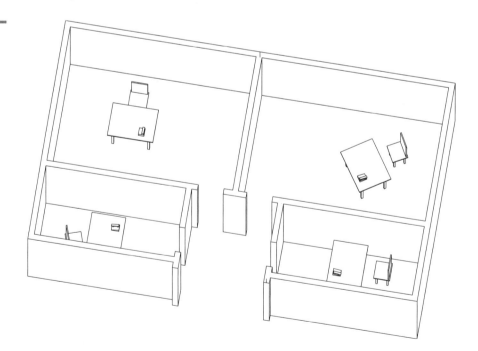

30. Save the model as TBOFF.
31. Open the OFFICE file and watch the results. The PHONE model has been added automatically to every table in the office. The orientation of the phones may be incorrect based on the orientation of the tables with which they were first attached using XREF. To correct the orientation, use the ROTATE command to swing the tables around as needed. Figure 13.32 shows the final layout.

Questions

1. How does the orientation of a symbol model in its own model file affect its orientation when it is inserted into another model?

2. How does the orientation of a symbol model when it is made into a block affect its orientation when it is inserted?

3. What option allows scaling of a 3D symbol independently in all three axes?

4. What is the benefit of using simple 3D symbols and then replacing them with more complex ones?

5. What is the procedure for replacing 3D symbols in a model?

6. Why is it convenient to use polylines to construct window frames?

7. You must take into consideration one extra factor when using the BASE command to create 3D symbols. What is it?

8. What must you always remember to do just before inserting a 3D symbol?

9. What 3D movement commands assist in the movement of objects in three-dimensional space?

Assignments

1. Use the previously created models given in the following list to assemble the kitchen table shown in Figure 13.33. Save the model as BKIT. It will be used in Chapter 14, Assignment 1; in Lab 15.C in Chapter 15; and in Chapter 17, Assignment 2.

3D SYMBOL	SOURCE
TABLE	Lab 5.B
CHAIR	Lab 5.C
COFMK	Lab 7.C
COFPT	Lab 8.A
COFMUG	Chapter 8, Assignment 1
SPOON	Chapter 8, Assignment 5

2. Assemble a nut and bolt, as shown in Figure 13.34. Use the previously created models given in the following list. Save the model as NBOLT. Remember to set the BASE point of the symbol during the creation stage.

3D SYMBOL	SOURCE
BOLT	Chapter 7, Assignment 1
NUT	Chapter 7, Assignment 5

3. Create a 3D symbol of a hexagon bolt head (see Figure 13.35). The model should fit within a 1-unit cubic area. Remember to add a 3D face to the top of the hexagon. Save it as BHEAD. This will be used in Chapter 14, Assignment 3.

Figure 13.33
Kitchen table layout

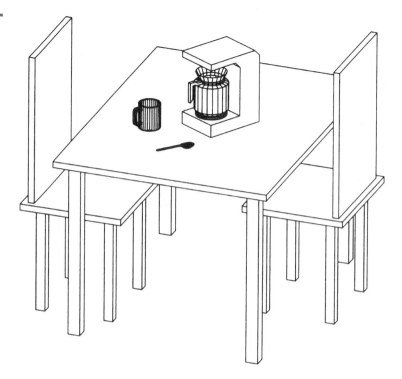

4. Generate the two common architectural models shown in Figure 13.36. Use 3D objects, such as the box and the pyramid, to perform the construction. Create the models using the full-size dimensions they would have if used on a house. Assume the lamppost would be placed beside a driveway and the coach light would

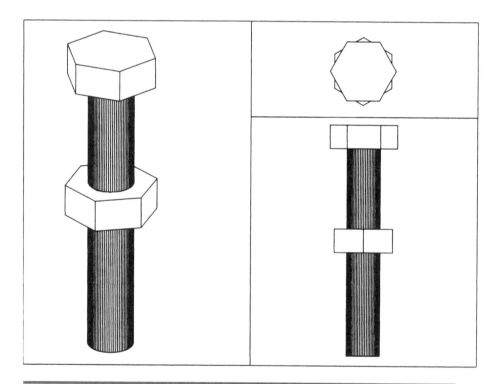

Figure 13.34
Nut and bolt assembly

Figure 13.35
Hexagon bolt head symbol

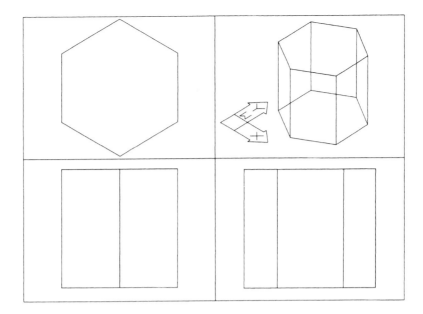

be placed beside the exterior entrances. Save the lamppost as LPOST and the coach light as COLIT.

5. Construct a grocery store checkout in a manner similar to Figure 13.5. Create a simple 3D symbol and perform the initial layout. Then, create the fully detailed checkout symbol and replace the simple symbol with the complex 3D symbol. Once you have completed the layout, try switching the symbols back and forth.

Figure 13.36
Lamppost and coach light models

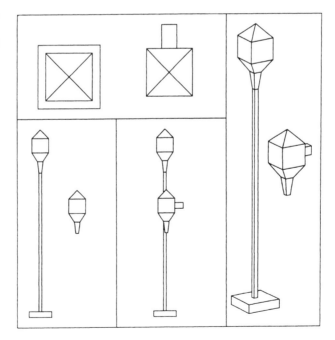

3D Parametric Design

Overview

This chapter discusses parametric design as it relates to 3D models. It is always useful to have on hand a model that can be used in several applications. In this chapter, we'll show how to create a model whose shape can be altered to suit various applications and we'll give specific examples of 3D parametric models.

Concepts Explored

- A description of parametric design
- The three parametric symbol types, their differences, and their uses
- Object snapping in the setting of the parametric parameters
- How to create and apply parametric symbols

14.1 Introduction

Parametric design creates a standard design that can be applied to differing sets of parameters. The standard design, then, is capable of changing and conforming to new parameters. The process followed during the creation of the standard design gives the model its parametric properties.

As Chapter 13 explained and illustrated, 3D symbols are extremely useful devices for saving time and labor. Here, in Chapter 14, we'll see how giving 3D symbols parametric properties makes their usefulness infinitely greater. We'll illustrate how parametric design techniques can be applied to 3D symbols, and we'll explain the process for creating 3D symbols that allows different parameters to be applied to them.

It should be noted that there are other Autodesk products that have more advanced parametric capabilities. One is Mechanical Desktop that works inside of AutoCAD. Chapter 24 gives you a brief overview of the program. Another Autodesk program is Inventor. It is a very sophisticated parametric modeler that works outside of AutoCAD.

The purpose of this chapter is to give you some exposure to parametric capabilities. Initially they seem cumbersome because it appears that they can be accomplished with other methods. But the intent is to introduce you to the concept and be able to apply them in the future when you do find a need. When you become more proficient, you'll find that their application is very efficient.

14.2 Parametric Symbol Types

The essence of parametric symbol design is AutoCAD's ability to scale 3D blocks independently in all three axes upon insertion. This ability creates three parametric symbol types: The first is referred to as 3ES, for 3 Equal axes Scaling; the second is referred to as 3US, for 3 Unequal axes Scaling; and the third is referred to as 2ES, for 2 Equal axes Scaling.

The parameters of a type 3ES parametric symbol allow it to be scaled uniformly in all three axes. Basically, the symbol can get larger or smaller, but its overall proportions remain the same. Because the scaling is equal, any complex symbol can be used, such as a large mug versus a small mug or a large carton versus a small carton, as shown in Figure 14.1. Once created, the model can be used over and over again at any size desired as long as each axis scaling remains equal. If a 3ES parametric symbol is inserted and the scaling is not equal, a distorted symbol results. While this result might be desirable in certain cases, keep in mind that the 3ES parametric symbol was designed for equal scaling in all three axes.

The second parametric symbol type, 3US, allows unequal scaling in all three axis directions. This ability means the symbol is much more versatile, but its shape is restricted. Because of its need to be scaled unequally in all three axes without distortion, the 3US parametric symbol must be shaped without features, like a box. At first glance, one may doubt that a featureless box can be of any use. In fact, however, the uses of a 3D symbol that can be stretched in any direction are almost endless (see Figure 14.2). You can form the box into blocks of any size or shape. You can stretch

Figure 14.1
3ES parametric symbols

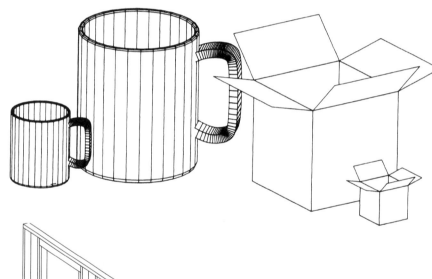

Figure 14.2
3US parametric symbols

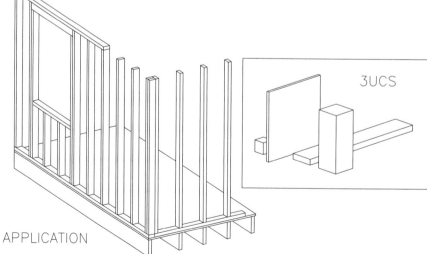

it into sheets of any thickness. You can use the box to create planks or posts of wood in any length simply by specifying different scales in each of the three axes. It is up to the user's need to define this symbol's boundaries.

Two of the scaling axes of our third parametric symbol type, 2ES, must remain equal, whereas the third can be any size. The 2ES is a combination of the 3ES and the 3US parametric symbol types. As a result, it can have a complex shape along two axes and be extruded or stretched along the third. This compromise between the 3US and the 3ES symbol types allows the 2ES symbol to take on unique shapes (like a 3ES) while retaining the ability to be stretched (similar to the 3US). The 2ES parametric symbol can be categorized according to how the third axis functions. In one category are 2ES symbols with a constant third axis. The two axes that define the profile of this kind of 2ES symbol are enlarged or reduced while the third axis remains constant or at the same thickness (see Figure 14.3). This type of 2ES symbol has limited applications.

In the other category is a much more versatile kind of 2ES symbol. Its two profile axes remain the same, whereas its third axis controls the transformation. Like the thickness property, this allows the user to take a profile and extrude it to any length, but with 2ES the user has more control and maneuverability. The profile can be any complex form, such as structural members, pipe of any diameter, and complicated moldings that are used in extruded aluminum window and door frames, and the complex profile can be extruded to any length, thereby allowing for quick construction of any model (see Figure 14.4).

Figure 14.3
2ES parametric symbols with third axis remaining constant

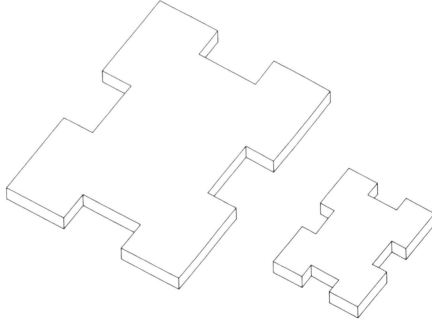

Figure 14.4
2ES parametric symbols with extrusion along the third axis

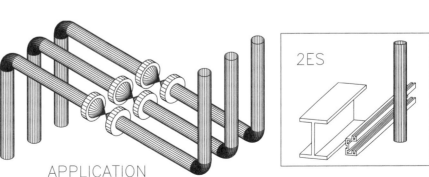

APPLICATION

2ES

Whenever you are going to create a 3D symbol, you should first categorize it by its parametric type. Give some thought to how you are going to apply it and how it could be best utilized before you create it. In this way, you'll design a more efficient and versatile 3D symbol. As always, remember that blocks that have unequal scaling cannot be exploded into their original objects.

14.3 **Object Snap and Scaling**

Once you have created a parametric symbol in 3D, you can scale it by snapping to an existing object to set the scaling distance along a particular axis. All that is required when using this simple technique is to have some type of object to snap to, so that the axis scaling can be set. Then you literally need only indicate the start and the end, and the 3D parametric symbol astonishingly stretches to conform to the indicated length. You'll find this technique extremely helpful when using 2ES symbols where lengths of materials are required. Items such as pipe, wood, or structural members can be assembled easily using this method.

Refer now to Figure 14.5, where the scaling method is illustrated. Part A of the figure shows two 3D symbols already in place. In this example, the symbols are two I-beams. The UCS is aligned to the face of one of the symbols. The faces of both the symbols are parallel and in line with each other.

In part B of Figure 14.5, the 3D parametric type 2ES symbol of an I-beam is inserted and is snapped onto the midpoint of the face of the lower I-beam. In part C, the inserted (using −INSERT) I-beam symbol is scaled in the Z axis to conform to indicated length by snapping to the midpoint of the upper I-beam's face. Thus, as Figure 14.5 shows, the actual steps from insertion to scaling are few.

The following labs give direct hands-on experience in the creation and application of two parametric symbols. You should be able to apply what you practice in these labs to the creation of other parametric symbols, whatever their type (3US, 3ES, or 2ES) and abilities.

Figure 14.5
Scaling a 3D symbol using snap points

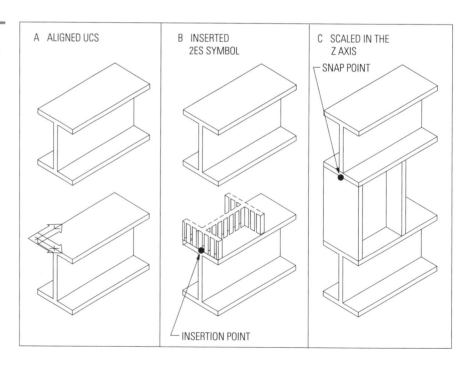

UCS and Scaling

The orientation of the UCS working plane is crucial for proper stretching along the Z axis. Stretching of 2ES parametric symbols usually occurs along the Z axis so it is particularly important to determine in which direction the Z axis is pointing during the scaling.

Lab 14.A   Parametric Cube and Deck

Purpose

Lab 14.A shows you how to create a type 3US parametric symbol. After you create a symbol of a cube, you will learn how to use it as a 3US parametric symbol to create a wooden deck.

Objectives

You will be able to:

- Construct a type 3US parametric symbol
- Apply the parametric symbol in the creation of a model

Primary Commands

INSERT–XYZ
BASE

Final Model

Figure 14.6 shows both the type 3US parametric symbol and the final model you'll be creating.

Procedure

1. Start a new model called PCUBE (Parametric CUBE) with the following settings or you can open file a3dex14a from the a3d2005 folder. This file has most of the settings already set. All you should need to do is display the necessary toolbars.

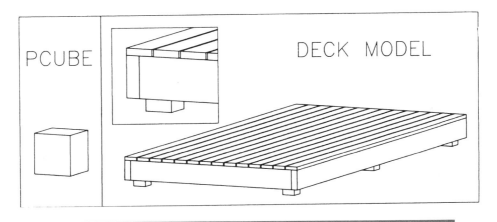

Figure 14.6
Type 3US parametric symbol and the final model

Units = architectural
Limits = −1″,−1″ to 1″,1″
Grid = 1″
Snap Incr. = 1″
Elevation = 0
Thickness = 1″
Current Layer = 0
UCS = WCS
UCSICON = On, Origin, and set to 2D display properties
UCSVP = 0 (always set before creation of viewports)
Fill = off

Creating the Parametric Cube

In this case, there is no need to create an orientation cube because the piece of geometry that the user is constructing is a cube.

2. A 3D surface object is going to be used for this symbol.
3. Use the AI_BOX command to create a surface model that is a 1″ cube (1 × 1 × 1), as shown in Figure 14.7.
4. Set the BASE point to 0.5,0,0 so that it is halfway along the X-axis cube.
5. Save the model as PCUBE.

Constructing the Deck

You are going to create a wooden deck using 4 × 4s, 2 × 6s, and 1 × 4 decking. The sizes used for the lumber are the nominal sizes as opposed to the actual sizes (see following list). This makes it easier to construct the deck at this point. Although you could use actual lumber sizes, you would have to change the lengths and positions accordingly. The deck itself is 10′ long, 4′11-1/4″ wide, and a total of 9″ high.

NOMINAL SIZE	ACTUAL SIZE
4 × 4	3-1/2 × 3-1/2 construction lumber
2 × 6	1-1/2 × 5-1/2 construction lumber
1 × 4	1 × 3-1/2 decking

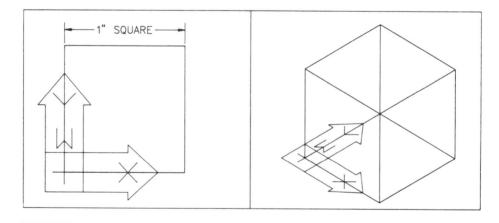

Figure 14.7
PCUBE model

6. Start a new model called DECK with the following settings or you can open file a3dex14adeck from the a3d2005 folder. This file has most of the settings already set. All you should need to do is display the necessary toolbars.

Units = architectural
Limits = −1′,−1′ to 11′,6′
Grid = 1′
Snap Incr. = 1/4″
Elevation = 0
Thickness = 8″
Current Layer = OCUBE
UCS = WCS
UCSICON = On, Origin, and set to 2D display properties
UCSVP = 0 (always set before creation of viewports)
Fill = off

Creating the Orientation Cube and Division Line

7. Using the LINE command, draw a box, as shown in Figure 14.8. The start should be at 0,0,0, and the box should be 10′ 0″ by 4′11-1/4″. This allows the deck boards to cover the area evenly.
8. Set the elevation to 5″ and the thickness to 0. This allows a line to be drawn around the orientation cube at the height of 5″ above the ground. This line, which we'll call the division line, will be used to insert the PCUBE model.
9. Using the LINE command, draw a line around the perimeter of the orientation cube. This is the division line.

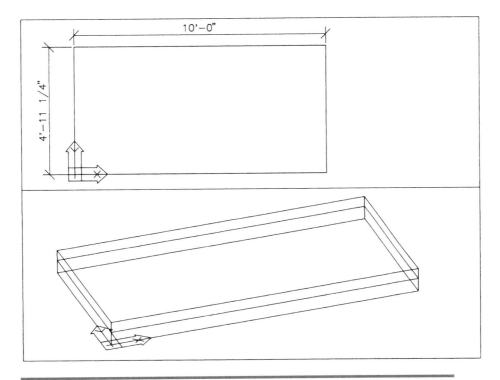

Figure 14.8
Orientation cube and division line

Using PCUBE for the Leg Columns

Now you are going to create a leg column that is 4″ square and 8″ high (see Figure 14.9).

10. Create a layer called LEG, and make it current.
11. Set the elevation to 0 and the thickness to 0.
12. Using the INSERT command, insert the PCUBE model:

Command: **–INSERT** (Note the use of the minus prefix)
Enter block name or [?] <cube>: **PCUBE** (You can enter the ~ symbol to use the File browser.)
Specify insertion point or [Scale/X/Y/Z/Rotate/PScale/PX/PY/PZ/PRotate]: **4,2,0**
Enter X scale factor, specify opposite corner, or [Corner/XYZ] <1>: **XYZ**
Specify X scale factor or [Corner] <1>: **4**
Enter Y scale factor <use X scale factor>: **4**
Specify Z scale factor or <use X scale factor>: **28**
Specify rotation angle <0>: **0**

13. Copy the newly created leg to the other three corners and the two center positions.
14. Save the model as DECK.

Using PCUBE to Create Support Joists

Now you are going to create supports that are 2″ × 6″ boards. To place the boards and set the length, use the division line to snap to.

15. Create a layer called SUPPORT, and make it active.

16. Use the SW Isometric View tool to display an axonometric view $(-1,-1,1)$ similar to the view in Figure 14.10. This makes it easier to place the supports.
17. Create a working plane that runs along the inside of the right side of the orientation cube with the Z axis pointing toward the left side of the cube. This allows

Figure 14.9
Inserting the PCUBE to create legs

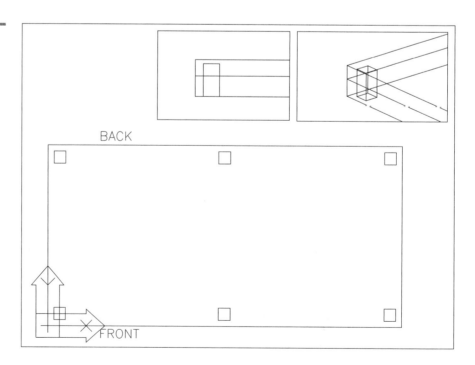

Figure 14.10
Using PCUBE to create supports

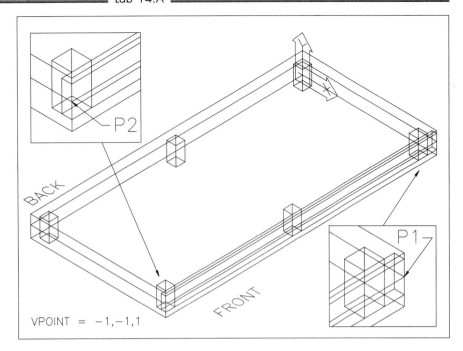

VPOINT = −1,−1,1

for the placement of the PCUBE and the desired stretching along the Z axis (see Figure 14.10). Save this working plane/UCS as IRIGHT (Inside RIGHT side). The correct placement of this working plane is crucial for proper stretching along the Z axis.

18. Use INSERT to add and form PCUBE into the front support member. (*Note:* The orientation of the PCUBE model during insertion will affect the direction of the Z scaling.)

Command: **–INSERT** (Note the use of the minus prefix)
Enter block name or [?] <cube>: **PUCUBE** (You can enter the ~ symbol to use the File browser.)
Specify insertion point or [Scale/X/Y/Z/Rotate/PScale/PX/PY/PZ/PRotate]: **R** (This is used to rotate the block 90 degrees.)
Specify rotation angle: **90**
Specify insertion point: **endpoint snap to the point labeled P1 shown in Figure 14.10**
Enter X scale factor, specify opposite corner, or [Corner/XYZ] <1>: **XYZ**
Specify X scale factor or [Corner] <1>: **6**
Enter Y scale factor <use X scale factor>: **2**
Specify Z scale factor or <use X scale factor>: **endpoint snap to the point labeled P2**

The length of the member is automatically entered based on points P1 and P2.
19. Add the remaining supports using the procedure just listed. Refer to Figure 14.11 for the locations.
20. Save the model as DECK.

Using PCUBE to Create the Decking

Now it is time to add the decking, which will be 4″ wide and 1″ high (see Figure 14.12).

21. Create a layer called DECKING, and make it active.

255

Figure 14.11
Adding the remaining supports

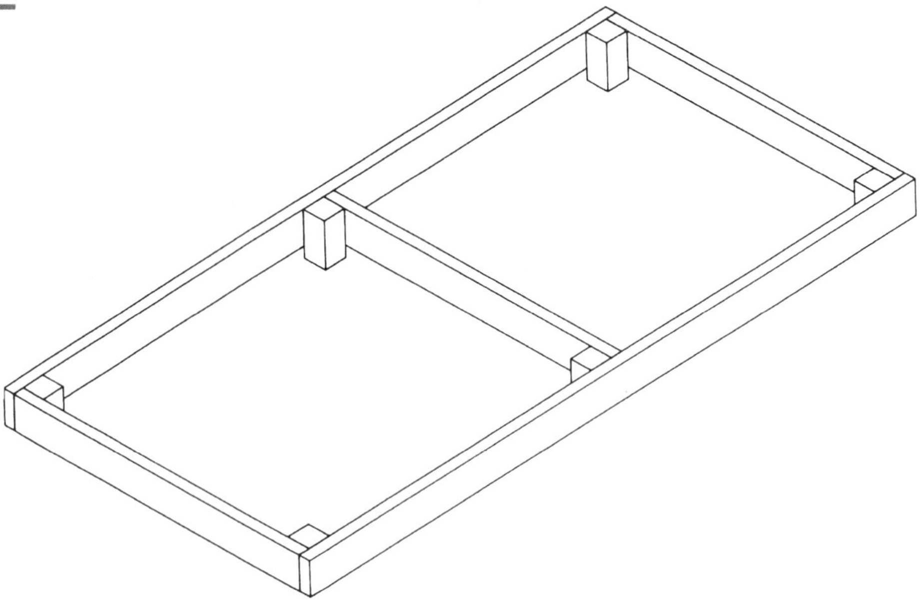

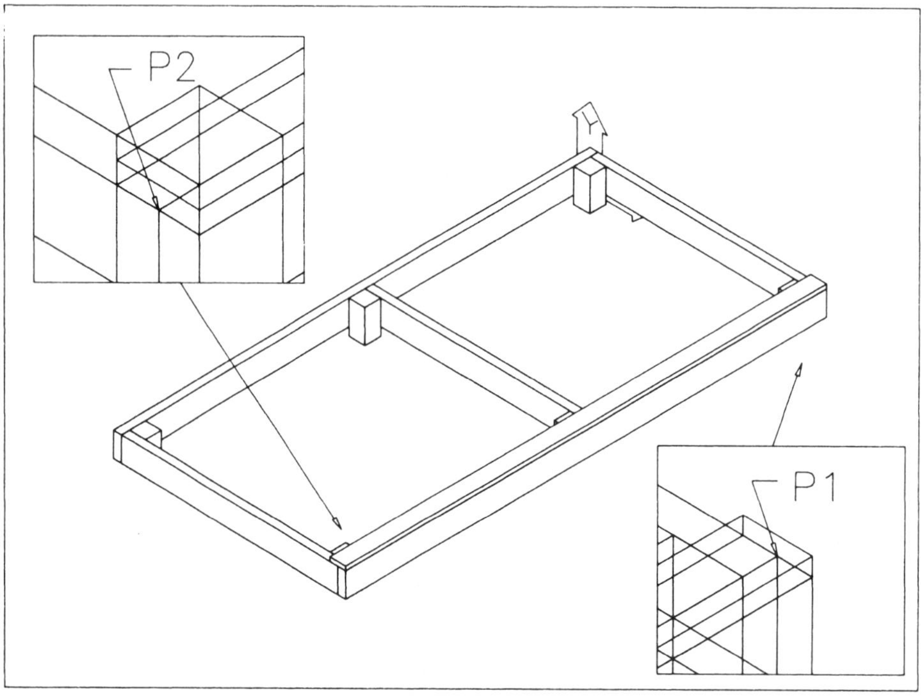

Figure 14.12
Using PCUBE to create the decking

22. Restore the IRIGHT working plane.
23. Using the INSERT command, insert the PCUBE model to use in the creation of the decking:

Command: **–INSERT** (Note the use of the minus prefix)
Enter block name or [?] <cube>: **PCUBE** (You can enter the ~ symbol to use the File browser.)
Specify insertion point or [Scale/X/Y/Z/Rotate/PScale/PX/PY/PZ/PRotate]: **endpoint snap to the point labeled P1, shown in Figure 14.12**

Enter X scale factor, specify opposite corner, or [Corner/XYZ] <1>: **XYZ**
Specify X scale factor or [Corner] <1>: **4**
Enter Y scale factor <use X scale factor>: **1**
Specify Z scale factor or <use X scale factor>: **endpoint snap to the point
    labeled P2**
Specify rotation angle <0>: **0**

> The length of the member is automatically entered based on points P1 and P2.

24. Use the ARRAY command to create the rest of the decking. The decking will
    have a 1/4″ gap between each plank.

Command: **ARRAY**
Select objects: **click the newly created deck member**
1 found
Select objects: **press Enter to continue**
Enter the type of array [Rectangular/Polar] <R>: **R**
Enter the number of rows (- - -) <1>: **1**
Enter the number of columns (|||) <1>: **14** (14 decking boards)
Specify the distance between columns (|||): −**4.25**

> The distance of −4.25 gives a gap of 1/4″ between the decking boards.

25. Save the model as DECK.
26. Turn off the OCUBE layer. Use the HIDE command and observe the model.
    It should be similar to the one shown in Figure 14.6.

You have just created an entire model from parametric 3D symbols. As you have
seen, using parametric symbols makes construction tasks much easier. Remember to
note that Lab 14.A used a 3US symbol, allowing unequal scaling in all three axes.

Lab 14.B   Parametric Pipe and Piping

Purpose

Lab 14.B shows you how to create a 3ES parametric symbol of a pipe elbow and a
symbol of a pipe that will be used as a 2ES parametric 3D symbol. You will create a
small piping system using the 3ES elbow and 2ES pipe symbols.

Objectives

You will be able to:

■ Construct a 2ES parametric symbol
■ Construct a 3ES parametric symbol
■ Apply the parametric symbols in the creation of a model

Primary Command

INSERT–XYZ

Final Model

Figure 14.13 shows the 2ES and 3ES parametric symbols and the final model you'll
be creating.

Procedure

1. Start a new model called ELBOW (piping ELBOW) with the following settings or you can open file a3dex14b from the a3d2005 folder. This file has most
   of the settings already set. All you should need to do is display the necessary
   toolbars.

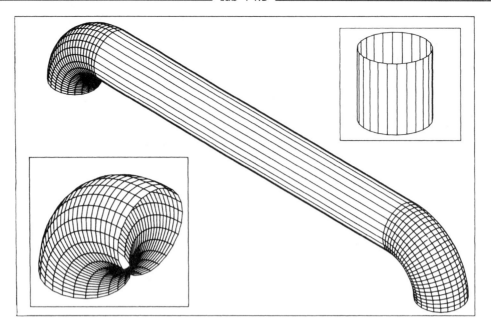

Figure 14.13
2ES and 3ES parametric symbols and the final model

Units = decimal
Limits = −1'',−1'' to 2'',2''
Grid = 0.5''
Snap Incr. = 0.5''
Elevation = 0
Thickness = 0''
Current Layer = PROFILE
UCS = WCS
UCSICON = On, Origin, and set to 2D display properties
UCSVP = 0 (always set before creation of viewports)
Fill = off

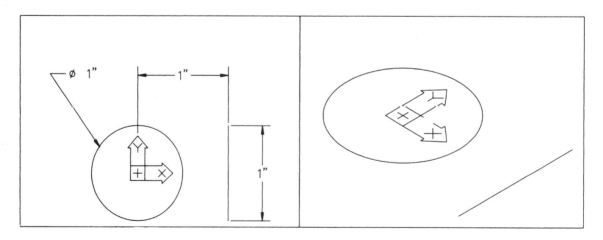

Figure 14.14
Profile of a circle and a line

Creating the Elbow Model

2. Using a circle and a line, draw the objects shown in Figure 14.14. The circle's center should be 0,0,0 and have a radius of 0.5''. The line should start at 1,−0.5,0 and end at 1,0.5,0.
3. Set the SURFTAB1 and SURFTAB2 variables to 24.
4. Create a layer called SURF, and make it current.
5. Using the REVSURF command, construct the model shown in Figure 14.15.

Command: **REVSURF**
Current wire frame density: **SURFTAB1 = 24 SURFTAB2 = 24**
Select object to revolve: **select the circle**
Select object that defines the axis of revolution: **select the line**
Specify start angle <0>: **0**
Specify included angle (+ =ccw, − =cw) <360>: **−90** (You may have to enter positive 90 degrees, depending on how the axis line was created and which end of the line you clicked earlier. Refer to Figure 14.15 for the desired outcome.)

Changing the Thickness

The thickness of the line that was used as the axis of revolution must be changed to 1.5''. It will be used as a working plane.

6. Using the PROPERTIES command (highlight object, right-click, select Properties), change the thickness of the line to 1.5'', as shown in Figure 14.16.
7. Create a working plane on the face of the extruded line, and set the current layer to PROFILE.
8. Draw a line 2.5'' long on the working plane, from the center of the elbow's circular face, as shown in Figure 14.16. Later in the lab, this line will be used as a snap point when adding the pipe symbol.
9. Set UCS to equal the WCS, and save the 3ES model as ELBOW.

Creating the 2ES Pipe Symbol

10. Start a new model called PIPE with the following settings or you can open file a3dex14bpipe from the a3d2005 folder. This file has most of the settings already set. All you should need to do is display the necessary toolbars.

Units = decimal
Limits = −1'',−1'' to 2'',2''
Grid = 0.5''
Snap Incr. = 0.5''

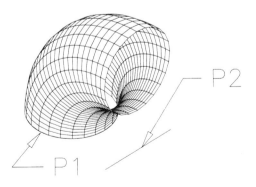

Figure 14.15
Creating a surface of revolution

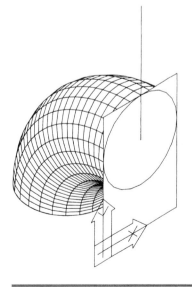

Figure 14.16
Adding a line to the elbow face

Elevation = 0
Thickness = 0''
Current Layer = PROFILE
UCS = WCS
UCSICON = On, Origin, and set to 2D display properties
UCSVP = 0 (always set before creation of viewports)
Fill = off

Creating the Pipe Model

The pipe model is only one unit high and one unit long. This allows the scaling that is required during insertion.

11. Using a circle and a line, draw the objects shown in Figure 14.17A. The circle's center should be at 0,0,0 and have a radius of 0.5''. The line should start at 0.5,0,0 and end at 0.5,0,1.
12. Set SURFTAB1 and SURFTAB2 variables to 24.
13. Create a layer called SURF, and make it current.
14. Using the TABSURF command, construct the model shown in Figure 14.17B.

Command: **TABSURF**

Select object for path curve: **select the circle** (It controls the path the polygons will follow.)

Select object for direction vector: **select the line near the end that touches the circle** (It controls the length of the polygons and the direction they will be pointing.)

> The end of the line that was selected controls the direction of the surfaces. If the surfaces are generated in the wrong direction, delete them and repeat the command. This time, however, select the other end of the line.

15. Make sure the BASE is set to 0,0,0 and save this 2ES model as PIPE.

Creating a Piping Model

Now you are going to assemble the two 3D symbols ELBOW and PIPE into a piping model. Remember, ELBOW is a 3ES parametric symbol, and PIPE is a 2ES parametric symbol.

16. Start a new model called PIPES with the following settings or you can open file a3dex14pipes from the a3d2005 folder. This file has most of the settings already set. All you should need to do is display the necessary toolbars.

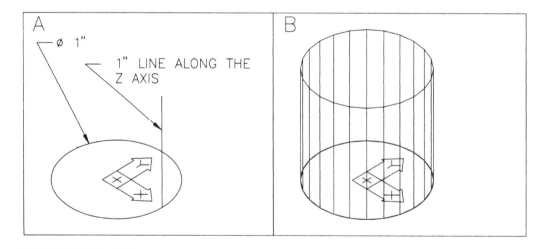

Figure 14.17
Creating the surfaced pipe

Units = decimal
Limits = −1″, −1″ to 10″,10″
Grid = 0.5″
Snap Incr. = 0.5″
Elevation = 0
Thickness = 0″
Current Layer = ELBOW
UCS = WCS
UCSICON = On, Origin, and set to 2D display properties
UCSVP = 0 (always set before creation of viewports)
Fill = off

Inserting the Elbow Model

17. Insert the model called ELBOW at the locations shown in Figure 14.18. Remember to use the Rotate option for one of the elbows.

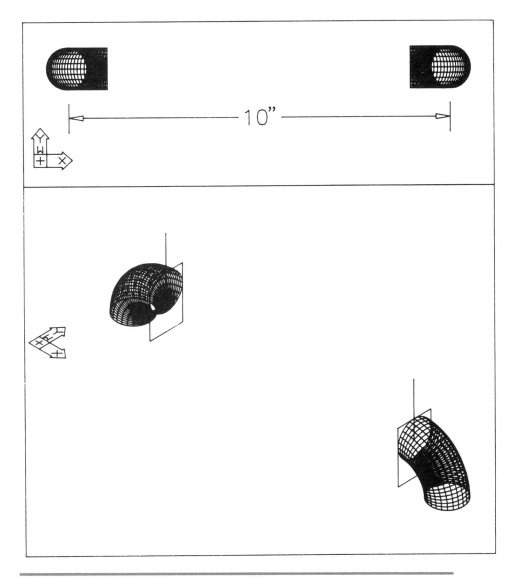

Figure 14.18
Inserting the 3ES symbol ELBOW

Inserting the Pipe Model

18. Create a working plane on the elbow, as shown in Figure 14.19.
19. Insert the 2ES symbol called PIPE:

Command: **–INSERT** (Note the use of the minus prefix)
Enter block name or [?] <cube>: **PIPE** (You can enter the ~ symbol to use the File browser.)
Specify insertion point or [Scale/X/Y/Z/Rotate/PScale/PX/PY/PZ/PRotate]: **endpoint snap to the lower endpoint of the line labeled P1, shown in Figure 14.19**
Enter X scale factor, specify opposite corner, or [Corner/XYZ] <1>: **XYZ**
Specify X scale factor or [Corner] <1>: **1**
Enter Y scale factor <use X scale factor>: **1**
Specify Z scale factor or <use X scale factor>: **endpoint snap to the lower endpoint of the line labeled P2, shown in Figure 14.20**
Specify rotation angle <0>: **0**

The length of the pipe is automatically entered based on points P1 and P2 and should look like the final length shown in Figure 14.21.

20. Freeze the layer called PROFILE.
21. Save the model as PIPES.
22. Use the VPOINT and the HIDE commands to move about the model and observe the display after it has the hidden edges removed. You can also use 3DORBIT and different shade modes to manipulate the display of the model.

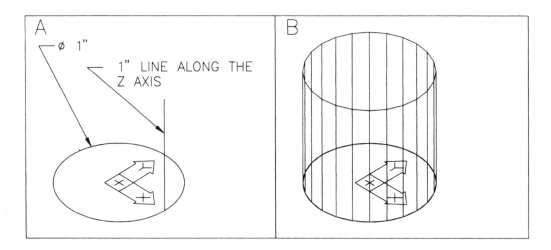

Figure 14.19
Inserting the 2ES symbol PIPE

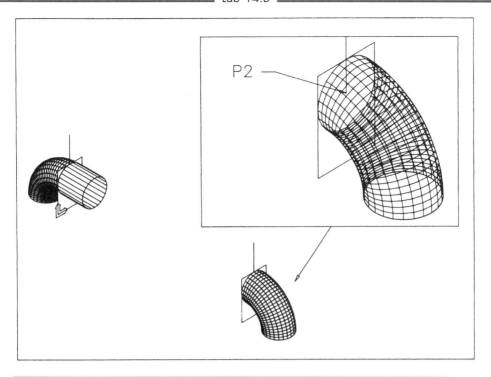

Figure 14.20
Scaling the length to point P2

Figure 14.21
The final length of pipe

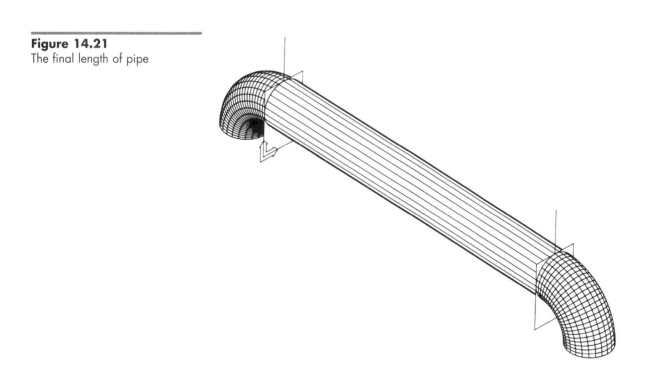

Questions

1. Explain what a parametric design represents?

2. What is a 3ES symbol?

3. What is the advantage of a 3US parametric symbol over a 3ES parametric symbol? What is the disadvantage?

4. What is the main feature of a 2ES parametric symbol?

5. How is snapping to existing objects an aid in the setting of parametric parameters when inserting a parametric symbol?

6. What option is used to allow independent scaling along the three axes when inserting a 3D symbol block?

Assignments

1. Create a carton, like the one illustrated in Figure 14.1, that is large enough to contain the mug model created in Chapter 8, Assignment 1 (COFMUG). This carton model is a 3ES parametric symbol. Save the model as CARTON. Now, restore the kitchen model created in Chapter 13, Assignment 1, called BKIT. Insert the 3ES symbol CARTON at an XYZ scale of 0.75 and place it on the table top. Then insert the mug model, COFMUG, into the box. It will also be XYZ scaled to 0.75. Save this scene as BKIT2. Display a view looking toward the open box so that the mug can be seen, and use the HIDE command. Figure 14.22 illustrates the final scene. (*Note:* All the 3D models in this scene are actually 3ES parametric symbols. They must be scaled equally in all three axes so that they retain their shapes and proportions.)

2. Generate a stud wall as shown in Figure 14.23. The entire wall should be constructed out of 2 × 4s (nominal size = 2 × 4, actual size = 1-1/2 × 3-1/2) and make use of the 3US symbol PCUBE, created in Lab 14.A.

Figure 14.22
A small mug in a small carton

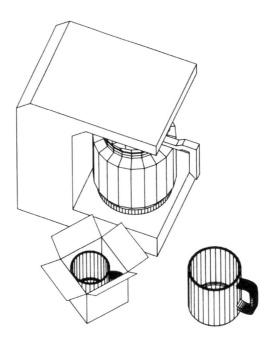

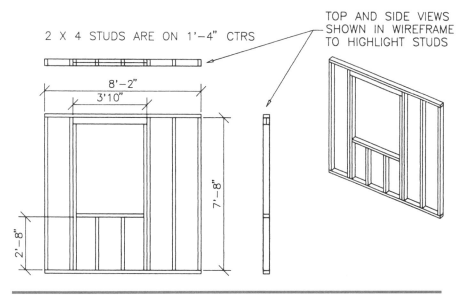

2 X 4 STUDS ARE ON 1'–4" CTRS

TOP AND SIDE VIEWS SHOWN IN WIREFRAME TO HIGHLIGHT STUDS

8'–2"

3'10"

7'–8"

2'–8"

Figure 14.23
Stud wall

Figure 14.24
Flange/bolt assembly

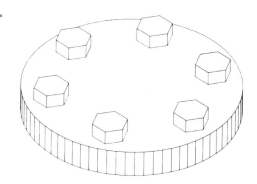

3. Draw the flange/bolt assembly shown in Figure 14.24. Use the model of the bolt head, BHEAD, created in Chapter 13, Assignment 3. The BHEAD model is a 2ES symbol. When inserting the BHEAD parametric symbol, be sure the XY scale is 1.125. This gives a size of 1-1/8″ across the flats. Use a Z scale of 0.5 to give a head thickness of 1/2″. The flange should be created using a circle of 8″ and a thickness of 1″.

4. Design a structure that could make use of the 3US parametric symbol PCUBE. Sketch the design first on paper, outlining where the parametric symbol can be used. Then create a 3D model using the parametric symbol.

5. Research to identify some 2ES parametric symbols and their applications. Undertake to create these 2ES symbols in AutoCAD.

6. Restore the model BKIT2 from Assignment 1 in this chapter. Try to put the entire kitchen table into a carton using a procedure similar to that used in Assignment 1. Orient the view so that the table can be seen inside the box.

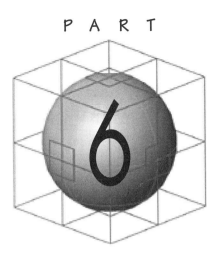

Presentation

Now that you can create a 3D model and visually move it about on the screen, it's time to study the various aspects of presentation. The presentation techniques we'll discuss in this part relate to both the appearance of the model on the video screen and the resultant hard copies. We'll also explore the enhancement features available within AutoCAD and the other software available to enhance the presentation of your model.

Displaying 3D Models for Presentation

Overview

In this chapter, we'll explore techniques that are not necessarily important in model creation but enhance the viewing of the model on the screen and prepare it for final presentation. For instance, you will learn how to create a camera's view of the model, which results in a picture that is closer to those images the human eye is accustomed to seeing. In addition, we'll explain techniques for clipping away unwanted features.

Concepts Explored

- The importance of perspective views, the principles behind them, and how they differ from axonometric views
- How the DVIEW command relates to an SLR camera
- The operation of the DVIEW options
- The way in which different lenses distort an image
- How to remove obstructing objects
- How to recognize a new form of the UCS icon
- How to create various perspective views
- How to use the 3D Orbit toolbar with DVIEW

15.1 Introduction

Up to this point, we have viewed models axonometrically. This type of viewing is extremely important in the construction stage. It is easier to tell if the model is drawn correctly when the lines that create the model are parallel to each other. But when we want to display a model, especially if it is something large like an architectural structure, axonometric display is less than visually pleasing. It is much more appealing to have the model displayed in a perspective view. An image with perspective is the ultimate in pictorial drawing. There is no substitute for a picture that depicts what the viewer's eyes would actually see, as Figure 15.1 shows. To compare the two ways of viewing, look at Figures 15.2 and 15.3. Figure 15.2 shows the axonometric view of a house model, and Figure 15.3 illustrates the way the human eye would perceive the same model.

Figure 15.1
Perspective display of a 3D
model of a house

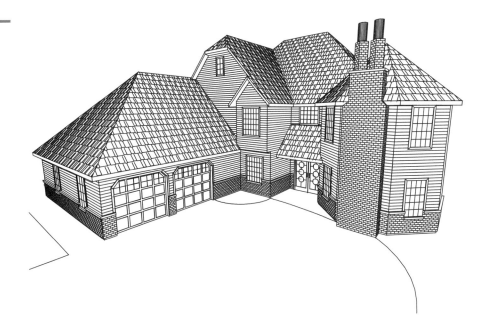

Figure 15.2
Axonometric display of a house

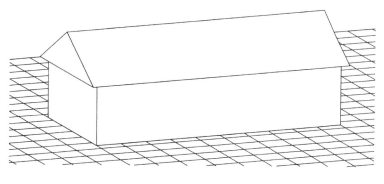

Figure 15.3
Perspective display of a house

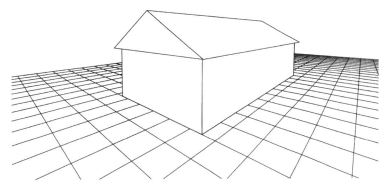

15.2 Perspective versus Axonometric Views

Axonometric (including isometric) drawings make use of parallel lines to generate a picture or 3D view of an object. Because the lines along one of the three axes are parallel to each other, the displayed view of the object remains uniform, regardless of the viewing distance. Obviously, although the overall displayed size can change, the proportional distance from each object remains the same. Axonometric views are created using the AutoCAD command VPOINT, or using 3DORBIT with parallel projection, which is explained in Chapter 3.

Figure 15.4
How the human eye perceives
objects

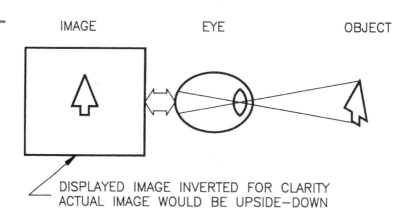

IMAGE   EYE   OBJECT

DISPLAYED IMAGE INVERTED FOR CLARITY
ACTUAL IMAGE WOULD BE UPSIDE-DOWN

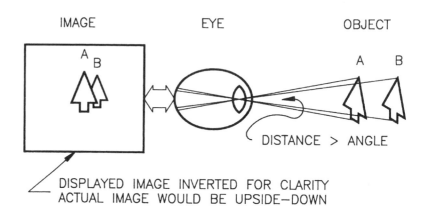

IMAGE   EYE   OBJECT

DISTANCE > ANGLE

DISPLAYED IMAGE INVERTED FOR CLARITY
ACTUAL IMAGE WOULD BE UPSIDE-DOWN

Perspective drawing is different. Perspective drawing attempts to simulate the view of a human's eye (refer to Figure 15.4). Because lines converge toward the eye as they pass the lens, an angle is formed from the extent of the object viewed. As the object's distance away from the eye increases, the extent angle decreases, as Figure 15.4 illustrates. Eventually, the angle is too small for the human eye to discern. This point is referred to as the *vanishing point*.

Thus, in perspective viewing, the farther an object is from the viewer, the smaller it appears, until it eventually blends into a dot. AutoCAD simulates this type of view with the command DVIEW, which stands for dynamic viewing, or by using 3DORBIT with perspective projection.

15.3 Center of Interest and the Station Point

When creating any perspective view, whether by drafting manually or by using CAD, you need two key points—the center of interest and the station point. The center of interest is the most important feature or component of the object or model. In other words, it is the part in an entire scene that draws your eye, such as the front door of a house. The station point represents where the viewer is standing, and it may be close, far away, or above or below. Refer to Figure 15.5. You can use the CAMERA command to set the station point (camera position) and the center of interest (camera target) for the DVIEW command. You can use the 3DORBITCTR to set the center of interest for the 3DORBIT command.

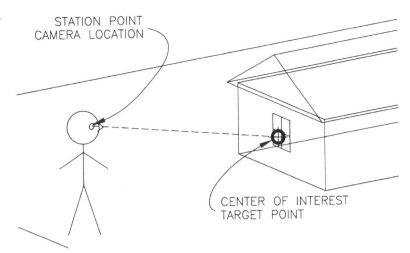

Figure 15.5
The center of interest and the station point

15.4 **DVIEW Command**

DVIEW, AutoCAD's first method for generating a perspective view of a three-dimensional model, has many features similar to those of a camera. Let's investigate how it works and what it can do. AutoCAD 2005 does not have menu access to the DVIEW command. To use the command, you must enter it on the command line.

Camera and DVIEW

Consider the operation of a 35-mm single-lens reflex (SLR) camera. When using an SLR camera with a 50-mm lens (similar to the human eye), you look at an object from a set distance, as in Figure 15.6. If you are too far away, you can either move

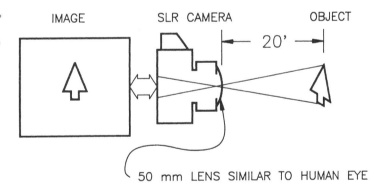

Figure 15.6
50-mm lens image versus 200-mm lens image

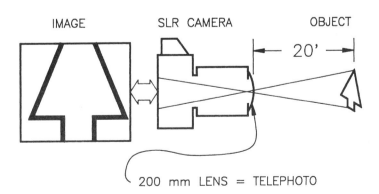

Figure 15.7

50-mm lens image versus 35-mm
lens image

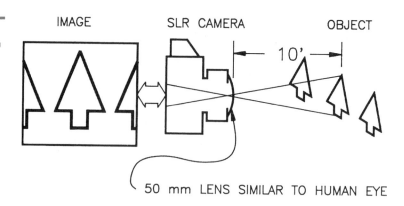

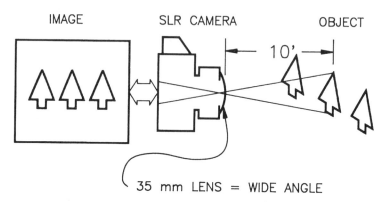

closer to decrease the distance or use a telephoto (zoom) lens (such as a 200-mm lens) to magnify the picture. If the view is larger than the frame, as in Figure 15.7, then you can use a wide-angle lens, such as a 35-mm lens. And if you want to change your viewing angle, you can simply turn the camera in your hand, as Figure 15.8 illustrates.

All these features of a regular 35-mm SLR camera can be simulated with AutoCAD's DVIEW command. AutoCAD refers to the center of interest as the *target point* and the stationary point as the *camera point*. Using DVIEW, the distance away from the model to be viewed can be set, and any length of telephoto lens can be selected. The camera can even be twisted, much like turning a hand-held camera. And there are other features in DVIEW not found on a regular camera, such as the Clip option. Clip can remove unwanted obstructions from the viewed picture. Wouldn't that be a wonderful feature to find on a regular camera? It would eliminate that large thumb in the foreground of your breathtaking shot of the Grand Canyon!

Figure 15.8

Turning the camera on an angle

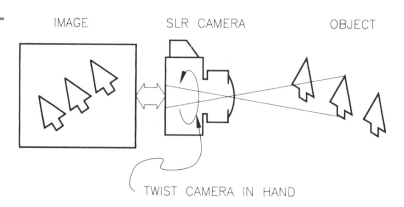

Figure 15.9
The vertical and horizontal slider bars

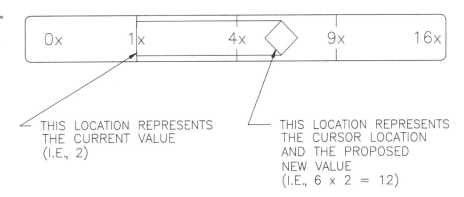

THIS LOCATION REPRESENTS
THE CURRENT VALUE
(I.E., 2)

THIS LOCATION REPRESENTS
THE CURSOR LOCATION
AND THE PROPOSED
NEW VALUE
(I.E., 6 x 2 = 12)

DVIEW's Camera-like Options

Using the DVIEW command allows you to display a preview of a model. Once you have achieved the desired preview, you can apply the view to the entire model. A similar feature is DVIEW's Drag option. The standard Drag option of most of the modifying commands allows you to see the object's movements while modification is actually taking place. The Drag option of DVIEW allows you to view the model three-dimensionally while selecting the desired view. You can see the model rotate, enlarge, shrink, twist, or turn.

With the Drag option, as with the DVIEW Camera, Target, and Pan options, you move the cursor/crosshair attached to the object in question. However, the DVIEW options that control Zoom and Distance also have slider bars that produce feedback on the bar to inform you of the desired values to be entered. The slider bar is shown in Figure 15.9. Depending on where the cursor is on the bar, the desired effect is applied to the image displayed. You can override the slider bar by entering values on the command line.

Selecting an Object

As mentioned previously, to apply the DVIEW options to a model, you must select a preview. You may do this using the Preview Selection Set. If desired, you may select the entire model or only those items that give definition to the model. For example, consider the finished house model illustrated in Figure 15.10, containing the dwelling walls, roof, windows, and doors. This entire model could be selected for dynamic manipulation, but the dynamic movement would be slow, especially if there are many objects in the model. Instead, only the objects that define the model need to be selected. These objects could be some of the walls and perhaps the roof and the

Figure 15.10
Entire house model

Figure 15.11
Selected objects for the Preview
selection set

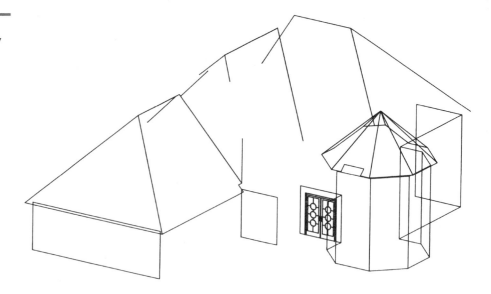

Figure 15.12
The DVIEWBLOCK command

front door, as Figure 15.11 shows. When selecting objects, choose the ones that would enable you to recognize the house's orientation when it is dynamically shifted.

As an alternative to the Preview selection set, AutoCAD has a built-in feature for manipulating the DVIEW environment. It is called the DVIEWBLOCK, and Figure 15.12 shows this three-dimensional block that can be manipulated within DVIEW. AutoCAD supplies a block model of a simple house for the DVIEW-BLOCK command. However, if desired, you can create a new three-dimensional block and name it to replace the original DVIEWBLOCK. The only restriction to the block you create is that it must fit within a one-unit cube. The DVIEWBLOCK is activated by pressing the Enter key when the prompt to select objects for DVIEW appears. Then the DVIEWBLOCK is displayed and can be manipulated. Once you complete the preview manipulation, you can apply it to the actual model.

Placing the Camera

As soon as the selection set is complete, depending on the previous settings, the model is displayed in the DVIEW environment. The first option of the DVIEW command to be activated is the Camera option. Here, use the cursor/crosshair to swing the model around its horizontal axis first and then around its vertical axis next. Either move the cursor device or type the appropriate angle on the command line to accomplish these swings. It is possible to toggle between angles by using the T suboption of the Camera option, which has the effect of switching from one angle to the other.

Selecting a Center of Interest

When you enter the DVIEW environment for the first time, the camera distance and the center of interest are selected automatically. To change the center of interest, use the Target option. This option is similar to the Camera option, except that moving along the cursor with the Target option causes the center of interest to swing about the camera location. The camera location becomes the pivot point. There is an easy way to think of the difference between the Camera and the Target options (see Figure 15.13). The Camera option gives a view similar to what you see when walking around an object while focusing on one spot of the object. The Target option gives a view similar to what you see when standing still but turning to look around from that stationary position.

Figure 15.13
The Camera option versus the
Target option

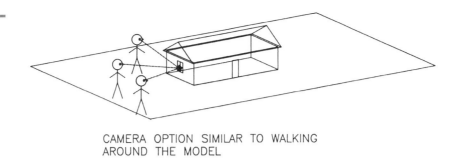

CAMERA OPTION SIMILAR TO WALKING
AROUND THE MODEL

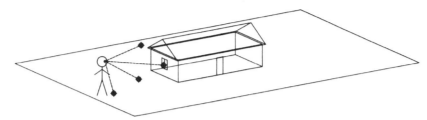

TARGET OPTION SIMILAR TO LOOKING
AROUND IN ONE SPOT

Activating the Perspective View

The perspective view is activated by using the Distance option, which changes the distance from the target point to the camera point, or how far the viewer is away from the center of interest. As soon as the Distance option is used, the view changes to perspective. If you're using the 2D wire UCS icon, you can tell if the perspective view has been activated by looking at the UCS icon: Instead of the usual L-shaped symbol (see Figure 15.14), it has changed to a perspective box (see Figure 15.15). If you're using the 3D icon, it becomes dashed when perspective is on. The 3D shade icon does not change appearance.

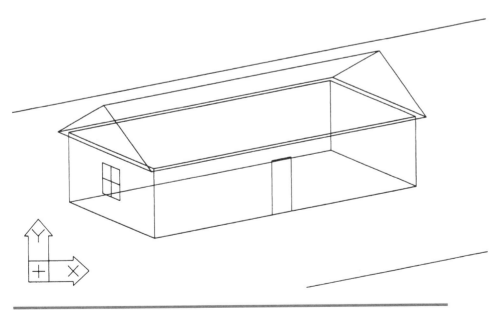

Figure 15.14
Axonometric UCS icon

Figure 15.15
Perspective icon

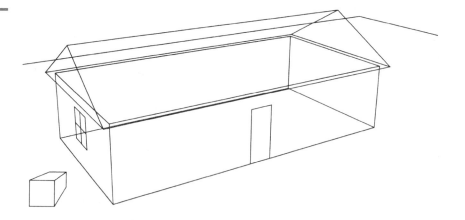

3D VIEWPOINT

Turning Off Perspective Viewing

Perspective viewing is created with the DVIEW command. To turn a perspective view off, use the Off option of the DVIEW command but remember to use the Save option of the VIEW command to save your DVIEW settings before you turn the view off so that you can restore them later. It's also possible to turn perspective view off by using the Project/Parallel option of the 3DORBIT command (right-click during the command).

The Distance option moves along the axis of vision, which runs along an imaginary line that passes through the camera point (stationary point) and the target point (center of interest). It is possible to have a distance that is too close to the object viewed. If the model suddenly disappears, it is likely that the distance setting is too close to the object.

When using this option, it is easier to enter the distance away from the object at the command line than to use the slider bar. If the operator was looking at a house, it may be desirable to set the distance preliminarily to 100′ or if the model to be viewed happens to be the size of a coffee mug, the preliminary distance could be 12″.

The slider bar uses a multiplicative factor with the Distance option. This means that whatever distance was previously set is multiplied by the slider bar the next time the Distance option is used. If the previous distance was 100′ away from the target point, the next time the slider bar is set to 2×, then the distance becomes 200′.

It is possible to reduce or enlarge a model without turning on the perspective. This is accomplished by using the Zoom option, which works as long as the Distance option has not been used.

The perspective can be turned off by using the Off option of the DVIEW command.

Choosing the Proper Lens

Once you have decided how far the viewer will be standing away from the model, your next step is to choose the proper lens with which to view the model. To do this, use the Zoom option. Activate the slider bar, and use it to adjust the camera's lens length. The 50-mm lens simulates what an unassisted human eye would see of the model at the set distance. An actual camera has set lens lengths, but the distance is

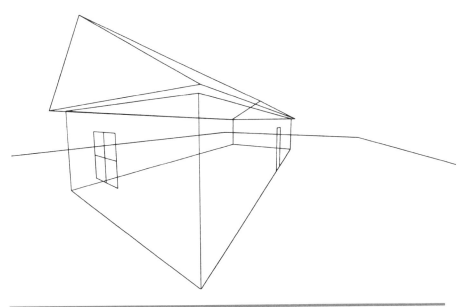

Figure 15.16
Model display distorted by too close a camera distance and too small a lens size

variable with DVIEW. If the view is too small, then increase the lens length, thereby increasing the magnification. If the view does not show enough of the model and its surroundings, then choose a smaller lens length. Keep in mind, however, that using too small a lens length can greatly distort the display of the model, as Figure 15.16 shows. If this happens—and it is not desirable—the distance from the camera to the target and the lens length should be increased. By alternating the Distance and Zoom options, you can achieve the most pleasing view.

Simultaneous Moving of the Camera and the Target

It is possible to move the camera and the target together. This is accomplished with either the Pan or the Twist option. The Pan option moves the camera and the target in a sliding fashion. The distance or the angle of view does not change. The Pan option used here functions much the same as the standard PAN command used outside of DVIEW. Using the Twist option has the same effect as manually turning a camera; it twists about the axis of vision.

Getting Rid of Unwanted Objects

Often, when model construction is finished and the desired view has been set, there is some part of the model that is obstructing the view of the center of interest. To alleviate this problem, the Clip option can be utilized. Its purpose and operation are quite simple. There are two clipping planes—front and back. These planes move along the axis of vision, parallel to the graphics screen. Whatever is in front of the front clipping plane toward the viewer is hidden from the display. Whatever is behind the back clipping plane away from the viewer is hidden from the display (see Figures 15.17 and 15.18). Both the front and back planes of the Clip option can be turned on and off, and they can be set any distance from the target point. Positive distances are in front of the target, and negative distances are behind the target.

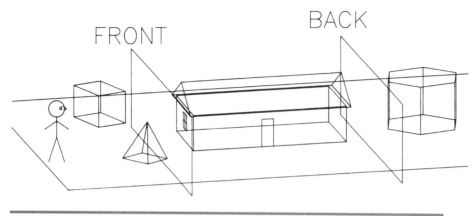

Figure 15.17
Removing obstructions with the Clip option

Figure 15.18
The display after the clipping planes have been applied

Another use for the Clip option is to "cut" through surfaces, which you may need to do when you want to see inside a model, such as a house or a mechanical assembly. When a clipping plane cuts through a surface, the edge that cuts through the surface is displayed as a line. This makes it easy to tell where the "cut" is taking place. This cutting affects only what is on display, not the actual construction of the geometry.

Locating the Camera and Target Exactly

When a specific view is desired (for instance, "I want to stand at the top of the stairs and look down into the entrance hall"), it can be achieved using the Points option. This option allows the user to click or enter exact X,Y,Z point locations of both the camera and the target. Filters and object snaps are functional, even when perspective is on. When the option is selected, perspective viewing is turned off to allow the user to specify a target point and a camera location. To ensure the proper view, you need to enter the distance option. Its default will be changed to the distance between the camera and target. Remember to set the proper zoom lens. Figure 15.19 shows a city model (created in the application project of Chapter 19). In this case, the target is the roof of the main entrance (560′,760′,50′) and the camera is located on the roof of a nearby building (285′,595′,105′). The calculated distance 325′ 4″ and a 50-mm lens were used. You can see the resulting view, just as if you were standing on the roof looking at the entrance.

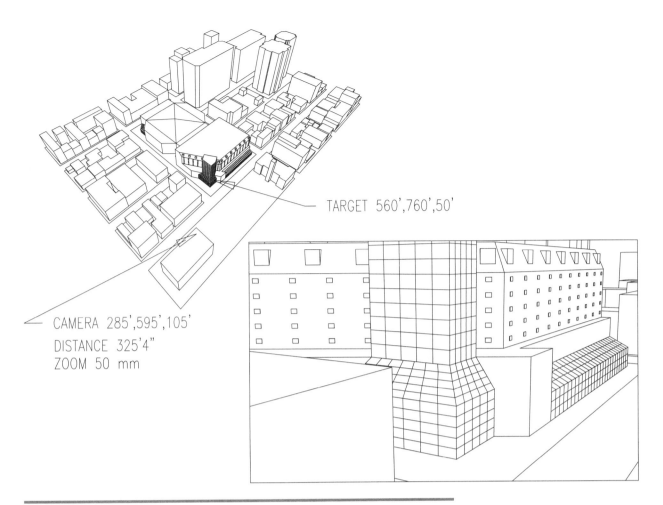

TARGET 560',760',50'

CAMERA 285',595',105'
DISTANCE 325'4"
ZOOM 50 mm

Figure 15.19
Locating the camera and target

Hiding the Preview

To generate a hidden line removal of the Preview Selection Set, select the Hide option while in the DVIEW command. The Hide option applies only to those surfaces that were selected for the DVIEW command.

Applying the Preview to the Entire Model

Once the desired view and effects have been achieved with the Preview selection set, you only need to exit from the DVIEW command. Then, all the effects, except the Hide option, are applied to the model. After exiting from the DVIEW command, you can invoke the HIDE command or use various shade modes.

DVIEW settings can be stored for later recall by saving the current view.

Note that there are some limitations when the perspective view is active: The ZOOM, PAN, and SKETCH commands do not function, and the pointing device cannot be used to enter coordinates. However, the two 3D viewing commands, 3DZOOM and 3DPAN, can be used to overcome the viewing limitations.

DVIEW Command Options Summarized

The various options of the DVIEW command follow:

OPTIONS	DESCRIPTION
<Enter>	Pressing Enter at the "Select objects" prompt activates the DVIEWBLOCK
CAmera	Places the camera in relation to the target
TArget	Places the target in relation to the camera
Distance	Sets the distance from the camera to the target
POints	Places the camera and the target using coordinates
PAn	Shifts the display
Zoom	Changes the size of the displayed view
TWist	Turns the camera
CLip	Temporarily removes unwanted features
Hide	Removes hidden lines
Off	Turns perspective view off
Undo	Reverses the effects of the last DVIEW operation
eXit	Leaves DVIEW and applies settings

15.5 Using the 3D ORBIT Toolbar with DVIEW

The 3D Orbit toolbar can be used to enhance the application of using the DVIEW command. As a beginner it's a good start to use the DVIEW command because the various options are very concrete and detailed, especially for setting the camera lens size. Once you're used to creating perspective views, you may want to only use 3DORBIT to create your view. Once you have set your view using the DVIEW command, you can use commands on the 3D Orbit toolbar to make changes to the view on the fly (see Figure 15.20).

There are several commands on the 3D Orbit toolbar that adjust DVIEW settings.

The 3DZOOM command adjusts the camera lens size.

The 3DPAN command slides the camera and target together.

The 3DSWIVEL command adjusts the target or center of interest by pivoting the camera up or down, left or right.

The 3DDISTANCE command adjusts the camera distance from the target or center of interest.

The 3DCLIP command adjusts the front and back clipping planes.

The 3DORBIT command moves the Points around the object. However, it does not allow as accurate control as the Points option of the DVIEW command. You will have more success using this option.

While the 3DORBIT command is active, you can right-click to bring up the context menu. From this menu you can switch projection modes between parallel and perspective. You can also use the More option to set Orbit Maintains Z. If the UCS is set to World, this option has the effect of

Figure 15.20
The 3D Orbit toolbar

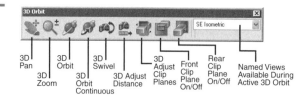

keeping your model on the "ground" while 3D Orbit takes place. This is useful if your model is a building.

3D VIEWPOINT

Perspective Views and Commands

There are several viewing commands that will not function when a perspective view is on the screen. The ZOOM and PAN commands are two of these. To get around this, use the 3D Orbit toolbar. It contains 3D Pan and 3D Zoom that will function with a perspective view.

 Lab 15.A **Dynamic Viewing with Exterior Perspective**

Purpose

Lab 15.A shows you how to create a perspective view of the exterior of a model. The basic dwelling model created in Lab 8.B, Chapter 8, will be your tool.

Objectives

You will be able to:

- Create an exterior perspective view of a model
- Understand the manipulation of the DVIEW command's options
- Save the perspective view settings for later retrieval

Primary Commands

DVIEW–Camera, Distance, Zoom
VIEW–Save
3DORBIT

Procedure

Initial Setup

1. Open the basic dwelling drawing that was created in Lab 8.B in Chapter 8. The file name is BDWELL. Make sure the shade mode is set to 2D wireframe. You'll find this works much better for initially setting the perspective view using the DVIEW command.
2. Align the UCS to the WCS, and turn on the UCS icon. Use the Properties option of the UCSICON command to set the display of the icon to 2D.
3. Display an isometric view using the SE Isometric View tool or the VPOINT command.

Command: **VPOINT**
Current view direction:
   VIEWDIR = 0.0000,0.0000,1.0000
Specify a view point or [Rotate] <display compass and tripod>: **1,–1,1**
Regenerating model

Creating the Preview Selection Set

4. Activate the DVIEW command:

Command: **DVIEW**
Select objects:

5. Select the objects for the Preview selection set (see Figure 15.21).

Figure 15.21
Selecting the Preview selection set

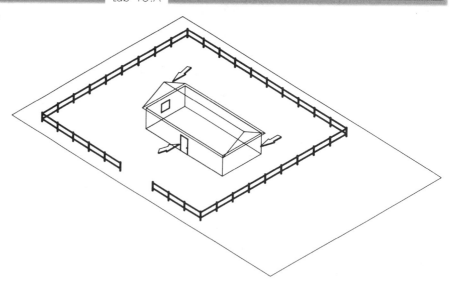

Figure 15.22
Selecting the desired camera view

Using the Camera Option

6. Now activate the Camera option. Move the cursor up and down and note how the preview model pivots about a horizontal axis. This is the angle from the X–Y plane.
7. Move the cursor from left to right until the display is similar to that shown in Figure 15.22. Press the click button at the desired location. (*Note:* The Camera option can be used as many times as necessary to achieve the desired view.)

Setting the Camera Distance

8. To choose the distance of the viewer from the model, use the Distance option. When you select this option, a slider bar appears, controlling the distance the camera is from the target. Move along the slider bar, observing the reduction and enlargement of the displayed model. Instead of using the slider bar to set the distance, however, enter the distance of 100′ at the command prompt:

CAmera/TArget/Distance/ . . . /CLip/Hide/OFF/Undo/<eXit>: **D**
New camera/target distance <current>: **100′**

If your UCS icon is set to display as 2D, it will change to a perspective box icon. Whenever the Distance option is selected, the view of the model changes from an axonometric view to a perspective view.

Using the Zoom Option to Get a Better Picture

9. The display now shows the view as it would appear to a person standing 100′ away from the model. To allow a closer look, you must change the type of lens used to view the model, which is accomplished with the Zoom option. When you select the Zoom option, a slider bar appears. Move the cursor along the bar. Note how the image gets larger or smaller. The distance from the model has not changed, only the size of the lens used to view the model has changed. As the size of the lens increases, the picture appears to be closer; as the size of the lens decreases, more of the overall model is seen. Set the lens length to 75 mm. When you're done, the display should look like Figure 15.23.

Figure 15.23
Using the Zoom option

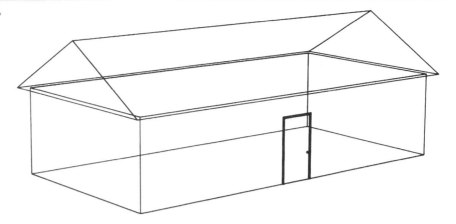

Command:
CAmera/TArget/Distance/ . . . /CLip/Hide/OFF/Undo/<eXit>: **ZOOM**
Adjust lens length <50 mm>: **75** (You may have to adjust the value, depending on your graphics screen, to achieve the same view as Figure 15.23.)

Applying the Preview to the Entire Model

10. Select the eXit option and observe the results. The display should look like Figure 15.24, where the manipulated DVIEW options have been applied to the entire model, achieving the desired perspective view. If the view on your screen is radically different than Figure 15.24, reenter DVIEW and adjust the settings as necessary.

Saving the Perspective Settings

11. It is always useful to save the settings of DVIEW, because they can be unique and hard to duplicate if lost. To save these settings, use the New option of the VIEW command. Save the view under the name PERSP1. The exact view with the DVIEW settings will be recalled if you use the Set Current option of the VIEW command.
12. Save the model as BDWELL.
13. Display the 3D Orbit toolbar using the View/Toolbars pull-down menu. Experiment using the 3D viewing commands, such as 3DPAN, 3DZOOM, and 3DDISTANCE.

Figure 15.24
Applying the DVIEW settings to the entire model

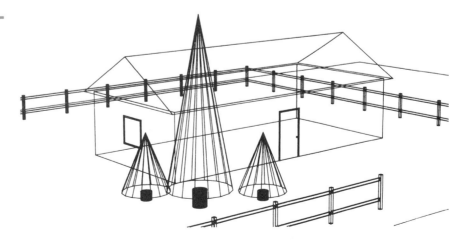

Lab 15.B

Dynamic Viewing with Removal of Obstructing Objects

Purpose

Lab 15.B shows you how to remove temporarily objects that are obstructing the best view of the model. The basic dwelling model created in Lab 8.B, Chapter 8, will be your tool.

Objectives

You will be able to:

- Create an exterior perspective view of a model
- Temporarily remove obstructing geometry from the model
- Save the current perspective view for later retrieval

Primary Commands

DVIEW–Camera, Distance, Zoom, Clip
VIEW–Save
3DORBIT

Procedure

Initial Setup

1. Open the basic dwelling drawing that was modified in Lab 15.A. The file name is BDWELL.
2. Align the UCS to the WCS, and turn on the UCS icon.
3. Use the VIEW command to set PERSP1 as the current view.

Creating the Preview Selection Set

4. Activate the DVIEW command:

Command: **DVIEW**
Select objects:

5. Select the objects for the Preview selection set. Select the roof, the walls, and the trees, as shown in Figure 15.25.

Using the Camera Option

6. Since the previous settings were restored when the view was restored, there is no need to move the camera.

Setting the Camera Distance

7. To achieve more of a perspective effect, select the Distance option and set the distance to 72′. You may have to adjust the distance depending on your screen. The value may be between 65′ and 75′.

Figure 15.25
Selecting the Preview selection set

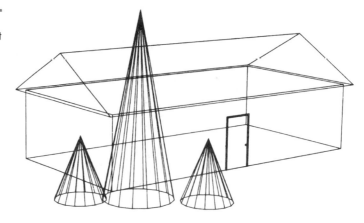

Figure 15.26
Achieving more of a perspective effect with new Distance and Zoom settings

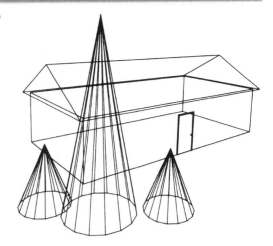

Using the Zoom Option to Get a Better Picture

8. Select the Zoom option, and set the lens length to 25 mm. The display should look like Figure 15.26.

Removing Obstructing Features

9. Note how the trees would be obstructing the view of the window. Use the Clip option to remedy this problem. Select the Clip option:

CAmera/TArget/Distance/POints/ . . . /CLip/Hide/OFF/Undo/<eXit>: **CL**
Back/Front/off: **F**
Eye/ON/OFF/<Distance from target> <1.0000>: **follow the next paragraph**

> Move the cursor along the slider bar and observe the results. Objects disappear or appear as the cursor moves. An imaginary clipping plane is being moved forward and backward over the model. Anything that lies between the plane and the view is temporarily hidden from the view. Set the plane so that the trees disappear from the model, as shown in Figure 15.27. If desired, you can use the back clipping plane to remove the objects that lie on the side of the plane away from the viewer.

Applying the Preview to the Entire Model

10. Select the eXit option. The display should look like Figure 15.28, where the Clip option of the DVIEW command has been applied to the entire model, achieving the desired perspective view. Note how all of the trees and part of the fence have been clipped away.

Saving the Perspective Settings

11. Use the New option of the VIEW command to save the current view, including the DVIEW settings. Save under the name PERSP2.

Figure 15.27
Using the Clip option to remove the trees

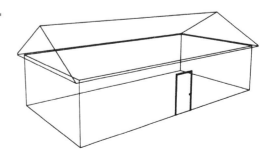

285

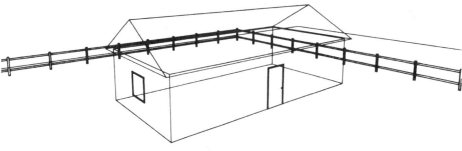

Figure 15.28
Applying the Clip feature to the entire model

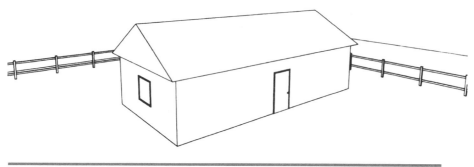

Figure 15.29
Using hidden line removal on the entire model

12. Save the model as BDWELL. Then, use the standard HIDE command on the model, and observe the results. They should be similar to Figure 15.29.

13. Display the 3D Orbit toolbar and experiment with turning the front clipping plane off and on using the Front Clip ON/OFF tool.

Lab 15.C   Dynamic Viewing with Interior View

Purpose

Lab 15.C shows you how to create an interior view and use a wide-angle lens to widen the pictured view. The basic kitchen model created in Assignment 1, Chapter 13, will be your tool.

Objectives

You will be able to:

- Create an interior perspective view of a model
- Pan the displayed image
- Make use of a wide-angle lens
- Use the Hide option

Primary Commands

DVIEW–Camera, Distance, Pan, Zoom, Hide
VIEW–Save

Procedure

Initial Setup

1. Open the basic kitchen drawing that was created in Assignment 1 in Chapter 13. The file name is BKIT.
2. Align the UCS to the WCS, and turn on the UCS icon.

3. Display an isometric view using the SE Isometric View tool or the VPOINT command.

Command: **VPOINT**
Current view direction:
  VIEWDIR = 0.0000,0.0000,1.0000
Specify a view point or [Rotate] <display compass and tripod>: **1,−1,1**
Regenerating model

Creating the Preview Selection Set

4. Activate the DVIEW command:

Command: **DVIEW**
Select objects:

5. Select the objects for the Preview selection set. Use the Window option to place a window around the coffeemaker, as shown in Figure 15.30.

Using the Camera Option

6. Now activate the Camera option. Use the cursor to place the angular location of the camera, as in Figure 15.31.

Picking a New Target

7. To select a new target point, use the Pan option. Click the center of the coffeepot as the base point and the center of the screen as the new location. Now, the coffeemaker is the new target location. This enables closer viewing of that particular area.

Setting the Camera Distance

8. Select the Distance option, and set the distance to 2′. The view is now very close, and it is difficult to make out features.

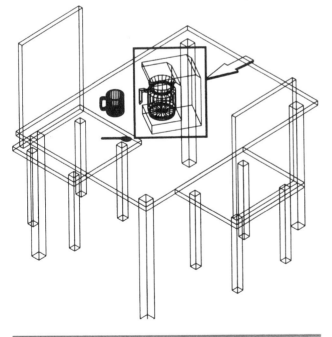

Figure 15.30
Selecting the Preview Selection Set using the Window option

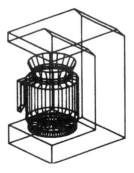

Figure 15.31
Getting the desired view by using the Camera option

287

Figure 15.32
Using a distance of 2′ and a
lens of 20 mm

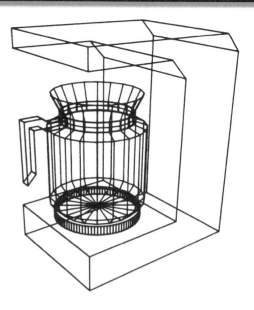

Using the Zoom Option to Get a Better Picture

9. Select the Zoom option, and set the lens length to 20 mm. This is a wide-angle lens, so it provides a larger viewing area. The display should look like Figure 15.32.

Using the Hide Option While in DVIEW

10. When it is desirable to view the Preview selection set with hidden line removal, use the DVIEW command's Hide option. Select the Hide option now and observe the results. Your screen should be similar to that of Figure 15.33.

Applying the Preview to the Entire Model

11. Select the eXit option. The display should look like Figure 15.34.

Figure 15.33
Using the Hide option within the
DVIEW environment

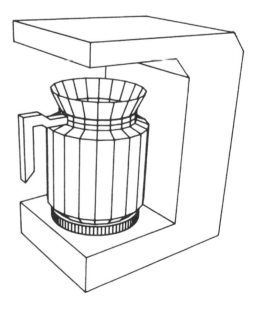

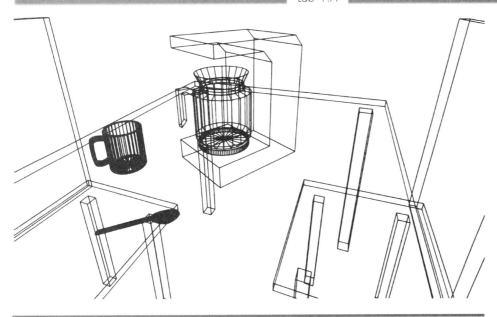

Figure 15.34
Applying the DVIEW settings to the entire model

Figure 15.35
Display showing the entire model with hidden lines removed

Saving the Perspective Settings

12. Use the New option of the VIEW command to save the current view as PERSP1.
13. Save the model as BKIT. Then, use the standard HIDE command on the model and observe the results. They should be similar to Figure 15.35.
14. Display the 3D Orbit toolbar and experiment with the 3D Adjust Distance tool.

Questions

1. What is the difference between an axonometric view and a perspective view?

2. In a perspective view, what effect does moving objects farther and farther away from the viewer have on the displayed view?

3. What causes the effect described in Question 2?

4. Explain the relationship between the center of interest and the station point.

5. What does the command DVIEW stand for? To what other AutoCAD feature is it similar?

6. Explain the purpose of slider bars and how they operate.

7. Explain the purpose of the Preview selection set.

8. Why might it be important to limit the items used in the Preview selection set?

9. Explain the function of the DVIEWBLOCK.

10. Which DVIEW options do you use to cause the perspective effect?

11. What happens to the UCS icon when a perspective view is being displayed?

12. How does the Distance option affect the location of the viewer?

13. What is the significance of the Zoom option?

14. Explain how the Clip option can be of use.

15. Identify the limitations of some of AutoCAD's commands when the perspective view has been activated.

Assignments

1. Create two lines of posts parallel to each other. Each line should be 10′ apart. In each line, there should be at least twenty 12′-high posts, 6′ apart from each other.

   First, display an axonometric view. Save the view as AXONA. Now, use the DVIEW command to create a view similar to the axonometric view, but make it a perspective view. Save this view as PERSPB.

   Split the screen into two horizontal viewports. Display the view AXONA in one viewport and the view PERSPB in the other. Compare the two views.

2. Using the file BDWELL, which was saved in Lab 15.B, create a perspective worm's-eye view of the house.

3. Insert the BKIT model (used in Lab 15.C) into the inside of the house model BDWELL (from Lab 15.B). Use the Clip option and a wide-angle lens to cut through the walls and view the kitchen scene. Use the HIDE command to enhance the effect.

4. Open the model NBOLT created in Chapter 13, Assignment 2. Use the Clip option of the DVIEW command to section the assembly.

5. Open the INCA model surfaced in Chapter 7, Assignment 2. Display a perspective view as if someone were standing close to the model and looking up, toward its top.

Plotting

Overview

In this chapter, you'll learn the techniques for making hard copies of wireframe and more complex models. (*Note:* The labs in this chapter have been designed so that you will be able to do them whether or not you have access to a plotter.)

Concepts Explored

- The importance of model plots
- How to create wireframe and hidden line removed plots
- The differences between axonometric and perspective plots
- What paper space represents
- How to work within paper space
- The creation of paper space viewports
- The creation of two-dimensional drawings from three-dimensional models
- How to plot three-dimensional models in single and multiple views

16.1 Introduction

Many experts believe that we are progressing toward a paperless society, where everyone will have access to computer monitors and be able to call up virtually anything for viewing. This may sound appealing and very efficient, but in most areas of industry today paper copies are still very much a necessity.

For instance, plots of 3D models are very effective presentation tools. If you can quickly generate multiple views of a model or even display what-if scenarios, illustrating different modifications to the model, then you can provide your client with a thorough and impressive presentation. But doing this on-screen usually isn't possible. Even though the screen does provide for on-the-fly changes during client-requested viewing, screens of a size that can be seen by many at one time are still very expensive. However, plotting the various views and scenarios onto large sheets is relatively cheap by comparison and still enables you to make impressive presentations.

Illustrators and artists also need paper copies. An illustrator creates a model—perhaps of a mechanical part or a commercial building—displays a desirable view, turns it into a perspective, and then plots it onto a sheet of paper. The illustrator then uses this plot as a guide when creating a manually drawn and

Figure 16.1
Multiview plot

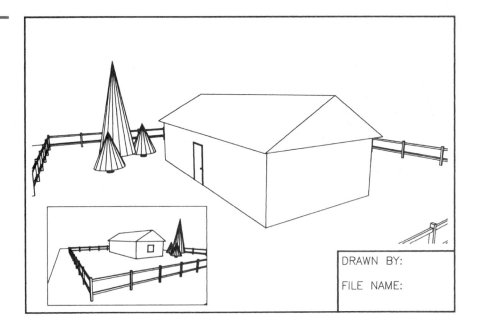

DRAWN BY:

FILE NAME:

painted rendering. The model does not have to be as complex as the final rendering; it merely has to have enough detail to give the illustrator a basis for the rendering.

Plots can be produced in a number of ways—using wireframe, hidden line removal, or axonometric, perspective, or multiple views (Figure 16.1). All these techniques are discussed in this chapter. In addition, paper space, which greatly reduces the complexity of these techniques, is introduced.

16.2 **Wireframe versus Hidden Line Removal**

The quickest way to display a model on the screen is in wireframe. Similarly, when plotting a model, leaving it in wireframe produces the fastest plot. However, this type of model is not the most desirable for presentation purposes. In most cases, hidden line removal is the most effective way to present a model illustration. Producing a plot of a wireframe representation requires no special settings. To plot with hidden lines removed, open the Plot dialog box. Under the shaded viewport options, there is a Shade plot drop-down list. From this list you can set the manner in which you want the plot to be shaded, such as hidden. If you have previously set the shade mode to shade the model, you can set the Shade plot to *As displayed*. (Paper space plot requirements are a little different; we'll discuss them later.) Also, recall that frozen layers are not used in the calculation of hidden line removal. So, to speed up hidden line removal during display or plotting, remember to first freeze layers that are not going to be shown.

3D VIEWPOINT

Hollow Arrowheads During Plotting
If you have arrowheads on your model and you plot the model with the Hide Lines option, the arrowheads will appear to be hollow.

16.3 Axonometric versus Perspective Representations

Axonometric representations of a model are to scale. This means that the objects are proportional to each other. The model can be dimensioned and plotted to a particular scale when it is generated as hard copy. On the other hand, perspective representations of a model are not to scale. This means that each object is not proportional to the other and that when objects are closer to the viewer they appear larger than when they are farther away from the viewer. Although this is what gives the representation its realistic look, it means that a perspective view cannot be dimensioned as such and is to no particular scale when plotted. Because of these differences between axonometric and perspective representations, the scaling of their plots is done differently.

Scaling a Single-View Plot

Plotting an axonometric representation in 3D is basically the same as 2D plotting. You select the desired view, and activate the PLOT command. When a specific scale is desired, you simply enter a scale in much the same way as for a 2D drawing (that is, 1 = 2 or 1/4″ = 1′, for example).

When plotting a perspective representation, you use the Fit to paper check box. The view is then scaled to fit a particular area of the drawing. In this way, the size of the final plot is based on the sheet area that you predefine.

16.4 Paper Space

There are two working environments within any drawing—model space and paper space. Model space is used for construction purposes. This is where the 3D model is built. The paper space environment is used to arrange multiple viewing areas on an imagined two-dimensional sheet of paper. Paper space can be thought of as an electronic cut-and-paste environment. In paper space, the viewports (floating) represent various pictures of the model. Each picture can be scaled, rotated, or written on, just as if the user had cut out various details and arranged them on a piece of paper.

Multiviews and Paper Space

Until Release 11, multiple-viewport displays could not be plotted as one unit. And, although not impossible, it was cumbersome to generate multiple views. Then came the introduction of paper space in AutoCAD. With paper space, you can create a layout of your desired views, set their scale, identify which views will be wireframe and which will be hidden, and, if desired, specify borders or labels for any or all of the views. You can also surround the entire layout with a border, such as a title block. Then, you can simply plot the layout without any complicated settings. The paper space layout stays with the drawing so that it can be used at any time.

There are two types of viewports: tiled and floating. Tiled viewports are multiple viewports created in model space arranged in a tiled format similar to a floor tile. You've used these in the creation of your models. Floating viewports are independent viewports created in paper space. These can be arranged anywhere on your paper space layout. There's a single toolbar for both tiled and floating viewports called Viewports. The tools contained in the toolbar "know" whether you're working in model or paper space and act accordingly. Some of the tools will only work in paper space.

Accessing Paper Space

The two working environments are accessed through the Model and Layout tabs at the bottom of the graphics screen. When the Model tab is active, the system variable called TILEMODE is set to 1. It allows the creation of tiled viewports using the VPORTS command. It allows construction to take place only in model space. This common mode was available in earlier versions of AutoCAD.

The Layout tabs are used to switch to paper space layout. When one of the Layout tabs is active, the system variable called TILEMODE is set to 0. This allows the creation of floating viewports.

You can switch back and forth between model environment and layout environment by using the tabs or the TILEMODE system variable.

When you first click on a Layout tab to enter paper space, the Page Setup dialog box appears. It is used to establish which output device (plotter/printer) will be used with the paper space layout. Once you establish those settings, a single floating viewport is created. Your current model space view will be displayed inside the floating viewport. You should create a layer for floating viewports before you create them so that they can be organized like any object in your drawing. Therefore, you will probably want to erase the automatically created viewport and create your own once you have a layer to put it on.

To create a viewport, use the Single Viewport tool from the Viewports toolbar or use the MVIEW command. This command works only when TILEMODE is set to 0. MVIEW stands for "Make VIEWport," which is exactly what it does. By selecting the various options, you can create any combination of viewports. These areas can be any size and can display any view of a model. Once you have placed the viewing areas, you can annotate and detail them in any fashion. As you might imagine, these floating viewports are very similar to the tiled viewports, except that each viewport created in paper space is considered an individual object. They can be any size, and they can overlap each other; hence the term *floating*. The border lines identifying their boundaries can be turned on or off. (Refer to the later section on initial paper space layout and plotting for information on the size of the model and the viewport border when plotting.) Each floating viewport contains a model space view of your model. Activating any floating viewport gives you access to model space.

You may add any type of objects in paper space, but these objects will only be present in the paper space environment; they are not added to the actual model. When you switch to TILEMODE = 1, any objects you created in paper space will not be shown. Then, when you switch back to paper space, with TILEMODE set to 0, the paper space objects will reappear.

PSPACE versus MSPACE

The power of paper space is increased by its ability to enter into any of the newly created floating viewports and alter the model contents in any way, such as changing the viewpoint, exactly as if you had switched back to the TILEMODE = 1 setting.

To activate a floating viewport, use the PAPER/MODEL toggle button on the status line. This is the same line that contains your SNAP and GRID buttons. When a layout tab is active (TILEMODE=0) and you've created a floating viewport, clicking on the PAPER/MODEL toggle button will switch back and forth between the paper space layout and the floating viewports. The toggle button displays which mode you're in: PAPER or MODEL. Remember, this is still within the layout.

There is a new feature introduced in AutoCAD 2005. It is called Viewport Maximize and it has its own tool button on the status line when you are in a paper space layout.

When a floating viewport is active and you click on the Maximize Viewport button, the viewport is maximized to fill the screen and switched to model space for model editing. If paper space is active and you double-click on the edge of the viewport, it will perform the same function as clicking on the Maximize Viewport button. Clicking on the button again will return you to the normal paper space layout.

PSPACE versus MSPACE Identification

There are several ways to identify which "space" you are in while TILEMODE is set to 0. The first method is to look at the status line. If the word PAPER is visible and black, then you're in paper space. If the word MODEL is visible and black, you're in model space.

The next method is to use the UCS icon. When you're in paper space, it takes on a new look, as shown in the column on the left. It appears in the lower-left corner of the screen.

3D VIEWPOINT

Accessing Floating Viewports

If a floating viewport lies completely within another floating viewport, you may find it impossible to access. To access it, you must turn off the larger viewport, using the MVIEW command.

The third method is to observe the behavior of the cursor. When in paper space, the cursor crosshair can roam all over the layout. When in model space, the cursor crosshair is limited to movement within the currently active viewport. When you move outside the viewport, it's displayed as an arrow. To activate a viewport, move the cursor within the viewport and click. The border of the viewport turns bold.

Exiting the Paper Space Environment

When you set TILEMODE back to 1 or click on the Model tab, you exit the paper space environment entirely and return to the common construction mode of model space. The screen returns to the settings originated before you entered paper space. The paper space settings and objects are not lost; they are simply stored until you return to paper space by again setting TILEMODE to 0 or by clicking a Layout tab. Any changes made to the model when TILEMODE is set to 1 is reflected in the viewports of paper space, even though they are turned off. When you return to paper space, you will be able to see the changes you made while in model space. At any time, you can switch back and forth between TILEMODE settings 0 and 1 by using the Model or Layout tabs, effectively switching between the two environments.

Initial Paper Space Layout and Plotting

The following outlines a method for setting up a paper space layout and plotting a model. This method could be used for any model.

1. The model has been constructed at this point. Create a layer for the floating viewports and another layer for your title block/border. Make the floating viewport layer current.

2. Click on a Layout tab. The first time you enter into paper space, the Page Setup dialog box creates a single floating viewport. Delete this viewport because this viewport is often not the desired size or in the desired location.

3. The paper space environment is a 2D environment and can be thought of as a flat piece of paper. Make your title block/border layer current and insert a border that represents the sheet of paper onto which the model will be plotted. This could be a standard title block and border. Most often, the scale of a paper space layout is plotted as 1:1, so the border should match the sheet at a scale of 1 to 1. The title block can be filled in now or later.

4. Make your viewport layer current and, within the inserted border, use the Single Viewport tool or the MVIEW command to create viewports that will display the various views that are desired. Remember that the viewports can be any size and can overlay each other. If the viewports are placed on their own layers, the border of a viewport can be turned off simply by turning off the layer on which its viewport was placed. When a layer the viewport is on is turned off, the border disappears and will not plot. However, the contents of the viewport will not be affected—they will still be visible and will plot.

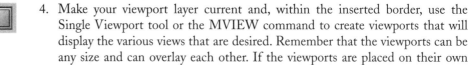

5. Switch to model space with the PAPER/MODEL toggle button and, using the various display commands, display the desired viewpoint and orientation. The scale of the model in the viewport can be set at this point or can also be set by modifying the viewport's properties. This is described in Step 7. A special ZOOM option, called XP, is available to do this. It will scale the model in relation to the paper space plot scale. Because you normally plot the paper space layout on a 1 = 1 scale, the XP scale is in proportion to that. For example, if you want a floor plan at a scale of 1/4″ = 1′ (1 = 48), then the XP scale value will be 1/48. Conversely, if a view is to be plotted at a scale of 2 = 1, the XP scale would be 2. To use this option, enter the desired viewport and type the following command:

Command: **ZOOM**
All/Center/Dynamic/Extents . . . /<Scale(X/XP)>: **1/48XP**

This model would be scaled to 1/4″ = 1′ when the paper space layout was plotted at a scale of 1 = 1. (*Note:* The XP option will work only when the TILE-MODE variable is set to 0.) Remember that the standard ZOOM command will not work with perspective views. To set the desired size of the perspective model, use the 3DDISTANCE command.

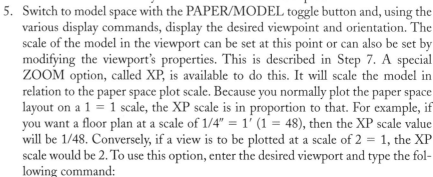

6. While still within the model environment, the layers in each viewport are independent. This means you can freeze different layers in different viewports, giving you any combination of displayed or not displayed layers. The command that controls the layers in the currently active viewport is called VPLAYER. You also can use the much more visual Layer Control. From the drop-down list, select Freeze or Thaw in current viewport icon. It's a sun symbol with a small rectangular box that represents a floating viewport. This freezes or thaws objects in only the active floating viewport.

7. Switch to paper space with the MODEL/PAPER toggle button. At this stage you can add any text or other annotation that you want. Remember that this is paper space and at a scale of 1 = 1.

You can also check or set the scale of any floating viewport. Click on the edge of a visible viewport to highlight it, right-click to bring up the context menu, and select Properties from the context menu. The Properties dialog box appears. Near the bottom of the dialog box there are settings for Standard and Custom scales. This sets the scale of the contents of the floating viewport.

8. To set the floating viewport that will plot with hidden lines removed, use the Properties dialog box again. At the bottom of the Properties dialog box for a

floating viewport, you'll find a Hide Plot setting. Setting Yes to this causes the viewport's contents to be plotted with hidden lines removed. Using this method allows you to decide which floating viewport will be plotted hidden and which will be plotted wireframe. (*Note:* The viewport border needs to be visible when this option is selected, but it does not have to be visible for plotting. Before plotting, turn the layer off that contains the viewport, and the viewport border will no longer be visible.)

9. Save the file with the paper space layout.
10. Use the PLOT command to alter the plot configuration. When in paper space, you can alter the plot configuration as you normally do, except the plot scale should be 1 = 1 and the Hide Objects option will have no effect because you will have already set it using the MVIEW command.

Once you have mastered the use of paper space—a process that should not take long—you will appreciate its power in setting up a drawing sheet. You might even wish to use paper space for all your construction and drawing, whether in 2D or 3D. Paper space is a very powerful feature; don't underestimate its uses. And remember its benefits! Paper space and the creation of independent viewports allow you to set up all plot scales directly within a drawing, and also to identify which detail will have hidden lines removed. When plotting from now on, you only need to plot to a scale of 1 = 1 and not worry if hidden line removal is turned on or off in the plot configuration.

Page Setup Manager

The Page Setup Manager was introduced in AutoCAD 2005. It specifies the page setup for the current layout. You can also create named page setups or import page setups from other drawings. To access the Page Setup Manager, right-click on the current Layout tab and click Page Setup Manager from the context menu. Figure 16.2A shows the Page Setup Manager dialog box. With the current layout name highlighted, clicking the Modify button brings up the Page Setup dialog box as shown in Figure 16.2B. You would use this new dialog box as you would the earlier version. All the settings are now contained on one page. Some settings are inaccessible because you are working with a paper space layout.

16.5 Working Drawings of Models

Once created, a model usually will either be prepared for final presentation (see Chapter 15) or used to create working drawings. A working drawing is a completely annotated 2D drawing that is used for the production of the modeled component. To add notes and text to a model is a simple process; you just create a paper space environment (see the 10-step procedure outlined earlier). The dimensioning of the 3D model is a more difficult process.

The easiest way to create a working drawing is to create 2D orthographic views of the model, put each view on its own layer, and then dimension those views. Unfortunately, you may have to doctor views to show hidden features with hidden lines. However, if you create a solid model, you can use the SOLVIEW and SOLDRAW commands explained in Chapter 11.

The second method for creating orthographic views involves the generation of a solid model using the Mechanical Desktop or Inventor program. These are separate application programs from Autodesk. Their purpose is to enhance the creation of 3D solid models through the use of parametric design. One of its features is the automatic creation of 2D drawings from a solid model (refer to Chapter 24).

Figure 16.2
Page Setup Manager dialog box

A

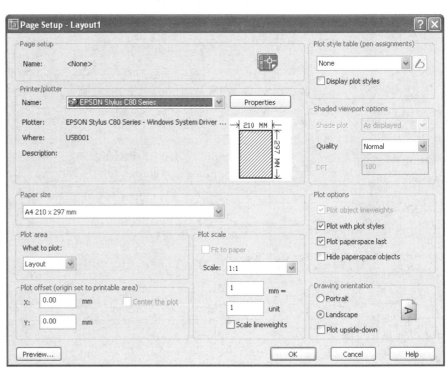

B

Lab 16.A   Paper Space Plot

Purpose

Lab 16.A familiarizes you with the paper space environment and helps you to appreciate how easy it is to lay out a multiple-view plot. You will make use of the ANGPLT model created in Chapter 7, Lab 7.B.

If you do not have access to a plotter, you can still do this lab.

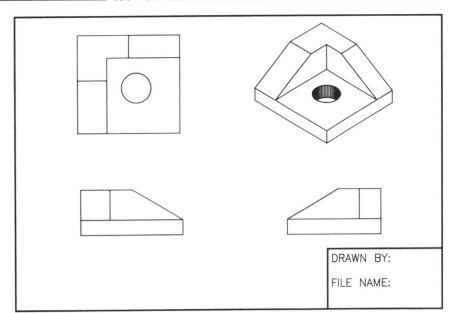

Figure 16.3
Multiview plot of the angle plate model

Objectives

You will be able to:

- Lay out a multiview plot in paper space
- Select which viewports will be plotted with hidden lines removed
- Switch back and forth between MSPACE and PSPACE

Primary Commands

TILEMODE
MVIEW
PSPACE
MSPACE
PLOT

Final Plot

Figure 16.3 shows the multiview plot of the angle plate model you'll be laying out.

Procedure

1. Create a title block as shown in Figure 16.4. If you already have a title block drawing file, you can use it. Just remember that it may not be the same size; you may have to make adjustments. This will be inserted into the paper space layout. Save the drawing as PSTB (Paper Space Title Block).
2. Open the ANGPLT model surfaced in Chapter 7, Lab 7.B.

Switching into the Paper Space Environment

3. Click the first layout tab at the bottom of the graphics screen to enter into the paper space environment. The first time you enter into paper space, the Page Setup dialog box creates a single floating viewport. Delete this viewport and create a layer for the floating viewports. It is commonly called VPORTS. If you have turned on the UCS icon, the paper space icon should be visible in the lower-left corner of the screen.

Switching Back to the Model Space Environment

4. Click the Model tab at the bottom of the graphics screen. The angle plate model should appear again, because you are back in the model space environment.

Figure 16.4
Title block named PSTB

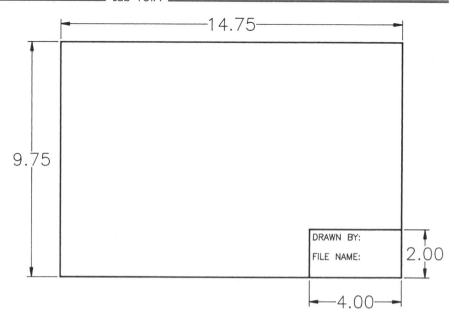

Recall that both environments are kept intact when you switch from one to the other.

5. Click the same layout tab you used earlier to return to your paper space layout.

Inserting the Title Block in Paper Space

6. Create a layer called TBLOCK, and make it current.
7. Using the INSERT command, place the title block with its lower-left corner at 0,0 and fill it in with the appropriate information (see Figure 16.5).

Figure 16.5
Title block inserted into paper space

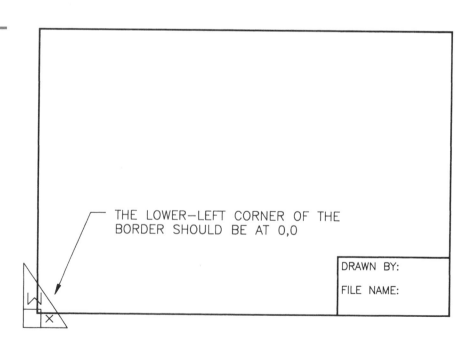

Figure 16.6

Four paper space viewports

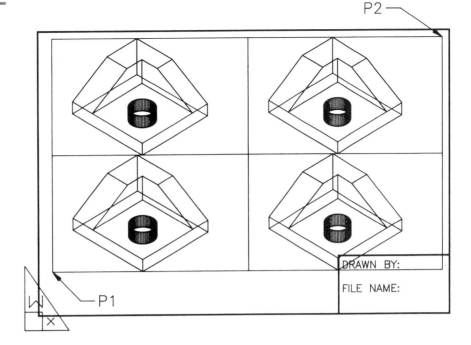

Creating Paper Space Viewports

8. Make the VPORTS layer current.

9. Using the Display Viewports dialog tool from the Viewports toolbar or the MVIEW command, create a four-viewport configuration:

Command: **MVIEW**
Switching to paper space
Specify corner of viewport or
[ON/OFF/Fit/Hideplot/Lock/Object/Polygonal/Restore/2/3/4] <Fit>: **4**
Specify first corner or [Fit] <Fit>: **0.5,1.5** (see Figure 16.6, P1)
Specify opposite corner: **14.5, 9.5** (see Figure 16.6, P2)

If you use a different title block and border, use the appropriate P1 and P2. Refer to the figure for proper locations.

You should now have four viewports, each displaying the last active viewport from model space, as shown in Figure 16.6.

Using MSPACE to Display Desired Viewpoints

To change the displayed view in any of the viewports, you must use the MSPACE command or use the MODEL/PAPER toggle button on the status line. This command switches to model space *within* the paper space environment, and allows access to the contents of the viewports.

10. Using the MSPACE command, enter into model space. Note how the cursor switched into one of the viewports. This is the currently active viewport.

11. Using the appropriate View tool or the VPOINT command, display the standard orthographic views—top, front, right-side, and axonometric (see Figure 16.7).

301

Figure 16.7

Multiviews in paper space set to 0.5XP

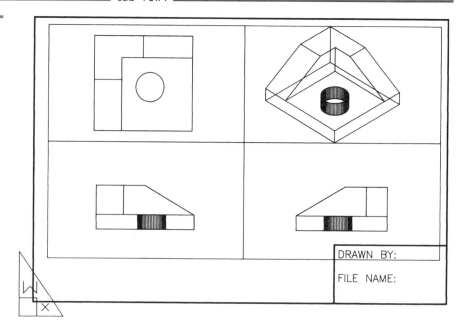

Setting the Scale

12. While still in MSPACE, go into each viewport by digitizing in the viewport, and set the scale using the XP option of the ZOOM command:

Command: **ZOOM**
All/Center/. . . . Window/ <Scale> (X/XP)>: **.5XP**

This sets the scale of the views at 1 = 2 when the paper space layout is plotted at a scale of 1 = 1 (see Figure 16.7).

Check the viewing scale of the floating viewport. Click the Model button to return to Paper (paper space). Click the edge of the viewport to highlight it and right-click to bring up the context menu. Select Properties from the menu.

When the Properties dialog box appears, scroll down to the bottom and look for the Standard Scale and Custom Scale settings. The Standard is set to 1:2 and the Custom is 0.5. This is what you set using the ZOOM XP command option.

Freezing the Viewport Object

Viewports created in paper space are considered objects. This means they can be scaled, stretched, or frozen when the layer they are on is frozen.

13. While in paper space, make layer 0 current.
14. Using the Layer Control, freeze the layer called VPORTS. Note how the outline of the viewport disappears, but the contents of the viewport do not. Remember, you can choose not to display the viewport border by freezing the layer that contains the viewport objects.
15. Thaw the VPORTS layer to display the viewport border again.

Removing Hidden Lines

To plot with hidden line removal in paper space, you must tell AutoCAD which viewports will be plotted with hidden lines removed. Use the PROPERTIES command to do this.

16. Click the edge of the viewport to highlight it and right-click to bring up the context menu. Select Properties from the menu. When the Properties dialog box appears, scroll down to the bottom and look for the Shade Plot setting. Change the setting to Hidden. Because of this selection, the contents of each viewport will be plotted with hidden lines removed. They won't show up hidden on the screen when you use Hideplot, only when plotted.
17. Freeze the layer called VPORTS.
18. Save the model as ANGPLT.

Plotting the Paper Space Layout

Note: If you do not have access to a plotter or printer, this is as far as you can go. If you do have access to a plotter, complete the following steps:

19. Set up the plotter in the usual fashion.
20. Use the PLOT command.
21. Set up the Plot configuration. (Recall that the Shade plot: Hidden option has no effect when plotting in paper space because you identify which viewport will be plotted with hidden line removal during the layout stage.) Also, be sure to plot this layout at a scale of 1 = 1.
22. Your final plot should look like Figure 16.3. Note how the text in the title block stayed the same size, whereas the model views plotted at half their actual size. This happened because the text was added in paper space and the model views were scaled using the XP option of the ZOOM command.

Lab 16.B   Paper Space Layout with Insert

Purpose

Lab 16.B familiarizes you with the process of manipulating viewports in paper space and shows you how paper space viewports can overlap each other. You will be using the BDWELL model from Chapter 8, Lab 8.B, again.

You do not have to have access to a plotter to do this lab.

Objectives

You will be able to:

- Lay out a master viewport with an overlapping viewport in paper space
- Select which viewports will be plotted with hidden lines removed
- Switch back and forth between MSPACE and PSPACE

Primary Commands

TILEMODE
MVIEW
PSPACE
MSPACE
PLOT

Final Plot

Figure 16.8 shows the final multiview perspective plot of the basic dwelling model.

Procedure

1. Open the model BDWELL created in Chapter 8, Lab 8.B.
2. Using the DVIEW command, display a perspective view similar to that shown in Figure 16.9.

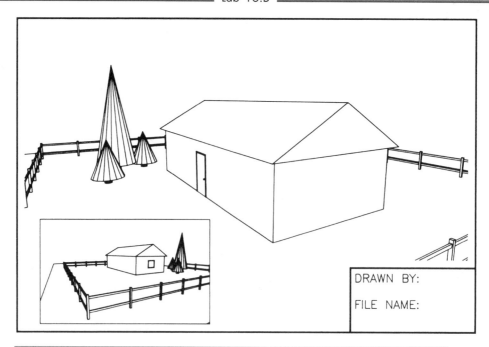

Figure 16.8
Multiview perspective plot of the basic dwelling model

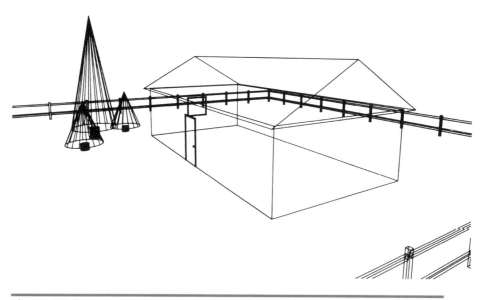

Figure 16.9
Perspective view of the basic dwelling

Switching into the Paper Space Environment

3. Click the first Layout tab at the bottom of the graphics screen to enter into the paper space environment. The first time you enter into paper space, the Page Setup dialog box creates a single floating viewport. Delete this viewport. If you have turned on the UCS icon, the paper space icon should be visible in the lower-left corner of the screen.

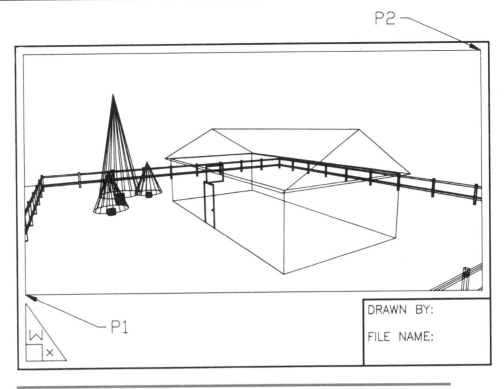

Figure 16.10
Single paper space viewport

Inserting the Title Block in Paper Space

4. Create a layer called TBLOCK, and make it current.
5. Using the INSERT command, place the title block that was created in Lab 16.A (PSTB from Step 1) with its lower-left corner at 0,0, and fill it in with the appropriate information.

Creating Paper Space Viewports

6. Create a layer called VPORT1, and make it active.

7. Using the Single Viewport tool from the Viewports toolbar or the MVIEW command, create one viewport that fits within the title block area, as shown in Figure 16.10.

   Command: **MVIEW**
   Switching to paper space
   Specify corner of viewport or
   [ON/OFF/Fit/Hideplot/Lock/Object/Polygonal/Restore /2/3/4] <Fit>: **1/4″,2-1/4″**
      (See Figure 16.10, P1.)
   Specify opposite corner: 1′2-1/2″,9-1/2″ (See Figure 16.10, P2.)

   If you use a different title block and border, use the appropriate P1 and P2. Refer to the figure for proper location.

8. Create a layer called VPORT2, and make it current.

9. Using the Single Viewport tool from the Viewports toolbar or the MVIEW command, create one viewport that overlaps the first viewport, as shown in Figure 16.11.

305

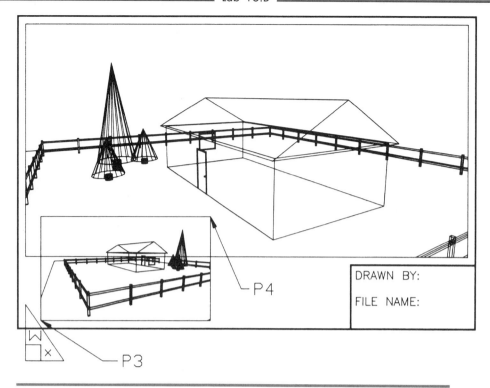

Figure 16.11
A small viewport overlapping onto a larger viewport

Command: **MVIEW**
Switching to paper space
Specify corner of viewport or
[ON/OFF/Fit/Hideplot/Lock/Object/Polygonal/Restore/2/3/4] <Fit>: **3/4″,1/4″**
   (See Figure 16.11, P3.)
Specify opposite corner: **6-1/4″,3-1/2″** (See Figure 16.11, P4. If you used a different title block, click the appropriate locations for P3 and P4.)

Switching to Model Space

10. Click the PAPER button on the status line or use the MSPACE command to switch to model space.
11. Make the small viewport active. The best way to do this is to click in the nonoverlapping area. Otherwise, AutoCAD does not know which viewport you are activating.
12. Using the DVIEW command, display a rear perspective view of the dwelling similar to the one shown in Figure 16.8.
13. Using the PSPACE command, switch back to paper space.

Removing Hidden Lines

To plot with hidden line removal in paper space, you must tell AutoCAD which viewports will be plotted with hidden lines removed. Use the PROPERTIES command to do this.

14. Click the edge of each viewport to highlight them and right-click to bring up the context menu. Select Properties from the menu. When the Properties dialog

box appears, scroll down to the bottom and look for the Shade Plot setting. Change the setting to Hidden. Because of this selection, the contents of each viewport will be plotted with hidden lines removed.

15. Freeze layer VPORT1 so that the border around the viewport will not be plotted.
16. Save the model as BDWEL2.

Plotting the Paper Space Layout

Note: If you do not have access to a plotter, this is as far as you can go.
      If you do have access to a plotter, complete the following steps:

17. Set up the plotter in the usual fashion.
18. Use the PLOT command.
19. Set up the Plot Configuration. (Recall that the Hide Lines option has no effect when plotting in paper space because you identified which viewport will be plotted with hidden line removal during the layout stage.) Be sure to plot this layout at a scale of 1 = 1.
20. The final plot should look like Figure 16.8.

Questions

1. In what way do artists make use of 3D model plots?
2. How do you activate hidden line removal when plotting?
3. In what way do frozen layers affect hidden line removed plots?
4. How is scaling affected by axonometric and perspective plots?
5. What does the system variable TILEMODE control?
6. What are the various functions of the MVIEW command?
7. Can the MVIEW command be used in model space?
8. What is the function of the PAPER/MODEL button on the status line?

Assignments

You'll be creating a hardcopy plot or a 2D drawing file using a DXB file in each of the following assignments.

1. Using the model scene BKIT (Basic KITchen) assembled in Chapter 13, Assignment 1, produce a paper space layout illustrating (a) the entire kitchen layout in perspective and (b) an overlapping view showing a close-up of the coffeemaker. Use MVIEW to make all the viewports plot with hidden lines removed. Save the model plus the layout as BKIT. Then, plot the layout.

2. Create an office layout using the models from Chapter 5 given in the following list. Use paper space to lay out several viewports looking around the scene. Use MVIEW to make all the viewports plot with hidden lines removed. Save the model plus layout as OFFC (OFFiCe layout). Then, plot the layout.

3D SYMBOL	SOURCE
TABLE	Lab 5.B
CHAIR	Lab 5.C
FCAB	Chapter 5, Assignment 1
BSHEL	Chapter 5, Assignment 2

3. With the duct models created in Chapter 8 (see following list), create an assembly. Use paper space to lay out four viewports that display the top, front, right-side, and isometric views. Use MVIEW to make all the viewports plot with hidden lines removed. Save the model plus layout as PIPA (PIPing Assembly). Then plot the layout.

3D SYMBOL	SOURCE
TDUCT	Chapter 8, Assignment 3
ODUCT	Chapter 8, Assignment 4

4. Create a paper space layout of a perspective view and an overlapping orthographic view of the side of a car, using the CAR model created in Chapter 8, Assignment 6. Use MVIEW to make all the viewports plot with hidden lines removed. Save the model and layout as SCAR (Sports CAR). Then plot the layout or create a 2D drawing using DXBIN.

5. Restore the ANGPLT model plotted in Lab 16.B. Turn off the paper space layer called VPORTS created in that lab and create a new layer, called VPORT2. On this new layer, create a paper space layout that has two viewports that are side by side. Display the same axonometric view in each. Set the left viewport to use hidden line removal and the right one to remain as a wireframe model. Save the model and new layout as ANGPLT. Then plot the layout.

Rendering

Overview

In this chapter, we explore the use of light, shadow, materials, and preferences in final renderings. The techniques for presenting drawings in enhanced fashions are explained, and the additional rendering procedures necessary for these effects are noted.

Concepts Explored

- The process involved in CAD rendering
- The Render utility and the different types of rendering
- Choosing and placing lights
- Attaching materials
- Applying mapping projection
- Setting preferences

17.1 Introduction

For AutoCAD users, rendering presents a design in an artistic form; it generates an image that gives a more representative view of their creations. In CAD, rendering is the process of taking an image made basically of lines and adding tones across the surfaces between those lines, which produces a more realistic form of the design. The tones range from light to dark and may be in black and white or a combination of other colors. Because the chances of selling the resulting product improve as the prototype design becomes more appealing, rendering is often the finishing touch that ensures the sale. An example of a rendered image is shown in Figure 17.1.

Performing renderings with three-dimensional models is an art in and of itself. Producing photorealistic images is a long process, but it no longer requires access to expensive hardware. This chapter introduces you to the range of possible rendering techniques and helps make your first attempt at rendering relatively easy. Here, you'll only get your feet wet, but you'll be able to see what you can accomplish with rendering given skill and opportunity. New terms that apply to rendering and various rendering types are discussed in the chapter.

Figure 17.1
A rendered image of an automobile

17.2 **AutoCAD and Rendering**

The Render utility is used to create basic to photorealistic images. It is more powerful than the Shade modes because it gives you control of lighting and the addition of materials. With the integrated enhancements of AutoCAD 2005, each light type can cast shadows, and materials can make use of bitmap images.

There are three rendering types: Render, Photo Real, and Photo Ray-Traced. Render is the fastest but does not show material maps or shadows. The next is Photo Real, which does show shadows and material maps. The third, Photo Ray-Traced, shows reflections, refractions, and more precise shadows.

Render Toolbar

The Render toolbar can be used to access all the commands related to rendering. The toolbar is displayed by checking the Render box from the Toolbars dialog box. The Toolbars dialog box is displayed by selecting Toolbars from the View pull-down menu. If you move the cursor onto a tool without clicking it, a tooltip may appear. Tooltips are words that describe the function of the tool. Tooltips can be turned on by checking the Show Tooltips box in the Toolbars dialog box.

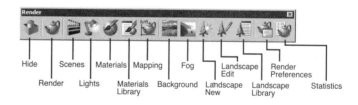

Rendering Procedures Outlined

To make rendering a relatively easy task, follow the procedure outlined next. Once you have committed the procedure to memory, you'll find the task of rendering to be a pleasurable experience. The outline of the procedure identifies major areas that will be explained in the text that follows.

1. Open the desired model to be rendered.
2. Create the desired pictorial views, whether axonometric or perspective. These should be stored under the VIEW command.

3. Specify (place) the desired number and type of lights to illuminate the view using the LIGHT command. Although it is possible to create a rendering without specifying lights (AutoCAD would then use default settings to create the rendering), placing lights gives you more control over the final rendering.

4. Load materials to be used with the RMAT command. First, however, you must extract materials from a material library that can be accessed through the RMAT command or the MATLIB command.

5. Assign material properties to objects, colors, or layers (to add highlights and bitmap images to the model) using the RMAT command.

6. Assemble scenes that contain the desired view and lights utilizing the SCENE command.

7. Set the rendering preferences, such as rendering type, background fog, and so on, using the RPREF command.

8. Select the desired scene, use the RENDER command, and click the Render button. The screen should display the model in a rendered form.

9. Save the image on disk using the SAVEIMG command so that it may be replayed at a later time. You can also render to a file using the Destination option of the Render dialog box.

10. Replay an image using the REPLAY command.

17.3 Creating the Pictorial View

You will need to manipulate the view of the model on the screen until the desired position is attained. When creating pictorial views of small components, it is often best to display them as axonometric views. When viewing an actual physical model, the human eye usually does not discern vanishing points on small, close objects. The simplest method for creating axonometric views is by using the VPOINT or the 3DORBIT command (refer to Chapter 3).

When creating renderings of large objects, such as buildings or large machinery, where vanishing points are readily discernible, display them as perspective views. Use the DVIEW command to generate perspective views (see Chapter 15).

Regardless of the viewpoint chosen, store the views so that they may later be selected to be placed into scenes. Both axonometric and perspective views can be stored using the VIEW command.

17.4 Choosing the Lights

The addition of lights varies the tones of the rendered image. When used in combination with materials, lights also create highlights and even cast shadows for an increasingly dramatic effect.

When lighting a scene, it is important to remember that the brightness of a surface is controlled by its relation to the light source. The closer the face is to being perpendicular to the source of the light, the brighter the surface will be. Two other factors govern the brightness of a surface—reflection and roughness. These are explained later, when we discuss material properties.

The four light types are ambient, distant, point, and spot. The ambient light type is referred to as background light. It creates an illumination that is all around the model and that lights every surface evenly. There is no specific source to ambient light, but you assign an intensity that controls the overall level of brightness. Note that in Figure 17.2A, an ambient setting of 1.0 illuminates the area uniformly. Ambient light is useful to brighten or darken a scene uniformly.

The distant light type simulates a light source that is a great distance from the model, such as the sun. Because the light source is treated as if it is far away, its light rays are projected parallel with each other. The distance away from the model has no effect on the light. Only the direction in which the light type is pointing and its intensity affect the lighted model. In Figure 17.2B, you can see that with the addition of a distant light source there is a distinct difference in the effect of lighting on the surfaces.

The point light type radiates light out from its source location, in an effect similar to that of a lightbulb. The distance that the point light is away from the model affects the amount of light reaching the model. This phenomenon is referred to as *falloff* or *attenuation* and is controlled by using the inverse linear and inverse square settings of the point light options. If it is set to "none," the point light will not fall off and will be at the same level of brightness regardless of the distance from the light to the surface. The Inverse Linear setting causes the light to diminish with distance, and Inverse Square causes it to diminish at a greater rate. The greater the amount of light that falls off, the farther the point light is from a surface. Light from point sources passes through surfaces and does not cast shadows. This light type illuminates a large space and is useful for accenting an area, emphasizing a feature, or adding highlights. Figure 17.2C shows the effect of a point light when light falloff

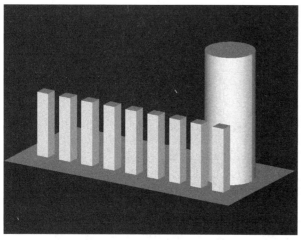

A   Ambient light

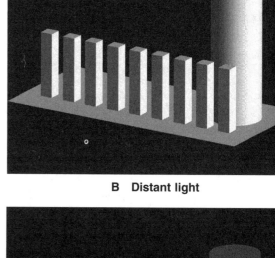

B   Distant light

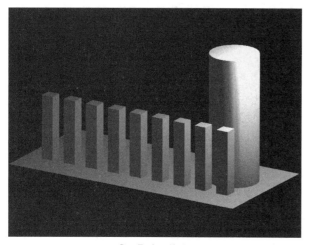

C   Point light

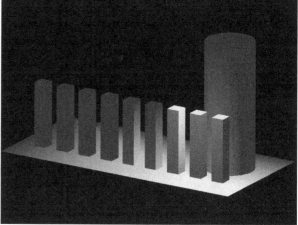

D   Spotlight

Figure 17.2
Behavior of light types

is turned on. The point light source is at the right, so the surfaces of objects going toward the left become darker with increasing distance.

The spotlight type simulates the effect of spotlights to create brightly lit areas. The spotlight's purpose is to generate a cone of light projecting from a source and falling on a particular area. Its intensity falls off as the distance from the source increases; therefore, it is particularly useful in highlighting areas or casting shadows (see Figure 17.2D).

Shadow Casting

The three main light types—Point, Distant, and Spot—each have shadow-casting capabilities. Each light-type dialog box has a check box to turn on shadow casting. Figure 17.3 shows the shadow-casting effect. Also note that there's a Shadow button when performing the rendering. It turns all the shadow generation for the render on or off. You must remember that even though you may have shadows turned on for light, it also needs to be turned on during rendering as well. This applies in the reverse as well.

Placing the Lights

In a scene to be rendered, it is important to place lights in a way that will cause changes in the surfaces to be lighted or shadowed. This is what makes the model stand out. A model can be rendered without placing any lights, but this usually results in a flat-toned image. It is best to include at least one light in any scene to be rendered.

When placing lights, direct a light to shine diagonally on the model from the left or right top of the screen. This produces a most desirable effect because it causes at least three tone levels. The first level, and the brightest one, appears on the surfaces that are closest to being perpendicular to the light. The other two levels are not as bright because they appear on surfaces that are more parallel and less perpendicular to the light source.

If the model is large, such as a house, more lights may be needed in order to accent areas. By casting more light, you can increase the contrast between light and dark in the scene. Light surfaces appear to project toward the viewer, and dark surfaces recede from the viewer. Ultimately, it is up to you to decide how much lighting best suits the model; however, remember that the more contrast between light and dark, the more the model stands out.

You may place a light type in one of three ways: select Lights from the Render pull-down menu, select the Lights tool from the Render toolbar menu, or type

Figure 17.3
Shadow casting

LIGHT at the command prompt. Any of these three methods will display the Lights dialog box, which is shown in Figure 17.4A. Note that the LIGHT command cannot be used in paper space.

Looking at Figure 17.4A, note that on the right side of the Lights dialog box are the Ambient Light settings. The intensity can be adjusted at any time.

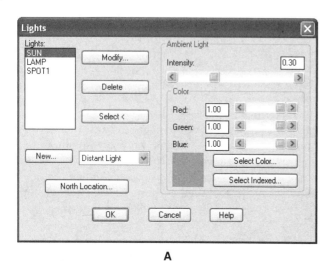

A

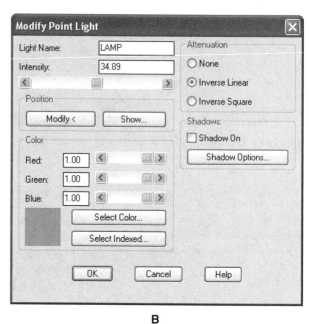

B

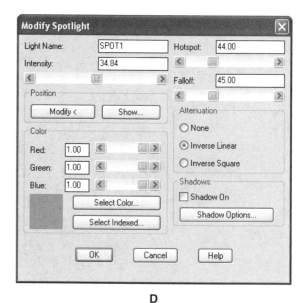

C

D

Figure 17.4
Lighting dialog boxes and the light blocks

314

The procedure to place a new light is as follows:

1. Click one of the three light types: point, distant, or spot.
2. Select NEW from the Lights dialog box.
3. Now a New Light dialog box appears depending on which type of light you chose. Now give a name to the light type. Give a unique name for each placement of light. Also, enter the Intensity. A value of 0 turns the light off. For point and spotlights, the value can be any real number. For distant lights, the value can be any real number between 0 and 1.

The following are some unique settings for each light type:

POINT   The New Point Light dialog box contains an Attenuation area (see Figure 17.4B), which controls the point light falloff; that is, the rate at which the point light intensity decreases as the distance from the light source increases. If you do not wish any decrease in light intensity, select the None box; if you want a gradual decrease, select the Inverse Linear box; and if you want a rapid decrease, select the Inverse Square box. To place the point light, use the Modify button; to check its location, use the Show button.

DISTANT   The distant light is normally used to simulate the sun. To assist in its placement, use image boxes to define the Azimuth and Altitude values (see Figure 17.4C). To identify the location toward which the sun is shining, use the Modify button.

SPOTLIGHT   The spotlight is used to highlight areas and cast shadows. To define the area on which the light falls, use the Hotspot and Falloff values (see Figure 17.4D). The Hotspot defines the area of the brightest and most definite shadow, whereas the Falloff value defines the area where the shadow gradually fades away. Like the point light, use the Modify and Show buttons to place the light by identifying the light location and the direction in which it's pointing.

4. To accept the light type settings and place the light, select the OK button. When a light is placed, a block with the light's unique name appears at the given coordinate location. The size of the block is governed by the Icon Scale setting in the Rendering Preferences dialog box (RPREF).
5. To modify a currently placed light, you can either click the light name from the list or use the Select option to select the light block required. This is done from the Lights dialog box.

Note: A file may have up to 500 lights contained in it.

17.5 **Material Properties**

Material properties control the way light is reflected from or absorbed by a surface. These properties can be attached to specific objects, colors, or layers. Figure 17.5 shows a tire on a car. The tire itself has a low reflection value and a high roughness value, giving it a flat, uniform tone. The hubcap has a high reflection value and a low roughness value, giving it a very shiny, polished look.

You can create your own material types or select previously created ones from a material library. Each material has a set of attributes that controls the behavior of light and color or the application of a bitmap image.

Using Materials

The creation and attachment of materials is performed from the Materials dialog box (see Figure 17.6A). The following is the procedure used to access and attach a material:

Figure 17.5
Flat and shiny surfaces

Figure 17.6
Material dialog boxes

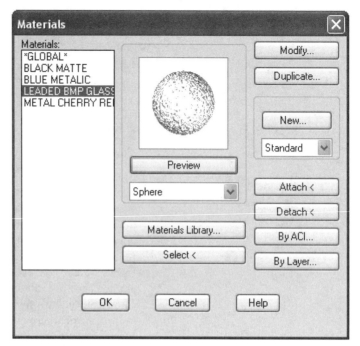

A

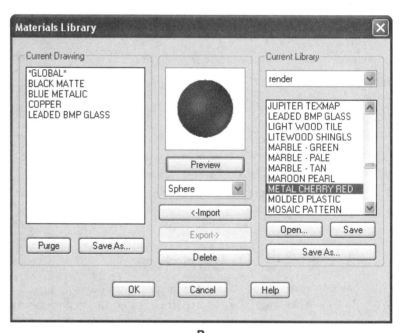

B

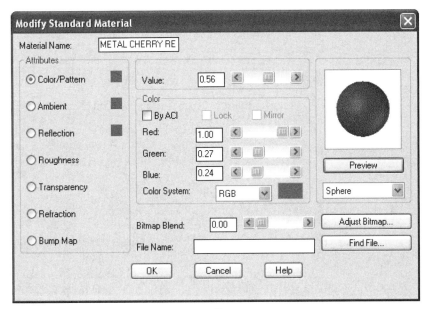

c

1. Use the RMAT command to display the Materials dialog box.
2. If materials were already included in the drawing, select them from the Materials list on the left side of the Materials dialog box. But if the drawing is new, you must import materials into the drawing. To do this, click the Materials Library button. You are presented with the Materials Library dialog box shown in Figure 17.6B.
3. Along the right side of the box is the Library list. Normally, it displays the default library, RENDER.MLI. Scroll through the list and highlight the desired materials to bring into your drawing. When you have highlighted the ones you want, click the Import button and these materials are brought into your drawing.
4. You can preview any single material that you highlight, either from the Materials list or the Library list.
5. You can save a drawing's Material list to its own library with the Save button. It allows you to create a library file with the extension .MLI that you can use in other drawings by opening it as a library.
6. Once you have created your materials list, use the OK button to return to the Materials dialog box.
7. Then, highlight the material you want to assign and click either the Attach, By ACI, or the By Layer buttons. The Attach button allows you to attach the material to a specific object. The By ACI button allows you to assign a material to a color in the drawing. The By Layer button allows you to assign a material to a specific layer.
8. If you select the Modify or New button, you are presented with a dialog box similar to that of Figure 17.6C. This allows you to create your own materials or to modify existing ones.

Modifying Materials

The following is a description of the different areas of the Modify Standard Material dialog box, as shown in Figure 17.6C.

317

Each material is given a unique name. Once you have created a new material or modified a previously created one, you can export it to the currently active library so that you may use it with other models.

Attributes

There are seven different attributes that control the rendering of a material.

Color/Pattern	Controls the main color of the material. It is often referred to as the Diffuse color. This area is in the light, and you must set the color to match the color you wish the material to be. You can also apply a bitmap image to the attribute to take the place of the color.
Ambient	Controls the color of the material that is in shadow. Usually a darker tone of the main color is used.
Reflection	Controls the color of the material that is in the brightest light. It is often referred to as the highlight, or specular, color. You can also apply a bitmap image to the attribute to take the place of the color.
Roughness	Controls the size of the highlight portion of the Reflection attribute. A low value means the material is highly reflective, and the highlight is small and intense. A high value means the material is rougher, and the highlight is spread over a larger surface.
Transparency	Controls the transparency of a material and the object to which it is attached. You can also apply a bitmap image to the attribute.
Refraction	Adjusts how refractive a material is. This attribute functions only if Photo Ray-Traced rendering is used.
Bump Map	Applies a bitmap image that causes the material surface to appear bumpy based on the bitmap. Light portions of the image appear to be raised above the surface.

Value

This area is used to adjust the strength of the associated attribute. To use the value, click the attribute and then adjust its strength value. For example, if you select the Transparency attribute, you can adjust how transparent the material will be by adjusting its value.

Color

You can adjust the color value of the three color attributes: main, ambient, and reflective.

By ACI	When this box is checked, the colors match the color of the object when it was created.
Lock	This setting locks the attribute colors to the main color.
Mirror	This setting applies to the Reflection attribute only and is used to create actual mirror images on the attached object.
Color System	This value determines what type of color system is to be used: RGB or HLS. RGB uses red, green, and blue to adjust the color. HLS uses hue, lightness, and saturation to adjust the color.
Color Swatch	The color swatch displays a dialog box needed to adjust the levels of the color system.

Bitmap

The Bitmap area controls the application of a bitmap image to one of these four attributes: Color/Pattern, Reflectivity, Transparency, and Bump Map.

Bitmap Blend	This value controls the strength of the image. The image is not shown at a value of 0 and is the strongest at 1.
File Name	The name of the bitmap image is stored here.
Adjust Bitmap	This setting is used to adjust the scale and orientation of the image.
Find File	This value is used to locate a bitmap image. You have seven different file types from which to choose: tga, bmp, tif, gif, jpg, png, and pcx.

Preview

You can see a preview of the current material using either a sphere or a cube.

Material Mapping

When you use a material that contains an image map, you need to make sure the object has the appropriate mapping projection applied. This is accomplished using the SETUV command. When you use this command, you are requested to select an object and then you are presented with a dialog box, as shown in Figure 17.7A.

Projection

Planar	Projects map parallel to the surface. Used on flat surfaces.
Cylindrical	Wraps map around a single axis. Used on cylindrical surfaces.
Spherical	Wraps map around all three axes. Used on spherical surfaces.
Solid	Special application used for materials having solid properties.

Adjust Coordinates

This area is used to make adjustments to the selected projection type so that you may change the orientation (see Figure 17.7B). You can alter the location of the planes or axes. By using the Picked Plane radio button or Pick Points button, you can identify the plane or axis on the object itself.

The Adjust Bitmap button displays the Adjust Object Bitmap Placement dialog box, as shown in Figure 17.7C. This dialog box is used to make adjustments to the bitmap image as it is applied to the selected object. The scale settings of U and V control the number of times the bitmap is copied across the object's surface. You can enter any value for either U or V. For example, a value of 1 copies the bitmap once, a value of 2 copies it twice, a value of 0.5 shows only half the bitmap image, and so on. The Offset settings of U and V can be used to shift the bitmap's placement on the object.

17.6 Scenes

Scenes are combinations of desired views, light types, and their placements that are stored under a scene name that can be restored at any time prior to rendering.

Creating Scenes

To create a scene, enter the Scenes dialog box shown in Figure 17.8A. The following procedure is used to create scenes:

1. Select New from the Scenes dialog box and the New Scene subdialog box appears, as shown in Figure 17.8B.
2. Enter a unique name for the new scene.
3. From the list of presaved views, highlight the single desired view.
4. From the list of preplaced lights, highlight as many lights as you desire.

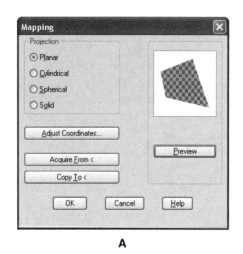

A

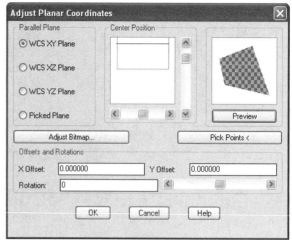

B

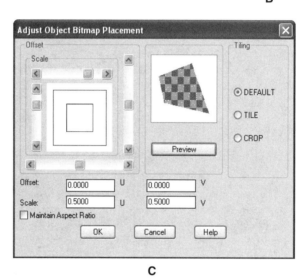

C

Figure 17.7
Mapping, Adjust Planar Coordinates, and Adjust Object Bitmap Placement dialog boxes

Figure 17.8
Scene dialog boxes

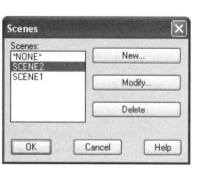

A

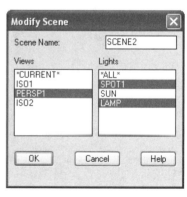

B

5. Select the OK button on the New Scene dialog box to return to the Scenes dialog box.
6. To use a scene, highlight its name and then select the OK button. When you use the RENDER command, the indicated scene is rendered.

17.7 Rendering Preferences

By making use of the options in the Rendering Preferences dialog box, you can control the rendering type, destination, edge smoothness, material, and more. There are default values to help speed up the rendering process. Settings that are subject to constant use should be recorded here. Figure 17.9A shows the Rendering Preferences dialog box. The following lists some of the options available:

Rendering Type	Sets the rendering type: Render, Photo Real, or Photo Ray-Traced. Render is the fastest but does not use shadows or material maps. Photo Real uses materials and shadows, whereas Photo Ray-Traced is the same as Photo Real but creates sharper shadows and makes use of refraction.
Rendering Procedure	Selects individual objects, identifies a rendering window, and skips the Render dialog box.
Scene to Render	Sets the scene to render from a list of previously created scenes.
Rendering Options	Controls the render display with various on/off toggles for smoothing, materials, shadows, and so on.
Destination	Sets where the final rendered image will be sent: viewport, render window, or file. With the file setting you can adjust the file type and image resolution.
Sub Sampling	Sets the level of pixel rendering and the speed of the rendering. At 1:1, every pixel is rendered, making it the most detailed and the longest procedure. At 8:1, only every 1 in 8 pixels is rendered. This gives the least detail but is the fastest way to check a sample rendering.
Background	Sets the type of background to use: solid, gradient, image, or merge (see Figure 17.9B).
Fog/Depth Cue	Enables the application of fading to simulate fog or depth cue. Fog traditionally uses a white color, and depth cuing uses black. However, you can use any color. Use Near and Far settings to establish where the fog starts and stops as well as the density of the fog.

17.8 Rendering the Model

The RENDER command renders a selected scene or the current display if no scene is selected. Figure 17.10A shows the Render dialog box. It is identical to the Render Preference dialog box so that you can make any changes to the next render. If the Skip Render dialog is checked, either in the Render Preferences dialog box or the Render dialog box, the Render dialog box will not appear the next time the Render command is used. To reset this, use the RPREF command.

If the image is rendered in a viewport, you can save the image to an external file by using the SAVEIMG command. Figure 17.10B shows the Save Image dialog box. To redisplay an image, use the REPLAY command. Figure 17.10C shows the Replay dialog box.

If you render to the Render window, the image is displayed in a separate window, as shown in Figure 17.11. This new window can be used to save the image as a BMP file or copy the image to the Windows clipboard. You can also display previously saved BMP images, print them, and resize the image using the Windows options.

321

Figure 17.9
The Rendering Preferences and
Background dialog boxes

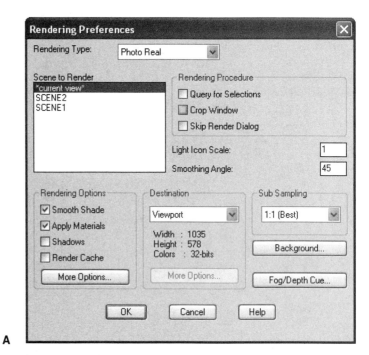

A

B

If you intend to render to a file, you can set the image size and file time before engaging the Render.

17.9 **Landscape Objects**

A landscape object is extended-object geometry with an image mapped onto it that you can place in a model scene. Basically, you place a simple geometric object in the model, and when you render the scene, it is replaced with a bitmap image. If you place a tree object, you will see simple lines to represent the tree; however, when you render the scene, the simple lines are replaced by a picture of a tree.

The LSNEW command is used to add a landscape object to your scene. Figure 17.12A shows the Landscape New dialog box. You can select from a list of objects,

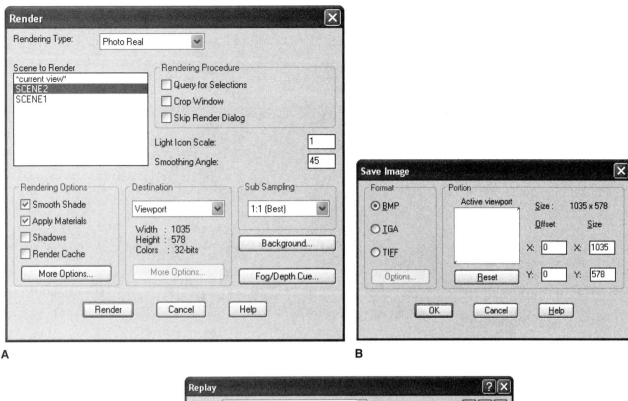

A

B

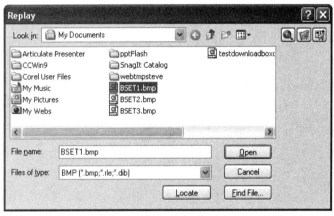

C

Figure 17.10
The Render, Save Image, and Replay dialog boxes

click the type geometry, and position the object. View Aligned is useful with objects such as trees.

The LSEDIT command is used to edit an existing landscape object. You can adjust its geometry and height.

The LSLIB command is used to access the landscape libraries that contain the objects (see Figure 17.12B). You can modify landscape objects or create your own.

Creating photorealistic renderings requires a great deal of time and experience, but such renderings can be very rewarding when the project is presented to others. Creating shaded images or basic renderings, on the other hand, is relatively easy, and these can be effective presentation tools as well. The following labs give you enough hands-on experience in the rendering of models to show you that rendering does not have to be an intimidating process.

323

Figure 17.11
The Render window

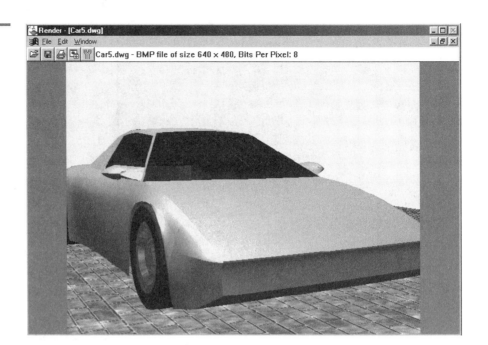

Figure 17.12A
Landscape New dialog box

Figure 17.12B
Landscape Library dialog box

Background and Fog

To add further realism to your rendered image, you can add a background to the final image as well as adding fog to the scene or background.

You can set the background using the Background button in the Render or Render Preferences dialog box or use the Background tool. The dialog box looks similar to Figure 17.13A. By default the background is set to the screen background set by the Options/Display dialog box. If you uncheck the AutoCAD Background box, you can set any color you want by using the Color slider bars. If you want to use a Bitmap image as the background, you can click the Image radio button and then use the Find File button to locate the desired background image.

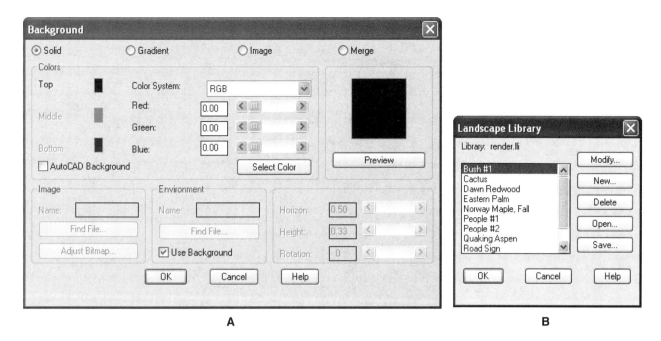

A   B

Figure 17.13
Background and Fog/Depth Cue dialog boxes

3D VIEWPOINT

Backgrounds

You can enable backgrounds to appear in a shaded viewport without rendering. This is set by enabling backgrounds from the Options dialog box, Systems tab, Properties button.

 You can set the fog using the Fog button in the Render or Render Preferences dialog box or use the Fog tool. The dialog box looks similar to Figure 17.13B. To turn off the fog function, click the Enable Fog button. This applies fog to the entire rendered objects. If you want the background to be foggy as well, click the Fog Background button.

You can adjust the color of the fog as well as the near and far distances, which sets where the fog starts and stops. The percentage values are used to set how dense the fog will be.

To start using fog, first adjust the rear clipping plane so that it's behind the objects. Use the 3D Adjust Clipping Planes tool on the 3D Orbit toolbar. Then, open the Fog dialog box, enable Fog, and set the Near distance to 0.75 and the Far distance to 1.00. After that, set the Near percentage to 0.00 and the Far percentage to 1.00. Perform a test rendering and then adjust your fog settings accordingly. Reduce the Far percentage if you want to be able to see a background image fogged.

Plotting Rendered Models

Plotting from model space is a good way to get a quick plot onto paper for review but it's not as efficient for presentation drawings. This is where you would use a paper space layout.

325

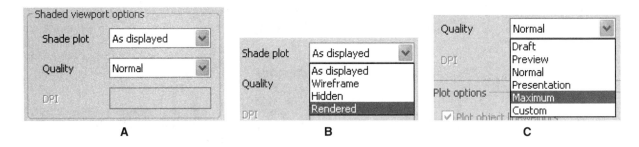

Figure 17.14
Shaded viewport options portion of the Plot dialog box.

The following is a description of a quick plot using model space and a more detailed layout using paper space.

1. To plot from model space, click the Plot tool.
2. Adjust your settings as space would for any plot.
3. Open the More options button (AutoCAD 2005).
4. Adjust the Shade Viewport Options section of the dialog box. Refer to Figure 17.14A and the following text.

> Set the Shade plot setting to Rendered (see Figure 17.14B).
> Set the Quality setting to the desire level (see Figure 17.14C).
>
> *Draft* Sets rendered and shaded model space views to be plotted as wireframe.
> *Preview* Sets rendered and shaded model space views to be plotted at one-fourth of the current device resolution, to a maximum of 150 dpi.
> *Normal* Sets rendered and shaded model space views to be plotted at one-half of the current device resolution, to a maximum of 300 dpi.
> *Presentation* Sets rendered and shaded model space views to be plotted at the current device resolution, to a maximum of 600 dpi.
> *Maximum* Sets rendered and shaded model space views to be plotted at the current device resolution with no maximum.
> *Custom* Sets rendered and shaded model space views to be plotted at the resolution setting that you specify in the DPI box, up to the current device resolution.

5. Plot your model. The model goes through the rendering process internally, before it is sent to the plotter. It is not required for you to render the model before plotting.

The process to plot a render model in paper space is similar to model space with some slight differences.

1. Select the floating viewport that contains the model view to be plotted/rendered and open the Properties pallette. You need to adjust the Shade property of the floating viewport to be rendered (see Figure 17.15A).

Figure 17.15
Floating viewport shade property and Shaded viewport options portion of Page Setup dialog box.

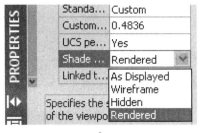

2. Right-click on the Layout tab for the paper space layout you want to plot and select Page Setup Manager. Highlight the proper layout and click the Modify button.
3. The Page Setup dialog box which is similar to the Plot dialog box, appears. The difference is that the Shade plot setting is inaccessible because you set it by the floating viewport properties (see Figure 17.15B). Set the Quality as described earlier in model space plotting.

Lab 17.A   Rendering with AutoCAD

Purpose

Lab 17.A shows you how to render a model using the RENDER utility. You will be rendering the BDWELL model created in Lab 8.B in Chapter 8.

Objectives

You will be able to:

- Select views and place lights
- Assemble a view and lights into a scene
- Display various model representations
- Save a rendered display and recall it

Primary Commands

LIGHT
SCENE
RPREF
SAVEIMG
REPLAY

Final Shaded Model

Figure 17.16 shows the initial rendered basic dwelling model.

Procedure

Initial Setup
1. Open the BDWELL model from Lab 13.B, Chapter 13.
2. Using the DVIEW command, display a perspective view similar to that shown in Figure 17.17. Use a Zoom lens of 25 mm.

3. Save the view settings by using the VIEW/NEW command. Give it the name PERSP2.

Figure 17.16
Rendering of the basic dwelling model

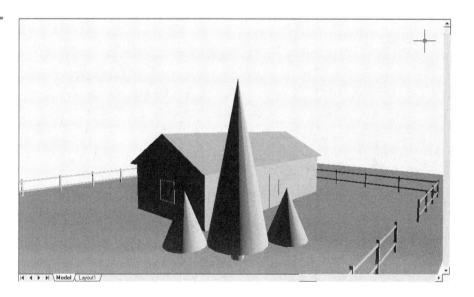

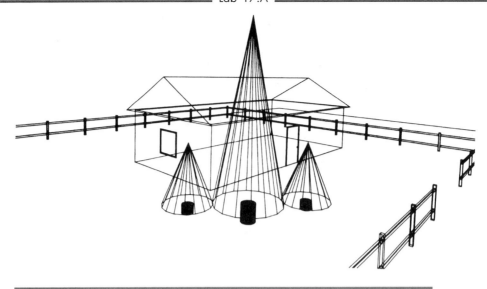

Figure 17.17
Perspective view of the basic dwelling model

Placing the Sun

4. Select the Light option from the View/Render pull-down menu. The Lights dialog box should appear on the screen.
5. Select Distant Light from the pop-up list. Click the New button, and the New Distant Light dialog box should appear.
6. Select the Light Name box, and enter the name of the light as SUN. This light represents a dawning sun shining on the dwelling. Enter an intensity of 1.
7. Select the Light Source Vector Modify button, and place the light at the following coordinates:

Enter light direction to <current>: **80′, 30′, 15′**
Enter light direction from <current>: **130′, −9′, 30′**

> The screen returns to the dialog box.
> Check the Shadow Casting box.

8. Select OK on the New Distant Light dialog box to return to the Lights dialog box. Do *not* exit from this box.

Placing Accent Lighting

9. Select Point Light from the pop-up list. Click the New button, and the New Point Light dialog box should appear.
10. Select the Light Name box, and enter the name of the light as ACCENT. This light adds some accent lighting to the side of the dwelling on which the sun does not shine, which brings out the features on that wall. Enter an intensity of 2.
11. Select the Position Modify button, and place the light at the following coordinates:

Enter light location <current>: **39′, 40′, 5′**

> The screen returns to the dialog box.

12. Select OK on the New Point Light dialog box to return to the Lights dialog box. Set the ambient light to 0.6 to brighten the scene. Select OK to exit from the Lights dialog box.

Observing the Placement of the Light Blocks

13. Display a plan view of the model. You should be able to see the newly placed light blocks.
14. Window in closer to see the names that are attached to the lights. These should match the names you gave them when creating the light types. (*Note:* The scale of these icons is controlled in the Render Preferences dialog box.)

Putting a Scene Together

15. Select Scene from the View/Render pull-down menu. The Scenes dialog box should appear.
16. Select New from the Scenes dialog box. The New Scene dialog box should appear.
17. Enter SCENE1 for the scene name.
18. Highlight PERSP2 as the View, and highlight both SUN and ACCENT for the lights.
19. Select OK to exit the New Scene dialog box and return to the Scenes dialog box.
20. Make sure that scene SCENE1 is highlighted, and then select OK to exit from the Scenes dialog box.

Checking the Rendering Preferences

21. Select Preferences from the View/Render pull-down menu. The Rendering Preferences dialog box should appear.
22. Check the following:

Render Type:	Render
Rendering Procedure:	Skip Render dialog is not checked
Rendering Options:	Leave Smooth Shade and Apply Materials checked
Destination:	Viewport
Icon scale:	200 (This enlarges the viewing size of the light blocks.)

23. Select OK to exit from the dialog box.

Rendering the Scene

24. Select Render from the View/Render pull-down menu. The screen should be rendered as shown in Figure 17.16. If you are using full screen rendering, use the space bar to return to the drawing editor screen.

Saving the Image

25. Select Tools/Display Image/Save from the Tools pull-down menu. The Save Image dialog box should appear.
26. Select the appropriate format for the graphics of the computer you are using. Normally, BMP should work.
27. Enter IMAGE1 as the image name, and select Save to save the image. The image is saved as a separate file with the extension dependent on the graphics format selected. If you selected BMP, then the extension would be BMP.

Replaying the Image

28. Select Tools/Display Image/View from the Tools pull-down menu. The Replay dialog box should appear. You may have to specify *.BMP as a pattern.

29. Highlight the IMAGE1 file, and select OPEN. The Image Specification dialog box should now appear. Select OK at this dialog box, and the rendered image should reappear on the screen.
30. Save the model as BDWELL.

Changing the Rendering Type

31. Using the RENDER command, set the Render Type to Photo Real and render the scene. The image should look like Figure 17.18. Note that the shading is more uniform.
32. Using the RENDER command, check the Shadows box so that it is on, and render the scene. The image should look like Figure 17.19. Note that the addition of shadows makes the scene more realistic.
33. Save the model as BDWELL. In the next lab you will add materials to the building for a rendering that looks even more realistic.

You may want to experiment with the light intensities to achieve a more desirable combination, or you could add more lights for different effects. Getting the best looking picture is all up to you. Try rendering directly to a file by changing the destination in the Render dialog box. Have fun!

Figure 17.18
Rendering using Photo Real

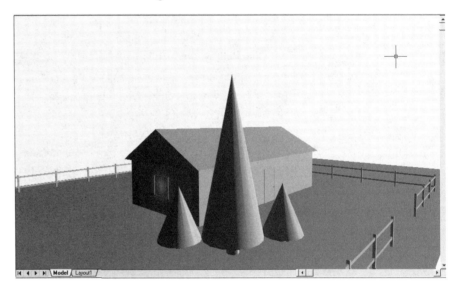

Figure 17.19
Rendering using Photo Real with
Shadows on

Lab 17.B   Creating a New Material

Purpose

In this lab you'll create a new grass material using a bitmap image. After following this lab you should be able to create any custom material by using bitmap images.

Objectives

You will be able to:

- Create a new material
- Add it to the material library
- Attach it to an object

Primary Command Procedure

RMAT

1. Start a new empty drawing and draw a polyline rectangle approximately 10′ × 10′ and turn it into a region. This will be used to test the material.

Creating a New Material

2. Use the Materials tool from the Render toolbar or the RMAT command to open the Materials dialog box (see Figure 17.20). Because this is a new drawing, there are no materials contained within the drawing.
3. At the right side of the dialog box there's a New button and below that button there's a Material type. It should be set to Standard. Click the New button. This displays the New Standard Material dialog box.
4. Review the Attributes column. These are used to create complex materials with various properties. For this exercise you're going to use a bitmap material. This greatly simplifies the process.
5. Enter GRASS as the name of the material.
6. At the bottom-right corner of the dialog box there are settings for bitmap images. Click the Find File button to locate the bitmap image file that you're going to use. Go to the a3d2005 folder and locate the GRASS1.JPG file. You may have to set the Files of type to *.jpg to see the file. When you open the file you'll return to the New Standard Material dialog box.

   Note that the bitmap image file name is now shown along with the path. It's important to note the path for materials. If you move the bitmap file or use a different computer, the bitmap file may not be found. Click the Preview button and you'll see the rendered grass.

Figure 17.20
Materials dialog box

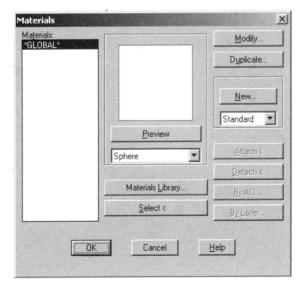

Tinting the Material Blue

7. Now you will alter the material to add a blue tint to the grass to make it appear similar to Kentucky bluegrass.

   Adjust the Bitmap blend value to 90. This means that the final rendering of the grass will use 90% of the bitmap and 10% of a color.

   Turn off the By ACI button and set the Blue color value to 1. Display the preview again and refer to Figure 17.21. You should see a tint of blue now. Using this method you can tint images any color. There is a limit to how much you can do with this method, but it's fast. Click OK to return to the Materials dialog box.

Adding the Material to the Library

8. Grass has now been added to the current drawing. However, it's only in this drawing. You need to save it in a material library to use it in other drawings.

   Click the Materials Library button. A dialog box similar to Figure 17.22 appears. Note the Grass material on the left. On the right is a list of materials in the Render.mli material library. Highlight Grass in the left list and click the

Figure 17.21
New Standard Material
dialog box

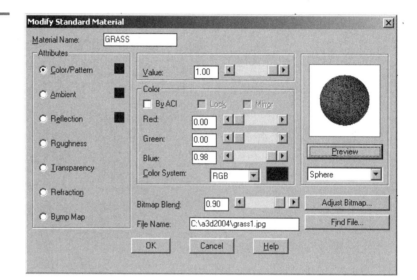

Figure 17.22
Materials Library dialog box

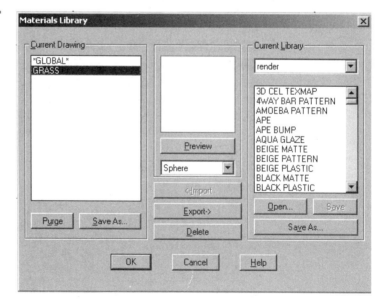

Export button. The name now appears in the right column. Click the Save button below the right list. This saves the material library with the new material. Click OK to go back to the Materials dialog box.

Attaching the Material

9. There are a number of ways to attach materials to objects. We'll use the simplest at this stage. With the GRASS material highlighted, click the Attach button and select the region in your drawing. Press Enter to go back to the dialog box and then click OK to exit.

Test Rendering

10. Display an isometric view using the SE Isometric View tool from the View toolbar.
11. Select the Render tool from the Render toolbar. Refer to Figure 17.23 for your settings. Click the Render button and refer to your screen and Figure 17.24 for the results.
12. Try adjusting the bitmap blend and colors to change the color of the grass.

Figure 17.23
Render dialog box

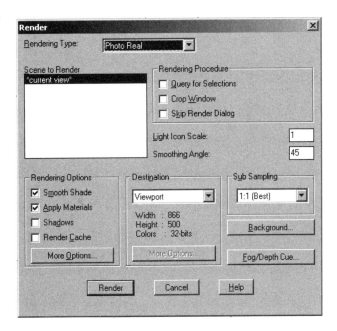

Figure 17.24
Rendered grass

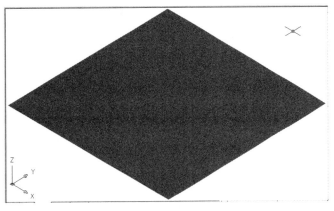

Lab 17.C   Adding Materials

Purpose

Lab 17.C shows you how to add materials to the surfaces in your model. You will use the model BDWELL from Lab 17.A.

Objectives

You will be able to:

- Import materials from the materials library
- Attach material to objects
- Adjust the mapping projection on an object
- Add landscape objects

Primary Commands

RMAT
SETUV
LSNEW

Procedure

Initial Setup

1. Open the BDWELL model from Lab 17.A and display an isometric view using the VPOINT command.

Attaching a Material

2. Use the RMAT command to display the Materials dialog box, as shown in Figure 17.25. *Note:* It won't have the materials list yet. You'll do this next using the Materials Library.
3. Select the Materials Library button and import the materials shown in Figure 17.25. The GRASS material was created in Lab 17.B and added to the material library.
4. In the Materials dialog box, highlight the BROWN BUMPY BRICK material and, using the Attach button, attach it to the rectangular box that represents the walls of the house.
5. Using the Render command, render SCENE1 with materials on. The resulting image should look like Figure 17.26. If you look carefully at the walls, you should be able to see a pattern of small bricks.
6. You are going to use mapping to change the scale of the brick bitmap image. Before you can make changes, use the REGEN command to restore the wireframe model.

Figure 17.25
Materials dialog box

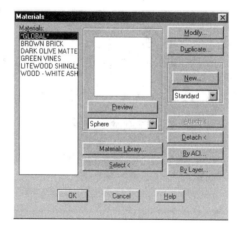

Figure 17.26
Rendered image with material streaks showing

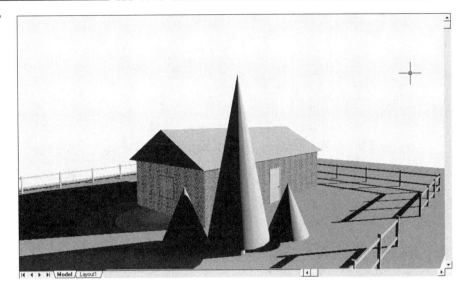

Use the SETUV command. Click one of the edges and press Enter. The Mapping dialog box appears, similar to Figure 17.27. Make sure the Planar Projection radio button is checked.

7. Click the Adjust Coordinates button to display the Adjust Planar Coordinates dialog box, as shown in Figure 17.28A.
8. Click the Adjust Bitmap button to display the Adjust Object Bitmap Placement dialog box, as shown in Figure 17.28B.
9. Observe the Scale boxes U and V. Normally they are both set to 1. This places the bitmap on the object at a scale of 1. Change both values to 0.25, as shown in Figure 17.28B. This enlarges the bitmap image as it is applied to the walls, making the bricks larger.
10. Click OK in each of the dialog boxes to close all of them. The scale of the mapping for the walls has now been changed.
11. Use the RENDER command again. The results should be similar to Figure 17.29.

Adding Roof Materials

12. Using the RMAT command, attach the LITEWOOD Shingles material to the roof object. If you like, adjust the mapping on the roof as you did with the walls.

Figure 17.27
Mapping dialog box

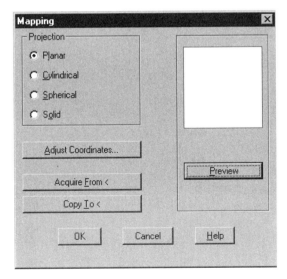

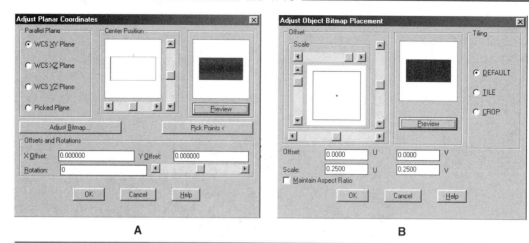

Figure 17.28
Adjust Planar Coordinates dialog box and Adjust Object Bitmap Placement dialog box

Figure 17.29
Rendered image with mapping project applied to front wall

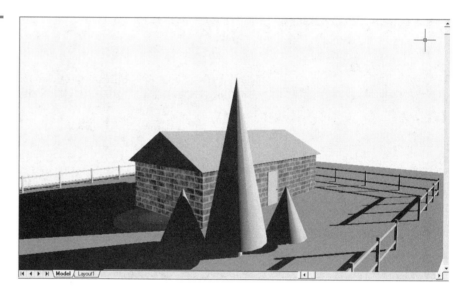

Adding Tree Material

13. There is no specific tree material. However, the Green Vines material applied to the trees does cause an interesting effect. Attach the Green Vines material to the trees.

Adding Lawn Material

14. Using the RMAT command, attach the GRASS material to the lawn.

Adding Fence Material

15. Using the RMAT command, attach the WOOD-WHITE ASH material to the fence blocks.

Rendering with Mapping Coordinates

16. Render the scene now that you have set the mapping projection. The image should look similar to Figure 17.30.
17. Save your drawing as BDWELL so that you retain your original drawing.

336

Figure 17.30
Rendered image with other materials applied

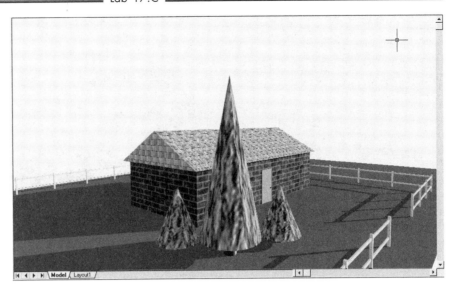

Adding Landscape Objects

18. Display a world plan view of the scene and set the UCS to World.
19. Erase the tree and trunk objects from the scene.
20. Use the LSNEW command to display the Landscape New dialog box, as shown in Figure 17.31.
21. Select the Dawn Redwood landscape object and click the Preview button to see what it looks like. Make sure the boxes are checked as shown in Figure 17.31 and that the scale is set to 100.
22. Using the Position button, place the tree at approximately 29'5", 34'8", 0'0", and click OK to leave the dialog box.
23. The maximum scale at which the landscape object can be set in the dialog box is 100. This is too small for your model. The way to get around this is to use the standard SCALE command and scale up the landscape symbol.

    Use the SCALE command and scale up the landscape symbol three times.
24. Render the scene again, making sure that you use the Photo Ray-Traced rendering type. The image should look similar to Figure 17.32.
25. Save the model as BDWELL2.

Figure 17.31
Landscape New dialog box

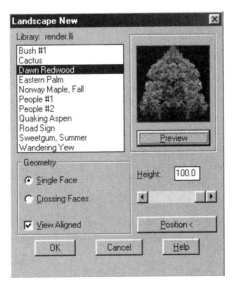

337

Figure 17.32
Rendered image showing tree landscape object

Questions

1. What is meant by CAD rendering?

2. How is rendering accomplished within AutoCAD?

3. List the four light types and explain their differences.

4. What is the purpose of assigning materials and how do you create them?

5. Why create scenes?

6. How are images saved and recalled?

7. What is the difference between the Shade mode and the RENDER command?

8. If a material were created with a high reflection value and a low roughness value, what would the surface be—flat or reflective?

Assignments

Note: To achieve a more favorable effect on any rendering, the colors you set for different elements of a model should differ. It would be wise to set the various colors before rendering the model.

For these assignments, do the following:

- Shade the scene within AutoCAD.
- Render the scene within AutoCAD. You'll need to create a scene and a view and place lights.
- Compare the results.

1. Create a scene by assembling a coffeemaker (use the COFMK model created in Lab 7.C, Chapter 7) and a coffeepot (use the COFPT model created in Lab 8.A, Chapter 8).

2. Create a scene using the kitchen model BKIT (created in Assignment 1, Chapter 13).

3. Add a shiny material to the nut and bolt assembly NBOLT (created in Assignment 2, Chapter 13).

4. Recall the DECK model created in Lab 14.A, Chapter 14, and generate the various rendered images.

5. Assign different materials to the pipe assembly model (PIPES) created in Lab 14.B, Chapter 14, to create the various rendered images.

Application Projects

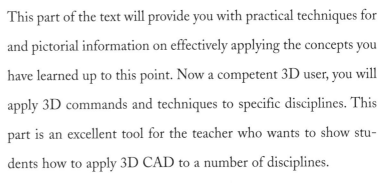

This part of the text will provide you with practical techniques for and pictorial information on effectively applying the concepts you have learned up to this point. Now a competent 3D user, you will apply 3D commands and techniques to specific disciplines. This part is an excellent tool for the teacher who wants to show students how to apply 3D CAD to a number of disciplines.

The following chapters take the form of self-contained projects and, as such, they do not have associated exercises or questions. However, they are easy to extend and will thoroughly explain the basic skills you need to be able to design a similar project on your own. The first project, found in Chapter 18, is extremely directed, allowing you to make few choices. In later chapters, the projects become increasingly complex and you will be making more and more decisions.

The projects in this part deal with wireframe, surface, and solid modeling.

C H A P T E R

Architectural Project: Residential Dwelling

Overview

This chapter walks you through the creation of a model of a residential dwelling, starting with the organization of the basic plan and then adding the various individual elements and library symbols until the final 3D rendering is complete. This residential dwelling project is not intended to teach the concepts involved in the design or the construction of a house; instead, it is meant to illustrate the techniques and procedures in the construction of a 3D model of a house. At the conclusion of this step-by-step project, you will be able to apply all the basic elements learned here to many more complex creations.

Concepts Explored

- Application of the AutoCAD features presented in the previous chapters
- Creation of a complex 3D model of a residential dwelling
- Generation of 3D symbols for insertion into the main model
- Production of ideally located perspective views
- Generation of shaded and rendered images

18.1 Introduction

In this chapter, we create an exterior model of a residential dwelling, as illustrated in Figure 18.1. The parameters of the dwelling have already been determined to allow easy construction of the model. However, new values (or even a new dwelling) can easily be substituted for the ones given in this project, allowing you to create a model of your own choosing. Also, although this project focuses on the construction techniques used in the creation of the exterior of the dwelling, it would not be more difficult (just more time-consuming) for you to complete the inside of the model as well.

When this model is finished, you should be able to view the house from any angle and look through the windows into the house. In addition, you should be able to hide the walls and roof at will, enabling you to see into the interior.

This exercise uses a combination of 3DFACES and regions. You can substitute one for the other, depending on which one you want to use. Regions are useful because you can easily create holes. But you must remember that they're side dependent. This means they can be viewed only from one side. Make sure the Z axis of the UCS is always pointing outward when you create a region.

340

Figure 18.1
Perspective display of the
residential dwelling project

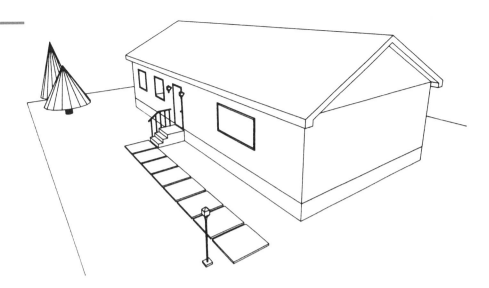

18.2 **Project Stages**

In this project, as in all CAD projects, it is important to organize the model before attempting any creation. The first step in organizing a model is determining the stages of model development. Some of these stages are necessary in all model creation, but others are unique to each model type. The order in which the stages are performed is usually unique to each model type as well.

PROJECT STAGES
1. Division of the architectural model (foundation, roof)
2. Layer designations (elevations)
3. Initial settings (units, base)
4. Initial architectural plan layout (plan extrusion)
5. Initial complex surface generation (roof peak)
6. 3D symbol creation (windows, doors, concrete steps)
7. Insertion of symbols
8. Complex surface generation (window openings)
9. Exterior features (steps, walkways)
10. Presentation display (creating a perspective view, rendering)

Stage 1: Model Division

At this point in the learning process, you are creating more complex models. To make creation more manageable, complex models need to be broken down into sections. This holds true for our residential dwelling model, and because this is an architectural project there are some obvious section divisions, as listed here:

- The foundation, which includes footings and the foundation wall
- The first floor, including all exterior walls
- The roof, including the soffits and fascia
- The windows, including trim and sills
- The doors, including the treads and handles
- The external features that would be attached to a house, such as steps and lights
- The temporary objects that facilitate model construction

Other divisions, such as extra floors or gabled windows, would be created depending on the type of house model to be constructed.

The name of the master model should be determined at this point. In this project, the master model will be called DWELL. Start a new drawing with this name.

Stage 2: Layer Designations

It is very important that layer designation takes place in the early stages of development. The ability to make objects visible or invisible is one of the most powerful features of CAD, and we want to utilize it in our 3D construction. The separation of layers facilitates both the construction and the display of the final model. Most of the layers will be named now, but some layers will not be created until a need for them becomes apparent during the actual 3D creation.

Before we create the layers, let's recall two important pieces of information that, if not utilized in advance of the modeling, will cost us too much time to correct. First, as anyone who has viewed or plotted a model with hidden features removed knows, the more complex the model, the longer it takes to remove the hidden features. Second, to alleviate this problem, AutoCAD ignores objects on a layer that are frozen during the process of hidden line removal. To make use of these two important facts, we'll divide the model in this project into viewing directions. Any view of the exterior of the house will normally show only two sides of the house as well as the roof section.

Viewing sides can be named either for compass directions (north, south, east, west) or for hand directions (left side, right side, front, rear). For this model, we use the hand directions. The geometry is broken into viewing sides so that any combination of sides can be frozen at any time. This simplifies the construction of the model and greatly speeds up the HIDE routine. Here are the designated abbreviations for the viewing sides:

ABBREVIATION	VIEWING SIDE
FR	front
RE	rear
RI	right
LE	left

When naming layers, remember that even though the name of the layer can have as many as 31 characters, only the first 8 characters of the layer name are visible on the status line. Taking this into consideration for our model, we use the first 8 characters of each layer as an abbreviation and the rest as a longer explanation of the layer.

The layers to be designated at the start of the model creation are as follows:

LAYER NAME	LAYER DESCRIPTION
LOT	Ground line and lot area
FR-FOUND	Front foundation
FR-1FLOR	Front first floor
FR-ROOF	Front roof
FR-WINDO	Front window
FR-DOOR	Front door
FR-FEATU	Front feature attached to wall
FR-TMPOR	Temporary front (for construction)
RE-FOUND	Rear foundation
RE-1FLOR	Rear first floor
RE-ROOF	Rear roof
RE-WINDO	Rear window

RE-DOOR	Rear door
RE-FEATU	Rear feature attached to wall
RE-TMPOR	Temporary rear (for construction)
RI-FOUND	Right foundation
RI-1FLOR	Right first floor
RI-ROOF	Right roof
RI-WINDO	Right window
RI-DOOR	Right door
RI-FEATU	Right feature attached to wall
RI-TMPOR	Temporary right (for construction)
LE-FOUND	Left foundation
LE-1FLOR	Left first floor
LE-ROOF	Left roof
LE-WINDO	Left window
LE-DOOR	Left door
LE-FEATU	Left feature attached to wall
LE-TMPOR	Temporary left (for construction)

Note: A quick way of either freezing/thawing or turning on/off layers can be accomplished by using wild card characters. Wild card characters are inserted in place of letters or groups of letters. The wild card question mark (?) can be substituted for any individual character and the wild card asterisk (*) can be substituted for any group of characters. Here is an example of combining the question mark and the asterisk in one command. The two question marks replace the first two characters in the layer name (FR, RE, RI, LE). The single asterisk replaces all the remaining characters after "-1FLOR":

Command: **–LAYER**
?/Make/Set/New/ON/OFF/Color/Ltype/Freeze/Thaw: **F**
Layer name(s) to Freeze: **??-1FLOR***

This command freezes all the first-floor layers.

Wild cards also can be used to add color designations for the various layers after all the layers have been created. For the purposes of our model construction, each section type is given its own separate color. At this point, it is not important which color goes with each section type; we simply want to give each a separate color to make it easier to distinguish what is on each layer. The section types and their colors are as follows:

SECTION TYPE	COLOR
FOUNDATION	1 (red)
1ST FLOOR	2 (yellow)
ROOF	3 (green)
WINDOW	4 (cyan)
DOOR	5 (blue)
FEATURE	6 (magenta)
TEMPORARY	7 (white)
LOT	12 (this might appear as blue-gray)

Now create the layers listed previously and assign each its appropriate color. *Note:* It is customary to use continuous linetype for all construction of 3D models. When you are creating a series of layers at one time, end the previous layer with a comma before you press Enter. A new layer will be created automatically without moving to the New button. Also remember that with AutoCAD 2005, you can save and restore layer states by name. In this way you can freeze different sides of your model and save each of those states. When it's time to plot the model, you can restore certain states to automatically freeze unwanted layers.

Stage 3: Initial Settings

The following is a list of settings that need to be entered before modeling can take place:

```
SETTINGS
Units = Architectural
Limits = 0',0' to 100',100'
Grid = 1'
Snap Incr. = 2"
Initial Elevation Thickness = 0'
Initial Thickness = 0'
UCS = WCS
UCSICON = On and set to 2D display properties
UCSVP = 0 (always set before creation of viewports)
UCS toolbar = displayed
View toolbar = displayed
```

Remember to ZOOM All, so that the display shows the set limits.

There may be other settings that you would like to set. If so, now is the time to set them, before we enter Stage 4.

Stage 4: Initial Architectural Plan Layout

Review the plan and elevation views shown in Figures 18.2 and 18.3, respectively. Then, proceed through the steps of this stage. REMEMBER TO SAVE YOUR DRAWING PERIODICALLY TO AVOID TIME LOSS!

Creating the Lot

Draw Ground line/Lot area on layer LOT using the 3DFACE or REGION command so that it appears as a surface (see Figure 18.2). Begin at the lower left corner, 0,0,0.

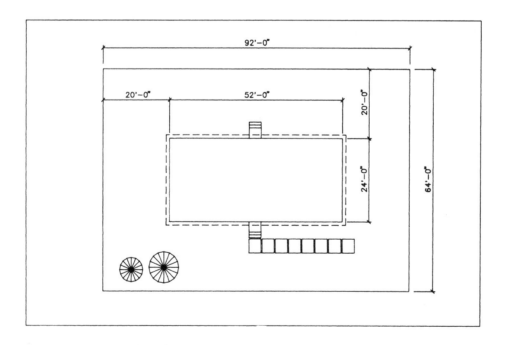

Figure 18.2
Plan view of the dwelling

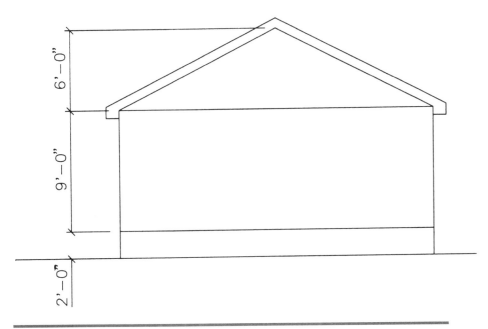

Figure 18.3
Side elevation view of the dwelling

Creating the Foundation

What goes on below the ground line is not of concern in this project, so the foundation starts at the ground line and extends 2′ above ground (see Figures 18.2 and 18.3). While still displaying the plan view, proceed.

```
SETTINGS
Elevation = 0′
Thickness = 2′
```

Using lines, draw the perimeter of the outside edge of the foundation. Remember to switch to the various view layers for the foundation: FR-FOUND, RI-FOUND, RE-FOUND, LE-FOUND.

Use the the SE Isometric View tool or the VPOINT command to see what you have created. It should look like Figure 18.4.

```
Command: VPOINT
Current view direction: VIEWDIR = 0.0000,0.0000,1.0000
Specify a view point or [Rotate] <display compass and tripod>: 1,−1,1
Return to the plan view.
Command: PLAN
Enter an option [Current ucs/Ucs/World] <Current>: W
```

Creating the First-Floor Walls

The commands in this step are similar to those used to create the foundation, but now set the elevation as well as the thickness. The first floor starts on top of the foundation and extends another 9′ into the air (see Figures 18.2 and 18.3).

```
SETTINGS
Elevation = 2′
Thickness = 9′
```

Again using lines, draw the perimeter of the first floor, switching to the proper layers as each side is drawn. Use the VPOINT command to see what you have created.

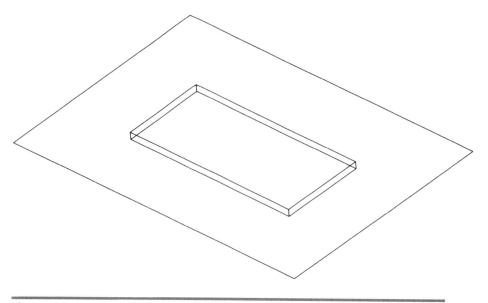

Figure 18.4
Isometric view of the foundation

Creating Working Planes

Now that we have some 3D extruded geometry, it will be very easy to create some working planes aligned to that geometry. Create four working planes, one for each viewing side (see Figure 18.5).

The following commands will create the first working plane—one for the front elevation. Remember to snap to key points when setting the UCS working planes.

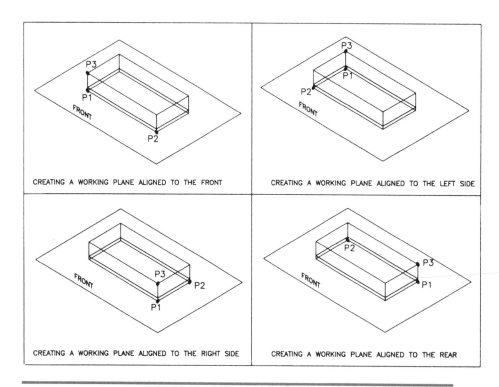

CREATING A WORKING PLANE ALIGNED TO THE FRONT

CREATING A WORKING PLANE ALIGNED TO THE LEFT SIDE

CREATING A WORKING PLANE ALIGNED TO THE RIGHT SIDE

CREATING A WORKING PLANE ALIGNED TO THE REAR

Figure 18.5
Creating the four working planes

346

Command: **UCS**
Current ucs name: *WORLD*
Enter an option [New/Move/orthoGraphic/Prev/Restore/Save/Del/Apply/?/World]
<World>: **New**
Specify origin of new UCS or [ZAxis/3point/OBject/Face/View/X/Y/Z] 0,0,0: **3**
Specify new origin point <0,0,0>: **refer to the front plane in Figure 18.5 for P1**
Specify point on positive portion of X-axis <default>: **refer to the front plane in Figure 18.5 for P2**
Specify point on positive Y portion of the UCS X-Y plane <default>: **refer to the front plane in Figure 18.5 for P3**

Use the UCS command to save the new working plane as FRONT. Switch to the plan view of the current UCS using the PLAN command, and save the view as FRONT using the VIEW command. Note the UCS icon. It should be easy to tell which working plane is active by observing the position of the icon.

Now create the other three working planes (rear, right, left), as illustrated in Figure 18.5. Save them and their matching views (REAR, RIGHT, LEFT).

Creating the Roof

The roof can be created very easily by extruding lines, similar to the way the walls were created. But the extrusion direction needs to be changed here. We'll do this by selecting a working plane that is perpendicular to the extrusion direction.

Begin this step by setting the elevation and the thickness:

SETTINGS
Elevation = 0'
Thickness = 1'

Now restore the UCS working plane RIGHT (see Figure 18.6). Note the UCS icon.

Freeze the FRont, REar, and LEft first-floor layers. By freezing these layers, we are ensuring that when we use the object snap modes, we will snap to the correct objects. When working in 3D space, it is possible to have objects (such as the right and left walls) completely overlap each other. If both left and right layers were on and you were looking at the right elevation, it would be impossible for you to tell to which side you might snap. So, to alleviate that difficulty, the layers containing the overlapping walls are frozen.

Restore the RIGHT view. Note that the icon has moved off the 0,0,0 point. This is because the icon cannot display fully. Use ZOOM 0.8× to fix the problem by reducing the displayed image to 80% of its current size on the screen. The displayed view should now be the same as in Figure 18.7.

Figure 18.6
Restoring the RIGHT working plane

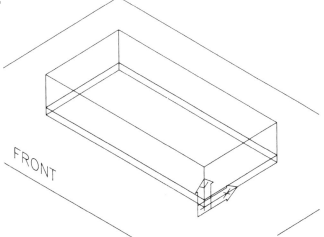

Figure 18.7
Displaying the right side parallel
to the screen

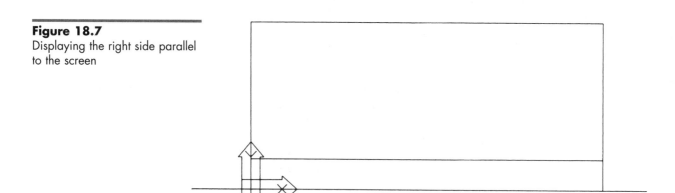

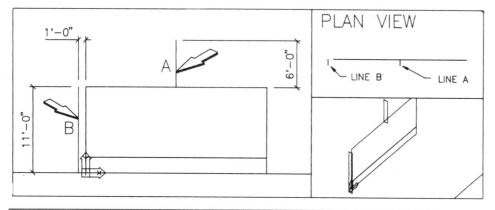

Figure 18.8
Adding temporary construction lines

Before the roof can be drawn, some temporary lines need to be created in order to set the height of the roof and the overhang. Switch to the RI-TMPOR layer and draw lines A and B as shown in the first box of Figure 18.8. Use the midpoint object snap for the start of line A and give the length using relative coordinates. Then, use the ID command to reference the lower left of the right foundation wall and use relative coordinates to give the start and finish of line B. Line B should be 11′ long and should run along the 0Z axis.

Use the SE Isometric View tool or VPOINT command to display an isometric view with coordinates 1,−1,1. Because a thickness of 1′ was used, the displayed view should look like the second box of Figure 18.8.

Now, to draw the roof line, switch to layer FR-ROOF.

    SETTINGS
    Elevation = 0′
    Thickness = −54′

The setting of 54′ represents the entire length of the roof, including the 1′ overhang on each end. The negative value causes the line to extrude back over the house.

Draw a line representing the roof by referring to Figure 18.9. Use endpoint object snap to P1 for the start. For the end of the line, select filter .*XY*, endpoint snap to P2, and enter a value of 1′ for the Z coordinate. In other words, use the X and Y coordinates from P2, but enter in the Z distance of 1′ for the overhang. Line C represents the underside of the roof.

To draw the top of the roof, as shown in Figure 18.10, use the OFFSET command with a distance of 8″, and use the FILLET command with a radius of 0 to

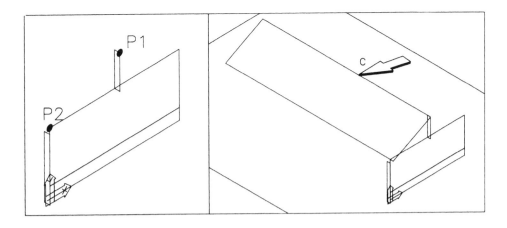

Figure 18.9
Adding one side of the roof

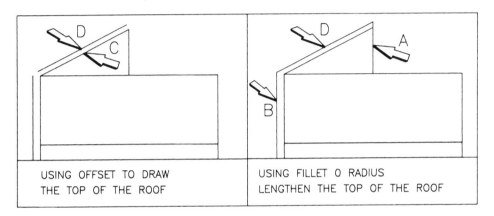

USING OFFSET TO DRAW
THE TOP OF THE ROOF

USING FILLET 0 RADIUS
LENGTHEN THE TOP OF THE ROOF

Figure 18.10
Creating the top of the roof

extend line D to line B and bring it in line with line A. Then, erase line B and trim line A back to the lower roof, which is line C.

Now draw the fascia and soffits (lines E, F, and G), as shown in Figure 18.11. Lines E, F, and G have a thickness of −54′.

We will mirror the roof half later.

Stage 5: Initial Complex Surface Generation

So far, our house model has walls and a roof, but the fascia ends of the roof and the space between the peak of the roof and the right wall (gable end) are not enclosed. To enclose these spaces, we'll need to use the 3DFACE command. Do the gable end first, because it is the easier of the two.

SETTINGS
Freeze layer FR-ROOF. The roof should disappear.
Make sure that the RI-TMPOR layer is on and thawed.
Switch to the RI-ROOF layer. The gable end surface is going to be placed on this layer.
Elevation = 0′
Thickness = 0′

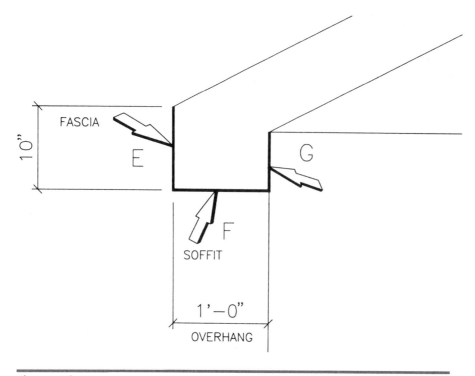

Figure 18.11
Adding in the fascia and soffits

FASCIA

10"

E

G

F

SOFFIT

1'—0"

OVERHANG

Creating the Gable End Surface

You can either create 3D faces or a region to form the gable. You may find the use of regions easier. To create a region, first draw a closed polyline as shown in Figure 18.12 and then use the REGION command to turn the polyline into a region. If you want to create 3D faces, select the 3DFACE command. Referring to Figure 18.12, endpoint snap to P1 and P3 on the top of the right wall and to P2 on the top of line A. Once you have input these three points, press the Enter key to complete the 3DFACE command, which places a surface in the peak area. (*Note:* The top of the temp line must be returned to a 6′ length before adding the gable.)

Figure 18.12
Adding the gable end with the
3DFACE command or regions

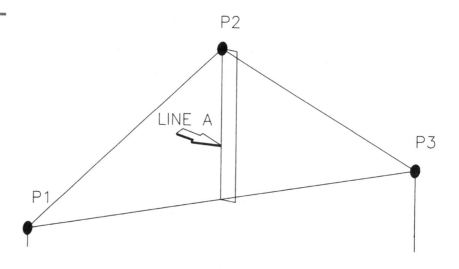

P2

P3

P1

LINE A

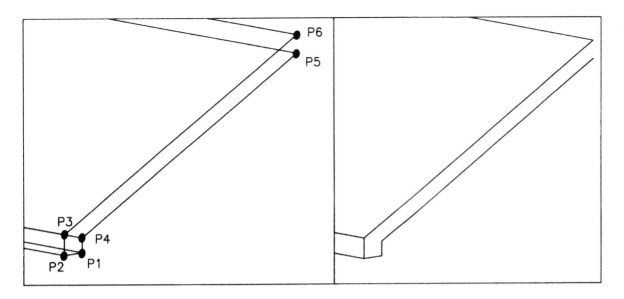

Figure 18.13
Adding the roof

Creating the Fascia End of the Roof

To create the fascia end of the roof, start with these settings:

> SETTINGS
> Thaw layer FR-ROOF.
> Switch to layer FR-ROOF. The fascia ends of the roof are going to be put on this layer.

You can either create 3D faces or a region to form the fascia. To create a region, first draw a closed polyline as shown in Figure 18.13 (close the polyline between P5 and P6) and then use the REGION command to turn the polyline into a region. If you want to create 3D faces, select the 3DFACE command. Referring to Figure 18.13, endpoint snap to P1 and P2. Before endpoint snapping to P3, select the Invisible Edge option. Now snap to P3 and P4. Do *not* exit from the 3DFACE command. Select the Invisible Edge option again and endpoint snap to P5 and P6. The 3DFACE command refers to them as points 3 and 4. Now press Enter to exit from the 3DFACE command. Half of the roof should now be complete. Try the HIDE command to see the effect.

Mirroring the Roof

Note: Settings do not need to be changed at this point.

Use the MIRROR command to select the roof components, including the region or 3D face on the roof fascia end. Exclude the temporary lines, the right wall, and the gable end region or 3D face. Use endpoint object snaps at P1 and P2, as shown in Figure 18.14, for the mirror line and respond No to the Delete Old Objects prompt. If you used regions to form the facia, use the UNION command to join them together as one region.

Modifying the Roof

Modify the roof, fascia, and soffits so that they are on their proper layers (that is, front roof slope on FR-ROOF layer, front fascia on FR-ROOF layer, roof peak on RI-ROOF layer, and so forth).

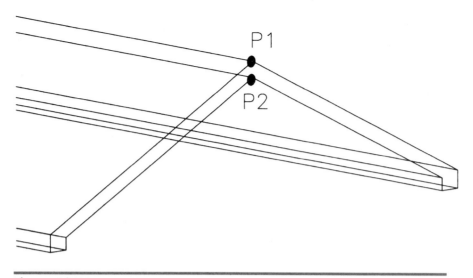

Figure 18.14
Mirroring one side of the roof to the other

Mirroring the 3D Faces or Regions

The right end of the building has 3D faces or regions on the ends of the roof and the peak space. It is time now to copy them to the left end of the building.

> SETTINGS
> Freeze layers FR-ROOF, RE-ROOF, RI-1FLOR.
> Thaw layers FR-1FLOR, RE-1FLOR.
> Make sure that layers RE-ROOF and LE-ROOF are thawed.
> Switch to layer RI-TMPOR.
> Restore the UCS working plane FRONT.

Using the midpoints on the front wall as shown in Figure 18.15, mirror all the 3D faces on the right wall to the left wall. Modify the mirrored objects so that they are on their proper layers.

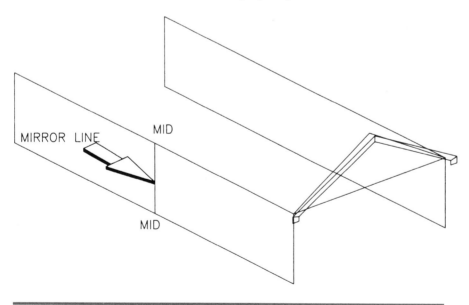

Figure 18.15
Mirroring one roof end to the other

352

Figure 18.16
The model in wireframe with
hidden lines removed

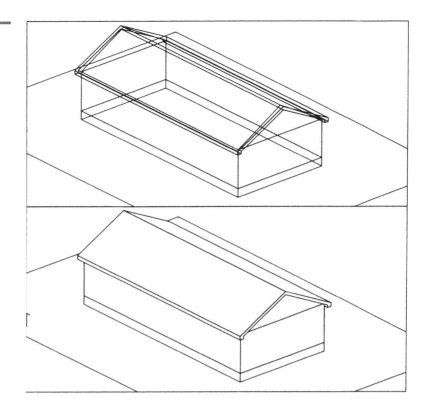

Thaw all layers except the temporary layers. The display should look like
Figure 18.16.

Save the model as DWELL.

The model should now have a surface over every area. Using the VPOINT command, move around the model—end to end, above, and below—and use the HIDE
command at each view to see the effect (which should be similar to Figure 18.16).
It is very important to note that regions are side dependent when rendering or using
shaded shade modes. What this means is that a rendered or shaded region is visible
only when viewed from the side it was created on (the positive Z axis of the UCS
during creation). If you view a region from the other side, it appears as if it is gone.
You may want to experiment with this by turning on Gouraud shading and then
using 3DORBIT to rotate around the model. If you find that a region disappears
when viewed from the exterior of the model, it means that the region must be turned
180 degrees. Check your model now to make sure there are no disappearing regions.
You have just created a semicomplex, fully surfaced 3D model. You have every right
to feel proud. But there's more to do! Exit from the model, and let's continue.

Stage 6: Symbol Generation

In this stage, we'll create individual 3D symbols, as shown in Figure 18.17. This
stage could have been performed earlier because, once created, 3D symbols are
independent and can be used at any time.

We'll create a 3D symbol of a concrete step here. If you read Chapter 13 in
sequence and performed Lab 13.A, you have already created 3D symbols for a 4′ × 3′6″
window (W4X3-6) and a 3′ × 6′8″ door (D3X6-8). To complete this project, two
more window symbols need to be created: one sized 5′ × 3′6″ (W5X3-6) and the
other sized 8′ × 3′6″ (W8X3-6). Refer to Figure 18.17 and follow the procedures
laid out in Lab 13.A. Once you have mastered those procedures, you can create any
number of window and door symbols.

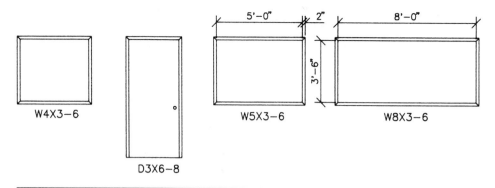

Figure 18.17
Window and door 3D symbols

As was stated in Chapter 13, when 3D symbols are inserted into a model they orient themselves to the current UCS based on the WCS of the drawing on which they were initially created. In other words, the *X, Y,* and *Z* WCS coordinates of the original 3D symbol drawing align to the current UCS of the model into which they are to be inserted (see Figure 18.18).

Start a new drawing called STEPS. This will be the original drawing for the 3D symbol of the concrete steps (see Figure 18.19).

SETTINGS
Units = Architectural
Limits = 0',0' to 5',6'
Grid = 6"
Snap Incr. = 2"
Thickness = 0'
Elevation = 0'
UCS = WCS
UCSICON = On and set to 2D display properties
UCSVP = 0 (always set before creation of viewports)
UCS toolbar = displayed
View toolbar = displayed
Layers = 0 (all construction will take place on layer 0)

Figure 18.18
Aligning the UCS for insertion

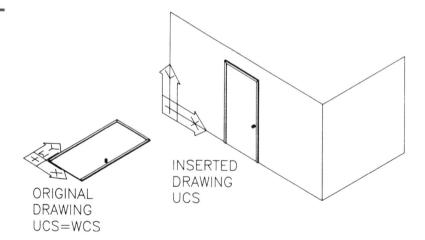

Figure 18.19
The layout of the steps

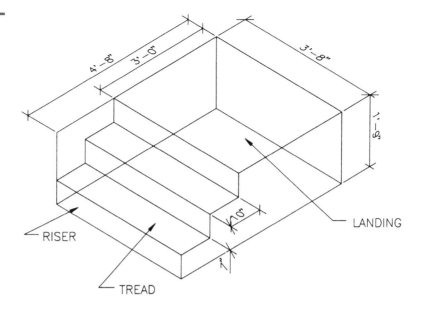

Creation of the Orientation Cube

Creating a box to surround the model that is about to be created is an excellent way to keep track of the orientation of the model and a quick way to create working planes (see Figure 18.20).

> SETTINGS
> Thickness = 1'9"
> Elevation = 0'

Draw a rectangle the same size as the concrete steps—with a width of 3'8" and a depth of 4'8". Use the SE Isometric View tool or VPOINT (coordinates 1,–1,1) to view the model. Save the view as ISO.

Use the UCS New 3POINT command to create a working plane on the right side of the box (see Figure 18.20). Save the UCS as SIDE.

Figure 18.20
Orientation cube and working plane

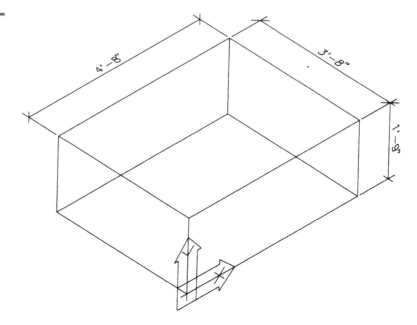

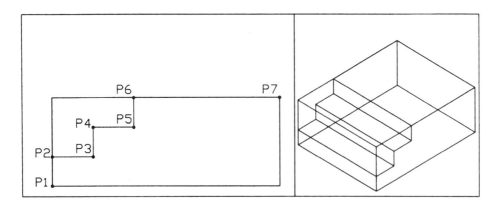

Figure 18.21
Adding the steps and viewing them from an isometric viewpoint

Creating Steps

Set only one setting for this step:

Thickness = −3'8"

Use the PLAN command to set the view to the current UCS. Draw the outline of the landing and the treads and risers as shown in Figure 18.21. Refer to Figure 18.19 for the sizes. Then, use the VIEW/Set Current command to redisplay the view ISO.

Creating Side Steps

First delete the top, front, and two side lines on the orientation box. Leave the back line for the back surface of the step. As before, you can use 3D faces or regions to form the stair sides. If using regions, create a closed polyline to trace around the steps and then turn it into a region using the REGION command. If you want to use 3D faces, use the 3DFACE command to place two surfaces—A and B—on the side of the step (see Figure 18.22). Use endpoint snap to snap to points A1 through A6.

Figure 18.22
Adding sides to the steps

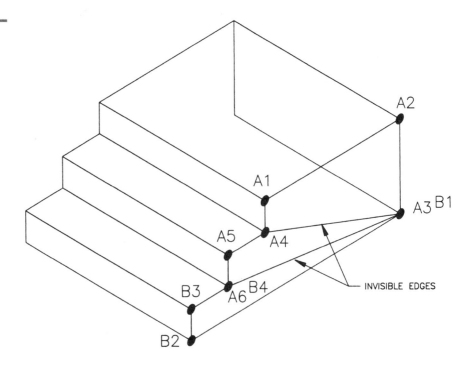

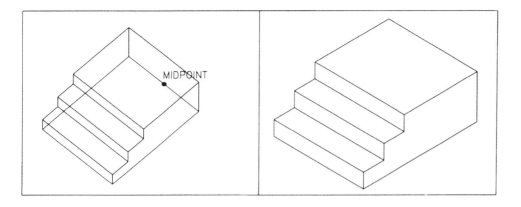

Figure 18.23
Setting the base and using hidden line removal

(*Note:* You must use the Invisible Edge option just before clicking points A3 and A6.) Exit the 3DFACE command, and then reenter it to add surface B. Refer to Figure 18.22 for the points. Remember to use the Invisible Edge option before clicking point B4.

Repeat the 3DFACE command or use a region to create the other side of the steps, or use the COPY command to copy the surfaces just created. If you use regions, check to make sure that you can see them using Gouraud shade mode.

Setting the Insertion Point

To insert the 3D symbol properly, you must set the insertion or base point before saving the drawing. Using the NE Isometric View tool or VPOINT command, display the rear of the steps. Use the BASE command to set the base point to the midpoint of the bottom of the rear line (see Figure 18.23). Set UCS = WCS. Save the model as STEP.

Use the 3DORBIT command to move about the model and use the HIDE command to observe each view. The views should be similar to those depicted in Figure 18.23. Exit from this model.

Repeat the steps in Stage 6 until you have created all the required 3D symbols.

Stage 7: Inserting Symbols

The following procedure details the insertion of the windows, door, and steps on the front of the dwelling. Repeat this procedure to generate the rest of the dwelling sides.

Open the master model for this project, DWELL, and enter the following settings:

    SETTINGS
    Freeze all layers except FR-FOUND, FR-1FLOR, FR-TMPOR, FR-WINDO,
        FR-DOOR.
    Thickness = 0'
    Elevation = 0'
    Current Layer = FR-TMPOR
    UCS = set to FRONT working plane
    Display = plan view of current UCS (FRONT)
    Fill = off

Referring to Figure 18.24, draw the temporary lines used to determine the insertion points for the windows, door, and steps.

357

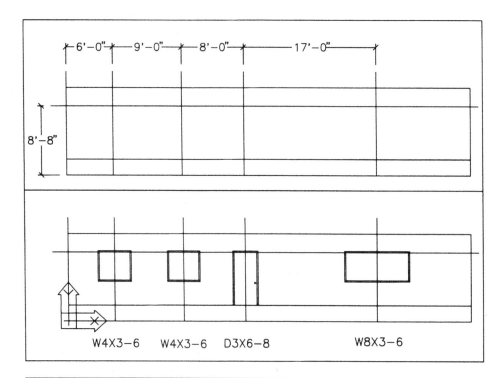

Figure 18.24
Temporary lines for insertion points and the inserted symbols

Window Insertion

Use this one new setting:

Current Layer = FR-WINDO

Use the INSERT command to place the windows on the wall. The block names are W4X3-6 and W8X3-6. Use insertion object snap for accurate placement (see Figure 18.24).

Door Insertion

The setting is

Current Layer = FR-DOOR

Use the INSERT command again to place the door, D3X6-8 (see Figure 18.24).

Step Insertion

We need to change the working plane at this point or the concrete steps will not have the proper orientation to the model. Try to insert the steps without changing the UCS. Observe the results, and then undo the insertion (see Figure 18.25).

    SETTINGS
    Current Layer = FR-FEATU
    UCS = WCS
    Display = restore view ISO

Use the INSERT command to place the STEP 3D symbol at the proper location. Use the endpoint object snap (see Figure 18.25).

358

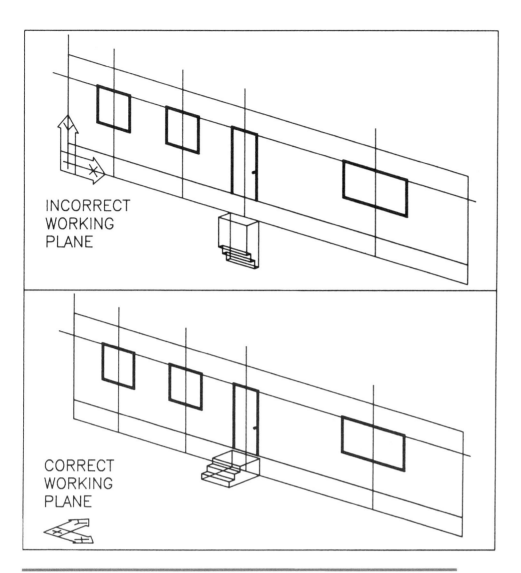

Figure 18.25
Using the incorrect working plane and using the correct working plane

At this point, the front elevation of the model is complete. It has windows, a door, and a set of steps. Using Figure 18.26 as your guide, complete the rest of the elevations. Remember to set the working plane to the side where you'll be inserting a symbol to ensure proper orientation of the 3D symbol. When you are done, save the model as DWELL.

Stage 8: Complex Surface Generation

If you use the HIDE command or different shade modes on the model at this point, the various features will be hidden but you will not be able to see through the windows. This is because we used the thickness property when creating the walls, so there is a complete surface over each window. What we have to do now is replace the walls created by lines with walls created by complex surfaces that allow openings where the windows appear. We will do this with the REGION command, one of the most useful 3D commands.

359

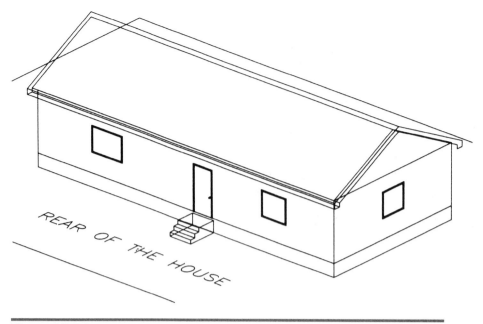

Figure 18.26
View of the rear left of the dwelling

Creating the Front Wall

The front wall will be replaced by a complex region.

```
SETTINGS
Freeze all layers except LE-1FLOR, RI-1FLOR, FR-1FLOR, FR-WINDO, FR-TMPOR.
Thickness = 0'
Elevation = 0'
Current Layer = FR-1FLOR
UCS = FRONT
```

Creating a Region Wall

You are now going to replace the front wall, which was created using a line with thickness, with a region. You will do this so that you can cut out openings for windows, enabling viewers to see inside the house model.

Erase the temporary lines that are on layer FR-TMPOR and make layer FR-TMPOR current. Using the PLINE command, draw a closed polyline around the perimeter of the wall, as shown in Figure 18.27. Use the original wall's corners as snap points.

Erase the previous wall that was created with a line with thickness and move the new polyline to the FR-1FLOR layer.

Use the REGION command to turn the polyline into a region.

Creating Window Openings

Using the window frames as guides, draw closed polylines around the perimeter of each window on the front wall (see Figure 18.28).

Use the REGION command to turn each new polyline into a region.
Use the SUBTRACT command to subtract the window regions from the wall region. This creates cutouts in the wall.

Figure 18.27
Polyline drawn around perimeter of wall

Figure 18.28
Polylines used for each window opening

Once you have replaced the solid wall with the regions that have openings for the windows, place a three-dimensional object inside the house in front of a window on the front wall. Use the HIDE command, and observe the results. You should be able to see the object through the window opening. Imagine how interesting the results would be if actual furniture were placed in the house!

Repeat the procedure outlined in Stage 8 for the other three sides.

Save the model as DWELL.

Stage 9: Exterior Features

This is the stage where we'll be adding features (such as railings, outside lamps, and walkways) to enhance the model. A variety of 3D commands can be used to generate these features. Some should be created as separate symbols to be inserted, while others can be created on the model itself. For example, as Figure 18.29 illustrates, railings and walkways can be created on the model very easily by using the 3D OBJECTS command and selecting the Box option. However, lamps and other similar features, which can be created by selecting the Sphere or Pyramid option of the 3D OBJECTS command, should be created as separate drawings to be used over and over again. (Recall that the lamppost and coach light were created in Chapter 13, Assignment 4.) For features you need to add to the model before proceeding to Stage 10, see Figures 18.29, 18.30, and 18.31.

When you are done, save the drawing as DWELL.

Figure 18.29
Front handrails and walkway

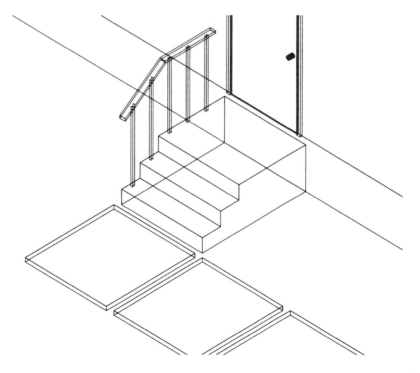

Figure 18.30
Front coach lamps, lamppost,
and trees

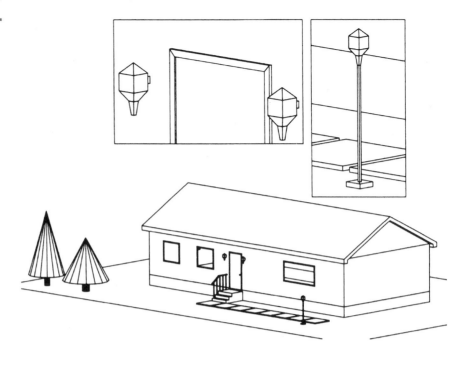

Figure 18.31
Rear coach lamp and steps

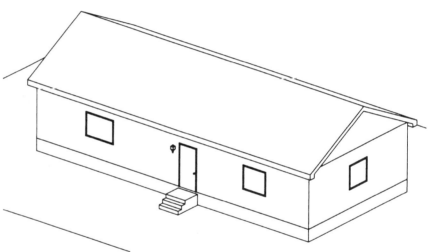

Stage 10: Presentation Display

The construction of the model is now complete and it is time to consider how to display the model for presentation purposes. Chapter 15 discusses the display and presentation of models in detail. What follows here is specific to this particular dwelling model.

First we establish the options for displaying a perspective of the house, showing the front right side from above, as in Figure 18.32.

    SETTINGS
Freeze all layers except the front and right-side layers, which are as follows:
    FR-FOUND, FR-1FLOR, FR-ROOF, FR-WINDO, FR-DOOR, FR-FEATU, RI-
    FOUND, RI-1FLOR, RI-ROOF, RI-WINDO, RI-DOOR, RI-FEATU.
Display = Isometric view (ISO)

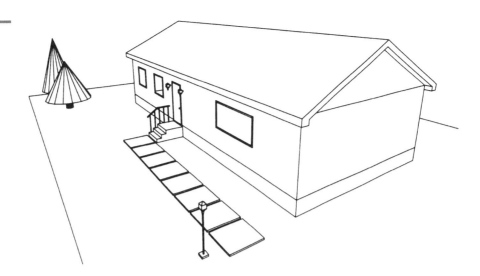

Figure 18.32
Perspective view of the model

Creating the Preview Selection Set

Activate the DVIEW command and select the front wall, side wall, roof sections, and the front door as the Preview selection set.

Using the Camera Option

Now activate the Camera option. Move the cursor up and down and left and right until you achieve the desired elevation and horizontal view. Figure 18.33 shows a sample view. Then click the left mouse button to accept the position.

Setting the Camera Distance

Using the Distance option, place the camera at the desired distance away from the model. A suggested distance is 80′.

Using the Zoom Option to Get a Better Picture

Select the Zoom option to change the lens length. Move the cursor along the slider bar or enter the length at the command line. A suggested length is 25 mm.

Applying the Preview to the Entire Model

Select the Exit option once you have created the desired view using the DVIEW options (see Figure 18.34). (*Note:* All the roof layers should be thawed at this point.)

Figure 18.33
View displayed with one possible location of the camera

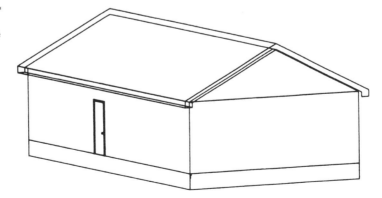

Figure 18.34
Applying the DVIEW settings to
the entire model

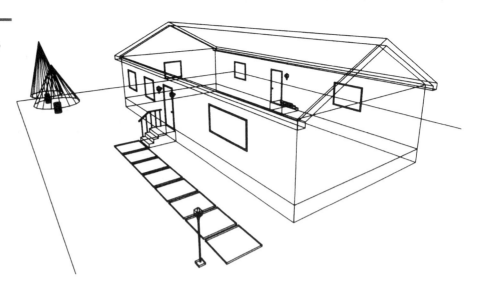

Saving the Perspective Settings

Select the VIEW command and save the current view as PERSP1. After you have done this, you can restore the perspective settings at any time using the VIEW command.

Using the HIDE Command

First, save the model as DWELL. Note that only the layers that can be seen from this view have been left thawed. This greatly saves on the time it takes to hide the model. Select the HIDE command or use the Hide shade mode and await the outcome. The display should be similar to Figure 18.1.

Applying Hatching

To enhance the hidden line removed view, use the BHATCH command to add various types of hatches to the model's surfaces. Remember that you need to set the UCS to each surface before performing the hatch. Once the model is hatched, use the HIDE command to see the results. You may have to move the hatch pattern slightly (1/6–1/8 inch) off the model's surface for them to appear when using Hide. Figure 18.35 shows a view of the model with some hatching applied to the surfaces. This will not have any effect on the rendered view but does enhance the model if you plan only to plot the model on paper.

Figure 18.35
Model with hatching applied

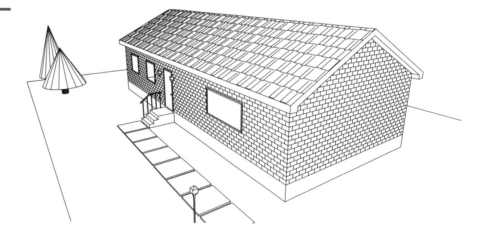

Rendering the Model

The project's final procedure is rendering the model in a way that creates a realistic image. This procedure should be thought of as your finishing touch, or what you can do to create truly impressive results. The rendering method you choose will be based on the level of realism required.

Rendering can be accomplished in one of three ways, depending on the available software. The lowest level of realism can be accomplished using the shade modes built into AutoCAD. You can produce a moderately realistic image that is sufficient for most purposes.

The next level of realism can be accomplished using the RENDER features built into AutoCAD. The main benefit of using the RENDER command instead of the shade modes is that it allows you to place lights to create different effects.

The highest level of realism can be achieved using Photo Real Rendering. Such rendering allows more flexibility in creating the final image and to have some special capabilities, such as casting shadows.

With each increasing level of realism, the number of steps required to create the image also increases. To learn more about rendering models, refer to Chapter 17.

Here are sample settings to create a rendering of our house model using the RENDER utility. The three lamps will appear as if they are turned on because we are rendering the house at night. The lights are placed for viewing the model at PERSP1. Figure 18.36 shows the rendered model.

Rendering Preferences: Use default settings, and set the Rendering options to Smooth Shading, Shadows On, and Render with Photo Real.

Lights:

NAME	TYPE	INTENSITY	FROM LOCATION	TO LOCATION
street	distant	0.5	14', −14',30'	69',43',0'
accent	point	23	105',42',5'	
lamp1	point	54	94'10",18'10",5'	

Figure 18.36
Rendered view of the house model

lamp2	point	54	63'11",29'1",8' (shadow on)
lamp3	point	54	69'1",29'1",8' (shadow on)
ambient		0.6	

Point Light Fall-off = inverse linear

You may want to add materials at this stage to add even more realism to your model. Refer to Lab 17.C in Chapter 17 for application of materials. See Figure 18.37 for a rendered image with some materials added.

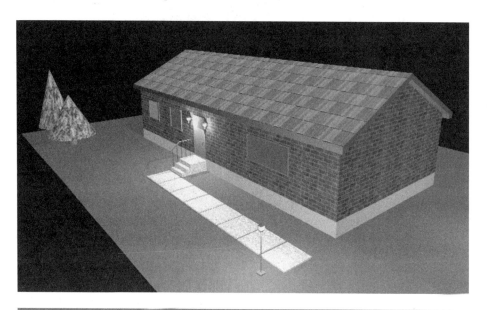

Figure 18.37
Rendered view of house model with some materials added

Architectural Project: Commercial Building

Overview

You will find this chapter to be very similar to Chapter 18 in both methodology and content, but the project you will be doing here is a much broader one. In this chapter, you will apply your newly learned commands and techniques to a commercial project that is more complex and that will require you to make more decisions about how to apply your knowledge. To prepare you for the demands of this project, you should complete the Chapter 18 project first.

This chapter's project is not intended to teach you how to design a building or to construct a city; instead, it will provide you with hands-on practice in constructing a model and placing it into a three-dimensional setting. Because this project demands a basic level of expertise in all the techniques and procedures of 3D manipulation, it will serve as your stepping stone to even more complex creations.

Concepts Explored

- Continued exploration of the AutoCAD features
- Creation of a complex 3D model of a commercial building and a city environment
- Generation of 3D symbols to be inserted into the model
- Production of ideally located perspective views
- Creation of shaded and rendered images

19.1 Introduction

The architectural project in this chapter involves the creation of an exterior model of a commercial building and its subsequent placement in a city environment, as illustrated in Figure 19.1. The building in question is referred to as a convention center, with one section of the structure used for conventions and the other used as an exhibition hall. Once you have constructed the building, you will develop a simplified city environment in which to place it. The parameters of both the building and its city have already been determined so that you can apply 3D construction techniques.

When this model is finished, you should be able to view the city from any angle. This should generate some impressive perspective views of the commercial building in its environment and illustrate how powerful such a presentation can be.

367

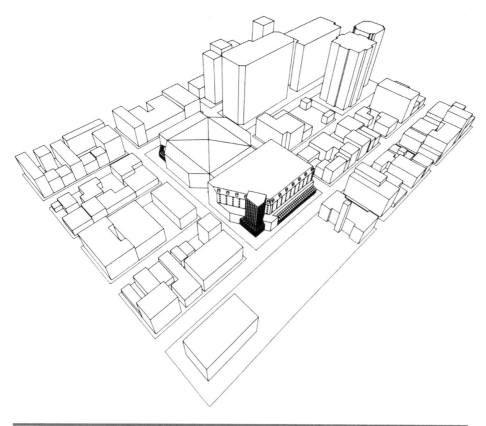

Figure 19.1
Perspective display of the commercial building in a city environment

This exercise makes use of the surfaces to create the model. However, if desired, you can use 3D solids. Just remember to keep the 3D solids you want with different materials separate.

19.2 **Project Stages**

Before we create it, we must organize the model. The importance of this first step was discussed in Chapter 18. As you should recall, we begin by determining the stages of development of the model. Some stages are common to all models; some stages are unique. The order in which the stages are performed depends on the particular model type.

Here are the stages in this project. Note that, after initial model division and layer designation, the stages will be done in two parts.

PROJECT STAGES
1. Division of the architectural model (walls, features)
2. Layer designations (elevations)

SECTION A: COMMERCIAL BUILDING CONSTRUCTION
3. Building settings (units, base)
4. Building layout (plan extrusion, wireframe)
5. Surface generation (walls, roof)
6. 3D symbol creation (windows, parametric cube)
7. Insertion of symbols

8. City settings (units, limits)
9. City blocks layout (using parametric cube)
10. Creation of buildings (using parametric cube)
11. Placement of the commercial building
12. Presentation display (creating a perspective view, rendering)

19.3 Initial Stages

Stage 1: Model Division

Because the model you are about to create is more complex, it needs to be broken down into more manageable sections. A breakdown of the two sections is listed next.

SECTION A: COMMERCIAL BUILDING CONSTRUCTION

- Roof areas
- Walls
- Windows
- Glass features (solariums)
- External features (steps)
- Temporary construction objects

SECTION B: CITY CONSTRUCTION

- Ground
- City blocks
- City block structures
- Surfaces of city block structures

Other divisions would be created if you chose to add extra elements.

The master model should be named at this point as well. In this project, the commercial building will be called CONV (CONVention center), and the city will be called CITY.

Stage 2: Layer Designations

As Chapter 18 noted, layer designation must take place in the early stages of development to facilitate the construction and later display of the final model. Most of the layers will be named now, but they will not all be created at this point. Some layers will not be created until they are actually needed during construction.

Because we want to use hide options to view or plot our complex model with hidden features removed and because AutoCAD ignores objects on a frozen layer during hidden line removal, thereby abbreviating the time that process takes, the model in this project is divided into individual city blocks (do not mistake these for AutoCAD blocks). Each block has its own designation. These designations allow you to freeze any number of city blocks, at any time, either for better viewing of the convention center or to speed up the processing time of the computer. Referring ahead to Figure 19.27, note that each block has a designated letter. Any construction taking place within that block will be on the layer for that block.

Recall that only the first 8 characters of a layer name are visible on the status line, even though the layer name can have as many as 31 characters. Because of this and for the sake of convenience, the names for the layers of this model have 8 or fewer characters. These names are self-explanatory; for example, A-WALLS would be the name of the layer containing the walls of the building on city block A.

369

Listed next are the layers you should create when starting the model. For section A (the commercial building construction), create the following layers. (*Note:* The layer names use F for the prefix because the commercial building occupies city block F.)

LAYER COLOR	LAYER NAME	LAYER DESCRIPTION
1	F-ROOF	Commercial building roofs
2	F-WALLS	Commercial building walls
3	F-WIN1	Commercial building windows (separate symbol)
4	F-WIN2	Commercial building windows (parametric cube)
5	F-GLASS	Commercial building glass structures
6	F-FEATU	Commercial building external features (steps)
7	F-WIRES	Commercial building wireframe construction
12	F-TMPOR	Temporary construction

For section B (the city construction), create these layers. (*Note:* Replace the * with the appropriate city block designation.)

LAYER COLOR	LAYER NAME	LAYER DESCRIPTION
4	*-CBLOCK	City block base (parametric cube)
5	*-STRUCT	City block buildings (parametric cube)
6	*-STSURF	City block surfaces as required (3D faces)

Give each section type its own color to make it easier to distinguish what is on each layer. The color you choose for each section type is not important at this point.

Remember: It is customary to use continuous linetype for all construction of 3D models.

19.4 **Section A: Commercial Building Construction**

Stage 3: Initial Settings

Start a new model called CONV. Create the layers listed in Stage 2, and assign the appropriate colors. Enter the following settings before beginning the model:

```
SETTINGS
Units = Architectural
Limits = 0',0' to 360',660'
Grid = 10'
Snap Incr. = 10'
Initial Elevation Thickness = 0'
Initial Thickness = 0'
UCS = WCS
UCSICON = On and set to 2D display properties
UCSVP = 0 (always set before creation of viewports)
UCS toolbar = displayed
View toolbar = displayed
```

Remember to ZOOM All, so that the display shows the set limits. In addition, if there are any other settings you would like to enter, now is the time to do so.

Note: To facilitate construction, start, intermediate, and end points are given where required. They are identified as P1, P2, and so forth. Simply enter each 3D point in sequence until the last point in the series has been entered. When exact coordinate numeric values are given, their locations are not shown on the related figures.

Stage 4: Building Layout

Review the plan and elevation views of the building shown in Figure 19.2. At this stage, most of the building will be constructed with extrusion and wireframe procedures. The missing surfaces will be added in Stage 5. Some advanced surface commands, such as EDGESURF, will be used to construct the many-paned, glassed-in areas.

Let's begin construction. First, we'll tackle the walls that represent the major structure of the convention section of the building. REMEMBER TO SAVE YOUR DRAWING PERIODICALLY.

Figure 19.2
Plan and elevation views of the building

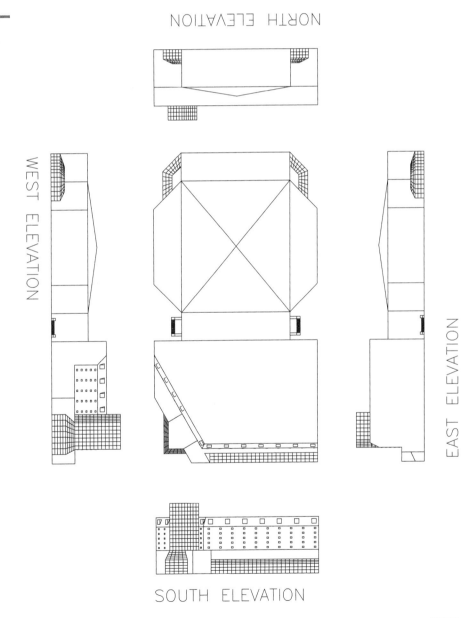

Creating the Major Structure of Convention Section

Create an orientation cube as a frame of reference. Use these settings:

```
SETTINGS
Layer = F-TMPOR
Elevation = 0'
Thickness = 120'
UCS = WCS
Viewports = Split the screen into two viewports, one above the other. The lower
    viewport should contain the plan view. The top viewport should contain an
    axonometric view (VPOINT = 2,−4,1).
```

Using the LINE command, draw the perimeter representing the orientation cube, as shown in Figure 19.3. The orientation cube is 360' in the X direction, 260' in the Y direction, and 120' in the Z direction. The lower-left corner must start at 0,0,0. (*Note:* When entering 3D coordinates, Z values may be left off as long as the elevation is set to the desired height.)

```
P1 = 0',0',0'          P2 = 360',0',0
P3 = 360',260',0'      P4 = 0,260',0'
CLOSE
```

Figure 19.3
Orientation cube

Creating the Rooftop of Convention Section

We now construct the top of the roof, including the sloped edge of the roof, out of wireframe. We'll surface it in Stage 5. The vertical wall that meets the sloped edge is constructed from a line with thickness (see Figure 19.4).

```
SETTINGS
Layer = F-WIRES
Elevation = 120'
Thickness = 0'
UCS = WCS
```

Using the LINE command, draw the perimeter representing the sloped edge of the roof (see Figure 19.4A).

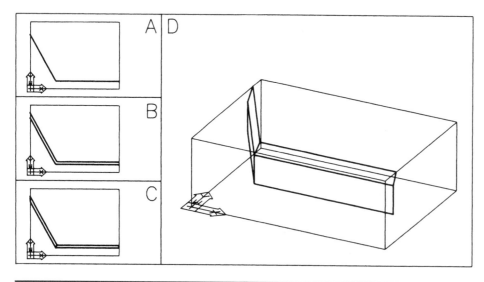

Figure 19.4
Wireframe representing the roof area

P1 = 360',40',120'
P2 = 108'8'',40',120'
P3 = 0',230'2'',120'

   SETTINGS
Layer = F-WALLS
Elevation = 50'
Thickness = 50'
UCS = WCS

Using the LINE command, draw the perimeter representing the vertical wall that meets the sloped edge of the roof (see Figure 19.4B).

P1 = 360',30',50'
P2 = 102'10'',30',50'
P3 = 0',210',50'

   SETTINGS
Layer = F-WIRES
Elevation = 0'
Thickness = 0'
UCS = WCS

Using the LINE command and endpoint object snap, add the sloped lines connecting the roof to the walls (see Figure 19.4C).

Creating the Extension Walls of Convention Section

The extension walls that run around the west and south wall are constructed now. The inner lines are wireframe, but the outer lines are extruded lines, because they represent a completely vertical wall.

   SETTINGS
Layer = F-WIRES
Elevation = 50'
Thickness = 0'
UCS = WCS

Using the LINE command, draw the walls representing the inner perimeter of the extension (see Figure 19.5A).

P1 = 360',30',50'
P2 = 102'10'',30',50'
P3 = 0',210',50'

   SETTINGS
Layer = F-WALLS
Elevation = 0'
Thickness = 50'
UCS = WCS

Using the LINE command, draw the walls representing the outer perimeter of the extension (see Figure 19.5B). For line 1, use the following points:

P1 = 360',20',0'
P2 = 108'7'',20',0'

For line 2, use these points:

P1 = 80',0',0'
P2 = 0',140',0'

373

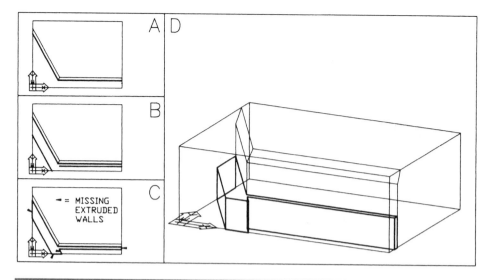

Figure 19.5
Creation of the extension walls

Using the LINE command, create the missing walls, as shown in Figures 19.5C and D. Remember that these are extruded lines.

Creating the South Glass Solarium in Convention Section

The south glass solarium at the front of the building is first constructed out of wireframe and then covered with meshes using the EDGESURF command.

```
SETTINGS
Layer = F-WIRES
Elevation = 0'
Thickness = 0'
UCS = WCS
```

Using the LINE command, construct the line representing the top of the solarium (see Figure 19.6A).

```
P1 = 360',20',30'
P2 = 120',20',30'
```

Using the LINE command again, construct the line representing the bottom and top of the vertical wall of the solarium (see Figure 19.6B). Use the following points for line 1:

```
P1 = 360',0',0'
P2 = 120',0',0'
```

For line 2, use these points:

```
P1 = 360',0',20'
P2 = 120',0',20'
```

Now add the missing lines as shown in Figure 19.6C. Use the LINE command and endpoint object snap.

```
SETTINGS
Layer = F-TMPOR
Freeze layer F-GLASS
```

374

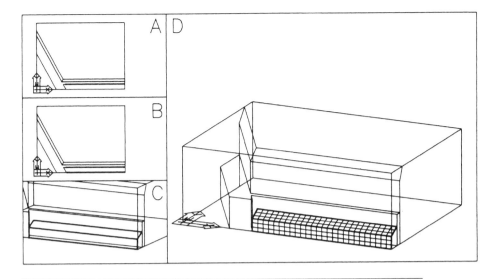

Figure 19.6
South solarium wireframe and mesh

SURFTAB1 = 26 (horizontal panes of glass)
SURFTAB2 = 3 (vertical panes of glass)

With the EDGESURF command, select groups of four lines to create a mesh (see Figure 19.6D). Select horizontal lines first so that SURFTAB1 controls the number of horizontal panes. After you have created the first mesh, use PROPERTIES to move it to the F-GLASS layer. This allows you to select the wireframe to create a new mesh without being obstructed by the previously created mesh. Now create the second mesh and move it to the F-GLASS layer.

Creating the West Glass Solarium in Convention Section

The west glass solarium at the angled side of the building is constructed in a manner similar to the construction of the south solarium.

```
    SETTINGS
Layer = F-WIRES
Elevation = 0'
Thickness = 0'
UCS = WCS
```

Using the LINE command, construct the line representing the top of the solarium (see Figure 19.7A).

```
P1 = 62'10",30',50'
P2 = 30',30',50'
P3 = 30',87'6",50'
```

Using the LINE command again, construct the line representing the bottom and top of the vertical wall of the solarium (see Figure 19.7B). For line 1, use these points:

```
P1 = 68'7",20',0'
P2 = 20',20',0'
P3 = 20',105',0'
```

375

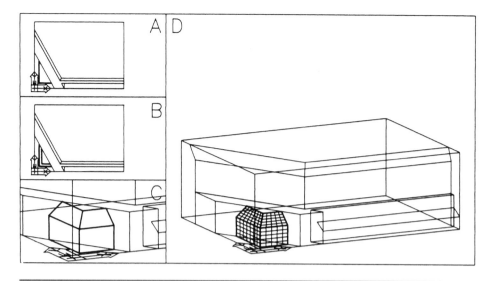

Figure 19.7
West solarium wireframe and mesh

For line 2, use these points:

P1 = 68'7",20',30'
P2 = 20',20',30'
P3 = 20',105',30'

Add the missing lines as shown in Figure 19.7C. Use the LINE command and endpoint object snap.

```
   SETTINGS
Layer = F-TMPOR
SURFTAB1 = 5 (horizontal panes of glass)
SURFTAB2 = 5 (vertical panes of glass)
Freeze layer F-GLASS
```

Using the EDGESURF command, select groups of four lines to create a mesh on the north face of the sloped surface. Select horizontal lines first so that SURFTAB1 controls the number of horizontal panes. After you have created the first mesh, use PROPERTIES to move it to the F-GLASS layer. Repeat this process for the north vertical face.

```
SURFTAB1 = 7 (horizontal panes of glass)
SURFTAB2 = 5 (vertical panes of glass)
```

Using the EDGESURF command again, select groups of four lines to create a mesh on the west face of the sloped surface. Select horizontal lines first so that SURFTAB1 controls the number of horizontal panes. Once you have created it, move the first mesh to the F-GLASS layer. Repeat this process for the west vertical face.

Thaw layer F-GLASS, observe the mesh, and then freeze the layer again.

Creating the Tower in Convention Section

The glass tower sits half on the west solarium and half on the extension. It will be constructed out of wireframe and then covered with a mesh using the EDGESURF command.

376

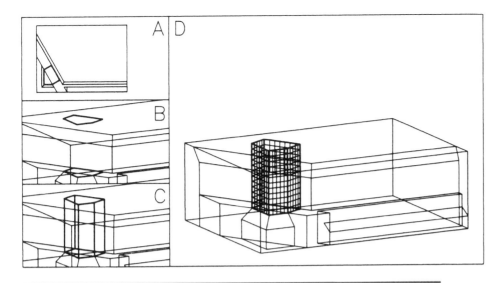

Figure 19.8
Glass tower construction

SETTINGS
Layer = F-WIRES
Elevation = 50′
Thickness = 0′
UCS = WCS

Using the LINE command, construct the lines shown in Figure 19.8A.

P1 = 93′,47′ 3″,50′   P2 = 62′10″,30′,50′
P3 = 30′,30′,50′   P4 = 30′,87′6″,50′
P5 = 60′2″,104′9″,50′

Using the LINE command again, construct the lines shown in Figure 19.8B, or copy the lines from Figure 19.8A to an elevation of 150′.

P1 = 93′,47′3″,150′   P2 = 62′10″,30′,150′
P3 = 30′,30′,150′   P4 = 30′,87′6″,150′
P5 = 60′2″,104′9″,150′

Using endpoint object snap, add the vertical lines as shown in Figure 19.8C.

SETTINGS
Layer = F-TMPOR
Freeze layer F-GLASS.
SURFTAB1 = 5 (horizontal panes of glass)
SURFTAB2 = 12 (vertical panes of glass)

Note: Use SURFTAB1 = 7 for the west and east tower faces.

Using the EDGESURF command, select groups of four lines to create a mesh on one side of the tower. Select horizontal lines first so that SURFTAB1 controls the number of horizontal panes. Use PROPERTIES to move the newly created first mesh to the F-GLASS layer. Repeat this process for the other four sides.

Thaw layer F-GLASS, observe the mesh, and then freeze the layer again.

Save the model as CONV.

Creating the Extruded Walls of Exhibition Center

The walls of the exhibition portion of the building are vertical, so they are created with lines that have thickness.

377

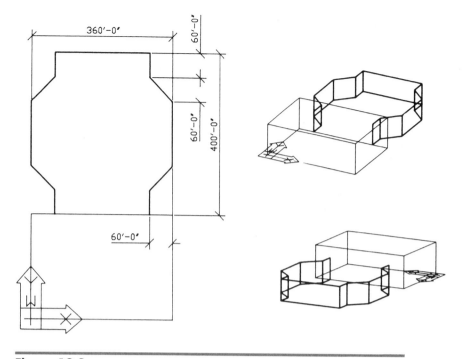

Figure 19.9
Extruded lines to create walls of the exhibition center

SETTINGS
Layer = F-WALLS
Elevation = 0′
Thickness = 100′
UCS = WCS

Using the LINE command, draw the perimeter representing the walls as shown in Figure 19.9. For clarity, the convention center portion of the building is not shown in Figures 19.9, 19.10, and 19.11.

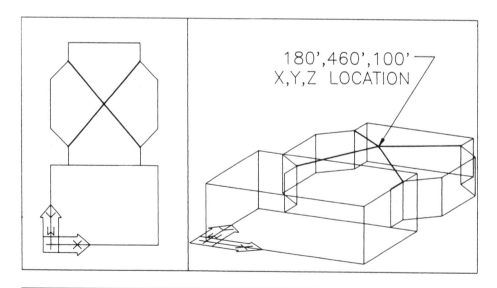

Figure 19.10
Wireframe of exhibition center roof

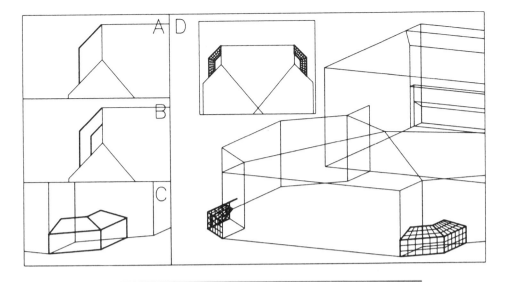

Figure 19.11
West and east solarium wireframe and mesh

Creating the Sloped Roof Structure of Exhibition Center

The sloped roof of the exhibition center will be constructed out of wireframe initially and then, in Stage 5, it will be covered with surfaces.

```
SETTINGS
Layer = F-WIRES
Elevation = 0'
Thickness = 0'
UCS = WCS
```

Using the LINE command, draw the four wires that represent the sloped structure of the roof as shown in Figure 19.10. The peak of the roof is numerically represented by the coordinates 180',460',100'. Use endpoint object snap to snap to the corners of the extruded walls, and then enter the coordinates for the peak. Be sure to work in the axonometric viewport so that the correct elevation is used as the endpoints.

Creating the West and East Glass Solariums in Exhibition Center

The exhibition center's solariums are constructed in a fashion similar to the way the west solarium of the convention center was constructed. A wireframe model is constructed first, and then it is covered with a mesh.

```
SETTINGS
Layer = F-WIRES
Elevation = 0'
Thickness = 0'
UCS = WCS
```

Using the LINE command, construct the top and bottom lines shown in Figure 19.11A. For the first line, use these points:

```
P1 = 20',560',0'
P2 = 20',620',0'
P3 = 60',660',0'
```

Use these points for the other line:

P1 = 20',560',20'
P2 = 20',620',20'
P3 = 60',660',20'

Using the LINE command again, construct the lines shown in Figure 19.11B.

P1 = 40',580',30'
P2 = 40',611'9",30'
P3 = 60',631'9",30'

Using endpoint object snap, add the missing sloped and vertical lines as shown in Figure 19.11C.

    SETTINGS
    Layer = F-TMPOR
    Freeze layer F-GLASS
    SURFTAB1 = 6 (horizontal panes of glass)
    SURFTAB2 = 3 (vertical panes of glass)

Using the EDGESURF command, select groups of four lines to create a mesh on one of the sloped surfaces. Select horizontal lines first so that SURFTAB1 controls the number of horizontal panes. When you have created the first mesh, use PROPERTIES to move it to the F-GLASS layer. Repeat this procedure for the other sloped surface. Thaw layer F-GLASS.

(Use the MIRROR command to mirror the west solarium to the east side.)

Observe the mesh, and then freeze the F-GLASS layer again.

Save the model as CONV.

Stage 5: Surface Generation

Now we need to add surfaces on the various portions of the building. We'll use the 3DFACE command to do this. Remember that 3D faces can be created with any three-dimensional coordinates and will not be forced to align to the current working plane. Thus, to add these surfaces, all we need to do is snap to the previously constructed wireframes. If you desire, you can use regions instead of 3D faces. Follow these steps to create 3D faces:

1. Using the 3DFACE command, add the missing surfaces by referring to Figures 19.12 and 19.13. Use object snap endpoint and intersection for most node points for the 3D faces.

    SETTINGS
    Layer = F-ROOF
    Elevation = 0'
    Thickness = 0'
    UCS = WCS

   Remember to use the Invisible Edge option of the 3DFACE command whenever necessary, so that no obstructing diagonal lines cross complex surfaces. (Refer to Section 7.3 of Chapter 7 if you need a refresher.)
2. Freeze the F-TMPOR layer and thaw the F-GLASS layer.
3. Save the model as CONV.
4. Using VPOINT or 3DORBIT, move around the model and use HIDE or Hide shade mode to observe the results. The model should look similar to Figure 19.14.

Figure 19.12
Surfaces to be added to the
convention center

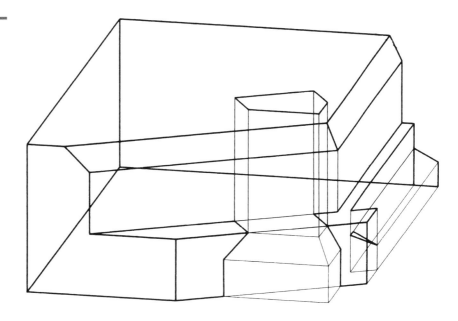

Figure 19.13
Surfaces to be added to the
exhibition center

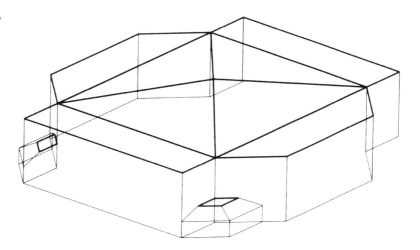

Stage 6: 3D Symbol Generation

At this point, we create and add the various 3D features that are needed for the building. We'll create two kinds of windows and a set of steps. If you desire, you can create more symbols and add them to the model for further enhancement. However, constructing the symbols specified here gives you sufficient practice in the necessary techniques. Once you become familiar with these procedures, there will be few limits to what you will be able to accomplish.

Creating the Parametric Cube

A parametric cube serves several functions in the construction of the building and the city. Its first function is to form windows that line the convention center. Later, it will be used to create the city block lots and the city's other buildings. (This portion of our project should serve as a convincing illustration of the usefulness of parametric symbol design.)

Start a new model called FCUBE (parametric Foot CUBE) with the following settings:

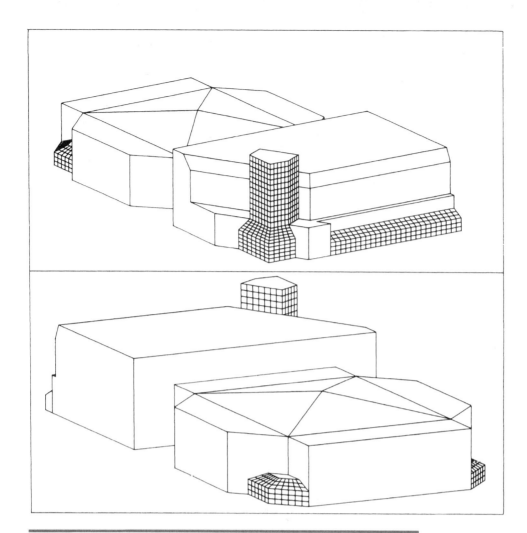

Figure 19.14
Model by the end of Stage 5

SETTINGS
Units = Architectural
Limits = −1′, −1′ to 1′,1′
Grid = 1′
Snap Incr. = 1′
Elevation = 0′
Thickness = 0′
Current Layer = 0
UCS = WCS

We are going to use a 3D surface object for this symbol. Use the AI_BOX command to create a surface model that is a 1-foot cube (1′ × 1′ × 1′), as shown in Figure 19.15. The lower-left corner should be at 0,0,0, and set the BASE point to 0,0,0. Then, save the model as FCUBE.

Creating the Sloped Window

A sloped window symbol will be placed along the sloped roof edge of the convention center. To construct it, start a new model called SWIN (Sloped WINdow) with the following settings:

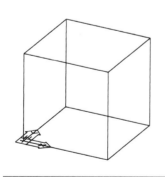

Figure 19.15
FCUBE model

382

Figure 19.16
SWIN model

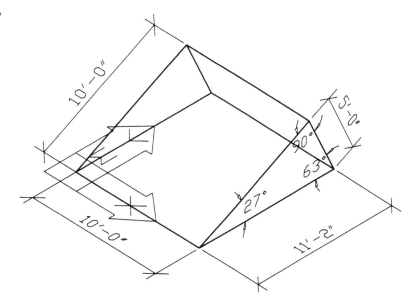

SETTINGS
Units = Architectural
Limits = −1′, −1′ to 12′,12′
Grid = 1′
Snap Incr. = 2″
Elevation = 0′
Thickness = 0′
Current Layer = 0
UCS = WCS

Using the LINE command, draw a wireframe of the illustration shown in Figure 19.16. (*Note:* The 63-degree angle and the length 11′2″ are approximate.)

Using the 3DFACE command, add surfaces to the sides and the top of the wireframe. Set the BASE point to 0,0,0. Then, save the model as SWIN.

Creating the Exhibition Steps

The concrete steps to the exhibition center are constructed with lines that have thickness and 3D faces (see Figure 19.17).

Start a new drawing called STEP2 with these settings:

SETTINGS
Units = Architectural
Limits = 0′,0′ to 35′,30′
Grid = 5′
Snap Incr. = 6″
Thickness = 5′10″
Elevation = 0′
UCS = WCS
UCSICON = On and set to 2D display properties
UCSVP = 0 (always set before creation of viewports)
UCS toolbar = displayed
View toolbar = displayed Layers = 0 (all construction will take place on layer 0)

Draw a rectangle the same size as the concrete steps—with a width of 30′ and a depth of 22′6″, as shown in Figure 19.18. Next, display an axonometric view of the cube.

Figure 19.17
Concrete step model

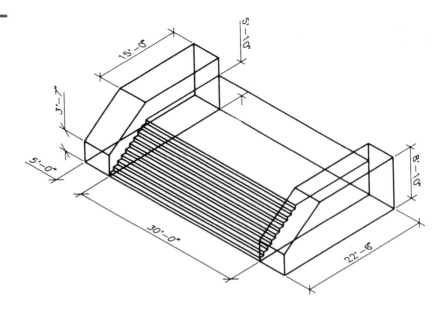

SETTING
Thickness = −30′

Create a working plane on the right side of the cube, as shown in Figure 19.19. Use the PLAN command to set the view to the current UCS. Draw the outline of the landing and the treads and risers, as shown in Figure 19.19.

SETTING
Thickness = 5′

Use the LINE command, and draw the sides of the steps, as shown in Figure 19.20.

Set the elevation to −30′ and the thickness to −5′ and draw in the other side of the steps, or use the COPY or MIRROR command and duplicate the first side.

Figure 19.18
Orientation cube and the working plane

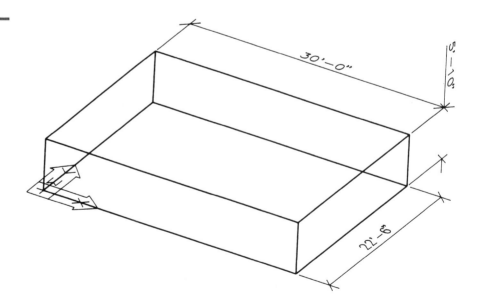

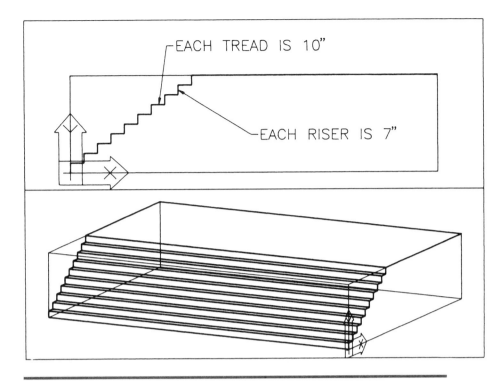

Figure 19.19
Adding the steps and viewing from an isometric viewpoint

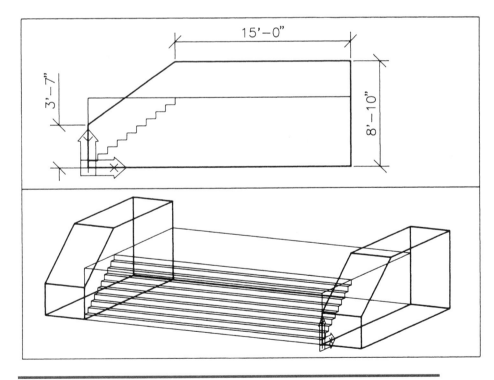

Figure 19.20
Sides of the steps

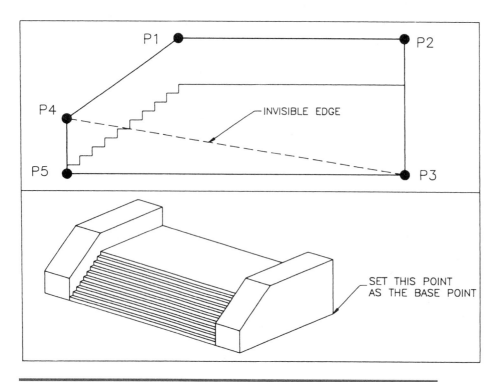

Figure 19.21
Adding surfaces to the sides

SETTING
Thickness = 0'

Delete the top, front, and two side lines of the orientation box. Leave the back line for the back surface of the step. You need to create surfaces on the two sides of the steps. You can use 3D faces or regions. To use regions, draw a closed polyline and turn it into a region. Remember you must reorient the UCS on each side of the step so that the regions face outward or they will not be visible when you shade or render.

To use 3D faces, refer to Figure 19.21 for the click points on the 3D faces. Use endpoint object snap to snap to points 1 through 5. *Note:* Remember to use the Invisible Edge option just before clicking P3.

Use the COPY command to copy the 3D faces to the other three sides. Then, set the BASE point to 35',22'6",0', as shown in Figure 19.21.

Use the HIDE command, and observe the results. The screen should look similar to Figure 19.21. Save the model as STEP2.

Stage 7: Inserting Symbols

In this stage, we'll add the two window types and the concrete steps to the building. If you constructed other symbols during the last stage, add them now as well.

Open the building model CONV.

Inserting the Sloped Window

The first symbol to be inserted is the sloped window. To have the proper orientation upon insertion, align the working plane to the sloped surface of the roof edge.

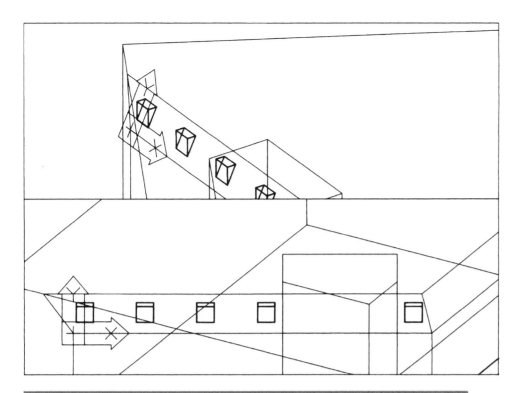

Figure 19.22
Sloped windows on the west side of the building

SETTINGS
Layer = F-WIN1
Elevation = 0'
Thickness = 0'
Freeze F-GLASS layer

Using the UCS command, align the UCS working plane to the sloped roof edge of the west side of the building, as shown in Figure 19.22.

Using the INSERT command, place the SWIN 3D symbol at the coordinates 1'6",6'2",0'. Leave the scale of the 3D symbol at 1 and the rotation at 0.

Using the ARRAY command, copy the window along the wall. The number of rows is 1, and the number of columns is 4. The distance between the columns is 35'.

Insert another sloped window on the right side of the tower, as shown in Figure 19.22. Place it at coordinates 191'6",6'2",0'.

Using the UCS command, align the UCS working plane to the sloped roof edge of the south side of the building, as shown in Figure 19.23.

Using the INSERT command, place the SWIN 3D symbol at coordinates 10'10",6'2",0'. Leave the scale of the 3D symbol at 1 and the rotation at 0.

Using the ARRAY command, copy the window along the wall. The number of rows is 1, and the number of columns is 7. The distance between the columns is 38'6".

Inserting the Second Window Type

The windows along the vertical walls of the convention center are created using the second window type. This window type is formed using the parametric cube FCUBE (see Figure 19.24).

Using the UCS command, align the UCS working plane to the west side of the building, as shown in Figure 19.24.

387

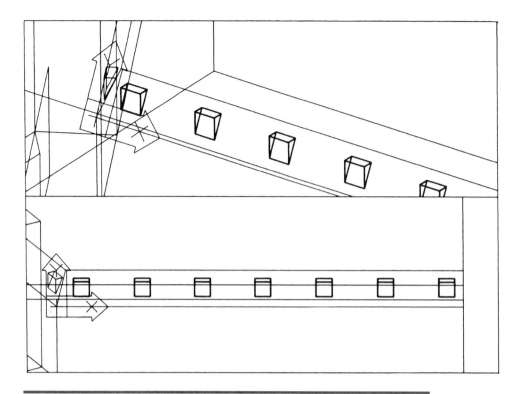

Figure 19.23
Sloped window on the south side of the building

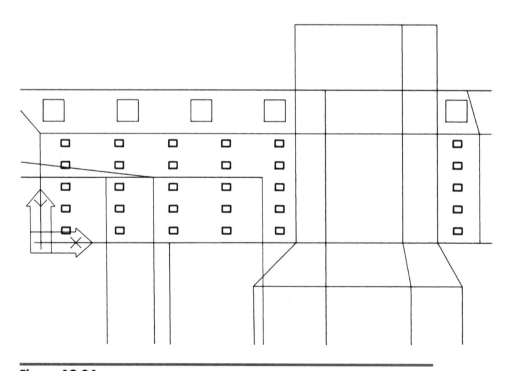

Figure 19.24
Parametric windows along the west side of the building

Using the INSERT command, place the FCUBE 3D symbol at coordinates 10′,4′,0′.

Use the XYZ option to allow scaling of the cube in all three axes:

$X = 4$
$Y = 3$
$Z = 0.3$

This creates a window 4′ wide, 3′ high, and 3.6″ thick.

Using the ARRAY command, copy the window along the wall. The number of rows is 5, and the number of columns is 5. The distance between the rows is 10′, and the distance between the columns is 25′5″.

Using the INSERT command, place the FCUBE 3D symbol at the right of the tower at coordinates 195′,4′,0′.

Use the XYZ option to allow scaling of the cube in all three axes:

$X = 4$
$Y = 3$
$Z = 0.3$

Using the ARRAY command, copy the window along the wall. The number of rows is 5, and the number of columns is 1. The distance between the rows is 10′.

Using the UCS command, align the UCS working plane to the south side of the building, as shown in Figure 19.25.

Using the INSERT command, place the FCUBE 3D symbol at the coordinates 10′,4′,0′.

Use the XYZ option to allow scaling of the cube in all three axes:

$X = 4$
$Y = 3$
$Z = 0.3$

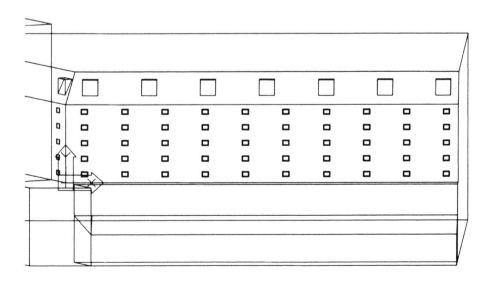

Figure 19.25
Parametric windows along the south side of the building

Using the ARRAY command, copy the window along the wall. The number of rows is 5, and the number of columns is 10. The distance between the rows is 10', and the distance between the columns is 26'4".

Inserting the Concrete Steps

A set of steps is placed on each side of the exhibition center where it joins the convention center. The working plane is set to match the WCS (see Figure 19.26).

```
SETTINGS
Layer = F-FEATU
Elevation = 0'
Thickness = 0'
UCS = WCS
Freeze layers F-WIN1 and F-WIN2
```

Using the INSERT command, first place the STEP2 3D symbol at coordinates 60',270',0', at a scale of 1 and a rotation of 270 degrees. Then place the symbol at coordinates 300',310',0' at a scale of 1 and a rotation of 90 degrees.

Save the model as CONV.

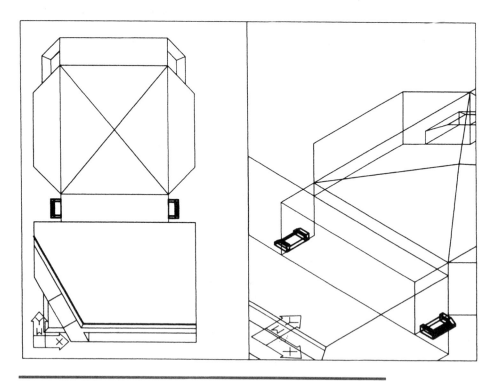

Figure 19.26
Placement of concrete steps

Section B: City Construction and Building Placement

Stage 8: City Settings

The following steps need to be completed before the modeling of the city blocks can begin.

Start a new model called CITY. Create the following layers and assign the appropriate colors:

LAYER COLOR	LAYER NAME	LAYER DESCRIPTION
3	GROUND	Ground surface (3D face)
4	*-CBLOCK	City block base (parametric cube)
5	*-STRUCT	City block buildings (parametric cube)
6	*-STSURF	City block surfaces as required (3D faces)

Replace the * with the appropriate city block designations A through P.

    SETTINGS
Units = Architectural
Limits = $-10'$, $-10'$ to 1760',1210'
Grid = 10
Snap Incr. = 10'
Initial Elevation = 0'
Initial Thickness = 0'
UCS = WCS
UCSICON = On and set to 2D display properties
UCSVP = 0 (always set before creating viewports)
UCS toolbar = displayed
View toolbar = displayed

Remember to ZOOM All, so that the display shows the set limits.

Are there other settings you would like to set? If so, now is the time to set them, before entering Stage 9. REMEMBER TO SAVE YOUR DRAWING PERIODICALLY.

Stage 9: City Blocks Layout

Figure 19.27 shows the plan views of the city blocks. These city blocks are constructed out of the parametric cube FCUBE. The city blocks A, B, C, D, E, H, I, J, K, L, M, O, and P are 400' × 200'. Blocks F, G, and N are made of modules sized 400' × 200' separated by street widths of 50'. Each block has a thickness of 6".

    SETTING
Layer = A-CBLOCK

Using the INSERT command, place FCUBE at coordinates 0',1000',0'.
Using the XYZ option, set the following scales. (You may use a 2D solid if desired.)

$X = 400$
$Y = 200$
$Z = -0.5$

Leave the rotation at 0.

The first city block has now been constructed at location A. Construct the remaining city blocks using the parametric 3D symbol FCUBE, as shown in Figure 19.27. All blocks are multiples of 400' × 200' with 50' street spacing. Remember to change the layer before the formation of each city block so that each block is on its own layer.

When you are done, save the model as CITY.

Figure 19.27
Plan views of the city blocks

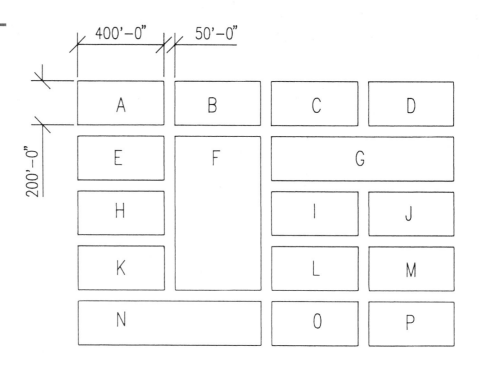

Stage 10: Creating Simple Buildings

Here we create simple buildings to represent the city setting into which the commercial building is inserted, as shown in Figure 19.28. Most of the buildings are constructed out of the FCUBF model. Those buildings with nonrectangular shapes are constructed out of lines with thickness and then covered with 3D faces.

Look at Figure 19.29 now. Note the enclosed numbers that are placed within each building area or near the area and directed to it. These numbers represent the

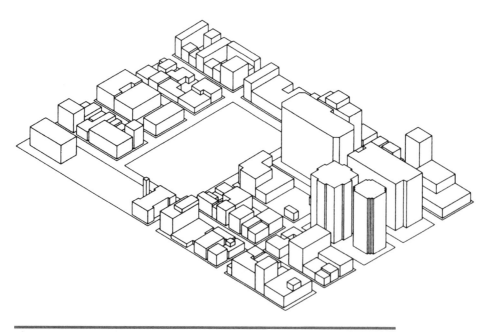

Figure 19.28
Isometric view of the city blocks

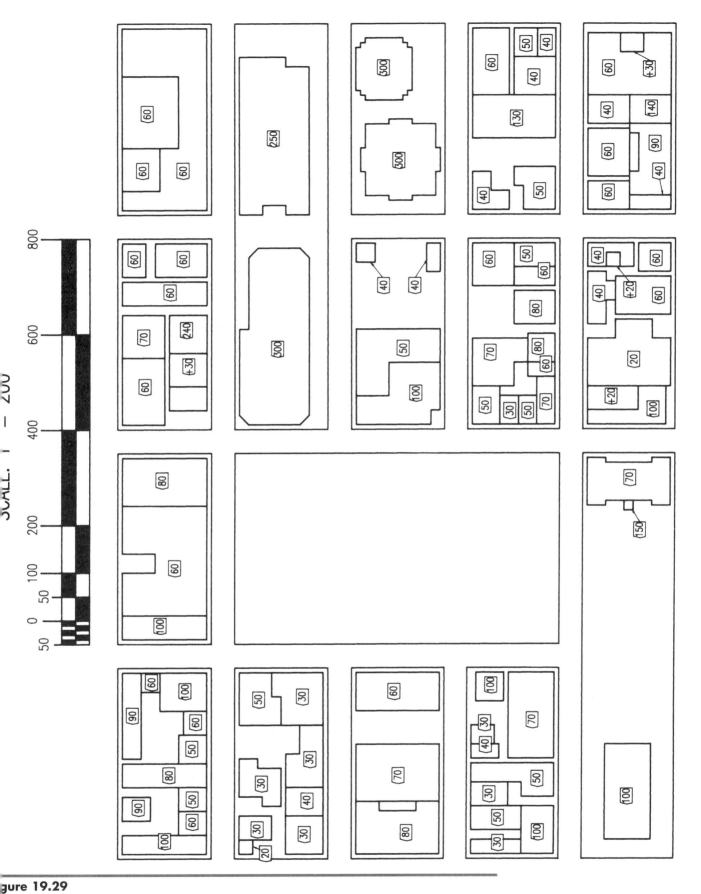

Figure 19.29
Plan view of the city buildings

393

roof elevation of each building (for example, "90" means that the roof is at an elevation of 90'). If there is a plus sign before the number, it means that this building structure is on top of another and is so many feet higher. (For example, +30 represents that the roof elevation is 30' above the elevation of the roof it is sitting on.)

The smallest division in the X or Y direction is 10'. The scale of the plan is $1'' = 200'$. The X and Y size of the buildings may be scaled directly from the plan. The scale bar on the drawing can be used to transfer the sizes as well.

```
SETTINGS
Layer = *-STRUCT (substitute * for city block letter as needed)
Elevation = 0'
Thickness = 0'
UCS = WCS
```

Refer to both Figures 19.28 and 19.29 as you create the buildings. Remember to change the layers as necessary. Layer *-STRUCT is for the FCUBE buildings and for the lines with thickness. Layer *-STSURF is for the 3D faces that are required to roof the nonrectangular buildings. Substitute * for city block letter as needed. (See layer creation in Stage 9.) Keep most of the elevations at 0'. However, to construct a building structure that is on top of another structure (indicated by a positive roof elevation number), set the elevation to the roof elevation of the bottom structure.

After you have created the simple buildings, save the model as CITY.

Stage 11: Placing the Commercial Building

Now it is time to insert the commercial building into the city setting.

```
SETTINGS
Layer = F-STRUCT
Elevation = 0'
Thickness = 0'
UCS = WCS
```

Using the INSERT command, place the CONV model at the coordinates 470',270',0'. Keep the scale to 1, and then rotate the building as necessary. See Figure 19.30 for the placement.

Save the model as CITY.

Stage 12: Presentation Display

The construction of the overall model is now complete, and we are ready to consider how to display the model for presentation purposes. Chapter 15 discusses presentation and display in detail; here, only the specifics for this commercial building model are given.

A project of this magnitude would be viewed in numerous ways. In fact, if you have access to Autodesk VIZ (see Chapter 25), you might consider creating an animated flyby of the city and the commercial building as an added challenge. However, we'll create only four perspective views for this project:

PERSP1: from above and to the southwest of the commercial building, looking at the commercial building

PERSP2: closer to the ground and closer to the southwest corner of the building, with emphasis on the glass tower and solarium

PERSP3: from the top of a building to the northwest of the exhibition center, looking toward the glass solarium on the northwest face of the exhibition center

PERSP4: from directly above the city, looking down

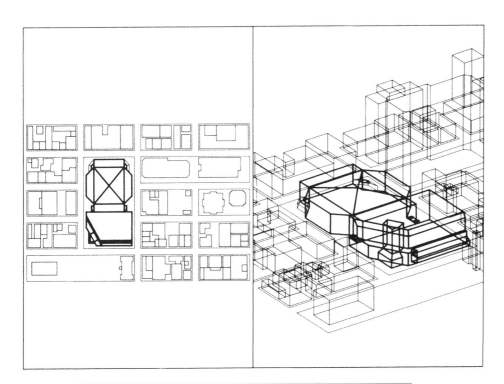

Figure 19.30
Commercial building placement

Creating the Preview Selection Set

When selecting objects for the Preview selection set, select only the commercial building, not the whole city. This makes it easier to modify the DVIEW settings to achieve the desired view. You may have to adjust the settings depending on your graphics.

Complete Steps 1 through 5 to create and save the four perspective views:

1. The following settings achieve the perspective view PERSP1 shown in Figure 19.31. Use the Points option of the DVIEW command to place the camera and the target points, and set the Distance and Zoom values.

   Points-Target = 699'9",1007'4", −161'5"
   Camera = −74'8",241'5",1078'
   Distance = 1650'
   Zoom = 22

   Exit the DVIEW command to apply the settings to the entire model.
   Using the VIEW command, save the perspective view as PERSP1.

2. The following settings achieve the perspective view PERSP2 shown in Figure 19.32. Use the Points option to place the camera and the target points, and set the Distance and Zoom values.

   Points-Target = 762'10",979'9",152'5"
   Camera = 447'8",563'6",14'8"
   Distance = 540'
   Zoom = 25

   Exit the DVIEW command to apply the settings to the entire model.
   Using the VIEW command, save the perspective view as PERSP2.

395

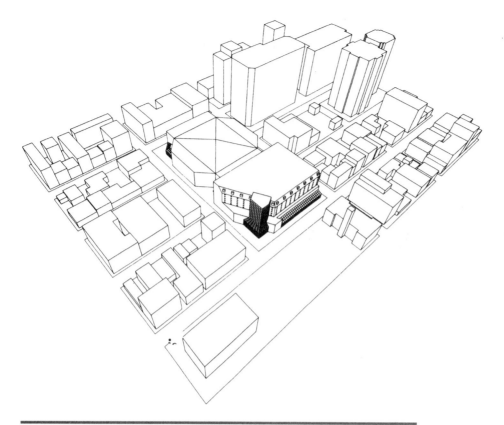

Figure 19.31
Perspective view PERSP1

Figure 19.32
Perspective view PERSP2

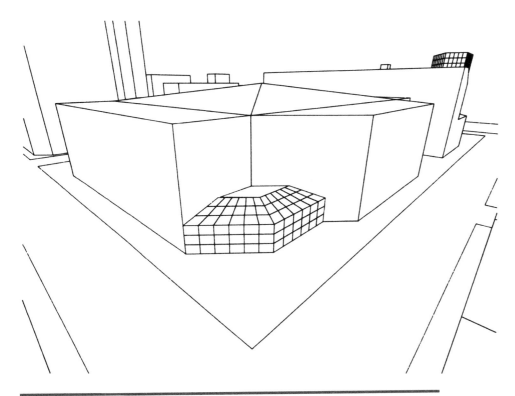

Figure 19.33
Perspective view PERSP3

3. The following settings achieve the perspective view PERSP3 shown in Figure 19.33. Use the Points option to place the camera and the target points, and set the Distance and Zoom values.

Points-Target = 560',1331'9'',30'
Camera = 440',1460',100'
Distance = 189'1''
Zoom = 20

Exit the DVIEW command to apply the settings to the entire model.
Using the VIEW command, save the perspective view as PERSP3.

4. The following settings achieve the perspective view PERSP4 as shown in Figure 19.34. Use the Points option to place the camera and the target points, and set the Distance and Zoom values.

Points-Target = 925',1083'9'',78'8''
Camera = 925',1083'9'',1078'8''
Distance = 1000'
Zoom = 15

Exit the DVIEW command to apply the settings to the entire model.
Using the VIEW command, save the perspective view as PERSP4.

5. Save the model as CITY.

Displaying the Model

Use the HIDE command to display the model. Then use various shade modes. Repeat the procedure with the previously saved views.

397

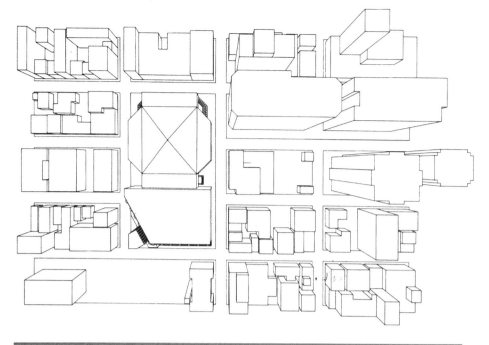

Figure 19.34
Perspective view PERSP4

Rendering the Model

Note: For a discussion on rendering models, see the final section in Chapter 18.

Here are sample settings to create a rendering of the city in the daytime using the RENDER utility. There is only one light, which represents the sun. See Figure 19.35 for an image plot of the rendered model.

Figure 19.35
Rendered view of the city model

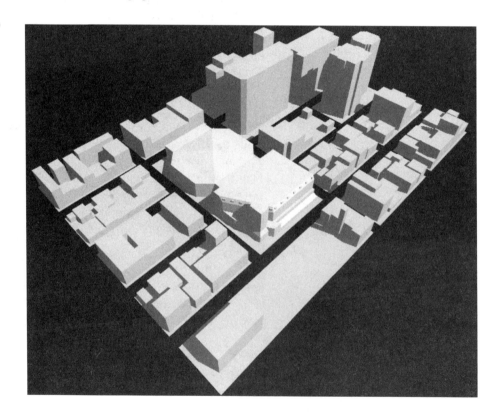

Rendering Preferences:			Use default settings. Turn Smooth Shading and Shadows On, and Render with Photo Real.	
Lights:			Make sure that you turn Shadows On when you create your Distant (Sun) light.	

NAME	TYPE	INTENSITY	FROM LOCATION	TO LOCATION
sun	distant	1.0	900′, 300′, 800′	700′, 900′, 0′
ambient		1.0		

Mechanical Project: Solid Modeling of a Split Pillow Block

Overview

In this chapter, you create a solid model of a common mechanical object—a split pillow block. The project illustrates techniques for creating holes in solids, forming unusual shapes, and adding curved and slotted solids.

Concepts Explored

- Continued reinforcement of AutoCAD features
- Creation of a complex 3D model of a mechanical object
- Generation of 3D symbols
- Use of 3D symbols to construct the final model
- Creation of paper space layouts of multiple views
- Final production of shaded and rendered images

20.1 Introduction

The project in this chapter creates a split pillow block model, illustrated in Figure 20.1, by generating individual parts and then assembling them into the final product. The parts are composed of curved, holed, and slotted solids, representing the complex aspects of mechanical design. When this model is finished, you should be

Figure 20.1
Axonometric display of assembled mechanical project

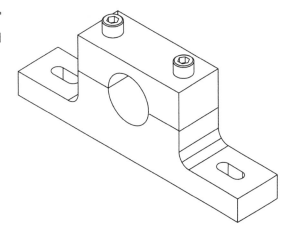

able to manipulate it completely within 3D space, view it from any location, explode the parts for better viewing, and reassemble them. As with the other projects in this text, the goal here is not to train you in the design of a particular mechanical component; rather, it is to facilitate your understanding and application of the methods of 3D creation.

20.2 Project Stages

A project involving the creation of a mechanical assembly should be an organized one. Even though this project does not have numerous parts, organizing the fabrication simplifies the modeling and reinforces the techniques you will need to apply to more complex models in the future. This project lends itself to obvious divisions: (1) the manufacture of the individual components, (2) their assembly, and (3) their disassembly. Within those divisions, the fabrication can be organized by the common creation techniques. Normally, the order of fabrication in a mechanical design is unique for every project. In this project, however, you will be able to apply some of the underlying commonalities to subsequent mechanical projects.

PROJECT STAGES
1. Division of mechanical model (parts)
2. Layer designations (surfaces, symbols)
3. Solid body fabrication
4. Slicing the solid in two
5. Assembly of the components
6. Presentation display (multiple views)
7. Disassembly of the model
8. Rendering the model

Stage 1: Mechanical Model Division

Creating a complex model is more easily accomplished if it can be done in sections. By identifying separate objects within the model, the creation task is simplified and the model is easier to manipulate after creation. The sections into which this model are divided are given in the following list:

- Creation of orientation cubes
- Creation of profiles
- Creation of extrusions
- Addition of features such as fillets

Stage 2: Layer Designations

As noted before, it is very important that layer designation take place early in the development stages. Being able to make objects visible or invisible facilitates the construction and later the display of the final model. Most of the layers are named now, but some layers are not created until 3D creation actually takes place.

In this model, assembly is broken down into the following parts:

Part 1: Upper YOKE (UYOKE model)
Part 2: Lower YOKE (LYOKE model)
Part 3: Connecting bolt (BOLT model)

Because only the first 8 characters of the layer name (which can have as many as 31 characters) are visible on the status line, the names for the layers of this model will have only 8 characters. For example, P1-SYM would represent the symbol for Part 1.

The layers to be created at the start of each model (UYOKE and LYOKE) are listed here:

LAYER COLOR	LAYER NAME	LAYER DESCRIPTION
**	P*-SYM	3D symbol model of individual part

Notes: The double asterisks (* *) identify a layer with multiple colors. Remember that the single asterisk (*) will be replaced by the appropriate part number.

For construction purposes, give each section type its own color. The separate colors makes it easier to distinguish what is on each layer. The color you choose for each section type is not important at this point.

Again, recall that it is customary to use continuous linetype for all construction.

Stage 3: Solid Body Fabrication

Initial Settings

Figure 20.2 illustrates the finished split pillow block model. Start the model called SPSOL (Split Pillow block SOLid) and enter the following settings:

```
Units = decimal
Limits = −1,−1 to 6,2
Grid = 0.125
Snap Incr. = 0.125
Elevation = 0
Thickness = 2
UCS = WCS
UCSICON = On and set to 2D display properties
UCSVP = 0 (always set before creation of viewports)
UCS toolbar = displayed
View toolbar = displayed
Display a plan (top) view (VPOINT 0,0,1)
Current layer = OCUBE
ISOLINES = 15
```

Figure 20.2
Solid model of split pillow block

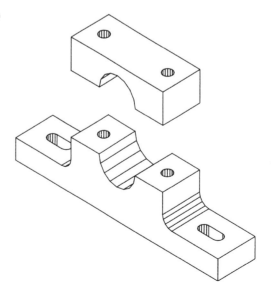

Figure 20.3

Orientation cube

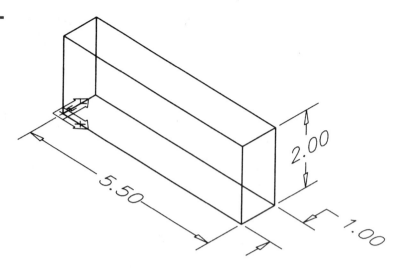

Creating the Orientation Cube

Using the LINE command, draw the orientation cube shown in Figure 20.3. The cube is 5.5″ along the *X* axis, 1″ along the *Y* axis, and 2″ along the *Z* axis. The lower-left corner starts at 0,0,0.

Creating the 2D Profile

Using the UCS command, create a working plane on the front face, as shown in Figure 20.4. Create a layer called PROFILE and make it current. Display a plan view of the current UCS. Set the thickness to 0. Using the PLINE command, draw a completely closed polyline representing the profile shown in Figure 20.4.

Extruding the Profile into a Solid

The 2D profile is turned into a 3D solid by means of the EXTRUDE command. Using the VPOINT command or the SE Isometric View tool, display an axonometric view (1,−1,1). Using the EXTRUDE command, select the profile to be extruded:

Figure 20.4

Setting the UCS and creating the 2D profile

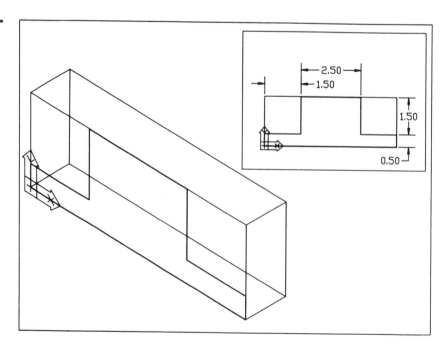

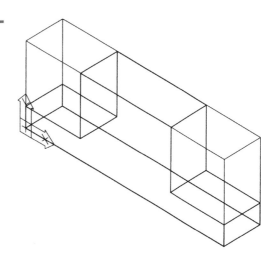

Figure 20.5
A 3D solid from the 2D profile

Command: **EXTRUDE**
Current wire frame density: ISOLINES = 4
Select objects: **click the polyline profile**
Specify height of extrusion or [Path]: **−1**
Specify angle of taper for extrusion <0>: **press Enter**

The command turns the profile into a 3D solid, as illustrated in Figure 20.5.

Creating a Hole Through the Solid

Using the CYLINDER command, create a solid cylinder that starts on the front face of the solid and extends to the rear of the solid (see Figure 20.6):

Command: **CYLINDER**
Current wire frame density: ISOLINES = 4
Specify center point for base of cylinder or [Elliptical] <0,0,0>: **2.75,1.25,0**
Specify radius for base of cylinder or [Diameter]: **0.5**
Specify height of cylinder or [Center of other end]: **−1**

Using the SUBTRACT command, subtract the cylinder from the main body:

Command: **SUBTRACT**
Select solids and regions to subtract from . . .
Select objects: **click the main body as the source solid**
Select solids and regions to subtract . . .
Select objects: **click the cylinder**

Figure 20.6
Subtracting the cylinder from the body

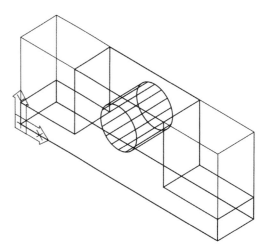

Figure 20.7
The hidden model showing the hole

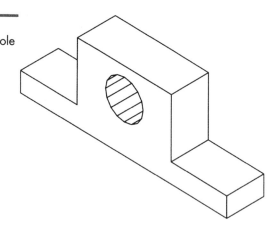

The display may not change but the cylinder was subtracted from the body. Try the
HIDE command to test the results. Your screen should look like Figure 20.7 when
the OCUBE is frozen.

Freeze the OCUBE layer and save the model as SPSOL.

Adding Two Top Bolt Holes

Using the UCS command, set the working plane to the top of the model, as shown
in Figure 20.8.

Using the CYLINDER command, place two cylinders inside the model, ex-
tending from the top to the bottom. Each cylinder has a radius of 0.125 (see Figure
20.8).

Command: **CYLINDER**
Current wire frame density: ISOLINES = 4
Specify center point for base of cylinder or [Elliptical] <0,0,0>: **0.375,0.5,0**
Specify radius for base of cylinder or [Diameter]: **0.125**
Specify height of cylinder or [Center of other end]: **−2**

Command: **CYLINDER**
Current wire frame density: ISOLINES = 4
Specify center point for base of cylinder or [Elliptical] <0,0,0>: **2.125,0.5,0**
Specify radius for base of cylinder or [Diameter]: **0.125**
Specify height of cylinder or [Center of other end]: **−2**

Using the SUBTRACT command, subtract the two newly created cylinders from
the body.

Figure 20.8
Subtracting the two cylinders
from the body

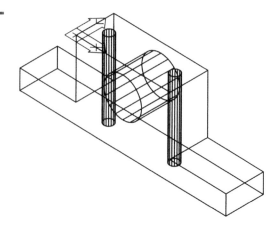

Figure 20.9
Creating the 2D profile

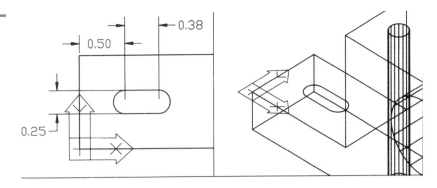

Adding Slots to the Base Using Extrusion

Using the UCS command, set the working plane to the top of the base of the body (see Figure 20.9) and display the plan view of the current UCS. Set both the elevation and the thickness to 0. Using the PLINE command, draw a closed polyline profile, as shown in Figure 20.9. Using the EXTRUDE command, extend the polyline profile into the base and turn it into a 3D solid as shown in Figure 20.10:

Command: **EXTRUDE**
Current wire frame density: ISOLINES = 4
Select objects: **click the slot profile**
Specify height of extrusion or [Path]: **−0.5**
Specify angle of taper for extrusion <0>: **press Enter**

Copy the slot solid to the other side of the base, as shown in Figure 20.11. Using the SUBTRACT command, subtract the slots from the body in order to create slotted holes in the body.

Adding Fillets to the Body

Display the previous axonometric view (1,−1,1). Using the FILLET command, create fillets that run along the edge of the body (see Figure 20.12):

Command: **FILLET**
Current settings: Mode = TRIM, Radius = 0.5000
Select first object or [Polyline/Radius/Trim]: **R**
Specify fillet radius <0.5000>: **0.25**
Command: **FILLET**

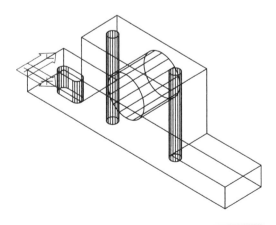

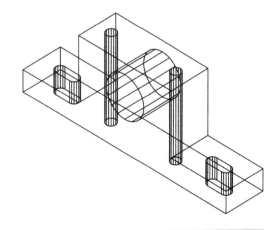

Figure 20.10
Creating a solid slot from a 2D profile

Figure 20.11
Copying the solid slot

407

Figure 20.12
Using the FILLET command to
create fillets

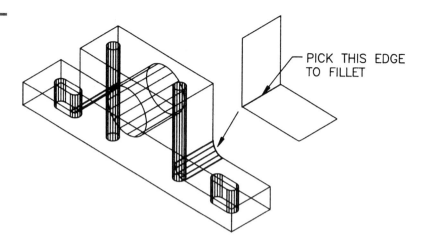

PICK THIS EDGE
TO FILLET

Current settings: Mode = TRIM, Radius = 0.2500
Select first object or [Polyline/Radius/Trim]: **select first edge**
Select second object: **select second edge**

Stage 4: Slicing the Solid in Two

The solid body is cut into two pieces: the upper yoke and the lower yoke. The cut is
accomplished with the SLICE command. Using the UCS command, set the UCS
to equal the WCS and then move the origin to 0,0,1.25. This sets the working plane
so that it intersects the body 3/4″ from the top, which is where the slice takes place.
The working plane is used as the slicing plane (see Figure 20.13). Using the SLICE
command, slice the single solid into two pieces:

Command: **SLICE**
Select objects: **click the solid body**
Specify first point on slicing plane by [Object/Zaxis/View/XY/YZ/ZX/3points]
<3points>: **XY**
Specify a point on the XY-plane 0,0,0: **press Enter**
Specify a point on desired side of the plane or [keep Both sides]: **B**

Separating the Two Solids

Using the MOVE command, separate the two solids. Move the top solid 1.5″ in the
Z direction (see Figure 20.14). Use the HIDE command to observe your finished
model. Save the model as SPSOL.

Figure 20.13
Slicing the solid along the
working plane

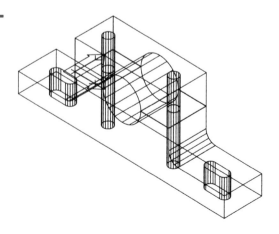

Figure 20.14
Separating the two solids

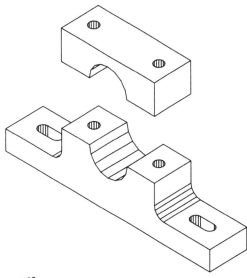

Creating Separate Part Files

You are going to create a file for each part.

Using the WBLOCK command, create a file called LYOKE (Lower Yoke) and select the lower solid part. Figure 20.15 shows the Write Block dialog box and settings. Your file folder may be different.

Using the WBLOCK command, create a file called UYOKE (UpperYoke) and select the upper solid part. Figure 20.16 shows the Write Block dialog box and settings. Your file folder may be different.

Stage 5: Assembling the Components

At this point in the project, all the required parts have been fabricated and are ready for assembly. Before we can insert the parts, a separate assembly file must be created. Call it SPB (Split Pillow Block).

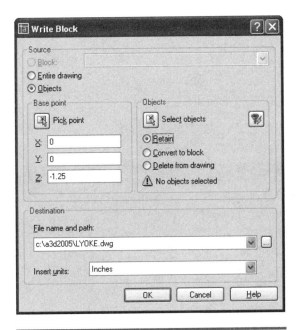

Figure 20.15
Write Block dialog box showing settings for LYOKE

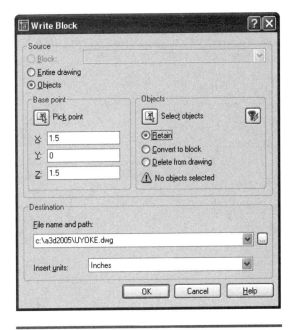

Figure 20.16
Write Block dialog box showing settings for UYOKE

Create the following layers and assign the appropriate colors. Then, enter the settings listed.

LAYER COLOR	LAYER NAME	LAYER DESCRIPTION
CYAN	P1-SYM	3D symbol model of Part 1
BLUE	P2-SYM	3D symbol model of Part 1
MAGENTA	P3-SYM	3D symbol model of Part 1

SETTINGS
Units = Decimal
Limits = −1,−1, to 6,2
Grid = 0.125
Snap Incr. = 0.125
Initial Elevation Thickness = 0
Initial Thickness = 0
UCS = WCS
UCSICON = On and set to 2D display properties
UCSVP = 0 (always set before creation of viewports)
UCS toolbar = displayed
View toolbar = displayed
Initial Layer = P2-SYM
VPOINT = 1,−1,1 (SE Isometric View tool)

Remember to ZOOM All, so that the display shows the set limits.

Inserting the Parts

Using the INSERT command, first insert Part 2, LYOKE (Lower YOKE), at the co-ordinates 0,0,0. Refer to Figure 20.17A and Figure 20.18 for the dialog box settings.

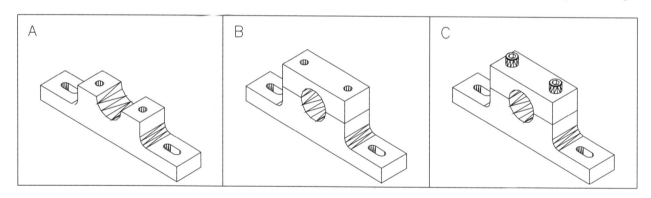

Figure 20.17
Assembly of parts

Figure 20.18
Insert dialog box for LYOKE

Scale = 1
Rotation = 0
    SETTINGS
Layer = P1-SYM
UCS = WCS

Second, insert Part 1, UYOKE (Upper YOKE), at the coordinates 1.5,0,1.25. Refer to Figure 20.17B and Figure 20.19 for the dialog box settings.

Scale = 1
Rotation = 0

    SETTINGS
Layer = P3-SYM
UCS = WCS

Third, insert Part 3, SOCSOL (connecting BOLT, created in Lab 10.C), at two sets of coordinates: 1.875,0.5,2 and 3.625,0.5,2. Refer to Figure 20.17C and Figure 20.20 for the dialog box settings.

Scale = 1
Rotation = 0

Figure 20.19
Insert dialog box for UYOKE

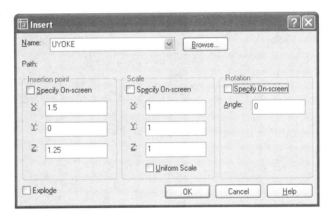

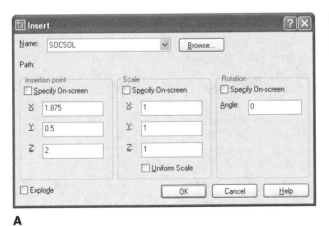

A

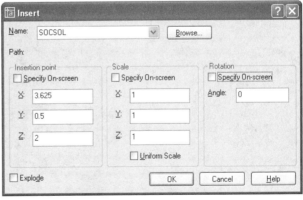

B

Figure 20.20
Insert dialog boxes for SOCSOL

Save the model as SPB. You have now created an assembled model of a split pillow block. It can be viewed from any location.

Stage 6: Presentation Display

To present the model of the split pillow block, four paper space viewports are created, each with its own scaled view of the model. If you have used paper space before now, turn off the layers containing the previously created viewports and create new ones as follows:

1. Using the TILEMODE command or clicking on a layout tab, switch to paper space by giving it the value of 0.
2. Create a layer called VPORTS, and make it active. Using the MVIEW command, split the screen into four equal viewports.
3. Using the MSPACE command, switch to model space and proceed to display the top, front, right-side, and isometric views of the model, as shown in Figure 20.21. By utilizing the XP option under the ZOOM command, the contents of each viewport are the same size. Set the XP value to 1. Depending on your printer/plotter, you may have to adjust the XP value.
4. Using the PSPACE command, switch to paper space.
5. Using the MVIEW command, set each viewport to Shadeplot = Hidden so that, when plotted, each viewport displays a hidden line removed plot.
6. Freeze the layer called VPORTS so that the border of the viewport is not visible and will not plot.
7. Save the model as SPB. Set the DISPSILH variable to 1. This displays only the silhouettes of the solids when hide is used.
8. If a plotter is available, plot the paper space layout.

Stage 7: Disassembling the Model

Depending on the usage, it is sometimes desirable to have an exploded view of an assembly. Here is how you would accomplish that:

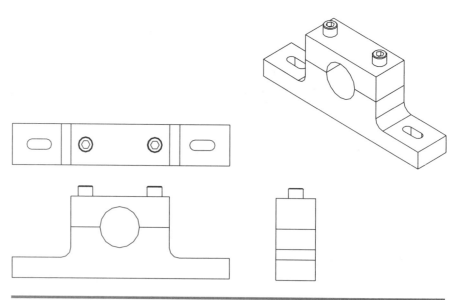

Figure 20.21
Four-view display of the model

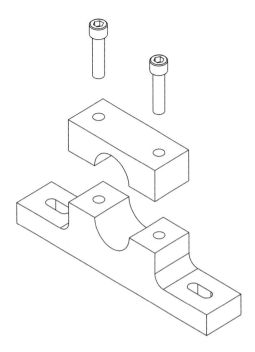

Figure 20.22
Exploded view of the split pillow block

1. Open model SPB.

   SETTINGS
   UCS = WCS
   TILEMODE = 1

2. Using the MOVE command, select the upper yoke and the connecting bolt parts. Use a displacement of 0,0,1.25 and press Enter for the second point.
3. Using the MOVE command, select the connecting bolt part. Use a displacement of 0,0,2, and press Enter for the second point.
4. Using View tools and the XP option of the ZOOM command, display the new views at a proper scale (see Figure 20.22).
5. Make sure the DISPSILH variable is set to 1. Save the model as SPB2. You now have an exploded view of the split pillow block assembly.
6. If a plotter is available, plot the paper space layout. If a plotter is unavailable, switch to model space, and use the HIDE command or the Hide shade mode in each viewport.

Stage 8: Rendering the Model

For general information about the rendering of models, refer to the final section in Chapter 18.

When performing your renderings, increase the FASCETRES variable. This makes curved solids smoother when rendering by adding more faces. Try a value of 2 to start.

The sample settings listed here create a rendering of the exploded split pillow block model using the RENDER utility. The settings place three lights so that their intensity can be increased or decreased to highlight any desired side. An image of the rendered model is shown in Figure 20.23.

Rendering Preferences: Use default settings, and set the Rendering options to Smooth Shading and Render using Photo Real.

413

Figure 20.23
Rendered view of the exploded
assembly

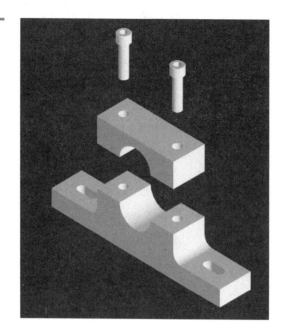

NAME	TYPE	INTENSITY	"FROM" LOCATION	"TO" LOCATION
front	distant	0.15	2.75,2.75,1.25	2.75,0,1.25
side	distant	1.0	8,0.5,1	5.5,0.5,1
top	distant	0.3	2.75,0.5,6	2.75,0.5,2
ambient		0.6		

Revisions

You may want to revise your solid models in some of the following areas:

- Make the socket-headed cap screw (SOCSOL) longer
- Fillet more of the edges of the upper and lower yoke to give it a more cast look
- Create a counterbore in the upper yoke to recess the cap screw

Mechanical Project: Solid Modeling of a Cellular Flip-phone

Overview

This chapter provides instruction on the creation of a cellular flip-phone using solid modeling techniques. The project reinforces skills gained in the previous chapters on solid modeling and demonstrates that using solid modeling can be easier than surface modeling, especially when adding holes to a model. This project uses filleting extensively, illustrating the ease with which it is possible in solid modeling.

Concepts Explored

- Extrusion of polylines to create a solid
- Filleting of edges of solid models and filleting behavior
- Creation of complex composite solids
- Generation of shaded and rendered images
- Possibilities of StereoLithography

21.1 Introduction

The mechanical project in this chapter requires you to use solid modeling to create the body of a cellular flip-phone. Figure 21.1 shows two views of the final model. If desired you could complete the project by creating all the pieces and assembling them into a complete flip-phone. The use of solid modeling to create this model also lends itself to the possibility of creating a physical prototype model using StereoLithography. By means of a laser, it is possible to create a tangible prototype of a 3D CAD model quickly. The process breaks down a CAD model into a series of "slices" of model data that is used to control a laser to form a prototype, slice by slice. One process, called StereoLithography Apparatus (SLA), uses a laser to harden a liquid polymer. Figure 21.27 at the end of this chapter demonstrates SLA. AutoCAD has the ability to create an ASCII text file of a solid model that can be used by SLA. The command to create the file is STLOUT.

21.2 Project Stages

This project is broken into several stages to facilitate creation.

PROJECT STAGES
1. Division of the solid model into component sections
2. Layer designations

Figure 21.1
Two views of flip-phone solid
model

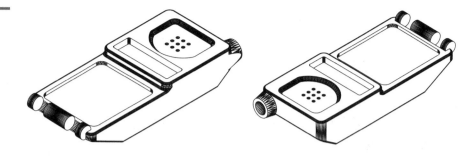

3. Creation of the extruded body
4. Rounding of vertical edges
5. Addition of hinge section
6. Rounding of horizontal body edges
7. Creation and subtraction of ear section
8. Creation and subtraction of display section
9. Creation and subtraction of control section
10. Addition of antenna section
11. Rendering the model
12. StereoLithography

Stage 1: Dividing the Solid Model

Creation of any complex solid model is easily accomplished if it can be done in logical sections. Figure 21.2 shows the profile views of the model. There are various distinct component sections into which the model can be broken, as listed here:

- Main body (used as the base)
- Hinge section

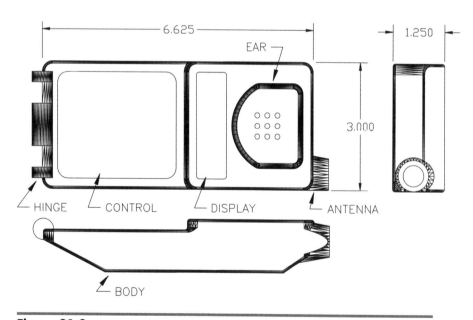

Figure 21.2
Profile views of the model

- Ear section
- Display section
- Control section
- Antenna section

Stage 2: Layer Designations

Using layers to differentiate between the various sections and components of a solid model facilitates creation and the display of the model. Layers can be frozen and thawed at will, making it easier to work on different parts of the model without other components obstructing views. The layers for this model are based on the component sections. Note that when one solid is added to another solid, it takes on the properties of the parent solid, including its color. So, don't be surprised if you add one solid to another and its color changes.

LAYER COLOR	LAYER NAME	LAYER DESCRIPTION
1	BODY	Main body of the phone
2	HINGE	Hinge solid before addition to the body
3	EAR	Ear solid before subtraction from the body
4	DISPLAY	Display solid before subtraction from the body
5	CONTROL	Control solid before subtraction from the body
6	ANTENNA	Antenna solid before addition to the body
7	OCUBE	Rectangular box to contain the model

Stage 3: Creating the Extruded Body

Initial Settings

Start a new model called PHONE. Create the layers listed previously, and assign the appropriate colors. Proceed with the following settings:

```
     SETTINGS
Units = Decimal
Limits = −1,−1 to 4,7
Grid = 0.125
Snap Incr. = 0.125
Initial Elevation = 0
Initial Thickness = 0
UCS = WCS
UCSICON = On and set to 2D display properties
UCSVP = 0 (always set before creation of viewports)
UCS toolbar = displayed
View toolbar = displayed
```

Remember to ZOOM All, so that the display shows the set limits. If you would like to choose any other settings, do so now before the creation of the orientation cube.

Creating the Orientation Cube

An orientation cube (profile shown in Figure 21.3) is created to define the three-dimensional boundaries of the body.

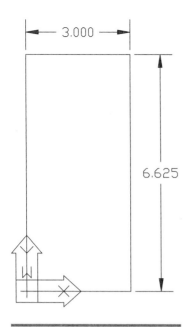

Figure 21.3
OCUBE profile

SETTINGS
Layer = OCUBE
Elevation = 0
Thickness = 1.25
UCS = WCS
VPOINT = 1,−1,1

Using the LINE command, draw the perimeter representing the orientation cube as shown in Figure 21.3. The lower-left corner must start at 0,0,0.

Creating the Body Profile

You are now going to create the profile of the body along the side of the orientation cube.

SETTINGS
Layer = BODY
Elevation = 0
Thickness = 0
UCS = set to the side of the body (Figure 21.4)

You may want to divide your screen into several viewports similar to the ones shown in Figure 21.4. Use the PLINE command to create the closed profile, as shown in Figure 21.4.

Extruding the Profile

Use the solid command EXTRUDE to create the extruded body, as shown in Figure 21.5. The thickness is −3 inches and there is no taper angle.

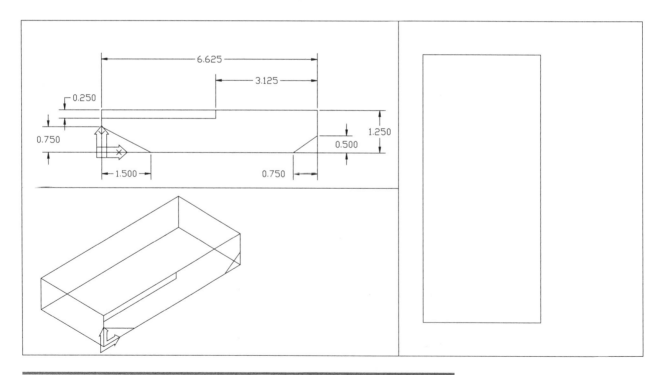

Figure 21.4
Profile of body

418

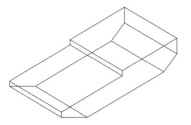

Figure 21.5
Extruded body

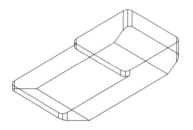

Figure 21.6
Rounding the vertical edges

Stage 4: Rounding Vertical Edges

Now that the body has been extruded, it is time to round (fillet) the vertical edges of the body. Because of the calculations involved when filleting a solid model, it should be broken down into small areas wherever possible.

Use the FILLET command and round the edges as shown in Figure 21.6. The radius is 0.25.

Stage 5: Adding the Hinge Section

The hinge section must be broken down into two parts. The first part is added to the body and the second part is removed from the body.

```
    SETTINGS
Layer = HINGE
Freeze the OCUBE layer
Elevation = 0
Thickness = 0
UCS = set to the side of the body (see Figure 21.7)
```

Using the CYLINDER command, create the solid cylinder as shown in Figure 21.7. Note that the start of the cylinder is −0.250 inch in the Z direction from the face of the body.

Using the UNION command, add the hinge cylinder to the body.

Now create the two solid cylinders that will be subtracted from the body. Refer to Figure 21.8 for their size and placement. Use the SUBTRACT command to subtract them from the body. The results should look like Figure 21.9. The HIDE command was used to help show what was subtracted.

Stage 6: Rounding the Horizontal Body Edges

At this stage extensive filleting to round the edges of the body takes place. Most of the body is rounded except for the hinge area and the area where the sloped edges meet the back. The filleting is broken into different steps to help clarify and simplify the process. Figures 21.10 through 21.13 illustrate each filleting step. The radius should be 0.06.

Figure 21.7
Solid cylinder creation

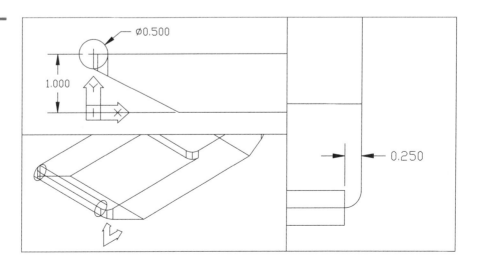

419

Figure 21.8
Subtracting the two cylinders
from the body

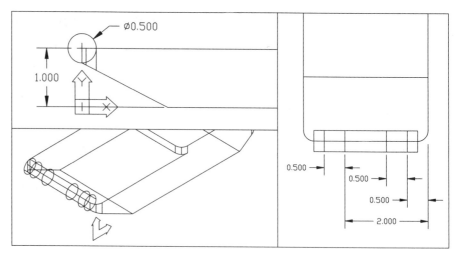

Figure 21.9
Results of subtracting cylinder
from the body

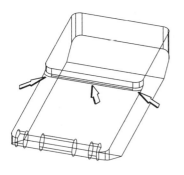

Figure 21.10
Fillet on inner edge and curve

Step 1   Figure 21.10 shows the filleting of the inner edge and curve.

Step 2   Figure 21.11 shows the filleting of the upper edge and curve. Remember to fillet both sides.

Step 3   Figure 21.12 shows the filleting of the top face edges. Remember to fillet all four edges at one time.

Step 4   Figure 21.13 shows the filleting of the bottom edges. All the bottom edges are filleted except for the curve that meets the hinge area and the two edges that are created where the slope meets the bottom.

Stage 7: Creating and Subtracting the Ear Section

You are going to create the ear section as a separate composite solid that includes the speaker holes. This composite solid is subtracted from the body.

```
     SETTINGS
Layer = EAR
Thaw the OCUBE layer
Freeze the BODY layer
Elevation = 0
Thickness = 0
UCS = set to the top of the OCUBE
```

Figure 21.11
Fillet on upper edge and curve

Figure 21.12
Fillet on top face edges

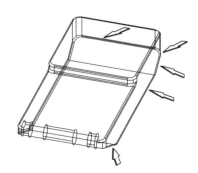

Figure 21.13
Fillet on bottom edges

420

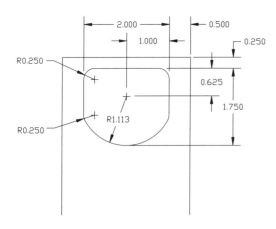

Figure 21.14
Creating the ear profile

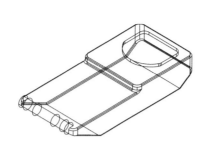

Figure 21.15
Extruding the ear profile

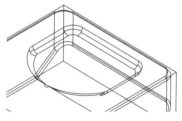

Figure 21.16
Fillet on lower edge of ear profile

You can use lines and arcs or polylines to create the ear profile. No matter what method you initially use, you must turn the geometry into one closed polyline. If you use lines and arcs, use the PEDIT command to turn them into one closed polyline. Proceed to create the profile and refer to Figure 21.14.

Freeze the OCUBE layer and thaw the BODY layer.

Using the EXTRUDE command, turn the profile into a solid. Use −0.125 for the extrusion thickness and 0 for the taper angle. See Figure 21.15 for the results.

Using the FILLET command, fillet the lower edge of the ear profile with a radius of 0.125 (see Figure 21.16).

Create the nine speaker holes using the CYLINDER command. The holes are 0.125 inch in diameter and 0.25 inch deep from the base of the ear solid. Each hole is 0.25 inch apart. Refer to Figure 21.17 for the center location of the pattern.

Once the holes are created, add them to the ear solid with the UNION command.

Using the SUBTRACT command, subtract the volume of the composite ear solid from the body. Use the HIDE command to observe the results.

Figure 21.17
Center location of speaker
hole pattern

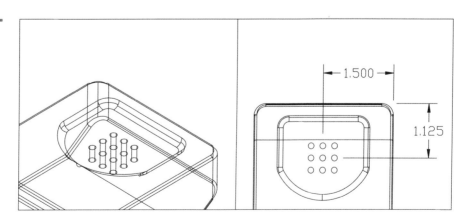

Figure 21.18
Creation of display solid

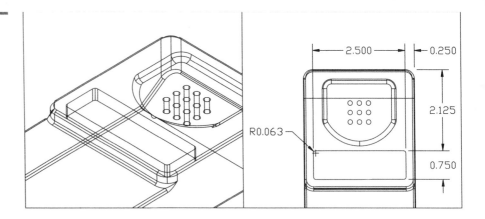

Stage 8: Creating and Subtracting the Display Section

Create the rectangular box solid that represents the display area of the phone. This is where the digital readout of numbers dialed would be displayed.

```
      SETTINGS
Layer = DISPLAY
Elevation = 0
Thickness = 0
UCS = set to the top of the body
```

Refer to Figure 21.18 and create a closed polyline. Use the EXTRUDE command to create a solid with a depth of –0.25″.

Use the SUBTRACT command to take away the volume of the display solid from the body.

Stage 9: Creating and Subtracting the Control Section

Create the rectangular box solid that represents the control area of the phone. This is where the control buttons would be installed.

```
      SETTINGS
Layer = CONTROL
Elevation = 0
Thickness = 0
UCS = set to the top control area
```

Refer to Figure 21.19 and create a closed polyline. Use the EXTRUDE command to create a solid with a depth of –0.125″.

Use the SUBTRACT command to take away the volume of the control solid from the body.

Stage 10: Adding the Antenna Section

You are now going to create the antenna section of the phone. This area would house the antenna casing. You are going to use a circle to create a tapered truncated cone.

Figure 21.19
Creation of control solid

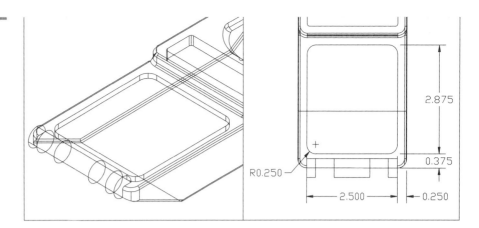

Figure 21.20
Creation of circle

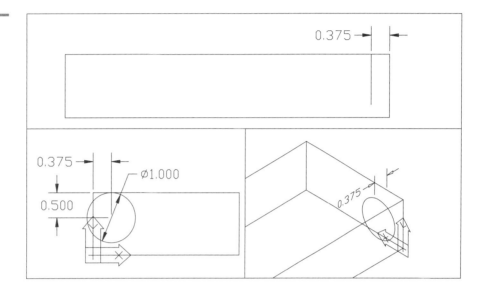

```
      SETTINGS
Layer = ANTENNA
Thaw the OCUBE layer
Freeze the BODY layer
Elevation = 0
Thickness = 0
UCS = set to the end of the OCUBE as shown in Figure 21.20
```

Use the CIRCLE command to draw the circle shown in Figure 21.20. Remember the center of the circle is −0.375" from the end face.

Use the EXTRUDE command to turn the circle into a solid truncated cone. Use a thickness of 0.75 and a taper angle of 10 degrees. Figure 21.21 shows the results of the extrusion. Note how the edge of the antenna cone protrudes past the OCUBE and body. You are going to clip off this protrusion with the use of another solid.

Using the BOX command, create a solid as shown in Figure 21.22. Now, create a UCS working plane along the side of the OCUBE to help with the creation. Once the creation of the box is completed, use the SUBTRACT command to take its volume away from the cone volume. Figure 21.23 shows the results.

Figure 21.21
Extrusion of circle

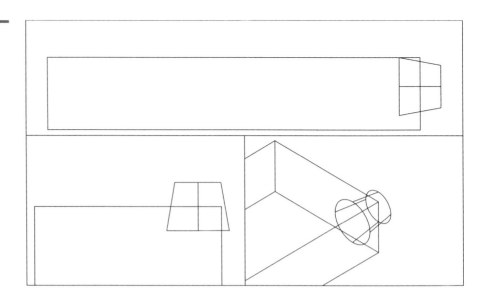

Figure 21.22
Creation of box solid

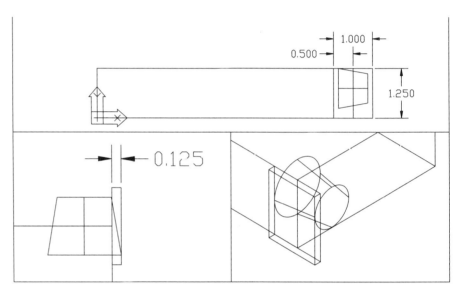

Figure 21.23
Subtracting box from cone

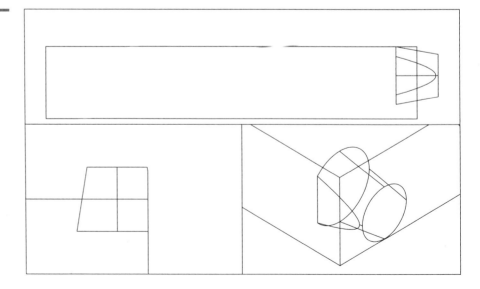

Figure 21.24
Results of subtraction

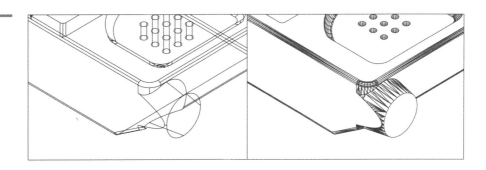

Figure 21.25
Subtracting a cylinder from
the body

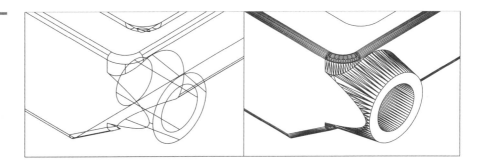

Using the UNION command, add the antenna solid to the body. Try the HIDE command to see the results. Figure 21.24 shows the wireframe display and the hidden display.

The antenna section requires a hole in it. Use the CYLINDER command to create a solid cylinder that is 0.5 inch in diameter and 0.625 inch deep. Place it in the center of the antenna section. Subtract the cylinder from the body. Figure 21.25 shows the results.

Stage 11: Rendering the Model

For general information about rendering models, refer to the final section in Chapter 18.

The sample settings here create a rendering of the phone solid model using the RENDER utility. The settings place two lights so the top and side surfaces may be highlighted. An image of the rendered model is shown in Figure 21.26.

Figure 21.26
Rendered view of flip-phone model

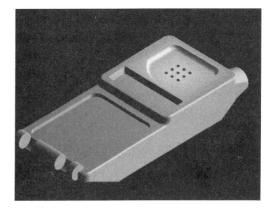

Lights:

NAME	TYPE	INTENSITY	FROM LOCATION	TO LOCATION
side	distant	1.00	5,6.5,2	2,4,1
top	point (inverse square)	1.24	1.5,5.5,3	
ambient		0.3		

Stage 12: StereoLithography

I wouldn't expect you to have access to a StereoLithography Apparatus (SLA), but if you refer to Figure 21.27 you can see the possible results of exporting your model using the STLOUT command.

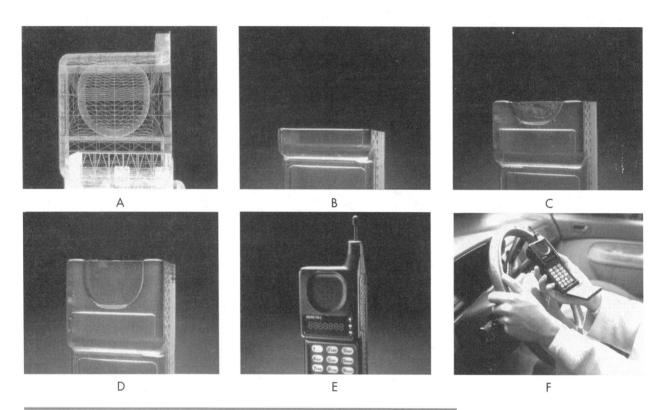

A   B   C

D   E   F

Figure 21.27
Physical model created from computer model using SLA. A is the 3D computer model of the cell phone body, A through D are creation of the StereoLithograph, E is the prototype, and F is the manufactured phone in use. (Note: the person using the phone is parked.)
Source: Courtesy of 3D Systems, Inc., Valencia, California.

Structural Project

Overview

In this project, you will model the structural members of a building. You will create and apply parametric (scalable) symbols and then compile the model with frames and supports represented by these symbols. (*A special note:* Third-party software that produces symbols similar to the ones you'll be creating in this project is available. By completing this project, however, you will learn how the symbols are produced and be able to create your own in future projects. Then, should you not have access to third-party software, all is not lost!)

Concepts Explored

- Continued use of AutoCAD features
- Creation of a complex three-dimensional model of the structural members of a commercial building
- Generation of 3D parametric symbols
- Use of 3D parametric symbols to create the model
- Discussion of 3D custom symbols and their creation for this project
- Production of ideally located perspective views
- Generation of shaded and rendered images

22.1 Introduction

Although this project generates the structural framing for a warehouse, it does not create all the structural members that would be required for this type of building. It does, however, construct the most common members, which illustrate the skills needed to create other structural members. Once this project is finished, you may want to construct other members to complete or enhance the model.

Like the other projects, this one is concerned with the application of three-dimensional modeling techniques, not with actual structural design. This project uses the structural discipline as a working environment to demonstrate the tools of three-dimensional modeling. In generating various 3D parametric models to compile the structure, the project demonstrates the usefulness of such symbols. And the presentation display stage again enables you to create views from any location and display them. For a sample view of the completed project, see Figure 22.1.

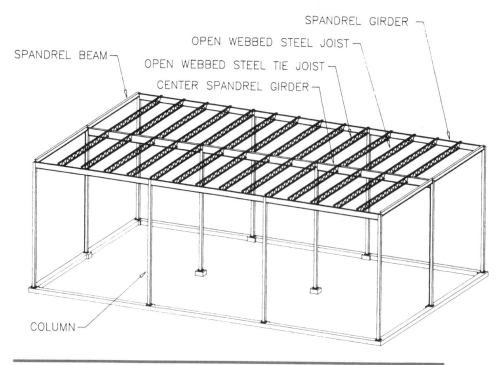

Figure 22.1
Axonometric view of the completed structural project

This exercise makes use of surfaces. However, you can substitute the use of 3D solids in your creation. Whenever thickness is used, you can use the EXTRUDE command instead. Remember that your profiles to be extruded must be closed polylines or regions.

22.2 **Project Stages**

Dividing a project into stages allows for an organized progression. And when similarities in project stages can be identified and exploited, a project can be completed more efficiently.

This project is broken into stages that apply not only to the erection of the structural form but also to the creation of each member.

PROJECT STAGES
1. Division of structural form (members)
2. Layer designations (surfaces, symbols)
3. Parametric symbol creation (beams, columns)
4. Custom symbol creation (joists)
5. Foundation construction
6. Structural member erection
7. Presentation display

Stage 1: Structural Form Division

As with our previous models, this model is divided into separate stages of creation to facilitate generation. The obvious areas to be sectioned are the individual members and the foundation. Thus, this model is divided into the following sections:

- Creation of the column parametric symbol (scalable)
- Creation of the spandrel girder parametric symbol (scalable)
- Creation of the spandrel beam parametric symbol (scalable)

428

- Creation of the center spandrel beam parametric symbol (scalable)
- Creation of the column pad and grout symbols (custom)
- Creation of the open-webbed steel joist symbol (custom)
- Creation of the open-webbed steel tie joist symbol (custom)
- Creation of orientation cubes
- Creation of the bayline grid
- Creation of the foundation
- Creation of the covering surfaces

If you plan to expand on the project model, this would be the ideal time to add further divisions. However, because you may be unfamiliar with the procedures that this type of project requires and, consequently, unsure of what additions you might like to make, it would certainly be acceptable to return to this planning stage at the end of the project to make any needed adjustments.

Stage 2: Layer Designations

To enable us to make objects visible and invisible (one of the most powerful features of CAD) and to facilitate construction and the later display of the final model, we name layers now. If you plan to make additions to the model, add their associated layers to our list if you can.

Even though the name of a layer can have as many as 31 characters, we use only the first 8 characters in our layer names because only these characters are visible on the status line. For example, 1-OWSJ represents the open-webbed steel joists for the ceiling of floor 1.

The layers to be created are listed next. Note that each layer in the main model is preceded by a number, representing the floor. Although there is only one floor in this project, there could be multiple floors in other projects. This stage, then, lays the procedural groundwork for future complex projects.

The main model (STRUCT) layers are listed here:

LAYER COLOR	LAYER NAME	LAYER DESCRIPTION
1	1-FNDEX	Foundation extrusions
1	1-FNDSUR	Foundation surfaces
2	1-COLUMN	Columns
3	1-SPGIRD	Spandrel girders
4	1-SPBEAM	Spandrel beams
5	1-CGIRD	Center girders
6	1-COLBAS	Column base plates and grout
7	1-OWSJ	Open-webbed steel joists
8	1-OWSTJ	Open-webbed steel tie joists
1	BGRID	Bayline grid

On the layer for parametric symbols (scalable), the parametric symbols have all their objects on layer 0.

The layers for the column base plates and group symbols (custom) are as follows:

LAYER COLOR	LAYER NAME	LAYER DESCRIPTION
3	BPLATE	Column support base plate
4	GROUT	Pad to foundation grout

The layers for the open-webbed steel joist symbols (custom) contain the symbols for both the open-webbed steel joist and the open-webbed steel tie joist.

LAYER COLOR	LAYER NAME	LAYER DESCRIPTION
1	ANGLE	Angle member extrusions
1	ANGSURF	Angle member surfaces
2	ROD	Connecting rod

| 3 | TEMPOR | Temporary construction |
| 7 | OCUBE | Orientation cube |

Give each section type its own color to make it easier to distinguish what is on each layer. Remember that it is customary to use continuous linetype for all 3D construction.

Stage 3: Creating the Parametric Symbols

Repeat the steps in this stage to create the parametric symbols for the four structural members. The processes for creating the symbols are basically identical, except for the location of the BASE points. These locations vary for each parametric symbol.

The four parametric symbols are named and described next. Each of the symbols is a 2ES parametric symbol, which is explained in Chapter 14.

SYMBOL NAME	DESCRIPTION
W8X24	Column
W14X26	Spandrel girder
W10X21	Spandrel beam
W18X55	Center spandrel girder

Initial Settings

Enter the following settings before modeling. For each symbol, create a new model, and call the model by the symbol name (W8X24, W14X26, W10X21, or W18X55). All creation takes place on layer 0, with color 7 (white).

```
       SETTINGS
Units = architectural
Limits = −1,−1 to 8,19
Grid = 1/2″
Snap Incr. = 1/2″
Initial Elevation = 0
Initial Thickness = 1″
UCS = WCS
UCSICON = On and set to 2D display properties
UCSVP = 0 (always set before creation of viewports)
UCS toolbar = displayed
View toolbar = displayed
```

Enter any other settings at this point. Remember to ZOOM All, so that the display shows the set limits.

Symbol Extension

Using the LINE command, draw the perimeter of the symbol as shown in Figure 22.2. Each symbol has a 1″ thickness along the Z axis. If you decide to create 3D extruded solids, remember to used closed polylines instead of standard lines. You may find that creation with 3D solids is actually easier than using objects with thickness.

Surface Creation

Using the 3DFACE command, place a surface on both ends of the extruded form.

Base Location

Using the BASE command, place the base point indicated for the model being created at this time.

Figure 22.2
2ES parametric symbols

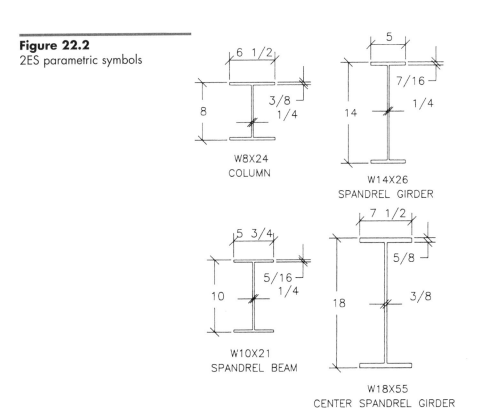

FILE	BASE (INCHES)
W8X24	3-1/4,4,0
W14X26	2-1/2,14,0
W10X21	2-7/8,10,0
W18X55	3-3/4,18,0

Save each model using its symbol name. Make sure you have repeated the steps in Stage 3 for all four 2ES parametric symbols.

Stage 4: Creating the Custom Symbols

The three custom symbols to be created for this project are the BASE plate (BASE), Open-Webbed Steel Joist (OWSJ), and the Open-Webbed Steel Tie Joist (OW-STJ). The requirements for these symbols are likely to change from project to project, so their creation processes are unique.

Creating the Base Plate and Grout Symbol

The first custom symbol to be created is the base plate and grout. The grout will eventually sit on the foundation, the plate will sit on the grout, and the columns will sit on the plate. Complete the numbered steps to create this symbol.

1. Start a new model called BASE and make the following layers:

LAYER COLOR	LAYER NAME	LAYER DESCRIPTION
3	BPLATE	Column support base plate
4	GROUT	Pad to foundation grout

SETTINGS
Units = architectural
Limits = −1″,−1″ to 14″,14″

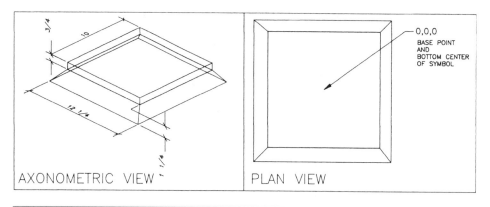

Figure 22.3
Finished symbol BASE

Grid = 1/2″
Snap Incr. = 1/2″
Initial Elevation Thickness = 0
Initial Thickness = 0
UCS = WCS
UCSICON = on and set to ORIGIN

Remember to ZOOM All, so that the display shows the set limits.

2. While on layer GROUT, use the LINE command to draw the perimeter of the grout in the plan view, as shown in Figure 22.3. Start the lower-left corner at −6-1/8,−6-1/8,0.

3. Using the ELEV command, set the elevation to 1-1/4″ and the thickness to 3/4″. Switch to layer BPLATE.

4. Using the LINE command, draw the perimeter of the base plate, as shown in Figure 22.3.

5. Using the 3DFACE command, add surfaces to the top of the plate.

6. Return to layer GROUT and create the four sloped sides of the grout using the 3DFACE command.

7. Using the BASE command, set the base point to 0,0,0.

8. Save the model as BASE.

Creating the Open-Webbed Steel Joist Symbol

Refer to Figures 22.4 and 22.5 for axonometric and orthographic views, respectively, of the custom symbol for the open webbed steel joist (OWSJ). Note that the connecting rods for this symbol are rectangular instead of round. If you use 3D solids for the connecting rods, you can use a polyline path and a circle for the profile. You can then use the EXTRUDE command to extrude the circle along the polyline path.

Figure 22.4
Axonometric view of finished
symbol OWSJ

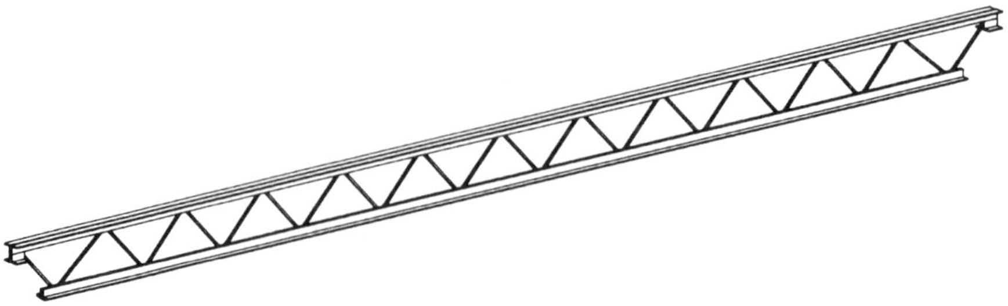

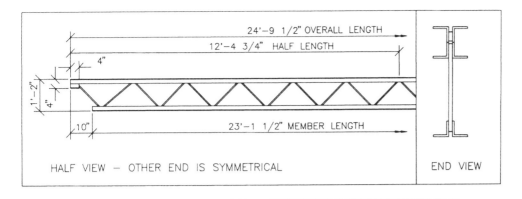

Figure 22.5
Orthographic views of symbol OWSJ

An orientation cube, a connecting rod, and several angle components must be created in order to model this symbol. Complete the numbered steps to create the symbol OWSJ.

1. Start a new model called OWSJ. Make the layers and enter the settings listed next.

LAYER COLOR	LAYER NAME	LAYER DESCRIPTION
1	ANGLE	Angle member extrusions
1	ANGSURF	Angle member surfaces
2	ROD	Connecting rod
3	TEMPOR	Temporary construction
7	OCUBE	Orientation cube

    SETTINGS
Units = architectural
Limits = −10″,−10″ to 30′,5′
Grid = 1″
Snap Incr. = 1/4″
Initial Elevation Thickness = 0
Initial Thickness = 0
UCS = WCS
UCSICON = On and set to 2D display properties
UCSVP = 0 (always set before creation of viewports)
UCS toolbar = displayed
View toolbar = displayed

Remember to ZOOM All, so that the display shows the set limits.

2. This step creates an orientation cube to define the 3D boundaries of the model.

    SETTINGS
Layer = OCUBE
Elevation = 0
Thickness = 1′2″
UCS = WCS

Using the LINE command, draw the perimeter representing the orientation cube as shown in Figure 22.6A. The orientation cube is 24′9-1/2″ in the *X* direction, 4-1/2″ in the *Y* direction, and 1′2″ in the *Z* direction. The lower-left corner must start at 0,0,0.

P1 = 0,0,0   P2 = 24′9-1/2″,0′,0′
P3 = 24′9-1/2″,4-1/2″,0′   P4 = 0′,4-1/2″,0′
CLOSE

433

Figure 22.6

Orientation cube and the new
working plane

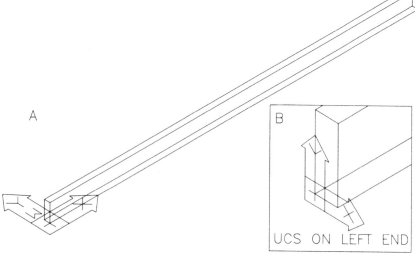

Change the working plane to the end of the orientation cube, as shown in Figure 22.6B.

3. This step creates three components made of angle iron. These are mirrored twice to create all the required angle components. All three components have the same dimensions for the X and Y axes. Only the dimensions for the Z axis change.

> SETTINGS
> Layer = ANGLE
> Elevation = 0
> Thickness = −24′9-1/2″

Using the LINE command, draw the first angle component as shown in Figure 22.7A.

Change the thickness to −4″.

Using the LINE command, draw the second angle component as shown in Figure 22.7B.

Change the elevation to −10″ and the thickness to −23′1-1/2″.

Using the LINE command, draw the third component as shown in Figure 22.7C.

Change both the elevation and the thickness back to 0.

Set the current layer to ANGSURF. Using the 3DFACE command, add a surface to all the exposed ends of the angle components.

Using the MIRROR command, mirror the three components as shown in Figure 22.7D.

Set the working plane to WCS. Mirror the left end components to the right end, as shown in Figure 22.8.

Save the model as OWSJ.

4. This step creates the square connecting rod. The rod is created at an angle of 45 degrees, except for the first two bends on each end (see Figure 22.9, line A and line C).

> SETTINGS
> Layer = TEMPOR
> Elevation = −2-1/2″
> Thickness = 0
> UCS = front plane, as shown in Figure 22.9A

Using the LINE command, draw line A, as shown in Figure 22.9. The coordinates for P1 are 3″,1′,−2-1/2″, and the coordinates for P2 are 1′2″,1″,−2-1/2″.

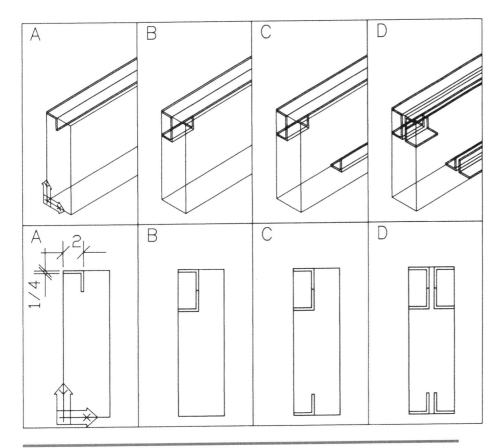

Figure 22.7
End views of angle components

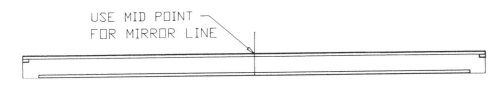

Figure 22.8
Angle components

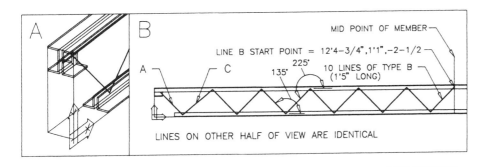

Figure 22.9
Creation of temporary lines

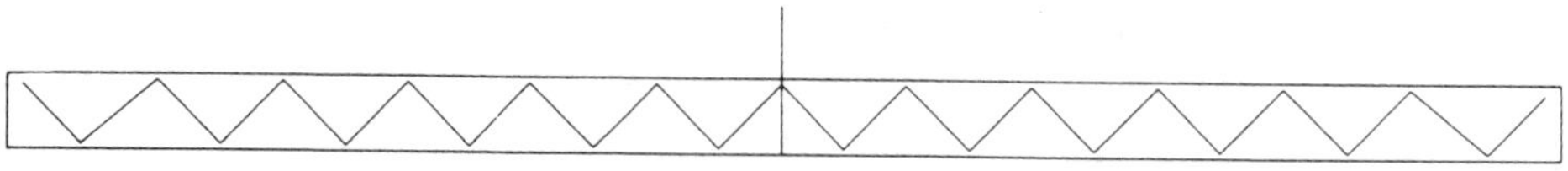

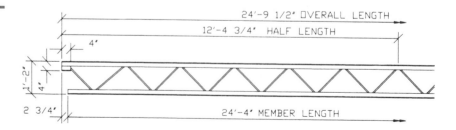

Figure 22.10
Connecting rod created by polyline

Using the LINE command again, draw the number of lines indicated as B from the center of the OCUBE at an angle of 45 degrees. Use relative coordinates @ 1'5"<225 and @ 1'5"<135 for each alternate line.

The last line, indicated as C, should be drawn by snapping onto the end of line A.

SETTINGS
Layer = ROD
Elevation = −2-1/2"
Thickness = 1/2"
Freeze all layers except the TEMPOR layer.

Using the PLINE command, draw the connecting rod (1/2" square) by endpoint object snapping to the ends of each of the temporary lines, as shown in Figure 22.10. The polyline should have a width of 1/2".

Freeze layers TEMPOR and OCUBE and turn on the other layers.

Set the UCS to the WCS, and set the BASE command to −1-1/4", 2-1/4", 10".

Save the model as OWSJ. Do *not* exit the drawing. This model will be used to create the symbol for the open-webbed steel tie joist as well.

If you wish, use the VPOINT and HIDE commands to move around and observe the newly created model. The model should look like Figure 22.4.

Creating the Open-Webbed Steel Tie Joist Symbol

To modify the open-webbed steel joist symbol to use as the symbol for the open-webbed steel tie joist, the two lower angle components need to be moved and then lengthened. Figure 22.11 shows the modifications. Complete the numbered steps to alter the symbol.

1. Set the UCS working plane to the left end of the OCUBE, as shown in Figure 22.12A.
2. Using the MOVE command, move the lower components a distance of 7-1/4" positively along the Z axis. This is illustrated in Figure 22.12B.
3. Using the CHPROP command, change the thickness of the angle components' extrusions to −24'4".

   Remember to replace/move the surfaces on either end of the angle extrusions.
4. Set the UCS to the WCS, and set the BASE command to −1-1/4", 2-1/4",10".
5. Save the model as OWSTJ (note the location of the *T* in the file name).

Figure 22.11
Open-webbed steel tie joist symbol

436

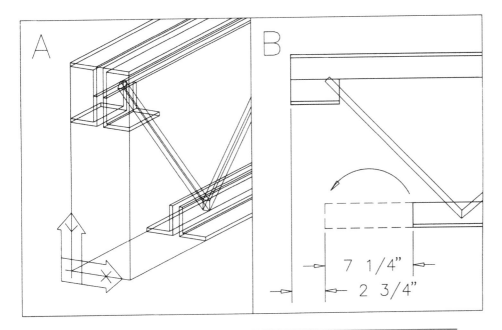

Figure 22.12
Increasing the length of the lower member

Stage 5: Constructing the Foundation

Now that all the symbols have been created, it is time to construct the foundation. It will be constructed out of lines with thickness and topped with surfaces using the 3DFACE command. The base plate and grout symbol will be added at this point as well.

Start a new model called STRUCT (STRUCTural model). Make the following layers and enter the settings listed below.

LAYER COLOR	LAYER NAME	LAYER DESCRIPTION
1	1-FNDEX	Foundation extrusions
1	1-FNDSUR	Foundation surfaces
2	1-COLUMN	Columns
3	1-SPGIRD	Spandrel girders
4	1-SPBEAM	Spandrel beams
5	1-CGIRD	Center girders
6	1-COLBAS	Column base plates and grout
7	1-OWSJ	Open-webbed steel joists
8	1-OWSTJ	Open-webbed steel tie joists
1	BGRID	Bayline grid

SETTINGS
Units = architectural
Limits = −5′,−5′ to 80′,55′
Grid = 5′
Snap Incr. = 5′
Initial Elevation Thickness = 0
Initial Thickness = 0
UCS = WCS
UCSICON = On and set to 2D display properties
UCSVP = 0 (always set before creation of viewports)

437

UCS toolbar = displayed
View toolbar = displayed

Remember to ZOOM All, so that the display shows the set limits.

Creating the Bayline Grid

The baylines that form the building grid are now laid out. They are 55′ long and spaced at 25′ intervals. They are drawn at an initial elevation of 10″ and later moved to an elevation of 1′. Snap to these grid lines when placing symbols.

      SETTINGS
Layer = BGRID
Elevation = 10″
Thickness = 0
UCS = WCS

Using the LINE command, draw the grid as shown in Figure 22.13.

Creating the Extruded Foundation

The extruded foundation is 10″ high and is topped with surfaces. The outer edge of the wall is 10″ from the grid, and the inner edge is 5″. The projections around the wall extend 5″ into the interior of the building. The two foundation pads that are in the middle of the building are 20″ square (see Figure 22.14).

      SETTINGS
Layer = 1-FNDEX
Elevation = 0
Thickness = 10″

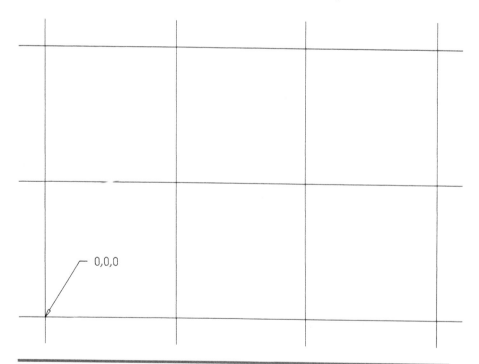

0,0,0

Figure 22.13
Bayline grid

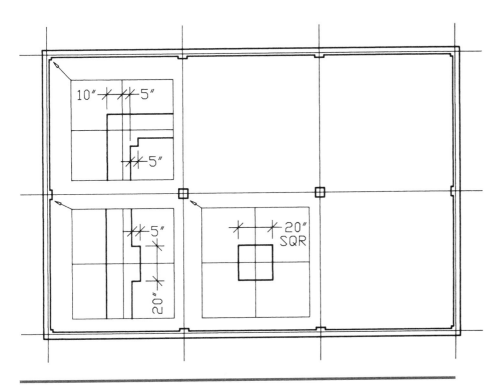

Figure 22.14
Extruded foundation

Using the LINE command, draw the extruded foundation, as shown in Figure 22.14. To use 3D solids, draw two closed polylines: inside and outside. Extrude them and subtract the inside from the outside. There is no need to add 3DFACES.

```
SETTINGS
Layer = 1-FNDSUR
Elevation = 10"
Thickness = 0
```

Using the 3DFACE command, create surfaces over the extruded foundation lines. Remember to use invisible edges where needed (see Figure 22.15).

The symbol BASE is now inserted.

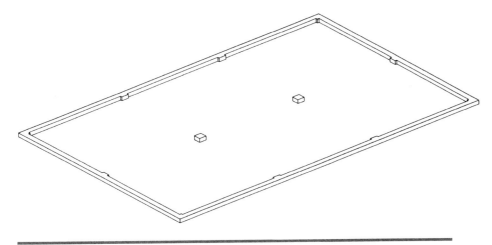

Figure 22.15
Foundation surface

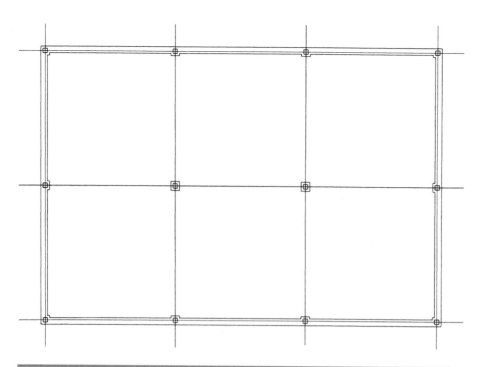

Figure 22.16
BASE symbol placement

```
            SETTINGS
Layer = 1-COLBAS
Elevation = 10″
Thickness = 0
UCS = WCS
Snap Incr. = 25′,25′
```

Using the INSERT command, place the BASE symbol at the intersection of each grid line, as shown in Figure 22.16. After you have placed one symbol, you can use the COPY command with the Multiple option to place the others.

Save the model as STRUCT.

Stage 6: Erecting the Structural Member

Placing the Column Symbol

The column parametric symbol is placed on top of the base plates at the intersection of the grid. Because the column symbol is a 2ES parametric symbol, we need to give a length upon insertion. The length of the column is 300″ (25′).

```
            SETTINGS
Layer = 1-COLUMN
Elevation = 1′
Thickness = 0
UCS = WCS
Snap Incr. = 25′,25′
```

Using the MOVE command, move the grid lines to an elevation of 1′. Using the −INSERT command, place the W8X24 (column) symbol at the intersection of each grid line, as shown in Figure 22.17. After placing one symbol, use the COPY

Figure 22.17
Placement of column symbol

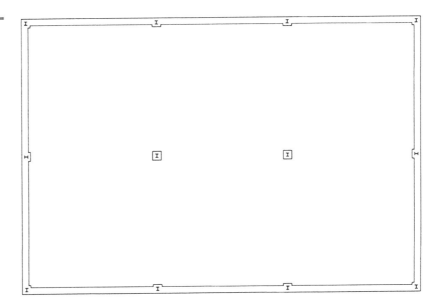

command with the Multiple option to place the others. (You could use the ARRAY command to perform the multiple copying if desired.) The orientation of a column depends on its location. Refer to Figure 22.17 to observe the orientation of each column. *Note:* When placing the block, do not use object snap; instead, use increment snap.

Command: −**INSERT** (Notice the use of the dash to execute a manual command.)
Enter block name or [?]: **W8X24** (You can enter the ~ symbol to use the File browser.)
Specify insertion point or [Scale/X/Y/Z/Rotate/PScale/PX/PY/PZ/PRotate]: **place the column symbol at the intersection of one of the grid lines; use increment snap so that the proper elevation is maintained**
Enter X scale factor, specify opposite corner, or [Corner/XYZ] <1>: **XYZ**
Specify X scale factor or [Corner] <1>: **1**
Enter Y scale factor <use X scale factor>: **1**
Specify Z scale factor or <use X scale factor>: **300** (300 inches = 25 feet)
Specify rotation angle <0>: **0**

Save the model as STRUCT.

Placing the Spandrel Girder Symbol

The spandrel girder parametric symbol is placed between each outer column and runs along the *X* axis of the WCS. Because it is a 2ES parametric symbol, we need to give a length upon insertion. The length of the girder is 299.75″ (24′11-3/4″).

        SETTINGS
    Layer = 1-SPGIRD
    Elevation = 0
    Thickness = 0
    UCS = WCS
    Snap Incr. = 1/8″,1/8″

The location and orientation of the UCS working plane is crucial to the placement of the remaining parametric symbols. The UCS commands for each placement are listed in detail. When you have completed them, refer to the associated figures to check that the location and orientation are correct.

441

Using the UCS command, rotate the UCS working plane to align with the upper-left beam when looking at a plan view. The command is as follows:

Command: **UCS**
Current ucs name: *NO NAME*
Enter an option [New/Move/orthoGraphic/Prev/Restore/Save/Del/Apply/?/World] <World>: **W**
Command: **UCS**
Current ucs name: *NO NAME*
Enter an option [New/Move/orthoGraphic/Prev/Restore/Save/Del/Apply/?/World] <World>: **N**
Specify origin of new UCS or [ZAxis/3point/OBject/Face/View/X/Y/Z] <0,0,0>: **Z**
Specify rotation angle about Z axis <90>: **90**
Command: **UCS**
Current ucs name: *NO NAME*
Enter an option [New/Move/orthoGraphic/Prev/Restore/Save/Del/Apply/?/World] <World>: **N**
Specify origin of new UCS or [ZAxis/3point/OBject/Face/View/X/Y/Z] <0,0,0>: **X**
Specify rotation angle about X axis <90>: **90**
Command: **UCS**
Current ucs name: *NO NAME*
Enter an option [New/Move/orthoGraphic/Prev/Restore/Save/Del/Apply/?/World] <World>: **N**
Specify origin of new UCS or [ZAxis/3point/OBject/Face/View/X/Y/Z] <0,0,0>: **using object snap endpoint, snap to the point indicated in Figure 22.18A**

Using the −INSERT command, place the W14X26 (spandrel girder) symbol at the center of the inside face of the column, as shown in Figure 22.18B. Once you have placed a symbol, use the COPY command with the Multiple option to place the others. Refer to Figure 22.19 for the correct placement of the symbols. Make sure the UCS is equal to the WCS before using the COPY command.

Command: **−INSERT** (Note the use of the dash to execute a manual command.)
Enter block name or [?]: **W14X26** (You can enter the ~ symbol to use the File browser.)

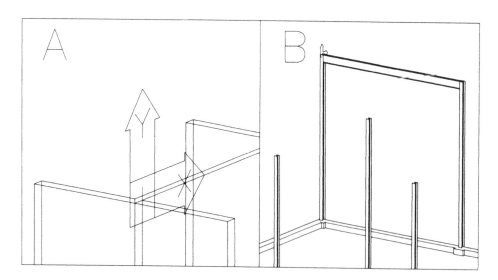

Figure 22.18
Placement of spandrel girder symbol

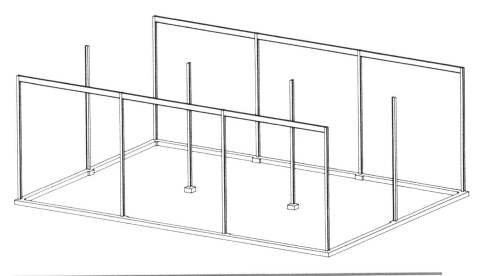

Figure 22.19
Copying of spandrel girder symbol

Specify insertion point or [Scale/X/Y/Z/Rotate/PScale/PX/PY/PZ/PRotate]: **3-3/8",0,0**
Enter X scale factor, specify opposite corner, or [Corner/XYZ] <1>: **XYZ**
Specify X scale factor or [Corner] <1>: **1**
Enter Y scale factor <use X scale factor>: **1**
Specify Z scale factor or <use X scale factor>: **299.75** (= 24′ 11-3/4″)
Specify rotation angle <0>: **0**

Save the model as STRUCT.

Placing the Spandrel Beam Symbol

The spandrel beam parametric symbol is placed between each outer column and runs along the *Y* axis of the WCS. Because it is a 2ES parametric symbol, we need to give a length upon insertion. The length of the beam is 295.875″ (24′ 7-⅞″).

```
    SETTINGS
Layer = 1-SPBEAM
Elevation = 0″
Thickness = 0
UCS = WCS
Snap Incr. = 1/8″,1/8″
Freeze layer 1-SPGIRD
```

Using the UCS command, rotate the UCS working plane to align with the upper-left beam when looking at a plan view. The command is as follows:

Command: **UCS**
Current ucs name: *NO NAME*
Enter an option [New/Move/orthoGraphic/Prev/Restore/Save/Del/Apply/?/World]
<World>: **W**
Command: **UCS**
Current ucs name: *NO NAME*
Enter an option [New/Move/orthoGraphic/Prev/Restore/Save/Del/Apply/?/World]
<World>: **N**
Specify origin of new UCS or [ZAxis/3point/OBject/Face/View/X/Y/Z] <0,0,0>: X
Specify rotation angle about X axis <90>: **90**

443

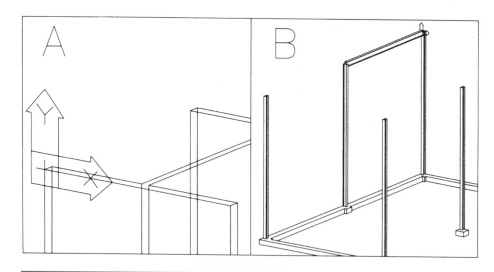

Figure 22.20
Placement of spandrel beam symbol

Command: **UCS**
Current ucs name: *NO NAME*
Enter an option [New/Move/orthoGraphic/Prev/Restore/Save/Del/Apply/?/World]
<World>: **N**
Specify origin of new UCS or [ZAxis/3point/OBject/Face/View/X/Y/Z] <0,0,0>: **using
    object snap endpoint, snap to the point indicated in Figure 22.20A**

Using the −INSERT command, place the W10X21 (spandrel beam) symbol at
the center of the face of the column, as shown in Figure 22.20B. Once you have
placed a symbol, use the COPY command with the Multiple option to place the
others. Refer to Figure 22.21 for the correct placement of the symbols. Make sure
the UCS is equal to the WCS before using the COPY command.

Command: −**INSERT** (Note the use of the dash to execute a manual command.)
Enter block name or [?]: **W10X21** (You can enter the ~ symbol to use the File browser.)

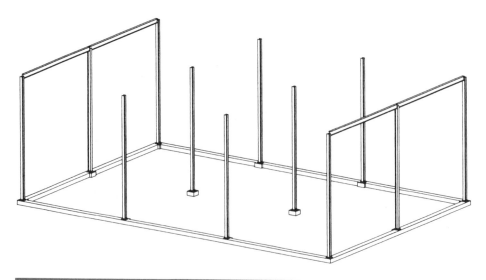

Figure 22.21
Copying of spandrel beam symbol

Specify insertion point or [Scale/X/Y/Z/Rotate/PScale/PX/PY/PZ/PRotate]: **3-1/4",4",0**
Enter X scale factor, specify opposite corner, or [Corner/XYZ] <1>: **XYZ**
Specify X scale factor or [Corner] <1>: **1**
Enter Y scale factor <use X scale factor>: **1**
Specify Z scale factor or <use X scale factor>: **295.875** (= 24' 7-7/8")
Specify rotation angle <0>: **0**

The spandrel beams are 4" above the columns so that their tops align with the tops of the joists when they are inserted later.

Placing the Central Spandrel Girder Symbol

The central spandrel girder symbol is placed between each center column and runs along the *Y* axis of the WCS. The two outer central girders are 24' 7-7/8" long, and the center central girder is 24' 11-3/4" long.

```
     SETTINGS
  Layer = 1-CGIRD
  Elevation = 0"
  Thickness = 0
  UCS = WCS
  Snap Incr. = 1/8",1/8"
  Freeze layer 1-SPBEAM
```

Using the UCS command, rotate the UCS working plane to align with the center-left beam when looking at a plan view. The command is as follows:

Command: **UCS**
Current ucs name: *NO NAME*
Enter an option [New/Move/orthoGraphic/Prev/Restore/Save/Del/Apply/?/World] <World>: **W**
Command: **UCS**
Current ucs name: *NO NAME*
Enter an option [New/Move/orthoGraphic/Prev/Restore/Save/Del/Apply/?/World] <World>: **N**
Specify origin of new UCS or [ZAxis/3point/OBject/Face/View/X/Y/Z] <0,0,0>: **Z**
Specify rotation angle about Z axis <90>: **90**
Command: **UCS**
Current ucs name: *NO NAME*
Enter an option [New/Move/orthoGraphic/Prev/Restore/Save/Del/Apply/?/World] <World>: **N**
Specify origin of new UCS or [ZAxis/3point/OBject/Face/View/X/Y/Z] <0,0,0>: **X**
Specify rotation angle about X axis <90>: **90**
Command: **UCS**
Current ucs name: *NO NAME*
Enter an option [New/Move/orthoGraphic/Prev/Restore/Save/Del/Apply/?/World] <World>: **N**
Specify origin of new UCS or [ZAxis/3point/OBject/Face/View/X/Y/Z] <0,0,0>: **using object snap endpoint, snap to the point indicated in Figure 22.22A**

Using the −INSERT command, place the W18X55 (center spandrel girder) symbol at the center of the face of the column as shown in Figure 22.22B. Once you have placed the first symbol, use the COPY command with the Multiple option to place another at the other end, as shown in Figure 22.23. *Remember:* The UCS must equal the WCS when using the COPY command.

Command: −**INSERT** (Note the use of the dash to execute a manual command.)
Enter block name or [?]: **W18X55** (You can enter the ~ symbol to use the File browser.)

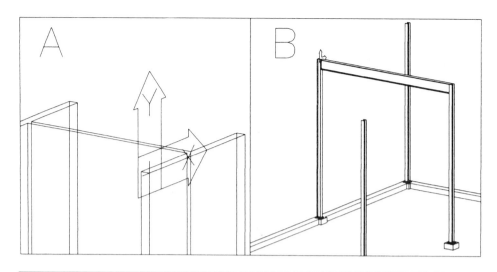

Figure 22.22
Placement of outer central spandrel girder symbol

Specify insertion point or [Scale/X/Y/Z/Rotate/PScale/PX/PY/PZ/PRotate]: **3-1/4",0,0**
Enter X scale factor, specify opposite corner, or [Corner/XYZ] <1>: **XYZ**
Specify X scale factor or [Corner] <1>: **1**
Enter Y scale factor <use X scale factor>: **1**
Specify Z scale factor or <use X scale factor>: **295.875** (= 24' 7-7/8")
Specify rotation angle <0>: **0**

The center girder is a different length, so it needs to be inserted at a new length and with a new origin for the UCS. The procedure is as follows:

Command: **UCS**
Current ucs name: *NO NAME*
Enter an option [New/Move/orthoGraphic/Prev/Restore/Save/Del/Apply/?/World]
<World>: **N**

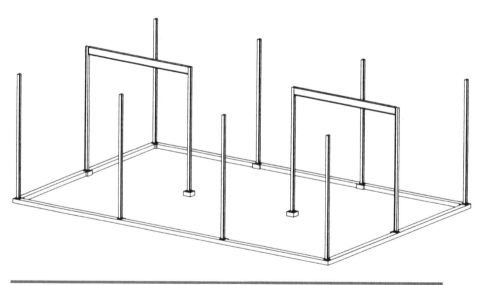

Figure 22.23
Copying of outer central spandrel girder symbol

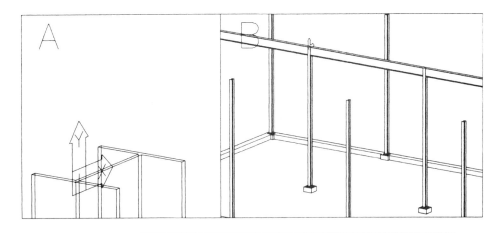

Figure 22.24
Placement of center central spandrel girder symbol

Specify origin of new UCS or [ZAxis/3point/OBject/Face/View/X/Y/Z] <0,0,0>: **using object snap endpoint, snap to the point indicated in Figure 22.24A**
Command: **−INSERT** (Note the use of the dash to execute a manual command.)
Enter block name or [?]: **W18X55**
Specify insertion point or [Scale/X/Y/Z/Rotate/PScale/PX/PY/PZ/PRotate]: **3-5/8″,0,0**
Enter X scale factor, specify opposite corner, or [Corner/XYZ]<1>: **XYZ**
Specify X scale factor or [Corner] <1>: **1**
Enter Y scale factor <use X scale factor>: **1**
Specify Z scale factor or <use X scale factor>: **299.75** (= 24′ 11-3/4″)
Specify rotation angle <0>: **0**

Save the model as STRUCT.

Placing the Open-Webbed Steel Tie Joist Symbol

The open-webbed steel tie joist symbol is custom designed for this project. This means that it is inserted at a constant scale for all axes. It is placed on the top of the inner four columns, as shown in Figure 22.25.

Figure 22.25
Placement of OWSTJ symbols

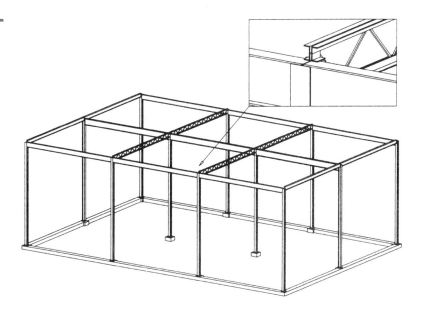

SETTINGS
Layer = 1-OWSTJ
Elevation = 0″
Thickness = 0
UCS = WCS
Snap Incr. = 1/8″,1/8″
Freeze layer 1-CGIRD

Use the INSERT command to place four OWSTJ symbols at the following coordinates. Each has an overall scale of 1 and a rotation of 90 degrees, as shown in Figure 22.25.

P1 = 25′,0′,26′   P2 = 25′,25′,26′
P3 = 50′,0′,26′   P4 = 50′,25′,26′

Placing the Open-Webbed Steel Joist Symbol

The open-webbed steel joist symbol is custom designed for this project. This means that it is inserted at a constant scale for all axes. It is placed on the top of the girders, as shown in Figure 22.26.

SETTINGS
Layer = 1-OWSJ
Elevation = 0″
Thickness = 0
UCS = WCS
Snap Incr. = 1/8″,1/8″
Freeze layer 1-OWSTJ
Thaw layers 1-CGIRD and 1-SPGIRD

Use the INSERT command to place four OWSJ symbols. Insert them at the coordinates listed below. Each has an overall scale of 1 and a rotation of 90 degrees, as shown in Figure 22.26.

P1 = 5′,0′,26′   P2 = 10′,0′,26′
P3 = 15′,0′,26′   P4 = 20′,0′,26′

Use the COPY command with the Multiple option to copy the six sets of four OWSJ symbols, as shown in Figure 22.27. (You could use the ARRAY command to perform the multiple copying if desired.)

Figure 22.26
Placement of OWSJ symbols

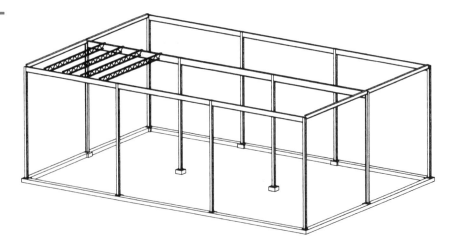

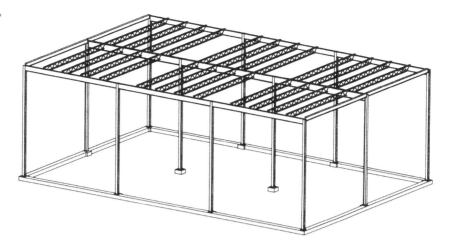

Figure 22.27
Copying of OWSJ symbols

Thaw the 1-SPBEAM and 1-OWSTJ layers, and save the model as STRUCT.

The model construction is now finished. You have created a model of the *initial* framework for the structural portion of a building, not a model of the complete structural framing. However, the techniques learned during this model construction should enable you to complete any type of structural project.

Stage 7: Presentation Display

With construction complete, the display of the model for presentation purposes must be considered. Figure 22.28 shows an axonometric view of the structural framework model. This type of viewing is necessary for construction purposes, but it is not as useful for presentation. For example, the viewer will have difficulty imagining the size of the building. Now look at Figure 22.29, which shows the perspective view. Here, the magnitude and realism of the structure are more effectively demonstrated.

We will create two perspective views of this project. The two views are described next. You may create other perspective views according to your needs (refer to Chapter 15 for a discussion of presentation and display).

PERSP1: from a height of 12′8″, to the right of the structure, and looking over the entire building

PERSP2: from a height of 6′, to the right of the structure, and looking upward, toward the open-webbed steel joists

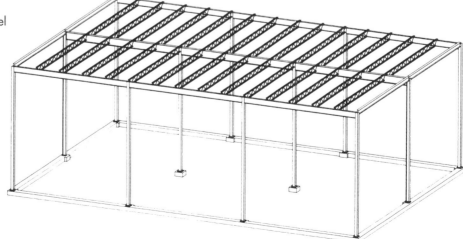

Figure 22.28
Axonometric view of the model

Figure 22.29
Perspective view of the model
(PERSP1)

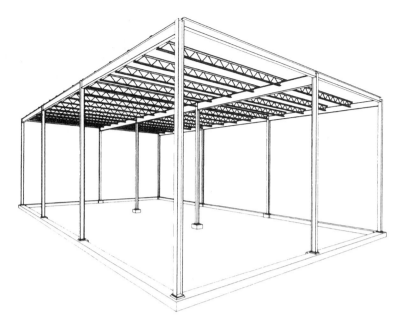

Creating the Preview Selection Set

When selecting objects for the Preview selection set, select only the columns, not the whole model. This makes manipulating in the DVIEW environment easier and quicker.

Completion of the following steps achieves the perspective view PERSP1, as shown in Figure 22.29.

1. Use the POINTS option to place the camera and the target points. Enter these settings:

   Points-Target = 36'2",27'6",12'8"
   Camera = 96'5",−17'2",12'8"
   Distance = 75'
   Zoom = 20

2. Exit the DVIEW command to apply the settings to the entire model.
3. Use the VIEW command to save the perspective view as PERSP1.

Completing the following steps achieves the perspective view PERSP2, as shown in Figure 22.30.

Figure 22.30
Perspective view of the model
(PERSP2)

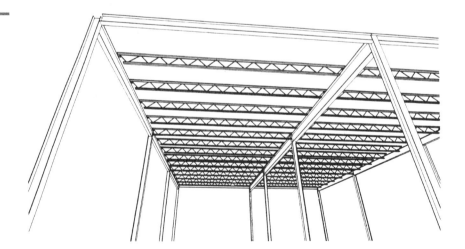

1. Use the POINTS option to place the camera and the target points. Enter these settings:

   Target = 66'9",12'5",25'
   Camera = 91',10',6'
   Distance = 28'8"
   Zoom = 20

2. Exit the DVIEW command to apply the settings to the entire model.
3. Use the VIEW command to save the perspective view as PERSP2.

   Save the model as STRUCT.

Displaying the Model

Use the HIDE command to display the model. Then use various shade modes. Repeat the procedure with the previously saved views.

Rendering the Model

If you need to review the discussion on rendering, turn back to the final section in Chapter 18.

The following sample settings create a rendering of the structure in the daytime using the RENDER utility. Only one light, representing the sun, is used. An image of the rendered model displaying PERSP1 is shown in Figure 22.31.

Rendering Preferences: Use default settings. Smooth Shading is not needed.
Lights:

NAME	TYPE	INTENSITY	FROM LOCATION	TO LOCATION
sun	distant	1.00	110', 0', 50'	37'6", 27'3", 10'
ambient		0.7		

Figure 22.31
Rendered view of the structural model

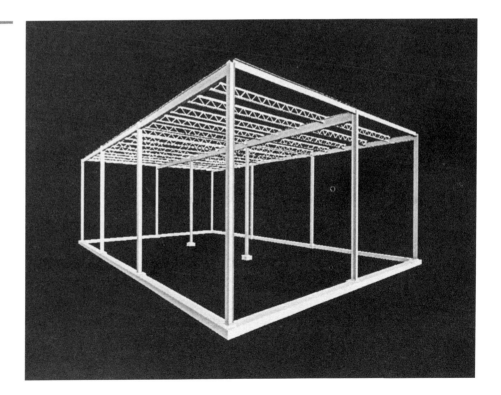

23 Civil Project

Overview

In this project, you use polygon mesh techniques to create a terrain model. You record varied topographical data as a text file and then learn how to use that text file to make the program create imagery automatically.

Concepts Explored

- Further application of AutoCAD features
- Generation of a complex three-dimensional terrain model
- Creation of a script/data file of topographical coordinates
- Generation of a polygon mesh terrain
- Exploration of polyline contours
- Creation of an elevation view of the contour lines

23.1 Introduction

The project in this chapter involves the creation of the terrain model shown in Figure 23.1. Although the data for this terrain model is supplied for you, you will acquire the skills you'll need to select a topographical map, determine the elevation coordinates, and create your own unique terrain model because the steps given here can be applied to any map.

Figure 23.1
Final terrain model

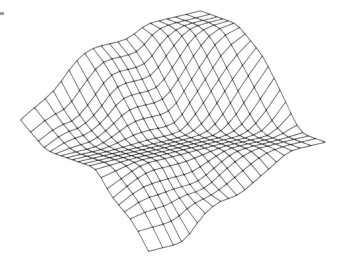

The coordinate values given in this project are kept simple, so as not to complicate the steps and risk you losing sight of the procedure. The theoretical topographical map measures 100 units by 100 units and shows contour lines at elevation intervals of 10 units (see Figure 23.2). You will convert this map into coordinated data in a text file that can be read into AutoCAD to create the terrain model automatically. You also use the data to create automatic profile lines that cut cross sections through the terrain so that when the models are finished and you are viewing the terrain, you are able to selectively view cross-section profiles.

As a point of interest, note that modern survey equipment can automatically store survey points similar to those used in this project. The data can then be transferred to the computer and used to create a topographical map.

23.2 Project Stages

Like any project, this one should be performed in an organized manner that allows efficient execution and easy repetition of the modeling process. To that end, this project is separated into stages that apply to the initial generation of a terrain model from topographical data and the subsequent generation of cross-section profiles.

PROJECT STAGES
1. Division of the terrain model
2. Layer designation
3. Development of the topographical data
4. Creation of the mesh script/data file
5. Creation of the polygon mesh terrain model
6. Creation of the profile script/data file
7. Creation of the profile model
8. Display of selected profiles

Stage 1: Dividing the Terrain Model

Any map could be selected for this project as long as it had distinct contour lines that indicate the various elevations. Refer to the contour map shown in Figure 23.2. The map's contour lines indicate that the highest elevation is at the top-right corner,

Figure 23.2
Contour map

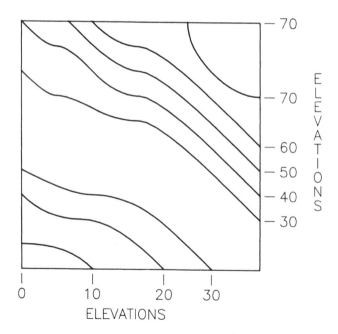

where there is a small plateau with an elevation of 70′. The terrain slopes downward and toward the left of the map, ending at an elevation of 0′ at the bottom-left corner of the map.

Stage 2: Layer Designations

This project needs only two layers. If other topographical features were added, or another map was substituted, then more layers would need to be named. Listed here are the layers to be created for this project:

LAYER COLOR	LAYER NAME	LAYER DESCRIPTION
1	CMESH	Contour MESH (representing the terrain)
2	PROFL	PROFile Lines (representing the cross-sectional profiles of the terrain)

Stage 3: Developing the Topographical Data

To create a three-dimensional model of the terrain of any map, you need to generate a series of coordinates. The coordinates are the X, Y, and Z locations of various points on the map. These coordinates must be extracted in a grid-type pattern so that the data reads into AutoCAD in the proper sequence.

Refer to Figures 23.2 and 23.3. The topographic contour lines in Figure 23.2 are converted to lines that correspond to the 10 by 10 unit division grid in Figure 23.3. The grid represents the format of the coordinate data to be placed into the data file. (*Note:* Any number of divisions could be used; however, the greater the number of divisions, the more accurate the model.)

The vertical lines of the grid represent each line of data as a cross section through the terrain. The lines travel from the left to the right, numbered 1 to 11. These lines also represent a location of 10′ along the X axis (that is, line 1 is 10′ along the X axis, line 2 is 20′ along the X axis, and so on).

The horizontal lines of the grid represent an individual field or coordinate of data along a line. There are 11 fields of data for each line, meaning that there are 11 X, Y, Z

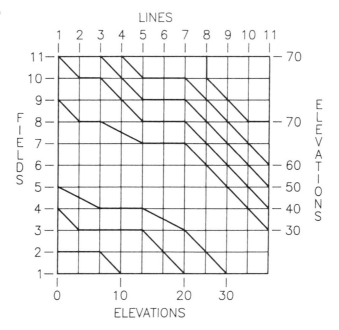

Figure 23.3
Stylized contour lines overlaid on a grid

455

Lines	Field 1	Field 2	Field 3	Field 4	Field 5	Field 6	Field 7	Field 8	Field 9	Field 10	Field 11
1	10, 10, 0	10, 20, 10	10, 30, 15	10, 40, 20	10, 50, 30	10, 60, 30	10, 70, 30	10, 80, 30	10, 90, 30	10, 100, 35	10, 110, 40
2	20, 10, 0	20, 20, 10	20, 30, 20	20, 40, 25	20, 50, 30	20, 60, 30	20, 70, 30	20, 80, 30	20, 90, 35	20, 100, 40	20, 110, 45
3	30, 10, 0	30, 20, 10	30, 30, 20	30, 40, 30	30, 50, 30	30, 60, 30	30, 70, 30	30, 80, 30	30, 90, 35	30, 100, 40	30, 110, 50
4	40, 10, 10	40, 20, 15	40, 30, 20	40, 40, 30	40, 50, 30	40, 60, 30	40, 70, 30	40, 80, 35	40, 90, 40	40, 100, 50	40, 110, 60
5	50, 10, 15	50, 20, 15	50, 30, 20	50, 40, 30	50, 50, 30	50, 60, 30	50, 70, 30	50, 80, 40	50, 90, 50	50, 100, 60	50, 110, 65
6	60, 10, 15	60, 20, 20	60, 30, 25	60, 40, 30	60, 50, 30	60, 60, 30	60, 70, 30	60, 80, 40	60, 90, 50	60, 100, 60	60, 110, 65
7	70, 10, 20	70, 20, 25	70, 30, 30	70, 40, 30	70, 50, 30	70, 60, 30	70, 70, 30	70, 80, 40	70, 90, 50	70, 100, 60	70, 110, 65
8	80, 10, 25	80, 20, 30	80, 30, 30	80, 40, 30	80, 50, 30	80, 60, 30	80, 70, 40	80, 80, 50	80, 90, 60	80, 100, 70	80, 110, 70
9	90, 10, 30	90, 20, 30	90, 30, 30	90, 40, 30	90, 50, 30	90, 60, 40	90, 70, 50	90, 80, 60	90, 90, 70	90, 100, 70	90, 110, 70
10	100, 10, 30	100, 20, 30	100, 30, 30	100, 40, 30	100, 50, 40	100, 60, 50	100, 70, 60	100, 80, 70	100, 90, 70	100, 100, 70	100, 110, 70
11	110, 10, 30	110, 20, 30	110, 30, 30	110, 40, 40	110, 50, 50	110, 60, 60	110, 70, 65	110, 80, 70	110, 90, 70	110, 100, 70	110, 110, 70

Table 23.1
Coordinate data for each topographical point

coordinate points for each of the 11 lines. The horizontal lines also represent location along the *Y* axis in the same way the vertical lines represent location along the *X* axis.

The next step is to take the coordinate location of each field location and tabulate the *X*, *Y*, and *Z* values. Refer to Figure 23.3 again and specifically observe the location of line 1, field 1. The elevation is 0, the *X* location is 10, and the *Y* location is 10. This means the coordinate data for that location is 10,10,0. Now refer to line 1, field 2, which coincides with the contour line for the elevation of 10′. This means that the coordinate data for line 1, field 2, is 10,20,10. This procedure would be followed to identify each coordinate location on the map. For this project, all the data has already been extracted and tabulated in Table 23.1. If you have selected your own map, then you must create a similar table.

Stage 4: Creating the Mesh Script/Data File

Once the data has been collected for each coordinate point, it needs to be placed into a file in a way that AutoCAD can read. This procedure creates a script file. A *script file* is a file containing a series of commands that AutoCAD can read and then perform.

The command that we are going to use in this project is the 3DMESH command. (This command is explained in Section 8.3 of Chapter 8.) AutoCAD refers to the function of the 3DMESH command as the creation of topographically rectangular polygon meshes. To use this command, you define the size of a grid and then enter the *X*, *Y*, and *Z* locations for each point on the grid. This places a surface mesh over the points. The script we are going to create enters such data automatically.

A script file must have the suffix .SCR for AutoCAD to recognize it. Our file is called MESH.SCR. The first line of the script activates the 3DMESH command and defines the size of the mesh. After that, each line represents a line from Table 23.1. Refer now to Table 23.2; the data file MESH.SCR should appear identical to this table.

Any text editor can be used to create the script, as long as it can create straight ASCII text that contains no formatting, such as justification or page breaks. If a word-processing program such as Corel WordPerfect or Microsoft Word is used, make sure that the data file is saved as DOS text.

In the script, there should be one (and only one) space placed between each field of data. Also, there should not be any extra blank lines at the bottom of the file or blank spaces at the end of each line. If an extra blank line or space is inserted, AutoCAD then tries to repeat the last command at that location in the script.

Table 23.2
Script file MESH.SCR

3DMESH   11   11

10, 10, 0 10, 20, 10 10, 30, 15 10, 40, 20 10, 50, 30 10, 60, 30 10, 70, 30
10, 80, 30 10, 90, 30 10, 100, 35 10, 110, 40

20, 10, 0 20, 20, 10 20, 30, 20 20, 40, 25 20, 50, 30 20, 60, 30 20, 70, 30
 20, 80, 30 20, 90, 35 20, 100, 40 20, 110, 45

30, 10, 0 30, 20, 10 30, 30, 20 30, 40, 30 30, 50, 30 30, 60, 30 30, 70, 30
30, 80, 30 30, 90, 35 30, 100, 40 30, 110, 50

40, 10, 10 40, 20, 15 40, 30, 20 40, 40, 30 40, 50, 30 40, 60, 30 40, 70, 30
40, 80, 35 40, 90, 40 40, 100, 50 40, 110, 60

50, 10, 15 50, 20, 15 50, 30, 20 50, 40, 30 50, 50, 30 50, 60, 30 50, 70, 30
50, 80, 40 50, 90, 50 50, 100, 60 50, 110, 65

60, 10, 15 60, 20, 20 60, 30, 25 60, 40, 30 60, 50, 30 60, 60, 30 60, 70, 30
60, 80, 40 60, 90, 50 60, 100, 60 60, 110, 65

70, 10, 20 70, 20, 25 70, 30, 30 70, 40, 30 70, 50, 30 70, 60, 30 70, 70, 30
70, 80, 40 70, 90, 50 70, 100, 60 70, 110, 65

80, 10, 25 80, 20, 30 80, 30, 30 80, 40, 30 80, 50, 30 80, 60, 30 80, 70, 40
80, 80, 50 80, 90, 60 80, 100, 70 80, 110, 70

90, 10, 30 90, 20, 30 90, 30, 30 90, 40, 30 90, 50, 30 90, 60, 40 90, 70, 50
90, 80, 60 90, 90, 70 90, 100, 70 90, 110, 70

100, 10, 30 100, 20, 30 100, 30, 30 100, 40, 30 100, 50, 40 100, 60, 50
100, 70, 60 100, 80, 70 100, 90, 70 100, 100, 70 100, 110, 70

110, 10, 30 110, 20, 30 110, 30, 30 110, 40, 40 110, 50, 50 110, 60, 60
110, 70, 65 110, 80, 70 110, 90, 70 110, 100, 70 110, 110, 70

Stage 5: Creating the Polygon Mesh Terrain Model

After the script file has been created, all that is needed to create the three-dimensional terrain is running the script.

Initial Settings

Start a new file called TERR (TERRain model). Create the two layers listed in Stage 2 and assign the appropriate colors. Then enter the settings.

```
     SETTINGS
Units = engineering
Limits = −10,−10 to 250,250
Grid = 10
Snap Incr. = 10
Initial Elevation Thickness = 0
Initial Thickness = 0
UCS = WCS
UCSICON = On and set to 2D display properties
UCSVP = 0 (always set before creation of viewports)
UCS toolbar = displayed
View toolbar = displayed
VPOINT = −2,−3,1 (set to an axonometric view)
Current Layer = CMESH
```

Figure 23.4
Rough terrain model from raw data

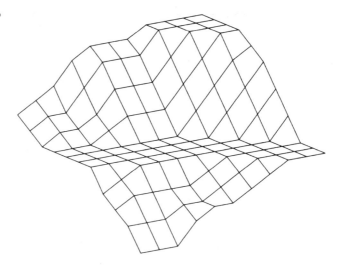

Running the Script

Using the SCRIPT command, enter MESH as the script file name. Now you can sit back and watch AutoCAD do its thing. AutoCAD reads each line of data and places each point on the screen. Then it places a mesh over the grid points forming the terrain. It's as simple as that. The resulting terrain model should look similar to Figure 23.4.

If some points on the grid look very much out of place, it is probably because some of the coordinate data is incorrect. In that case, use UNDO to remove the terrain model, save the file as TERR, and go back and correct the script file. Once you have corrected the script, reenter the TERR file, and run the script again.

Smoothing the Terrain

The terrain created from the raw data has a rough, jagged appearance. You can modify the appearance of the terrain using the PEDIT command. PEDIT modifies both polylines and polygon meshes. Before you can use PEDIT to modify the mesh, you need to adjust two variables that control the number of mesh surfaces: SURFV and SURFU. They represent the number of mesh surfaces in the two axes (V and U). Change both SURFV and SURFU to 20. Use the PEDIT command, select the surface, and then use the Smooth Surface option of the PEDIT command to change the number of mesh surfaces and to smooth their edges. The results should look similar to Figure 23.5.

Figure 23.5
Enhanced terrain model

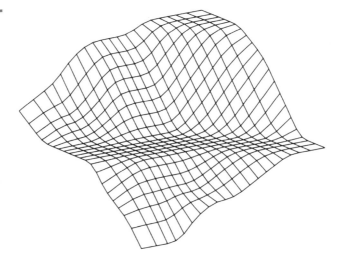

Save the modified mesh as TERR. Use the VPOINT command to move about the terrain, observing it from any location. Return to VPOINT –2,–3,1, and shade the terrain. The results should be interesting.

Stage 6: Creating the Profile Script/Data File

You can use the same data entered to create the terrain mesh to create profile lines showing the cross section through the terrain. You do this by modifying the original data file so that it automatically creates 3D polylines instead of 3D polygon meshes. The modification is a simple procedure: Replace the 3DMESH line with the 3DPOLY command at the beginning of the file and add two blank lines between each line of data. Refer to Table 23.3 to discover what the modified file should look like.

Copying the Original Data

Exit AutoCAD and copy the original script file MESH.SCR to a new file called MESH2.SCR.

Editing the Data

Use a text editor to modify the data so that it looks exactly like the data shown in Table 23.3. *Note:* This script needs one blank line at the end of the file to exit from the 3DPOLY command. The other rules regarding extra spaces and lines still apply.

Table 23.3 Script file MESH2.SCR	3DPOLY
	10, 10, 0 10, 20, 10 10, 30, 15 10, 40, 20 10, 50, 30 10, 60, 30 10, 70, 30
	10, 80, 30 10, 90, 30 10, 100, 35 10, 110, 40
	20, 10, 0 20, 20, 10 20, 30, 20 20, 40, 25 20, 50, 30 20, 60, 30 20, 70, 30
	20, 80, 30 20, 90, 35 20, 100, 40 20, 110, 45
	30, 10, 0 30, 20, 10 30, 30, 20 30, 40, 30 30, 50, 30 30, 60, 30 30, 70, 30
	30, 80, 30 30, 90, 35 30, 100, 40 30, 110, 50
	40, 10, 10 40, 20, 15 40, 30, 20 40, 40, 30 40, 50, 30 40, 60, 30 40, 70, 30
	40, 80, 35 40, 90, 40 40, 100, 50 40, 110, 60
	50, 10, 15 50, 20, 15 50, 30, 20 50, 40, 30 50, 50, 30 50, 60, 30 50, 70, 30
	50, 80, 40 50, 90, 50 50, 100, 60 50, 110, 65
	60, 10, 15 60, 20, 20 60, 30, 25 60, 40, 30 60, 50, 30 60, 60, 30 60, 70, 30
	60, 80, 40 60, 90, 50 60, 100, 60 60, 110, 65
	70, 10, 20 70, 20, 25 70, 30, 30 70, 40, 30 70, 50, 30 70, 60, 30 70, 70, 30
	70, 80, 40 70, 90, 50 70, 100, 60 70, 110, 65
	80, 10, 25 80, 20, 30 80, 30, 30 80, 40, 30 80, 50, 30 80, 60, 30 80, 70, 40
	80, 80, 50 80, 90, 60 80, 100, 70 80, 110, 70
	90, 10, 30 90, 20, 30 90, 30, 30 90, 40, 30 90, 50, 30 90, 60, 40 90, 70, 50
	90, 80, 60 90, 90, 70 90, 100, 70 90, 110, 70
	100, 10, 30 100, 20, 30 100, 30, 30 100, 40, 30 100, 50, 40 100, 60, 50
	100, 70, 60 100, 80, 70 100, 90, 70 100, 100, 70 100, 110, 70
	110, 10, 30 110, 20, 30 110, 30, 30 110, 40, 40 110, 50, 50 110, 60, 60
	110, 70, 65 110, 80, 70 110, 90, 70 110, 100, 70 110, 110, 70

Figure 23.6
Rough profile lines from raw data

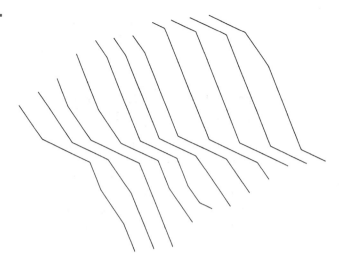

Stage 7: Creating the Profile Model

Create the terrain profiles in the same manner you created the terrain model.

1. Open the original model TERR.
2. Freeze the CMESH layer, and make the PROFL layer current.
3. Run the newly modified script MESH2. The resulting 3D polylines should look like Figure 23.6.

Smoothing the Profile Lines

As with the terrain model, the profile lines created from raw data are somewhat ragged and need to be smoothed. The technique to smooth them is identical to the technique you used earlier on the mesh.

1. Select the PEDIT command and click one of the polylines.
2. Use the Spline option to smooth the line.
3. Repeat for the other 10 lines. The resulting figure should appear similar to Figure 23.7.
4. Save the modified mesh as TERR.

Figure 23.7
Enhanced profile lines

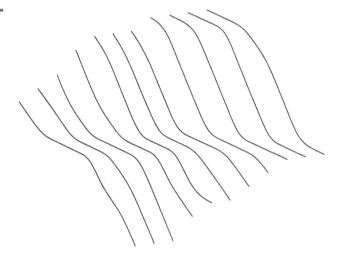

Stage 8: Displaying Selected Profiles

The next step is to display a cross-sectional view of the profiles and then selectively display each profile in turn. To allow the display of a single profile while hiding the rest, place each profile on its own layer.

1. Create layers for each profile line—a total of 11.

COLOR	LAYER
1	PLINE1
2	PLINE2
3	PLINE3
4	PLINE4
5	PLINE5
6	PLINE6
7	PLINE7
8	PLINE8
9	PLINE9
10	PLINE10
11	PLINE11

2. Using the PROPERTIES command, move each profile line to its own layer.
3. Save the model as TERR.
4. Using the VPOINT command, set the coordinates to −1,0,0 and ZOOM Extents. This gives an elevation view of the profile lines that should be similar to Figure 23.8.
5. Freeze all layers except PLINE1. The cross-section profile of PLINE1 should now be easy to interpret.
6. Proceed to display each profile line in turn and observe the cross section.

   The project is finished: You have created a topographical polygon mesh of a selected terrain and then created and displayed a series of cross-section profiles on that terrain. You now have the skills to recreate any terrain of your choice. Practice the procedures by translating a small portion of any contour map into a 3D topographic model. For a real challenge, try to translate a portion of a contour map of the Rocky Mountains or the Appalachians.

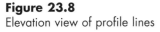

Figure 23.8
Elevation view of profile lines

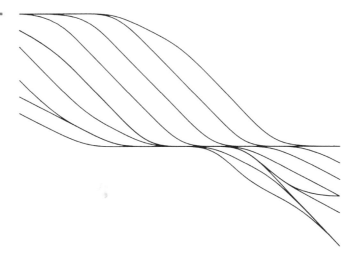

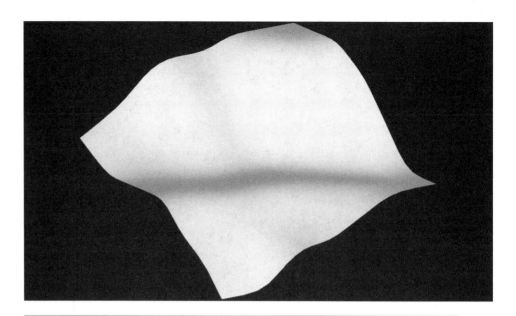

Figure 23.9
Rendered view of the terrain model

23.3 **Rendering**

To create a rendering, redisplay the terrain mesh, only set the Rendering Preferences to Smooth Shading, and then render the model. No lights are needed to give a representative view. Figure 23.9 shows an image of the rendered view. (If necessary, return to Chapter 17 for a review of the rendering process.)

P A R T

Application Programs

This final section, encompassing Chapters 24 and 25, explores two add-on programs that, although not provided with Auto-CAD software, act as a complement to it. In the same way that specialized menus and libraries make AutoCAD more valuable to specific users, add-ons like these can add capabilities that neither program could achieve on its own.

Mechanical Desktop, Inventor, and Autodesk VIZ, the three application programs explored here, point the way to the future for AutoCAD, and, in showing the extraordinary abilities of the programs, it seems fitting that we saved them, like a rich dessert, for last.

Mechanical Desktop and Inventor

24.1 Introduction

Mechanical Desktop and Inventor are a 3D, feature-based, parametric modeler. You can, therefore, create models of 3D parts by making use of 2D sketches. From these parts, you can create detail drawings and assemblies. Figure 24.1 shows the model creation progression in a simplified form.

Mechanical Desktop is designed to operate inside AutoCAD. It is fully integrated and makes use of the AutoCAD graphic interface. However, it has its own toolbars and a special interface called the Desktop Browser. Caution must be taken when using some of the standard AutoCAD commands. You should be familiar with the basics of drawing with AutoCAD before attempting to use Mechanical Desktop.

Inventor is a separate program from AutoCAD; however, its operation is very similar to Mechanical Desktop. The design process is the same for both. The main differences lie in the menu and tool options.

In this chapter, you are introduced to the Mechanical Desktop design process.

24.2 Design Process

To create in 3D, you must understand some basic concepts and terms. To help to understand them, let's review the design process. As you follow through this text, you will build on these concepts, going into greater detail. For now, familiarize yourself with the following basic principles.

Parts and Assemblies

Ultimately your goal is to create a complete part or an assembly of parts. The program operates in two environments: one for single parts (part environment) and one for parts that will be formed into assemblies (part/assembly environment). To begin with, you will use the single-part mode to learn how to use Mechanical Desktop. Once you're comfortable, you'll move on to creating assemblies. Figure 24.2 shows a part and an assembly.

Parametric Design

When you create a part, you determine the size, shape, and position of its various features. By assigning editable numeric values for size, shape, and position, you can alter the design of the part at any time for a variety of functions. This ability to alter

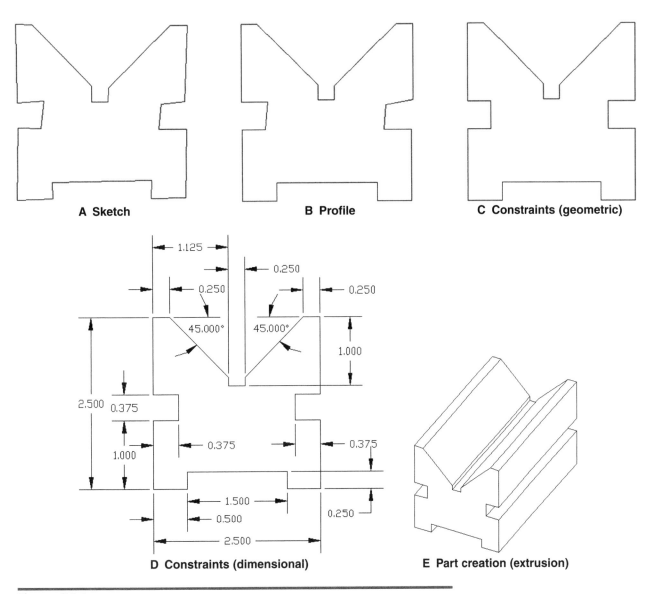

A Sketch   **B** Profile   **C** Constraints (geometric)

D Constraints (dimensional)   **E** Part creation (extrusion)

Figure 24.1
Model creation progression simplified

the design is referred to as parametric design. Figure 24.3 shows a single part with its design altered by changing the values of its features.

Feature-Driven Aspects

A part is created through the use of specific features that describe its shape. This aspect is referred to as feature driven. The features are the 3D shapes that form the part. Features are created through actions such as revolve, extrude, and sweep, using profiles shown in Figure 24.4. There are also standard features such as holes and fillets that can be added.

Profiles and Sketches

Profiles are the shapes that can be turned into features through such actions as extrude or revolve. Profiles are one of the most significant elements of the part design.

Figure 24.2
Single part and assembly

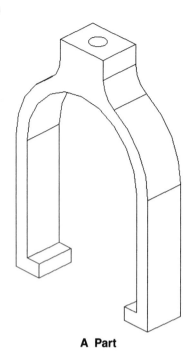

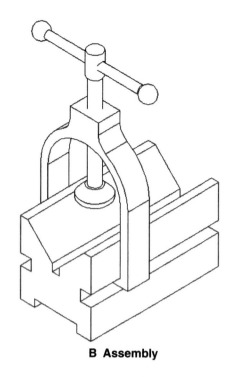

A Part

B Assembly

Figure 24.3
A part altered through
parametric design

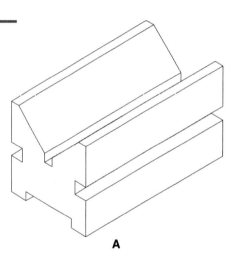

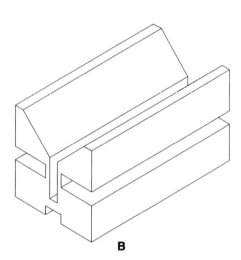

A

B

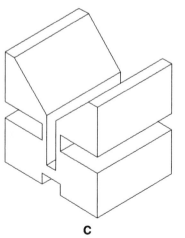

C

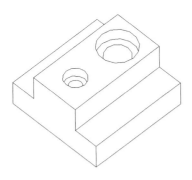

Figure 24.4
A part created with specific features

To create a profile, you first sketch it roughly and then turn it into a profile with constraints. Constraints control the shape (geometric) and size (dimensions) of the profile. This feature is another application of parametric design. Figure 24.5 shows an initial sketch and the profile with constraints.

Detail Drawings

Once your part is completed, you can use it to create fully annotated (notes and dimensions) multiview drawings, as shown in Figure 24.6. These drawings are created with a base view and other views based on it. Dimensions and notes are applied through automatic and manual means.

Assembly Drawings

Assembly drawings can be created with a variety of views, including exploded views, as shown in Figure 24.7; assembly views are created through the use of scenes. Part balloons and a bill of materials (BOMs) can also be added.

Advanced Features

There are a number of advanced features than can be used to enhance your design. Table-driven parts that use a spreadsheet can create a variety of standard parts, such as nuts and bolts, from one part. 3D surface models and shells can be used to form such items as castings or thin-walled plastic parts.

AutoCAD Standards

You must be very careful which standard AutoCAD commands you use when working with Mechanical Desktop. Because Mechanical Desktop is a parametric design program, you must use its commands when performing editing that involves the shape or size of a part or an assembly.

Tips

■ At the sketching stage, you can use any AutoCAD command to create or modify the geometry of your sketch. You can also use AutoCAD commands to modify a sketch even after it has been consumed by a feature, but the changes to the part are reflected only after an update to the part.

Figure 24.5
Profile created from a sketch

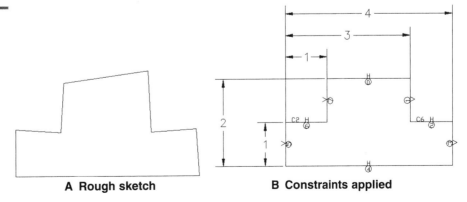

A Rough sketch　　　　　**B Constraints applied**

467

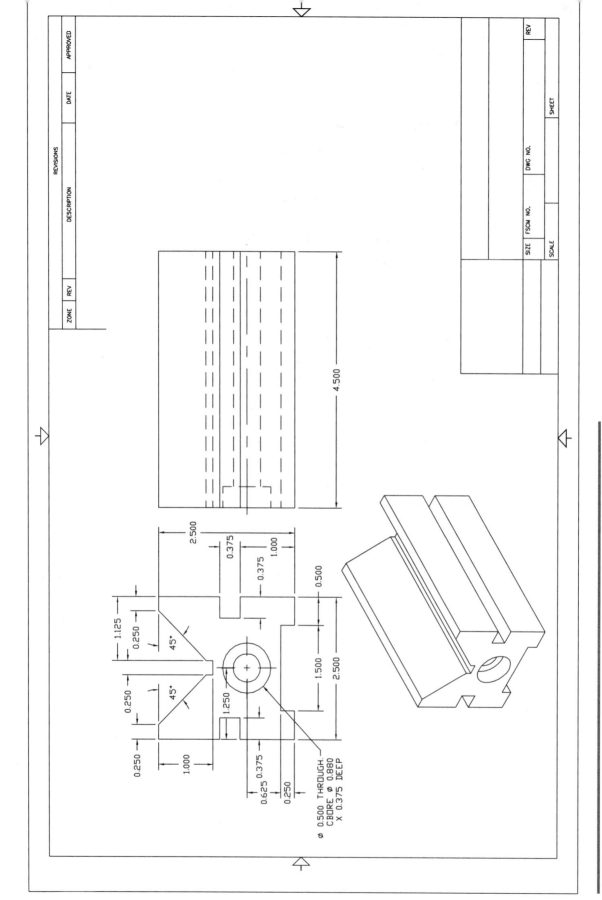

Figure 24.6
Detail drawing created from 3D part

Figure 24.7
Assembly drawing showing part
balloons and bill of materials

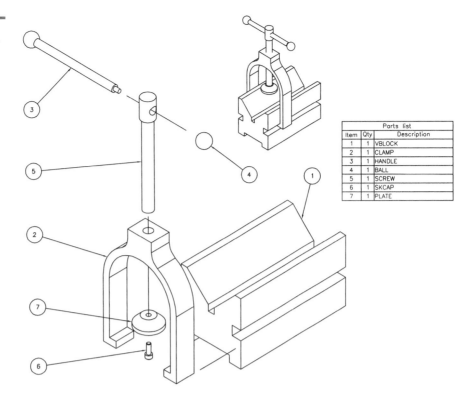

Parts list		
Item	Qty	Description
1	1	VBLOCK
2	1	CLAMP
3	1	HANDLE
4	1	BALL
5	1	SCREW
6	1	SKCAP
7	1	PLATE

■ Do *not* use AutoCAD dimensions, because they are not parametric and will not alter the shape or size of a part. Always use Mechanical Desktop dimensions.

■ Do *not* use the UCS command to move your sketch plane, because it is not associated with your part. Use sketch planes to control the UCS orientation.

■ Do *not* use the AutoCAD EXPLODE command, because it deletes the part definition from the Mechanical Desktop drawing, rendering it useless.

■ Do *not* use AutoCAD INSERT, WBLOCK, XREF, and XBIND to manipulate external part files. Using them corrupts the Mechanical Desktop data. Use the Assembly Catalog to perform such functions.

24.3 Interacting with Mechanical Desktop

When you start Mechanical Desktop, the standard AutoCAD toolbars are replaced with four toolbars and the Desktop Browser, as shown in Figure 24.8. Functionality has also been added to the standard set of pull-downs (content added, not replaced).

Toolbars
Mechanical Desktop

The Mechanical Desktop toolbar has been designed to replace many of the commands found in the AutoCAD standard and Object Properties toolbars, with the addition of new specialized tools.

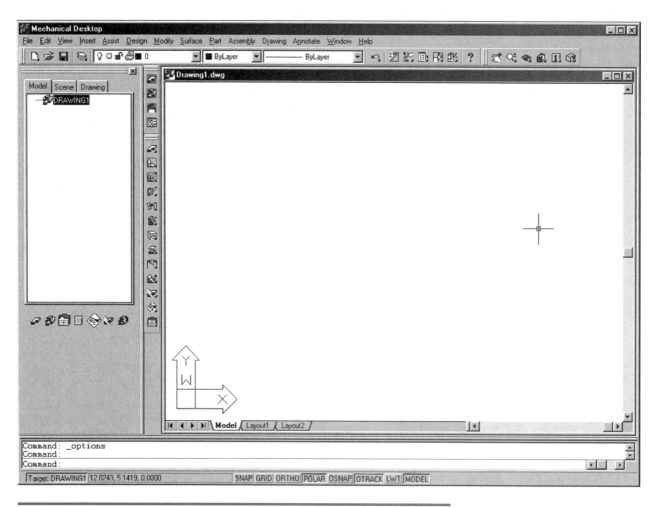

Figure 24.8
Mechanical Desktop screen layout

Desktop View

Desktop View is used to give you control over how you view your models. This includes real-time PAN and ZOOM, dynamic 3D rotation, and rendering commands.

Desktop Tools

The Desktop Tools toolbar is used as a toggle quick access to Part modeling, Assembly modeling, Scenes, and Drawing Layout toolbars. When you click one of the Desktop Tools, the associated toolbar is displayed. Figure 24.9 shows the toolbars associated with Desktop Tools.

Note: If you start in single-part environment, only Part Modeling, Toolbody, and Drawing Layout are available.

Part Modeling

The Part Modeling toolbar is displayed by default. It is replaced with the appropriate toolbar when you select a different Desktop tool, as explained previously. The Part Modeling toolbar is used to create and modify sketches, profiles, and features. It also updates and changes the visibility of a part.

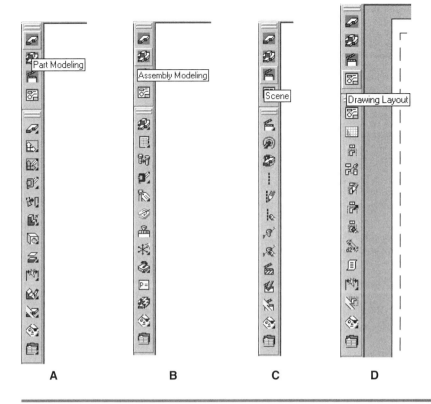

Figure 24.9
Flyouts on the Desktop Tools toolbar

Assembly

The Assembly toolbar is used to create and modify assemblies and subassemblies. It accesses the Assembly Catalog and allows you to update and change the visibility of assemblies.

Toolbody (only in Part Environment)

Toolbody is used to create, constrain, and modify combined parts. It accesses Part Catalog and allows you to update and change the display of toolbodies.

Scene

The Scene toolbar is used to create, modify, and manage scenes. Scenes are used to create an exploded view of an assembly. Scenes are used to create views without destroying the constraints applied to the assembly.

Drawing Layout

The Drawing Layout toolbar is used to create and modify drawing views and to insert and edit balloons, parts lists (BOMs), and annotations.

Desktop Browser

The Desktop Browser keeps track of all the features in sequence used to create a part and all of the parts that participate in an assembly, with their 3D constraint relationships. You can modify parts and assemblies through the use of the browser.

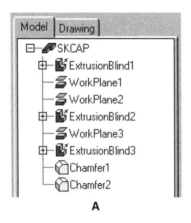

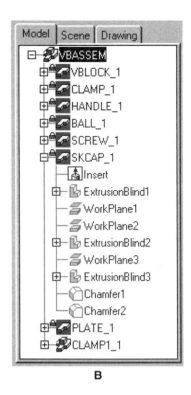

A   B

Figure 24.10
Single Part environment and Part/Assembly environment Desktop Browsers

(Figure 24.10 shows the browsers for the Single Part environment and the Part/Assembly environment.) One browser per session handles both part and assemblies. Between the environments the browser changes slightly.

Assembly: Model, Scene, Drawing
Part: Model, Drawing

Because your first exposure is going to be with single parts, we will concentrate on the browser for the Single Part environment. Both browser environments operate basically the same way except for the added functionality of the Part/Assembly environment.

24.4 **Using the Desktop Browser**

When you create your first sketch, a part is automatically named, numbered, and represented in the browser. Because the sketch is the first step, it is nested first under the part name (see Figure 24.11A). As you add more features, these are added to the part to form a hierarchy, showing the process used to design the part (see Figure 24.11B).

Expanding and Collapsing Hierarchy Levels

You can expand or collapse hierarchy levels by using the plus (+) or minus (−) signs. You can collapse the entire hierarchy by right-clicking the part name and choosing Collapse from the menu.

Figure 24.11
Using the Desktop Browser

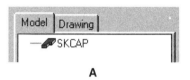

A

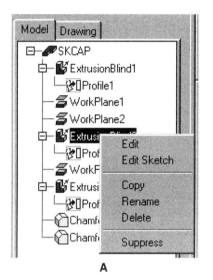

B

Figure 24.12
Browser command menus

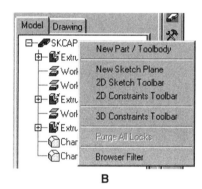

A   B

Browser Commands

Access most of the Mechanical Desktop commands by either right-clicking on an existing object in the browser or right-clicking in the browser background. Figure 24.12 shows the two browser command menus.

24.5 Interacting with Inventor

Even though Inventor is a separate program from AutoCAD and Mechanical Desktop, there are many similarities. This means the transition from AutoCAD into Inventor is not as complicated as you might first imagine.

The screen is divided into two main user elements: the application window and the graphics window (see Figure 24.13). The applications window contains the pull-down menus, command bar, docked toolbars, and command panels. The graphics window contains the modeling environment. You can have multiple graphics windows, each displaying different modeling environments. One window could display a single part, while another displays an entire assembly.

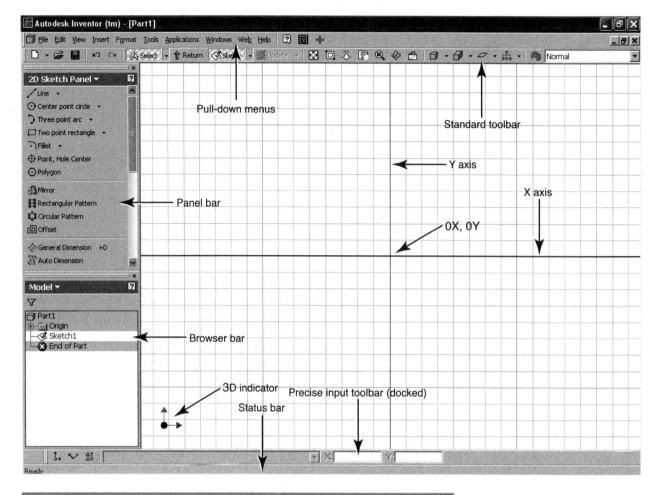

Figure 24.13
Autodesk Inventor Part screen layout

When you start a new part, the pull-down menus and toolbars are customized for the part modeling environment. Since the first stage in creating a part is to sketch the shape of the part, Inventor automatically goes into sketch mode. The purpose of this section is to provide an overview.

Pull-Down Menus

The pull-down menus lie at the top of the Inventor application window. Even though they contain various commands, you'll probably find yourself using a toolbar, panel bar, or context menu for most of your commands. The pull-down menu heads may stay the same between different modeling environments, such as part modeling or assembly modeling, but their contents change with the different environments.

Toolbars

Inventor uses a series of toolbars to perform most of the commands. Only the toolbars relevant to the active graphics window and environment are displayable. To display or hide a toolbar, you can use the View/Toolbar pull-down menu item or right-click on a blank spot on a toolbar to bring up the context menu. You can also drag toolbars around the application window to arrange them in a format that suits you.